U
SYRN

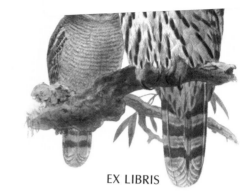

EX LIBRIS

THE LAW AND PRACTICE OF
LOCAL AUTHORITY MEETINGS

THE LAW AND PRACTICE
OF
LOCAL AUTHORITY MEETINGS

RAYMOND S. B. KNOWLES

D.P.A., A.C.I.S., F.I.P.M.

ICSA PUBLISHING

CAMBRIDGE

Published by ICSA Publishing Limited
Fitzwilliam House, 32 Trumpington Street,
Cambridge CB2 1QY, England
and
27 South Main Street, Wolfeboro,
New Hampshire, 03894–2069, USA

First published as *The Law and Practice relating to Local Authority Meetings* 1978
First (revised) edition 1987

© Raymond Knowles 1978, 1987

British Library Cataloguing in Publication Data

Knowles, Raymond S. B.
    The law and practice of local authority
    meetings.—[Rev. and substantially
    expanded ed.]
    1. Local government—England 2. Parliamentary
    practice—England
    I. Title   II. Knowles, Raymond S. B. Law
    and practice relating to local authority
    meetings
    352'.00047   KD4746

    ISBN 0-902197-51-7

Library of Congress Cataloging-in-Publication Data

Knowles, Raymond Stewart Brown.
    The law and practice of local authority meetings.

    Rev. ed. of: The law and practice relating to the
local authority meetings. c1978.
    Includes bibliographical references and index.
    1. Local government—Law and legislation—Great
Britain.   2. Parliamentary practice—Great Britain.
I. Knowles, Raymond Stewart Brown.   The law and
practice relating to the local authority meeting.
II. Title.
KD4759.K57   1987   342.42'09   87–3771
ISBN 0–902197–51–7   344.2029

Designed by Geoff Green
Typeset by Wyvern Typesetting Ltd, Bristol
Printed in Great Britain by
St Edmundsbury Press, Bury St Edmunds, Suffolk

CONTENTS

PREFACE

This book is a completely revised and substantially expanded edition of a work which was first published in 1978 under a slightly different title. It is not a legal textbook in the ordinary sense, though admittedly it has some of the trappings – the tables of cases and statutes – associated with a book written for lawyers. It was impossible to prepare a book relating to such subject matter without including references to common law and statutory rules governing meetings procedure. First and foremost, however, this book is intended as a manual for practitioners: for those in the public service whose task it is to attend and advise at meetings and so facilitate the transaction of business.

The law and practice of local authority meetings is far less static than one might imagine. Indeed, over recent years there have been significant changes. The Local Government (Access to Information) Act 1985 in particular gave substantial new powers of public access to the agenda and accompanying papers for local authority meetings and of admission to meetings of subcommittees. And many issues relating to local authority meetings have come before the courts during the last few years: it is now clear, for example, that councillors cannot be denied access to committees to which they have not been appointed if they can show a 'need to know' for the reasonable performance of their duties as members of the local authority. All this and much else has involved changes in the original text.

A mass of material, much of it unavailable elsewhere, is brought together here within the covers of a single volume. More than that, however, the book is designed as a readable narrative for all concerned with the management of local authorities (and the considerable number of bodies associated with local government), the National Health Service and the water industry.

I am grateful to many people (far more than I can mention individually) who in various ways helped in the preparation of this work or were associated with the earlier edition. I am indebted, too, to a large number of local authorities who generously responded to requests for information about their conventions and practices.

Special thanks are due to Colin Child, County Secretary of East Sussex County Council (currently Chairman of the Local Government Administrators Panel of the Institute of Chartered Secretaries and Administrators) who read the proofs of the manuscript and made several helpful suggestions which I was able to incorporate: but I take sole responsibility, of course, for the opinions expressed and for any errors which may have gone undetected. It would be ungracious of me, also, not to acknowledge a debt to the tutors and students who attended NALGO's annual committee administration courses during the ten-year period when I was privileged to be a member of a panel of otherwise distinguished tutors: consciously and, no doubt, unconsciously too, I have made use of the wisdom which flowed out of stimulating discussions on the law and practice of local authority meetings that often went on deep into the night on well-remembered occasions at Downing College, Cambridge (where the courses are usually held).

This edition appears under the imprint of a new publisher and this has meant that the book now enjoys the imprimatur of the Institute of Chartered Secretaries and Administrators. I am delighted that this is so for a number of reasons, including the fact that it is wholly fitting that ICSA – which now provides the recognised professional qualification for administrators in local government – should be associated with a book which deals with subject matter of cardinal importance to chartered secretaries serving with local authorities.

After the main text of this book had been typeset the Education (No. 2) Act 1986 received Royal Assent. The Act affects Chapter 13 (13.50–13.51) in providing, *inter alia*, in Part II for a new constitution for school governing bodies designed to ensure that (a) no special interest will predominate, (b) there will be an equal number of parents and local education authority governors, (c) the existing statutory rights of representation of head-teachers, other teachers, foundation governors and other local authorities are preserved, (d) additional members are appointed to give a broadly-based membership, and (e) there is representation from the local business community.

Raymond S. B. Knowles
Long Ditton, Surrey, February 1987

TABLE OF CASES

TABLE OF STATUTES

TABLE OF STATUTORY INSTRUMENTS

REFERENCES TO MODEL STANDING ORDERS

* Not specifically referred to or outside the scope of the law and practice of
  meetings

PART ONE

GENERAL PRINCIPLES

1

INTRODUCTION

Local government structure

1.1. This work is concerned primarily, but not exclusively, with the law and practice relating to meetings of local authorities and associated bodies in England and Wales and of their committees and subcommittees. Though the local government system is somewhat different in Scotland and substantially so in Northern Ireland, the meetings procedures which the local authorities there follow have much in common with the practice of local authorities in England and Wales. For example, the Local Government (Scotland) Act 1973 and the Local Government (Northern Ireland) Act 1972 contain many rules similar to those in the Local Government Act 1972, which is the principal Act prescribing the relevant statutory provisions governing the conduct of local authority business in England and Wales. Readers in the United Kingdom outside England and Wales may, therefore, have little difficulty in applying what is said in these pages to their own perception of local differences of statutory and common law.

Administrative areas

1.2. In *England*, exclusive of Greater London and the Isles of Scilly,[1] the country is divided into *counties* and *districts*. The counties are either *metropolitan* or *shire* counties and within the former there are *metropolitan districts* and elsewhere *non-metropolitan districts*. Some districts are known as *boroughs* or *cities*, mostly for historical reasons. Within the shire counties particularly there are rural *parishes*.

1.3. *Wales* is also divided into *counties* and *districts* and each district comprises one or more *communities*.

---

[1] For the Isles of Scilly there is a special council constituted by order of the Secretary of State for the Environment: Local Government Act 1972, s.265.

1.4. *Greater London* comprises the areas of the *London boroughs,* the *City of London,* and the *Inner and Middle Temples.*[2] The 12 London boroughs whose areas, together with the City, formed the former administrative county of London, are known as *inner London boroughs;* the remaining area of Greater London comprises *outer London boroughs.*

Local authorities

1.5. For each county, except a metropolitan one and the Greater London area as a totality,[3] and for each borough or district and the City of London, there is an elected local authority known as a *principal council.* The term *local authority* means throughout this work a principal council or a local council, i.e. *parish or community council*[4] or one of the new authorities established as a consequence of the abolition of the Greater London Council and the metropolitan county councils:[5]

(a) the *Inner London Education Authority,* a directly elected *ad hoc* authority, charged with responsibilities as a local education authority for the whole inner London area;[6]

(b) the several *statutory joint authorities* set up to discharge certain of the functions previously administered by the abolished authorities;[7]

(c) the *residuary bodies* whose job it is to wind up the affairs of the abolished authorities.[8]

1.6. For every parish there must be, and for every community there may be, a meeting of electors, i.e. a *parish meeting* or a *community meeting,* for purposes of discussing local affairs.[9] These meetings have power to exercise certain limited functions but are not regarded as local authorities.

---

[2] 'It is doubtful whether in the world of local government the Temples have any precise legal position': Herbert Morrison, *How London is Governed,* p. 3.

[3] The structure of local government established in England and Wales by the Local Government Act 1972 and in Greater London by the London Government Act 1963 was changed in 1986 by the Local Government Act 1985 which abolished the Greater London Council and the six metropolitan county councils (though the administrative *areas* of Greater London and the metropolitan counties were not abolished).

[4] Local Government Act 1972, s.270(1).

[5] Local Government Act 1985, s.105(1).

[6] *Ibid.* ss.18–22.

[7] *Ibid.* ss.23–28.

[8] *Ibid.* ss.57–67; and see 14.4–14.8. For certain purposes a residuary body is a principal council: *ibid.* sch.13, para.12.

[9] Local Government Act 1972, ss.9, 27.

Local authority meetings

Definition of 'meeting'

1.7. The definition of a meeting as 'a gathering or assembly of two or more persons for a lawful common purpose'[10] needs no modification in its application to local government, for one person cannot in any sense constitute a meeting.[11] A meeting implies literally the coming together of two or more persons; and in the context of local government this is assuredly so because there are certain legal formalities to be observed which require a plurality of persons to be present (see 1.35) in order that there shall be a valid and lawful decision. These legal formalities include the need for a meeting to be properly convened and constituted: see 1.31.

1.8. Not only must there be at least two persons present to constitute a meeting; there must also be someone in control to regulate the deliberations of those present. These requirements (that there must be at least two persons and someone in control) are 'axiomatic and universal'.[12] Thus it could be argued – at least for local government purposes – that no meeting can practically consist of less than three persons: if there are two only, the one who is chairman (and there must be a chairman) could decide every issue as he wished because of his statutory power to give a second or casting vote (see 7.114) in the event of an equality of votes, i.e. if he voted one way in the first place, and the other member the other way!

1.9. The person entrusted with authority to regulate the conduct of a meeting is usually styled the *chairman* (but see 7.10) and in the case of council meetings the chairman is the *chairman of the council* (or the *mayor*[13] in the case of those councils which have been permitted to retain their former status or assume that of one of their predecessors; or in the case of the London boroughs never lost that status).

---

[10] *Sharp* v. *Dawes* (1876) 2 QBD 26, where a meeting was defined as 'the coming together of at least two persons for any lawful purpose'.

[11] The few exceptional cases where one person can constitute a meeting (as, e.g. under the Companies Act, which provides that 'one member of the company present in person or by proxy shall be deemed to constitute a meeting') have no application to local government.

[12] Sebag Shaw and Dennis Smith, *The Law of Meetings* (1947). There is no specific judicial authority for the view that there must be a chairman but common law rules and statutes clearly imply that someone must preside at a meeting.

[13] The ancient title of *mayor*, enjoyed by the chairmen of borough councils, has been preserved along with some other offices of dignity by the Local Government Act 1972, ss.245, 246. This includes the distinctive title of *Lord Mayor* conferred on the holders of the mayoralty in certain boroughs.

Local authority meetings are private meetings

1.10. Generally meetings may be either public or private. A *public meeting* has been defined[14] as:

> Any meeting *bona fide* and lawfully held for a lawful purpose and for the furtherance or discussion of any matter of public concern, whether admission thereto be general or restricted.

This is a wide definition: it includes any meeting in a public place[15] and any meeting on private premises[16] which the public or a section of the public are permitted to attend, whether on payment or otherwise. It might seem that local authority meetings could thus be held to be public meetings, but the public's right of admission is conferred by statute:[17] it is not a common law right: see 3.1, 3.2. The fact that local authorities permitted the public to attend council and sometimes committee meetings even before the law conferred upon the public a right of access did not affect the position.[18]

Purpose of meeting

1.11. It is always important that the purposes of a meeting should be defined at the time it is convened. We are not concerned, of course, with assemblies for social intercourse or solely for civic ceremonial (although some council meetings may embrace both incidentally) but primarily with meetings for the transaction of local authority business. In the case of all formal meetings there will be an agenda or at least a clear understanding as to the terms of reference of the committee or subcommittee, working party, panel, or whatever it may be.

1.12. There are other meetings, less formally structured, where the objective may be less well defined, e.g. where local authority representatives receive a deputation of electors or seek to negotiate with a trade union on some matter in dispute. In those cases the authority's representatives must

---

[14] Law of Libel Amendment Act 1888, s.4.

[15] A *'public place'* is any highway, public park or garden, any sea beach and any public bridge, road, lane, footway, square, court, alley or passage, whether a thoroughfare or not, and includes any open space to which, for the time being, the public have or are permitted to have access, whether on payment or otherwise: Public Order Act 1936, s.9(1).

[16] *'Private premises'* are defined as 'premises to which the public have access (whether on payment or otherwise) only by permission of the owner, occupier or lessee of the premises': *ibid.*

[17] Local Government Act 1972, ss.100A, 100E, added by Local Government (Access to Information) Act 1985, as regards principal councils: see generally Chapter 3.

[18] See *Tenby Corporation* v. *Mason* (1908) 1 Ch.457, where the House of Lords held that the public had no right to attend a council meeting: see 3.1.

understand precisely what is to be their role: they must know the parameters within which discussion is to range, and obviously the extent of their power, if any, to bind the council. Unless these things are understood beforehand (with perhaps also a plan of tactics to be adopted depending upon the trend in discussion), the meeting may well be regarded as unsatisfactory on one or other or both sides, or the local authority representatives may find they have unintentionally committed their council to embark on an unwanted course of action.

1.13. Where one local authority joins with another or others and/or with other agencies for the discussion or co-ordination of some matter in which each is interested, the need for a clear definition of the purpose of the meeting (or, if of continuing concern: the joint committee or other body set up) is particularly important. Such a meeting or committee or body has invariably a diffuse set of objectives which are not necessarily related to one another and not immediately identifiable in terms of responsibility to one set of decision-makers.[19]

1.14. Although in most cases the objectives of a meeting will be to reach a decision this may not always be so. For example, in 1974 Kent County Council experimented with occasional meetings for *discussion only* 'to give members of the council an opportunity of debating matters of concern to the county . . . without the pressure of the need for decision-taking': the first two such meetings discussed a county-wide transportation plan and a county energy policy.[20]

Regulation by law

1.15. The convention, constitution and conduct of meetings (whether related to local government or not) are governed partly by statute and partly by common law. The principal statute as regards local authority meetings is the Local Government Act 1972 but there are other enactments which regulate the constitution of particular committees of local authorities. In total, however, the statutory provisions (although extremely detailed in certain respects) affect a comparatively small part of the relevant law. The standing orders which local authorities are empowered to make usually seek to regulate all other matters which would fall to be dealt with otherwise in accordance with the practices and conventions recognised at common law.

---

[19] For a discussion of the problems inherent in multi-organisations (outside the scope of this work) see: R. J. P. Harris and D. J. Scott, 'Perspectives on Multi-Organizational Design' 8 *Local Government Studies* 31.

[20] *Municipal and Public Services Journal* (14 June 1974), p. 722.

Types of meeting

1.16. There are two broad categories of meetings within the sphere of local government. These can most easily but not altogether satisfactorily be termed *formal* and *informal*. A *formal meeting* is one convened in the manner prescribed by law to enable councillors (sometimes with co-opted members) to transact local authority business with the object of reaching decisions – or formulating recommendations as a basis for decisions – which are intended to commit the authority as a whole. An *informal meeting* is any other meeting for the consideration or transaction of business which may or may not comprise councillors or at least comprise them exclusively: it may be a meeting convened solely for purposes of exploratory discussions between councillors and officers or between councillors and representatives of other bodies, and either not intended to be clothed with legal formality or by its nature cannot bind the local authority.

1.17. The main general principles governing formal meetings (of the full assembly particularly) are outlined in the paragraphs immediately following. Formal meetings of committees, and of gatherings akin to committees, are dealt with in Chapter 4, where there is a discussion of informal meetings of the kind increasingly common since the reorganisation of local government in England and Wales in 1974.

Formal meetings

1.18. Formal meetings are those of (a) *principal councils*, i.e. the councils of counties and districts in England and Wales and the London boroughs; (b) the new authorities created under the Local Government Act 1985, i.e., the *Inner London Education Authority*, the *statutory joint authorities*, and the *residuary bodies*; (c) *parish councils and parish meetings* in England and *community councils* and *community meetings* in Wales; and (d) their *committees and subcommittees*. Each must be convened and constituted in the manner prescribed by statute and/or standing orders.[21]

Special meetings

1.19. There are, in effect, three types of special council meeting: the *annual* meeting; an *extraordinary* meeting; and a meeting convened for *a specific purpose*. Each is regulated by statute in varying respects, particularly as regards its convention (dealt with in Chapter 6).

---

[21] See generally Local Government Act 1972, s.99, and sch.12; and London Government Act 1963, s.1.

1.20. The obligation upon local authorities to hold an annual meeting in every year is referred to below (see 1.23). The law also requires that certain business shall be transacted at an annual meeting (see 6.19).

1.21. An extraordinary meeting of the full assembly is one convened otherwise than by direction of the council as a whole, i.e. either by the chairman on his own initiative or upon the requisition of a prescribed number of council members[22] (see 6.5). Although there was earlier provision, in the Local Government Act 1933, for such meetings, the term 'extraordinary' meeting is used in the 1972 Act for the first time to refer to meetings convened in these circumstances.

1.22. An example of a council meeting convened for a specific purpose is one called to consider a proposal of a local authority to promote or oppose any local or personal Bill in Parliament.[23] Meetings of this character are dealt with in Chapter 13.

1.23. A principal and parish council is required to hold in every year an annual meeting of the full assembly,[24] and a parish meeting must assemble annually.[25] But a community meeting is under no such obligation. The annual meeting of a principal and parish council must be held within the period prescribed by statute, varying according to whether it is election year;[26] the parish meeting must assemble 'on some day between March 1 and June 1, both inclusive'.[27]

1.24. Each principal, parish and community council and parish meeting may hold, in addition to the annual meeting (or any other meeting it is required to hold) such other, i.e. ordinary meetings of the full assembly as it may determine.[28] It is difficult to understand why it has been thought necessary to provide legislative power to do something which local authorities could surely do in any case: however, in the case of a parish council there is an obligation to hold not less than three meetings in

---

[22] Local Government Act 1972, sch. 12, paras.3, 9, 25. There is provision also for the calling of meetings of a parish and community meeting in similar circumstances but the term *extraordinary* meeting is not used: *ibid.* paras.15, 30.

[23] *Ibid.* s.239.

[24] Local Government Act 1972, sch.12: principal councils, para.1(1); parish councils, para.7(1); community councils, para.23(1).

[25] *Ibid.* para.14(1).

[26] Except in the year of election of councillors a principal council may hold its annual meeting on such day in March, April or May as it thinks fit (*ibid.* sch.12, paras.1(2) (b), (3) (a)) and a parish council on such day in May as it may determine (*ibid.* para.7(2)). In the election year the annual meeting of a principal council must be held 'on the eighth day after the retirement of councillors or such other day within 21 days immediately following the day of retirement as the council may fix'; in the case of parish councils 'on or within 14 days after the day on which the councillors elected at that election take office' (*ibid.* para.7(2)).

[27] *Ibid.* sch.12, para.14(1).

[28] *Ibid.* sch.12: principal councils, para.2(1); parish councils, para.8(1); community councils, para.24(1); parish meetings, para.14(2); community meetings, para.30(1).

addition to the annual meeting,[29] with discretion to determine the hour and days;[30] and in the case of a parish which does not have a separate parish council the parish meeting must (subject to any provision made by a grouping order) assemble at least twice a year.[31] Some authorities fix the dates by standing orders; others determine them each year at the annual meeting.

Time of meeting

1.25. The time of meeting is not specifically prescribed. In the case of principal councils the 'annual meeting . . . shall be held at such hour as the council may fix, or if no hour is so fixed at 12 noon',[32] which presumably means that, in the unlikely event of a principal council convening an annual meeting without specifying the time of the meeting, it would necessarily be at 12 noon but the notice might still be held to be void for uncertainty. A parish and a community council's annual meeting may, somewhat similarly, be held 'at such hour as the council may fix or, if no hour is so fixed, six o'clock in the evening'.[33] The proceedings at a parish or community meeting must not commence earlier than 6.00 p.m.[34]

Meetings on Sunday

1.26. There appears to be no reason in law why a local authority should not meet on a Sunday, although there may be practical and other reasons why the practice should be regarded as undesirable.[35]

Frequency of meeting

1.27. Provided a local authority holds its statutory annual meeting and observes the requirements about other meetings (see 1.24), it can decide as it wishes upon the frequency of meetings,[36] i.e. it does not necessarily need to space out equally the ordinary meetings – though it may wish to do so in order to arrange a convenient and regular committee cycle (see 10.1). The frequency of meetings will obviously be determined by the volume and

---

[29] *Ibid.* para.8(1).
[30] *Ibid.* para.8(2).
[31] *Ibid.* para.14(3).
[32] *Ibid.* para.1(4).
[33] *Ibid.* paras.7(3), 23(3).
[34] *Ibid.* paras.14(4), 32(1).
[35] An opinion to the contrary appears in the *Justice of the Peace and Local Government Review* of 21 September 1963, but no grounds for the opinion are advanced.
[36] Local Government Act 1972, sch.12, paras.2(1), 8(1), 24(1).

incidence of business. District councils in the main meet monthly while some county councils meet quarterly, but all authorities dispense with meetings of the full assembly for the holiday period in the summer when, the expression goes, the council is 'in recess'. It is common practice for the dates of ordinary meetings to be fixed in advance at the annual meeting of a council.[37]

Place of meeting

1.28. Meetings of a principal council must be held 'at such place, either within or without their areas as they may direct';[38] so, too, may meetings of a parish council and a community council except that the meetings must 'not be held in premises licensed for the sale of intoxicating liquor unless no other suitable room is available either free of charge or at a reasonable cost'.[39] This discriminatory prohibition against the holding of a meeting on licensed premises applies also to parish meetings[40] although the statute is otherwise silent as to place.

1.29. These statutory provisions apply also to *committee meetings*.[41] Thus any local authority committee meeting may be held anywhere, either within or without its area, as the council or committee may decide – except in the case of committees of a parish council or parish meeting or of a community council, which must not be held on licensed premises unless no other accommodation is available free or at reasonable cost.

1.30. Notwithstanding the above, there is an assumption throughout this work that local authority meetings will take place ordinarily at the authority's offices. Sometimes, however – particularly in the case of committees or subcommittees – a meeting will be arranged at a defined location on the highway for purposes, perhaps, of making an inspection of a site which is the subject of a planning application. The reasons for meetings of this character are numerous. In all such instances care must be taken to avoid obstruction of the highway, for that would constitute an offence.[42] Highways exist for purposes of passage and anyone using a highway for some other purpose is in theory a trespasser; but so long as the meeting is not likely to interfere with the right of passage or lead to a breach of the peace then there is no reason why a local authority should feel

---

[37] This does not, of course, dispense with the necessity of public notice and individual summons on each occasion.

[38] Local Government Act 1972, sch.12, para.4(1).

[39] *Ibid.* paras.10(1), 26(1).

[40] *Ibid.* para.14(5).

[41] *Ibid.* s.99 applies the provisions of sch.12 to committees and subcommittees.

[42] If a person, without lawful authority or excuse, in any way wilfully obstructs the free passage along a highway he is guilty of an offence (Highways Act 1980, s.137).

inhibited from arranging such a meeting. It may be thought prudent, of course, depending on circumstances, to advise people living in the vicinity of the meeting so as to avoid unnecessary concern or speculation when they see a gathering outside their premises.

Requisites of a valid meeting

1.31. In order to constitute a valid meeting there must be three essentials:

(a) a plurality of persons present: see 1.7;

(b) someone in the chair: see 1.8; and

(c) a lawful common purpose: see 1.10.

In addition, in relation to local authority meetings, there must be compliance with statutory requirements, and standing orders, as to the time or period within which a meeting must be held (see 1.18) and, in certain cases, as to the place of meeting (see 1.28). Each meeting must also be:

(d) properly convened, i.e. there must be public notice of the meeting and a summons sent to every person entitled to attend (see 6.2); and

(e) properly constituted (see 1.37), i.e.:

    (i)   the proper person must be in the chair (see 7.24 *et seq.*); and

    (ii) the requisite quorum of members must be present (see 7.31).

Any irregularity in the convening, constitution or conduct of a meeting may, according to its nature (i.e. whether a council or committee or subcommittee meeting), invalidate all or part of the proceedings. But want of service of the summons will not ordinarily affect the meeting's validity and there is a presumption in law (i.e. until the contrary is proved) that, once the minutes have been drawn up and signed, the meeting was properly convened and held and the members present duly qualified; and even if there was a vacancy among the members or a defect in the election or qualification of any member, the proceedings are not thereby invalidated.[43]

1.32. It follows from the previous paragraph that if a number of councillors choose to meet of their own accord, their informal gathering together does not constitute a meeting for the lawful transaction of business. Most local authorities are prepared to allow the use of council accommodation for informal meetings of such a character, but there have been circumstances where permission has been refused. In 1981 some 11 Labour councillors in the London Borough of Southwark were initially denied

---

[43] This appears to be the effect of s.82 of the Local Government Act 1972, which provides that 'the acts and proceedings of any person elected to an office under this Act and acting in that office shall, notwithstanding his disqualification or want of qualification, be as valid and effectual as if he had been qualified': see 5.2.

facilities by the controlling Labour group to meet in council-owned premises because the councillors had been expelled from membership of the Labour Party (after opposing the policy of the Labour caucus on the council), although the group subsequently relented. It is undoubtedly a matter for the local authority's discretion whether and when to allow the use of council-owned premises; and if – as we shall see (e.g. 5.6, 5.67, 9.3) – a single councillor has precious little right as an individual member, it may seem to follow that a number of them can claim no right by mere multiplication[44] (although there might be some kind of right, extra-legal perhaps, in a number of councillors who wanted to meet for the purpose of framing a requisition for the calling of an extraordinary meeting of the council: see 6.5). Local authorities may think it prudent to agree a code of practice for the use of council accommodation for informal meeting purposes – governing, for example, the use for party group meetings and by individual councillors who wished to meet their constituents.

Decision-making

Determination of questions

1.33. As already indicated (see 1.14.), most local authority meetings are held to reach a decision on an item or items of business: to decide a question, in the phraseology of statute.[45] Our concern in this work is primarily with procedural and associated matters,[46] but it may be relevant to indicate briefly the three stages in the process of decision-making: first, an identification of the need for a decision; secondly, an examination of the various courses of action which would lead to a solution of the need, as well as consideration and analysis of the costs and consequences; and finally, the choice of the most appropriate solution available. This rational or systematic approach to decision-making cannot always be pursued. There may be insufficient time to assemble and consider all the pros and cons, even if there could be perfect knowledge of all possibilities and their consequences. There is also the influence of political dogma. Much has been done, organisationally and otherwise, to improve the quality of decision-making in local government, but any detailed examination of these developments other than that set out in Chapter 4 would be beyond the scope of this work.

---

[44] See Raymond S. B. Knowles, 'A Collective of Councillors' (1981) 145 *Local Government Review* 443.

[45] Local Government Act 1972, sch.12, Pt VI, para.39(1).

[46] A useful summary of legal considerations will be found in T. I. McLeod, *A Councillor's Guide to the Legal Framework of Decision-Making* (Barry Rose Publishers Ltd, 1983).

Voting

1.34. Voting at every local authority meeting is ordinarily by show of hands or as otherwise prescribed by standing orders (see 7.98). This is expressly required by law in the case of parish and community councils unless standing orders otherwise provide, but no method of voting is laid down by statute in the case of principal councils (where in some cases a mechanical system is now used) or in the case of parish and community meetings. Every person presiding at any local authority meeting – of the full assembly, committee or subcommittee – may exercise a second or casting vote. The whole matter of voting is considered in detail, including the question of recording votes on 'requisition', in Chapter 7.

Majority present and voting

1.35. There is a general principle governing by law the manner in which an authority shall reach a decision. This is that, save where other prescriptions apply[47] in particular circumstances:[48]

> . . . all questions coming or arising before a local authority shall be decided by a majority of the members of the authority present and voting thereon at a meeting of the authority.

1.36. This means that every decision which falls to be taken by a local authority (unless it is one which an officer has been empowered to make: see 4.8) can lawfully be reached only by the full assembly at a properly constituted council meeting or by a committee or subcommittee acting under delegated powers, and then only upon the affirmative vote of a majority of the members *present and actually voting*. Thus an authority of, say, 100 members may properly be committed to a course of action at a council meeting at which no more than the prescribed quorum (see 7.31) is present (say 25 council members, which would represent the quorum in the case of a principal council of that membership), of whom only three trouble to put up their hand in favour when a vote is taken and two vote against: or – a more extreme example – if one member votes in favour and no one else troubles to vote against.

1.37. Several important consequences flow from this principle. It means that *there can be no possibility of local government by referendum*:[49] the local

---

[47] For example, a majority of the whole number of council members is required for a resolution to promote or oppose a Bill: Local Government Act 1972, s.239, and see 7.139.

[48] Local Government Act 1972, sch.12, para.39.

[49] The archaic requirement has been repealed which formerly compelled borough and urban district councils contemplating the promotion of a private Bill in Parliament to convene a town's meeting to test support among the electorate for the proposition: Local Government Act 1933, s.255.

authority in full assembly or by a committee or subcommittee (or through the agency of another local authority or a joint committee) alone can make a decision on a matter which falls to be discharged by the authority at member level. And it must do it *at a properly constituted meeting*. It cannot make a decision by asking councillors by circular letter to signify through the post acceptance or rejection of a projected course of action. Nor can it do so by any informal gathering of its members (see 1.32). Nor may it lawfully purport to empower an individual council member to make a decision.[50] Nor may any individual council member vote by proxy:[51] he must be present at a meeting if he wishes his vote to count. Nor at a council or committee or subcommittee meeting can an officer vote in the decision-making process: even though the council, committee or subcommittee may be discussing a matter on which it has empowered the officer to act, it is to be presumed from its discussing the matter at a meeting that the council, committee or subcommittee concerned has revoked, albeit temporarily, the act of delegation.[52] There must be a properly convened assembly of council members (in council or committee or subcommittee) so that a decision can be made in circumstances where the cut and thrust of debate and argument and counter-argument can take place if council members are so minded: the fact that most members may take no part in the proceedings or abstain from voting does not affect the position.

1.38. The questions to be decided are questions of every kind (except, as indicated already (1.35), those for which some special procedure and/or majority vote is required): the same principle applies whether the decision is concerned with major policy or administrative detail. The law does not make such distinctions but, of course, the local authority can do so by delegating to committees, subcommittees or officers, as it thinks appropriate, the power to make decisions on matters of lesser importance (see 4.8, 9.80). Even before the law permitted such delegation, officers in practice operated either under extra-legal authority to act within certain defined administrative spheres or by presumption in law as agents of their authority.

---

[50] See, however, 5.63 concerning the conventional authority presumed to reside in a committee chairman to make decisions on behalf of his committee.

[51] A *proxy* is a person appointed by someone to act and vote for him at a meeting. The term is also applied to the instrument by which such person is appointed. There is no common law right to vote by proxy (*Harben* v. *Phillips* (1883) 23 Ch.D.14) and no statutory right conferred in respect of local authority meetings.

[52] A local authority or committee which has arranged for the discharge of any of its functions by a committee, subcommittee, or officer, or other local authority, is not precluded from exercising those functions: Local Government Act 1972, s.101(4).

The 'Wednesbury' principle

1.39. There is another procedural consideration which a local authority must take into account in the course of arriving at a decision. If a decision is not to be challenged and declared of no effect on grounds of unreasonableness and therefore *ultra vires* (see 1.40), it must comply with what is known as the *Wednesbury* principle. This principle was enunciated in *Associated Provincial Picture Houses Ltd* v. *Wednesbury Corporation* (1948).[53] Lord Greene summarised it thus:

> . . . the court is entitled to investigate the action of the local authority with a view to seeing whether it has taken into account matters which it ought not to take into account or, conversely, has refused to take into account or neglected to take into account matters which it ought to take into account. Once that question is answered in favour of the local authority, it may still be possible to say that the local authority, nevertheless, has come to a conclusion so unreasonable that no reasonable authority could ever have come to it. In such a case . . . the court can interfere. The power of the court to interfere in each case is not that of an appellate authority to override a decision of the local authority but is that of a judicial authority which is concerned, and concerned only, to see whether the local authority has contravened the law by acting in excess of the powers which Parliament has confided in it.

The local authority's advisers clearly have a responsibility to ensure that, in reaching a decision, the council or a committee addresses its mind only to matters that it ought to take into account or does not refuse or neglect to take account of such matters and is not influenced by matters that are irrelevant. The minutes of proceedings at a meeting might usefully recite the considerations taken into account by the council, committee or subcommittee in reaching its decision, but see 12.32, 13.18.

Decision must be intra vires

1.40. Although a decision may have been made in a procedurally correct manner it will still be *ultra vires* if it is one which the local authority has no power to make. A detailed discussion of the doctrine of *ultra vires* would be beyond the scope of this work but, briefly, it means that a local authority can lawfully do only those things which it is obliged to do by law or which it is permitted or assumed to be permitted by law to do. In the course of years the courts have adopted a more liberal attitude to the *assumed* powers of a local authority – in tune, it might be said, with present-day recognition that local government is concerned with more than the mere carrying out of

[53] [1948] 1 KB 223.

specific powers and duties.[54] And in s.111 of the Local Government Act 1972, authorities now have power to do anything (whether or not involving expenditure, borrowing or lending money or the acquisition or disposal of any property or rights) calculated to facilitate or be conducive or incidental to the discharge of any of their functions. Furthermore, there is power in s.137 enabling any local authority, subject to certain restrictions (particularly the exclusion of expenditure which the authority is otherwise permitted or obliged to make), to incur expenditure up to the product of a 2p rate[55] which in its opinion is in the interests of its area or any part of the area or all or some of its inhabitants.[56]

'Blanket' resolutions on policy

1.41. One other matter relating to the effectiveness of a decision needs to be touched upon here. It is in order – indeed, there is much to commend the practice – for a local authority to pass a resolution setting out its general policy on any issue in order to ensure consistency in decision-making. But whatever rules or guidelines on policy the authority may establish in this way, the general principle (though there is an exception: see the next paragraph) is that a local authority must not so rigidly apply them that it precludes proper consideration of the merits or otherwise of individual questions that arise for decision within the general policy or guidelines.[57]

1.42. There is, however, at least one instance where the law permits the passing of a rigid blanket resolution. The Lotteries and Amusement Act 1976, sch.3, para.2, and the Gaming Act 1968, sch.9, para.3, concerned with the licensing of permits for commercial provision of amusements with prizes and permits for gaming machines, expressly allow policy resolutions by the local authority declaring, for example, that it will not issue or renew any permits in respect of premises of a specified class. It is evident, however, that the court will interpret the statutory rules strictly.[58]

---

[54] 'Local government is more than the sum of the particular services provided. It is an essential part of English democratic government.': *Report of the Royal Commission on Local Government in England* (1969), Cmnd 4040, p. 146 – a sentiment endorsed by the Widdicombe Committee in its interim report (see 1.52).

[55] The Widdicombe Report (see 1.52) has recommended that the 2p should be increased to 4p for London borough and metropolitan district councils.

[56] There appears to be no need for a local authority to pass a resolution specifically invoking s.137, although it may be prudent to do so. It is no bad thing as a rule for a local authority to indicate the legal power or duty under which it is proposing to take action.

[57] See, e.g. *R. v. Port of London Authority ex-parte Kynoch Ltd* [1919] 1 KB 176, and other cases on fettering discretion by self-created rules of policy.

[58] See *R. v. Herrod ex-parte Leeds City District Council* [1976] 1 All ER 272; and *Walker v. Leeds City Council* [1976] 3 All ER 709.

Maladministration

1.43. A further factor to be mentioned in relation to decision-making is the possibility of a local authority being declared guilty of maladministration. Under the Local Government Act 1974, Part III, it is open to an aggrieved individual to take a complaint of maladministration, through a councillor, against a local authority[59] (but not a parish or community council or a parish or community meeting), a police or a water authority, or one of the authority's committees, to a local commissioner of either the Commission for Local Administration in England or the Commission for Local Administration in Wales, as the case may be. The Act does not define *maladministration* (it is for the ombudsman to decide whether maladministration has occurred) but it refers, for example, to the way in which an authority's decision has been made.[60] It covers administrative action or inaction based on or influenced by improper considerations or conduct (e.g. arbitrariness, malice or bias, including unfair discrimination), neglect, unjustified delay, incompetence, failure to observe relevant rules or procedures, failure to take relevant considerations into account, failure to establish or review procedures when there is a duty or obligation to do so, and the use of faulty systems. There are certain matters expressly excluded from the ombudsman's jurisdiction and he has no power to compel a local authority to redress or compensate anyone whose interests have been prejudiced through maladministration; but clearly opprobrium attaches to any authority which does not at least ensure that steps are taken to avoid in future the reason for maladministration.

1.44. Widdicombe has suggested some changes in the ombudsman system.[61] The law should be amended, it says, to enable the local ombudsman to consider complaints received direct from members of the public; there should be a new statutory right for complainants to apply to the county or, in Scotland, the sheriff court for a remedy where the complainant is dissatisfied with the remedy offered by a local authority following a finding of maladministration leading to injustice; the exclusions from the ombudsman's jurisdiction should be modified; the local

---

[59] See 5.44 concerning the possibility of maladministration by an individual councillor.

[60] 'If circumstances are not properly reported or if facts are omitted from a report to a committee the authority itself might be found guilty of maladministration in its decision-making. The ombudsman may find maladministration if serious complaints are not reported to the appropriate committee. Promises made by the authority and not fulfilled may result in a finding of maladministration. Procrastination and even, perhaps, undue haste may also produce an adverse finding by the ombudsman. These issues have now to be kept very much in the forefront of the mind of those who write reports and draft minutes.' R. G. Brooke, 'Modern Approach to Committee Practice' (1979) 143 *Local Government Review* 3.

[61] Widdicombe Report, paras.9.64–9.82. As to Widdicombe, see 1.52.

ombudsmen should be given new powers to investigate individual cases on their own initiative; and the government should reconsider (a) the case for charging the costs of the service direct to central government funds and (b) the need for the existence of the representative bodies whose task, *inter alia*, is to review and pass on to local authorities any general conclusions reached by the ombudsmen about their operations.

Variation of decisions

1.45. Decisions once made may, so far as practicable and lawful, be subsequently varied or rescinded although standing orders ordinarily seek to limit the frequency of change in this respect (see 2.13). Clearly it would be impracticable for an authority to purport to rescind a resolution upon which action had been taken which could not be undone; and unlawful to purport to rescind a resolution so as to disadvantage a third party who has properly relied on the decision unless, of course, the law permits the revocation or amendment of the decision when compensation may be payable. As to the position regarding committee and subcommittee decisions: see 11.34 *et seq.*

When does a resolution become effective?

1.46. In most instances the decision of a local authority takes effect immediately the resolution is properly passed. In certain circumstances, however, a decision cannot be acted upon until specific formalities have been observed: by-laws made by an authority are of no validity until confirmed by the confirming body;[62] a decision to sell land is ineffective until the formal deed has been executed; and in some cases a decision does not take effect until formal notification has been served upon those affected by it, e.g. a decision to dismiss an employee, or a decision granting planning permission (see 1.47).

1.47. There have been several cases on whether resolution or notification amounts to a grant of planning permission.[63] In *R.* v. *West Oxfordshire District Council ex-parte C. H. Pearce Homes Ltd* (1986),[64] however, the issue was clearly decided. Woolf J said:

Suffice it to say that even in the absence of authority I would, from my

---

[62] By-laws for good rule and government are made by simple resolution of the local authority, but the by-laws must be 'made under the common seal of the authority' and do not have effect until confirmed by the appropriate confirming authority: Local Government Act 1972, s.236(3).

[63] See particularly *Slough Estates* v. *Slough Borough Council* [1969] 2 Ch. p. 315 A/B.

[64] (1986) 150 LG. Rev. 119.

examination of the [planning] code, find a clear indication that it is the notification which amounts to the grant, and that where the notification is preceded by a resolution of the authority that resolution should be regarded as a resolution that planning permission should be granted and that the resolution is intended to be implemented by the notification which amounts to the grant. Accordingly, until there has been notification, an applicant for planning permission has not received permission.

This distinction between the resolution and the administrative act which gives the resolution full effect is important for several reasons. The local authority can change its mind after the resolution and before formal notification to revoke its decision;[65] and thus, of course, compensation for any revocation of planning permission cannot arise until after formal notification of the decision.

1.48. While it is important, as a general rule, that where a decision is to take effect on a certain future date the resolution should specifically include that date, the resolution may not necessarily be defective if it does not – provided the local authority's intention is clear, e.g. in the minute as distinct from the resolution itself. Thus in *Sheffield City Council* v. *Graingers Wines Ltd* (1977)[66] it was held that there had been sufficient compliance with statute even though a resolution under s.17 of the General Rate Act 1967 (relating to the rating of unoccupied property) did not in its terms state when the resolution was to take effect and despite provision in s.17(2), as amended by the Local Government Act 1972, s.15(1), that:

> the day to be specified in a resolution under subs. (1) of this section shall be . . . the first day of a rate period for that area beginning after the date on which the resolution is passed.

The Court of Appeal considered this was a serious omission but, while the trial judge held that it was fatal, the Court of Appeal took the view that, in the circumstances of the case, it was not: neither justice nor common sense required the court to isolate the resolution from its context to 'make that violent extraction of the kernel from the nut in which it shelters'.

Continuing validity of resolution

1.49. As a general rule there is no need for a local authority to pass a new resolution to replace one passed under legislation which, though repealed,

---

[65] In *R.* v. *Yeovil Borough Council ex-parte Trustees of Elim Pentecostal Church* (1972) 23 P & CR 39, there was a change of heart by the planning authority, which had previously resolved to grant planning permission, and the applicant's application for an order of mandamus requiring the council to issue planning permission was refused.

[66] (1977) 141 LG. Rev. 179, and see p. 660; (1977) WLR 1119.

is re-enacted to similar effect. Thus, for example, a resolution to apply the provisions of s.19 of the Local Government (Miscellaneous Provisions) Act 1982 (which concerned the registration of food hawkers and premises) is of continuing effect by virtue of the Interpretation Act 1978, ss.16 and 17, despite the repeal of s.19 of the 1982 Act and its re-enactment in Pt IV of the Food Act 1984.

1.50. The Interpretation Act 1978 provides in s.16 that where an Act repeals an enactment the repeal does not, unless the contrary intention appears, affect the previous operation of the enactment repealed or anything done thereunder; and s.17 provides that where an Act is repealed, with or without modification, then unless the contrary intention appears, any reference in any other enactment to the Act repealed is to be construed as a reference to the re-enacted provisions.

Inaccurate notification of a decision

1.51. What if an officer of the local authority misinterprets the terms of a decision to a third party or provides an inaccurate notification of the decision? Is the authority bound by its decision as minuted or by the officer's notification of its terms? A discussion of the concept of *estoppel* is outside the scope of this book but, so far as planning is concerned, this view of Michael Albery, Q.C.,[67] is of interest:

> It is submitted . . . that where planning permission is granted or refused by a corporate body, the grant or refusal is constituted by the appropriate resolution of that body or of its delegated committee. On the other hand, the applicant is entitled to assume that notice of such decision received from the officer of such body entrusted with the conduct of such matters correctly represents the decision. He is not bound to call for a minute of the resolution in order to check such accuracy. If the applicant acts, as will usually happen, to his detriment on the faith of such notice, and perhaps even if he does not, the planning authority will be estopped from denying the accuracy of such notice. This estoppel will enure for the benefit of the applicant's successors in title, in that for conveyancing purposes the notice can be treated as conveying the terms of the permission. But an applicant who has reason to suspect that the notice is less favourable to him than the resolution of which it purports to give notice is entitled to obtain copies of and to rely on the resolution itself, but not of course the application or surrounding correspondence unless these are incorporated into the resolution by reference. ‚

---

[67] (1974) 90 *Law Quarterly Review* 351, 360; and see 'The Legal Effects of Statements by Planning Officers', *ibid.* in which it is quoted. See also *Southend-on-Sea Corporation* v. *Hodgson (Wickford) Ltd* (1961) 2 All ER 46; and *Lever Finance Ltd* v. *Westminster (City) London Borough Council* (1971) 1 QB 222 (1971) JPL 115; discussed in S. H. Bailey, C. A. Cross and J. F. Garner, *Cases and Materials in Administrative Law* (1977), p. 259.

Conduct of local authority business

Widdicombe report

1.52. The Widdicombe Committee's report on *The Conduct of Local Authority Business* (Cmnd 9797)[68] was published as the manuscript of this edition was about to be sent to the publishers – just in time to allow the inclusion of brief reference to those of its recommendations which relate to the subject matter of this work. The committee of inquiry had been set up early in 1985 by the then Environment Secretary because of Government concern over what it suspected was widespread political abuse in the internal working of local government. Its terms of reference were:

> To inquire into practices and procedures governing the conduct of local authority business in Great Britain, with particular reference to:
> (a)   the rights and responsibilities of elected members;
> (b)   the respective roles of elected members and officers;
> (c)   the need to clarify the limits and conditions governing discretionary spending by local authorities;
> and to make any necessary recommendations for strengthening the democratic process.

The Government has decided to delay any decision on the proposals until after the end of 1986 so as to provide time for a wide-ranging debate and substantive responses on the whole Widdicombe package of 88 recommendations.

1.53. Widdicombe's principal proposals are referred to generally and in regard to political activity in Chapter 4; on public and member access to committee meetings and documents in Chapter 3; on matters relating to local authority membership and councillors' role and relationships and co-option in Chapter 5; and on committee membership and the delegation to committee chairmen in Chapter 9. Other matters are noted elsewhere where relevant throughout this work.

---

[68] The committee's main report was supplemented by four research volumes: vol. 1: *The Political Organisation of Local Authorities* (Cmnd 9798); vol. 2: *The Local Government Councillor* (Cmnd 9799); vol. 3: *The Local Government Elector* (Cmnd 9800); vol. 4: *Aspects of Local Democracy* (Cmnd 9801). The committee issued an interim report, *Local Government Publicity*, in August 1985, and certain of its recommendations were subsequently enacted in the Local Government Act 1986.

2

STANDING ORDERS

Statutory provisions

General power

2.1. Local authorities are given statutory power, i.e. they *may* make standing orders:[1]

(a) for the regulation of council proceedings and business; and

(b) regarding the quorum, proceedings and place of meeting of their committees and subcommittees;[2]

but are *compelled* to make standing orders as to contracts for the supply of goods or materials or for the execution of works.[3] Authorities appointing a joint committee may together make standing orders regarding the quorum, proceedings and business of the joint committee.[4]

Model standing orders

2.2. A model set of standing orders for the guidance of local authorities in regulating their proceedings and business was issued by the former Ministry of Housing and Local Government in 1963 and reprinted in 1973. Although the model is out of date in many respects – it is based on the now long ago repealed Local Government Act 1933 – there is no immediate intention on the part of the Department of the Environment to publish an updated version; accordingly, this work includes references where appropriate to the existing model.

---

[1] Local Government Act 1972, sch.12, para.42, which appears to be intended to relate solely to council meetings even though s.99 provides that sch.12 shall apply also to committees.

[2] *Ibid.* s.106. It might seem that s.99 and sch.12 together are sufficiently widely drawn to cover the making of standing orders for committees.

[3] *Ibid.* s.135(2). Thereunder *Model Standing Orders: Contracts*, 3rd edn, has been published: HMSO 1983; and see D.o.E. circular 15/83 and WO 25/83.

[4] *Ibid.* s.106.

No obligation to make standing orders

2.3. Although there is thus no obligation upon local authorities to make standing orders for the regulation of their proceedings and business in council or committee or subcommittee meetings, all authorities do so. If, however, no standing orders were made, then – except in so far as an authority's proceedings and business are not regulated by statute – common law provisions would apply: indeed, common law rules apply wherever standing orders are silent on a particular point.

2.4. Model standing order no. 36 provides that:

> The standing order of the council headed 'Rules of debate' (except those parts which relate to standing and to speaking more than once) and the standing order headed 'Interest of members in contracts and other matters' shall, with any necessary modification, apply to committee and subcommittee meetings.

If an authority does not make standing orders affecting its committees (or if two or more authorities appointing a joint committee do not make standing orders governing the joint committee),[5] or if the standing orders made in either case do not cover such matters, then the committees (or joint committee) or subcommittee of either may themselves determine the quorum, proceedings and place of meeting.[6]

Variation and revocation

2.5. There is express power enabling a local authority to vary or revoke the standing orders it makes.[7] As standing orders are made by simple resolution of the authority, so too, may their variation or revocation. Where a standing order has been revoked the resolution effecting the revocation may itself be rescinded, in which case the original standing order becomes again operative.[8]

[5] *Ibid.* s.106.

[6] In determining its own quorum, proceedings and place of meeting, however, the committee, joint committee or subcommittee should – on the analogy of *Picea Holdings* v. *London Rent Assessment Board* [1971] 2 QB 216 – follow the practice of the parent local authority or authorities. At common law if no quorum is fixed, all acts of a committee must be done in the presence of all members of the committee (*re The Liverpool Household Stores Association Ltd* (1890) 59 SJ Ch.616); but in local government the statutory provision that all questions coming before the local authority must be decided by a majority of those present and voting at a properly constituted meeting (Local Government Act 1972, sch.12, para.39, as applied to committees by s.99) clearly overrides the common law rule.

[7] Local Government Act 1972, sch.12, para.42, gives power to vary or revoke standing orders and this, by para.44(1), applies to standing orders affecting committees, joint committees, and subcommittees just as it applies to standing orders affecting the full council. Section 106, which provides power enabling standing orders to be made as regards committees, does not specifically provide for variation or revocation.

[8] *Weir* v. *Fermanagh County Council* [1913] 1 IR 63, p. 93.

2.6. There is much to be said for putting some procedural brake upon the too easy amendment of standing orders. Model standing order no. 39, for example, provides that:

> Any motion to add to, vary or revoke these standing orders shall when proposed and seconded stand adjourned without discussion to the next ordinary meeting of the council.

Some authorities stipulate that standing orders shall be altered or rescinded only upon the recommendation of the committee charged with the review of standing orders, while others require that a certain period of prior notice shall be given before formal amendment. Thus, in *Mayer* v. *Burslem Local Board* (1875)[9] a local board had made the following by-law:

> That no resolution of the local board be altered or rescinded unless one month's notice be given by the clerk to each member of the board, setting forth the proposed alteration, nor unless there be at least as many members of the board present at the meeting as were present at the meeting when such resolution was adopted.

Blackburn J said that the last part of this by-law might be invalid but that the first part was valid and was *a very salutary and competent by-law*.

Suspension

2.7. Although there is no specific power enabling an authority to *suspend* its standing orders, i.e. to decide, by resolution, that for a special purpose or for a period of time, one or other of its standing orders shall be of no effect, there is general acknowledgement that this can properly be done. Model standing order no. 40, for example, provides:

> (1) Subject to paragraph (2) of this standing order, any standing orders may be suspended so far as regards any business at the meeting where its suspension is moved. (2) A motion to suspend standing orders shall not be moved without notice . . . unless there shall be present at least [one half of the whole number of the] members of the council.

The suspension must be by resolution: it cannot be implied.[10] And despite the terms of the model standing order, notice of an intention to suspend any standing order ought surely to be given in the agenda for the meeting at which the suspension is to be moved. Widdicombe expressed this view:[11]

> We think it undesirable that procedural rules should be capable of change in

[9] (1875) 39 JPN 437.
[10] See *R.* v. *Hereford Corporation ex-parte Harrower and Others* [1970] 3 All ER 461; and see 2.10.
[11] Widdicombe Report, para.5.126.

mid-meeting by suspension of standing orders. Some safeguards are required. We are not convinced that . . . the model standing orders . . . are of themselves sufficient, and propose that standing orders should not be capable of suspension or amendment without advance notice of motion except on the vote of two-thirds of the membership of the council. All standing orders should be statutorily required to include such a limitation.

A two-thirds majority would need, of course, a change in the law because a local authority needs only a majority of those present and voting at a meeting to reach a decision: see 1.35.

Validity

2.8. Local authorities could quite properly make standing orders without express statutory power to do so: every constituted body has an inherent right to regulate its own proceedings though necessarily within the law. The fact that standing orders are made under statutory power and authority does not give them the force of law: they are not by-laws nor can they impose penalties; and if they purport to override or are in conflict with the law they are *ultra vires*.[12] Even a standing order which goes beyond what the law strictly requires may be *ultra vires*, e.g. a standing order which requires a councillor to be excluded from the *council chamber* or *committee room* and not merely from the *meeting* during consideration of a matter in which he has a pecuniary interest.[13] In other words, where a statute deals specifically with a subject-matter, standing orders cannot lawfully go further; but where this is not so the local authority is free to apply a standing order to the subject-matter (see 9.55, where *R. v. Newham London Borough Council ex-parte Haggerty* (1986) is discussed, in which it was held that as there is no statutory delimitation on the eligibility of councillors for committee membership, it is open to an authority by standing orders to establish its own criteria for membership).

Enforceability

2.9. There is authority for the view that a local authority is bound to observe its own standing orders.[14] In *R. v. Hereford Corporation ex-parte Harrower & Others* (1970),[15] Lord Parker CJ said:

It is quite clear that there is a statutory duty on the local authority to comply

---

[12] In *R. v. Teddington UDC* (1928) 92 JPN 208, a standing order requiring a two-thirds majority to rescind a resolution was held *ultra vires* in view of the Public Health Act 1875, sch.1, Pt (1), r.7 (see now Local Government Act 1972, sch.12, para.39). See also *Mayer* v. *Burslem Local Board, supra.*

[13] I.e. a standing order made under the Local Government Act 1972, s.94.(4): see 5.32.

[14] *R. v. Woolwich Borough Council* (1922) 87 JP 30; 128 LT 374.

[15] [1970] 3 All ER 461, p. 1427.

with standing orders as they exist at the time and if those standing orders have not been suspended then there is a duty to comply with them.

This case was concerned with standing orders in respect of contracts and not in regard to the regulation of internal domestic business. In a more recent case, however, the court made an order of *certiorari* to quash a decision of the Conservative group on the council suspending all Labour opposition councillors from committee membership because the decision to do so contravened the council's standing orders.[16]

2.10. In *Hereford, supra*, the local authority had suspended its standing orders by implication. The council had decided, quite openly, to invite tenders for the installation of central heating in certain flats from only the local electricity and gas boards and the National Coal Board, but omitted to suspend its standing orders which provided for open competitive and not select tendering. The court held that, although the council could properly suspend its standing orders, it could do this only by formal resolution of the council and not by implication. It also emerged from this case that if an authority acts contrary to its standing orders, the ratepayers have sufficient legal right to enable them to seek an order of mandamus against the authority.

2.11. The effective power of a local authority to enforce compliance with standing orders by its individual council members is limited; it might therefore be thought imprudent for an authority to make a standing order which could be flouted with impunity. Thus, to take the example of a ban on smoking at meetings, it would probably be unlawful for the council to order a member out of a council meeting who persisted in smoking in defiance of a standing order prohibiting it, because he has a lawful right to be present subject to temporary exclusion for disorderly conduct; and it is at least open to doubt whether smoking in contravention of a standing order could be classed as disorderly conduct.[17] The position as regards officers is quite different: compliance with standing orders can be an express or implied part of the contract of service, and breach of standing orders could be dealt with as an act of indiscipline.

[16] *R.* v. *Rushmore Borough Council ex-parte Crawford*: *The Times*, 28 November 1981. But for the provision in standing orders the council could have deprived the councillors of committee membership (*Manton* v. *Brighton Corporation* [1951] 2 KB 392): see 9.61.

[17] It is submitted, however, that a local authority could properly ban smoking in that part of the council chamber or committee room allocated to the public. Whether it would be appropriate to do so if councillors themselves persisted in smoking is a matter for consideration.

Procedural considerations

Formal making of standing orders

2.12. Standing orders are made by simple resolution: necessarily by the council in full assembly as regards standing orders which apply to the authority's proceedings and business generally; or by a committee or subcommittee where the council itself has not made standing orders relating to its committees and the committee or subcommittee wishes formally to regulate committee or subcommittee proceedings. Standing orders made by a committee or subcommittee cannot override the standing orders of the local authority (see 2.4). The form which standing orders take is dealt with below (see 2.22).

2.13. Although no special formalities need be observed for the making of standing orders (there is no approval of a confirmatory body to be sought), it may be thought desirable 'that an authority should regard the making of its standing orders (since they are to have continuing validity) as a matter of some seriousness'.[18] The general law affecting the convening of a council meeting requires notice to be given of the intention to make standing orders in the summons to the council meeting at which the motion is to be put. It is competent, as indicated in 2.6, for an authority to decide that, before any amendment of standing order comes into force, it should be confirmed by a subsequent meeting (but it would not be correct to require a special majority at either meeting).[19]

2.14. In practice the standing orders will be drafted by officers to meet the wishes and needs of the local authority and the draft may first need to be approved by the appropriate committee (a policy or general purposes committee) and submitted by recommendation to the full assembly for approval.

Amendment of standing orders

2.15. It follows that, subject to what has been said above, standing orders may be varied or revoked or suspended by simple resolution with similar lack of formality provided that due notice is given beforehand. Where the standing orders prescribe the procedure for amendment, the procedure should be followed (see 2.6) provided it does not purport to override the law.

---

[18] W. Eric Jackson, *The Secretarial Practice of Local Authorities* (1953), pp. 170–71.
[19] See *R. v. Teddington UDC, supra,* and see 2.6.

Periodical review

2.16. Ideally each local authority should undertake a regular review of its standing orders,[20] annually or at some other predetermined interval of time. No great changes are likely to be called for in those which deal with the rules of debate, but it may be necessary to take account of changes in the law and organisational structure (including particularly the committee system).

Supply to members

2.17. Councillors (and co-opted members, too) must be provided with an up-to-date copy of standing orders. Model standing order no. 41 is to the following effect:

> A printed copy of these standing orders, and of such statutory provisions as regulate the proceedings and business of the council shall be given to each member of the council by the town clerk/clerk of the council upon delivery to him of the member's declaration of acceptance of office on the member's being first elected to the council.

Content

What should be included

2.18. What is included in standing orders is entirely a matter for determination by each local authority, although enforcement is an inhibiting consideration (see 2.11). The main purpose is always to provide for the better regulation of proceedings at meetings – with which, of course, this work is primarily concerned – but some authorities now incorporate staffing and financial regulations and a variety of provisions relating to the corporate structure and organisation of the authority and the processes and procedures of its committee system. Often, however, there are well established practices or conventions governing the conduct of local authority business which are not incorporated in formal standing orders: see 2.19.

Conventions

2.19. Widdicombe said it saw an important role for local conventions in dealing with those matters where the need is for clear rules but which are

[20] See J. H. Warren, *Municipal Administration* (1948), 2nd edn, pp. 63–64.

not sufficiently susceptible to legal definition to lend themselves to standing orders and on which there is too great a variety of local circumstances
for national codes of conduct to be appropriate.[21] It recommended that
each local authority should draw up and make publicly available a list of
the conventions it observes in relation, for example, to the following:

> (a) the detailed basis on which committee places are apportioned among
>   councillors;
> (b) channels for councillors' contact with officers;
> (c) the relationship between committee chairmen and chief officers;
> (d) responsibility for agenda;
> (e) the rights of councillors to obtain information and advice from
>   officers;
> (f) any arrangements for informal working groups or regular briefing
>   meetings with officers which are not formally constituted as commit-
>   tees of the council;
> (g) attendance of officers at party groups;
> (h) the allocation of support services to councillors;
> (i) the status of any staff attached to the political groups or individual
>   councillors.

Widdicombe did not believe that conventions should necessarily be given
the force of law:

> The danger of giving them a statutory status would be that the conventions
> would be over cautious and avoid some of the more problematic relationships.
> Even without statutory status, the local ombudsman would generally take
> such conventions into account in deciding whether maladministration had
> occurred. The extent to which local authorities develop conventions, and their
> content, could usefully be monitored to see whether greater formalisation of
> their status appears desirable.

2.20. There may be thought to be advantages in the codification of
conventions in a single document – if only to guide newly elected
councillors and newly recruited officers – just as, later (see 12.50), it is
suggested that a local authority's decisions on policy or important principle
should be separately recorded for ease of reference if of continuing effect.

Basis for co-ordination

2.21. It is submitted that only standing orders can provide effectively for
the unification and co-ordination of an authority's committee system. This
can be secured, in a simple way, by the expedient of requiring each
committee to submit reports and recommendations to the full assembly on

---

[21] Widdicombe Report, paras.5.128–5.131.

matters that come before it. The full assembly is not, however, an efficient co-ordinator and never has been. Even the smallest authorities have long recognised that other measures need to be enforced if co-ordination is to be wholly effective. At the other extreme, the role of standing orders is of critical importance: as, for example, where committees are entrusted with extensive delegation or where, as is usual nowadays, there is a policy committee or similar machinery which may act as a filter through which the policy proposals of committees must pass or as an innovator of policy proposals for submission to the full assembly. Examples of standing orders for this purpose are given later.

Form

2.22. Standing orders should be easy to understand[22] though often they are not for a variety of reasons. Sometimes, because they are couched in the words of a statute or, in a misguided attempt to secure precision, the phraseology is so complex that an authority has to produce an explanatory note for the convenience of council members to show the intention. A useful expedient for the convenience of members is a summary of the standing orders or their interpretation in diagrammatic form, something akin to algorithms.[23]

2.23. Standing orders should be bound together within covers of suitable size so that they may be referred to easily at meetings. The date when the standing orders were made or last reviewed should be shown together with the date when they became effective; and in the case of a loose-leaf system (which has much to commend it for ease of updating) there should be an indication of the date when each standing order was approved. The orders should be grouped in a logical sequence, and – a recommendation made in the model standing orders – it is a convenient practice for appropriate extracts from statutes to be printed in a distinctive typeface, such as italics, at the head of each standing order.

---

[22] In the October 1977 issue of *District Councils Review*, a correspondent complained that he had been faced with a standing order in these terms: 'Irrespective of all other provisions of these standing orders no amendment shall without the prior permission of the chairman of the council be moved at a council meeting which would relate to a decision which is reported to the council at that meeting as having been taken by a committee and where that committee had taken the decision in accordance with powers delegated to it by the council whether those powers were delegated either generally or specifically'. This presumably meant: 'An amendment to the decision of a committee taken under delegated powers cannot be moved at a council meeting without the permission of the chairman'.

[23] See Ian McKay, 'On a Point of Order' (1973) 137 *Local Government Review* 826.

3

ADMISSION OF PRESS AND PUBLIC

Introduction

Origin of right of admission

3.1. The right of members of the public to attend local authority meetings has been acquired gradually over the years. At the beginning of the century council meetings were regarded at common law as private meetings even though the local authority in full assembly was transacting public business. The local authority's entitlement to exclude the public, and press representatives, from their meetings was affirmed in *Tenby Corporation* v. *Mason* in 1908,[1] which arose out of the Tenby authority's refusal to allow a local newspaper reporter to attend council meetings after, it was alleged by the council, the reporter had produced seriously inaccurate reports of the proceedings. As a result of the court judgment, Parliament passed the Local Authorities (Admission of the Press to Meetings) Act 1908 which gave a right to 'duly accredited representatives of the press' to be admitted to council meetings, but in s.5 provided that 'nothing in this Act shall be construed so as to prohibit a local authority from admitting the public to its meetings'.[2] And so council meetings were open meetings only so far as the local authority thought fit to allow the public to attend.

3.2. It was nearly 50 years later, in the Public Bodies (Admission to Meetings) Act 1960, that the public was accorded a specific right to be admitted to the meetings of local authorities and certain other bodies to which it applied. Then, in the reorganisation of local government in the 1970s, the Local Government Act 1972 extended that right to permit the public to attend meetings of local authority committees. A major develop-

[1] (1908) 6 LGR 233.
[2] Even earlier it had been held in *Purcell* v. *Sowler* (1877) 2 CPD 215, that at common law an authority might expressly or impliedly consent to the attendance of non-members at its meetings.

ment occurred when the Local Government (Access to Information) Act 1985, which applies only to principal councils (see 1.5), extended this right of admission to subcommittees by additions to the 1972 Act and made detailed provisions obliging those authorities to supply the public with agenda and reports in advance of all meetings – again by adding new provisions to the 1972 Act.

Admission of the public

General principle

3.3 Thus now every principal council and its committee and subcommittee meetings[3] must be open to the public,[4] except when the public is excluded – as it must be – because *confidential information* (see 3.6) might otherwise be disclosed during an item of business or – as it may be – if information within one of the statutorily specified categories of *exempt information* (see 3.7) might be disclosed. The general principle underlying the 1985 Act is that meetings should in general be open to the public, including the Press.[5] Widdicombe, however, has suggested some restriction consonant with its view (see 4.19) that purely deliberative committees (including, significantly, the policy and resources committee) which do not make decisions could comprise councillors of one party only. It says:[6]

> What concerns us about the 1985 Act is that it applies equally to committees that have no decision-taking powers but are purely deliberative. We think that this is misconceived, and that the same distinction between decision-taking and deliberative committees should be made with regard to access to information as with regard to committee membership. It is a simple reality, which no legislation can alter, that politicians will develop policy options in confidence before presenting the final choice for public decision. We do not think this unreasonable. If the law prevents them from conducting such discussions in private in formal committees, then they will conduct them less formally elsewhere. We have heard that some local authorities have been creating new informal mechanisms expressly to avoid the effects of the 1985 Act. It is unsatisfactory to force policy deliberation out of the formal committee system into groupings of indeterminate status. It is also unnecessary. No decision can be taken by a local authority without it eventually being referred to a decision-taking committee or the council, where there will be full public access to the meeting and the documentation. Given this basic safeguard, we can see no

---

[3] As to what is a *committee* or a *subcommittee* for local government purposes: see Chapter 9.
[4] This does not confer an *absolute* right of admission on every member of the public who may wish to be pesent: see 3.11.
[5] See D.o.E. circular 6/86 (WO circular 11/86), para.3.
[6] Widdicombe Report, para.5.63.

benefit in applying the Act also to deliberative committees. We would not in any way wish to discourage individual local authorities from opening deliberative committees to the public and press if that is appropriate to their particular circumstances, but do not believe that they should be required by law to do so.

Meetings open to the public

3.4. The meetings required to be open to the public and Press are those of principal councils as defined in the 1972 Act, of the new authorities established by the Local Government Act 1985, and of certain other authorities,[7] and of the committees and subcommittees of all such authorities. Parish and community councils remain subject, as regards the admission of the public to meetings, to the provisions of the Public Bodies (Admission to Meetings) Act 1960 as extended by the Local Government Act 1972, s.100.[8] This means that their council and any committee meetings must be open to the public unless by resolution excluded from the whole or part of any meeting 'whenever publicity would be prejudicial to the public interest by reason of the confidential nature of the business to be transacted or for other special reasons stated in the resolution and arising from the nature of the business or of the proceedings'.

Notice of meetings

3.5. Public notice must be given of meetings of a principal council and its committees and subcommittees,[9] and copies of the agenda and accompanying reports must be made available to the public: otherwise the transaction of business is prohibited (see more particularly Chapter 6). These requirements arising out of the Local Government (Access to Information) Act 1985 are of particular significance in the case of committee and subcommittee meetings because there is elsewhere an obligation upon local authorities to give public notice of council meetings.[10]

---

[7] This means, in addition to the principal councils listed at 1.5: the Inner London Education Authority, a joint authority, the common council of the City of London, a joint board or joint committee if a body corporate discharging the functions of two or more principal councils, a combined police authority which is a body corporate, and a combined fire authority: Local Government Act 1972, s.100J, added by Local Government (Access to Information) Act 1985.

[8] So, too, do the council of the Isles of Scilly and joint boards or joint committees which discharge functions of any of these bodies (or of any of these bodies and of a principal council or a new authority established under the Local Government Act 1985): Local Government (Access to Information) Act 1985, s.4 and sch.2, para.4(2).

[9] Local Government Act 1972, s.100A(6), added by Local Government (Access to Information) Act 1985.

[10] *Ibid.* s.100B.

'Closed' meetings

3.6. The transaction of confidential information which requires principal local authorities to exclude the public means:[11]

(a) information furnished to the council by a government department upon terms, however expressed, which forbid the disclosure of the information to the public; and

(b) information the disclosure of which to the public is prohibited by or under any enactment or by the order of a court.

In either case, the reference to the obligation of confidence is to be construed accordingly. Because there is a statutory requirement upon the local authority or a committee or subcommittee to exclude the public in these circumstances there may be no need for a resolution to that effect to be passed beforehand.

3.7. Local authorities may by resolution[12] – they have discretion in the matter[13] – close meetings if it is likely that otherwise information within one of the specified categories of 'exempt information' would be disclosed. These categories[14] of exempt information cover such matters as personal information, financial and business affairs of people or companies, action likely to lead to a prosecution, and industrial disputes affecting the authority as employer. The full list of descriptions of exempt information is set out in the appendix to this chapter. The Secretary of State has power to amend the list[15] and will consider doing so if experience shows that it has been too widely or too narrowly drawn in the first instance.[16]

---

[11] Local Government Act 1972, s.100A(3), added by Local Government (Access to Information) Act 1985.

[12] Local Government Act 1972, s.100A(4).

[13] In exercising this discretion an authority should bear in mind the underlying principle of 'open government' and thus exclude the public only if satisfied it is right to do so, having regard to the information to be disclosed: D.o.E. circular 6/86, para.9.

[14] Local Government Act 1972, s.100I; and see the appendix to this chapter.

[15] *Ibid.* s.100I.

[16] Under the Public Bodies (Admission to Meetings) Act 1960, s.1(2), which previously applied to all local authorities but no longer to principal councils, the power to exclude the Press and public was very widely drawn in general terms: see 3.4. When the Bill was before the Commons on 5 February 1960, Margaret Thatcher, one of the sponsors of the Bill, said it had been found impossible to draft a clause which would cover all individual cases where the public should be excluded. The 1985 Act sought to overcome that 'impossibility' but it is interesting now to see how closely the terms of the 'exempt information' follow what Mrs Thatcher said in the Commons in 1960:

There are two prongs to this clause. Publicity would be prejudicial for two main groups of reasons. The first group is where the matters under discussion are of a confidential nature. They may relate to personal circumstances of individual electors. They may relate to a confidential communication from a Government department asking local authorities for their opinion on a subject which the minister would not like to be discussed in open session until he is a good deal further on and has received the views of local authorities. There is another group of subjects which perhaps could not be

3.8. A resolution for the foregoing purpose must:

(a) identify the proceedings, or the part of the proceedings, to which it applies; and

(b) state the description, in terms of sch.12A to the Local Government Act 1972, of the 'exempt information' giving rise to the exclusion of the public.

Where such a resolution is passed the local authority may lawfully exclude the public during the proceedings to which the resolution applies.[17]

Exclusion must be reasonable

3.9. Although a local authority when exercising its discretion to exclude the public from a meeting must justify its action by reference to the statutory list of items of 'exempt information', it is submitted that it must still act reasonably.[18] It clearly cannot by subterfuge exclude the public in circumstances where it is required to admit it, e.g. by failing to give requisite notice of the meeting or by deciding to meet in a place that is manifestly inadequate to accommodate members of the public (see 3.11).

Who are the public?

3.10. The right of admission to local authority meetings applies to the public generally,[19] i.e. it is not restricted to ratepayers or electors or local residents. Only electors, however, are entitled to be present at parish and community meetings.[20]

16 cont.

> strictly termed confidential but where it would be clearly prejudicial to the public interest to discuss them in open session. They may relate to staff matters, to legal proceedings, to contracts, the discussion of which tender to accept and other such matters. On this prong the press has to be excluded for a special reason which would need to be stated in the resolution for exclusion. Where the matter is confidential it would not need to be specified further in the resolution for exclusion. Where it was for a special reason, that reason would need to be specified in broad general terms in the resolution for exclusion.

[17] Local Government Act 1972, s.100A(5), added by Local Government (Access to Information) Act 1985.

[18] The scope for judicial review of a local authority's discretion in this respect is probably limited. Blackwell's *Law of Meetings*, 9th edn, by Vincent Powell-Smith, quotes (p. 24) Lord Halsbury, LC, in *Westminster Corporation* v. *London and North Western Rail Co.* [1905] AC 426 p. 179: 'Where the legislature has confided the power to a particular body, with a discretion how it is to be used, it is beyond the power of any court to contest that discretion'; and *Sharp* v. *Wakefield* [1891] AC 173 p. 179: such a discretion must be exercised judicially 'according to the rules of reason and justice, not according to private opinion . . . it is not to be arbitrary, vague, and fanciful, but legal and regular'.

[19] The point was made by Sir Jocelyn Simon, Solicitor-General, during the passage of the Bill through Parliament: House of Commons Official Report, col. 162: 30 March 1960.

[20] Local Government Act 1972, ss.13(1), 32(1).

Adequacy of accommodation

3.11. There are obviously practical limits to the right of the public to be admitted. How much space is set aside is a matter for the local authority's discretion. During the passage of what was to become the Public Bodies (Admission to Meetings) Act 1960 it was said[21] that:

> ... the duty imposed on a local authority ... will be to choose a room big enough to take some members of the public and some reporters. It will not have to provide accommodation for an unlimited number of each ... The usual way in which any body whose deliberations are open to the public complies with its obligations is by providing reasonable but limited accommodation for members of the public and then allocating it on the basis of first come, first served.

3.12. If a local authority or a committee decides to meet in a very small room and then says in effect 'We cannot have the public in because there is no room' it would be acting in bad faith; and in such an event, the Lord Chief Justice has said,[22] the authority would not be beyond the long arm of their Lordships' court. It would seem, therefore, that where a council or a committee is to discuss a matter in which it knows there is considerable public interest, it must either provide more accommodation for the public than is ordinarily available or at least ensure that the accommodation is no less than that ordinarily available.

Admission of Press representatives

Substantially same rights as public

3.13. Representatives of the Press enjoy no rights of admission[23] to local authority meetings greater than those conferred upon the public except that an authority is required, as far as practicable, to provide 'duly

---

[21] By the Solicitor-General: House of Commons Official Report, cols. 119–20: 30 March 1960. Note, too, the words 'so far as practicable' in Local Government Act 1972, s.100(1).

[22] This was one of several matters considered in *R. v. Liverpool City Council, ex-parte Liverpool Taxi Fleet Operators' Association* [1975] 1 All ER 379; [1975] 1 WLR 701; 119SJ 166; (1974) 73 LGR 143, DC.

[23] During the passage of the Public Bodies (Admission to Meetings) Bill through Parliament, the Solicitor-General made it clear in the Commons on 30 March 1960 that the Press should not be admitted at the expense of the public. Nor vice versa. At an earlier occasion, Henry Brooke, the then Minister of Housing and Local Government, said: 'If the public gallery is full, that does not entitle members of the public to occupy the seats set aside for the press, nor would it be proper if members of the press attended ... in enormous numbers, to say that only reporters could come in and that provision could not be made for the public.'

accredited representatives of newspapers'[24] with reasonable facilities (see next paragraph).

Facilities for the Press

3.14. While a meeting is open to the public, duly accredited representatives of newspapers attending the meeting for the purpose of reporting the proceedings for those newspapers must, as far as practicable, be afforded reasonable facilities for taking their report and, unless the meeting is held in premises not belonging to the council or not on the telephone, for telephoning the report at their own expense.[25] Principal authorities must, on request and on payment of postage or other necessary charges for transmission, supply for the benefit of any newspaper:

(a) a copy of the agenda for a meeting and accompanying reports;

(b) such further statements or particulars, if any, as are necessary to indicate the nature of the items included in the agenda; and

(c) if the proper officer thinks fit in the case of any item, copies of any other documents supplied to members of the council in connection with the item.[26]

Photography, live broadcasts and tape recordings

3.15. While there is no absolute prohibition, it is expressly provided[27] that 'nothing . . . shall require a principal council to permit the taking of photographs of any proceedings, or the use of any means to enable persons not present to see or hear any proceedings (whether at the time or later), or the making of any oral report on any proceedings as they take place'. This, it is submitted, does not refer only to press or similar representatives: it means that a principal council could deny a councillor or a member of the public the right.[28]

---

[24] 'Duly accredited representatives of newspapers' is not defined in the Local Government Act 1972 (nor in the Local Government (Access to Information) Act 1985 which amended it), but 'newspaper' includes (a) a news agency which systematically carries on the business of selling and supplying reports or information to newspapers; and (b) any organisation which is systematically engaged in collecting news (i) for sound or television broadcasts; or (ii) for programmes to be included in a cable programme service which is or does not require to be licensed: Local Government Act 1972, s.100K(1), added by Local Government (Access to Information) Act 1985.

[25] Local Government Act 1972, s.100A(6)(c), added by Local Government (Access to Information) Act 1985.

[26] Local Government Act 1972, s.100B(7), added by Local Government (Access to Information) Act 1985. The charge which is permitted to be made is a charge for *transmission* and not a charge for the documents themselves.

[27] *Ibid.* s.100A(7).

[28] See B. E. H. Cotter, 'The Admission of Press and Public to Meetings of Local Authorities' (1974) 138 *Local Government Review* 174.

Other considerations

Qualified privilege of documents provided

3.16. Where any accessible document for a local authority meeting (a) is supplied to, or open to inspection by, a member of the public, or (b) is supplied for the benefit of any newspaper, the publication thereby of any defamatory matter contained in the document is privileged unless the publication is proved to be made with malice.[29]

Exclusion of public and Press in event of disorder

3.17. The statutory obligation upon principal councils to admit the public, and the Press, to their meetings is 'without prejudice to any power of exclusion to suppress or prevent disorderly conduct or other misbehaviour at a meeting' (and see 7.121 *et seq.* where the whole question of disorderly conduct at meetings is considered).

3.18. If the chairman of a meeting thinks it desirable or necessary to adjourn the meeting because of disorder among the public present (see 7.125) the council, committee or subcommittee cannot afterwards resume proceedings with the public still debarred from admission on the assumption that readmission would again lead to disorder, because this would be a contravention of the public's right of admission. But identifiable miscreants, whether individuals or a group, could properly be excluded if persisting in disorder when business proceeded.

3.19. There appears to be no right for the Press or public upon readmission, or at the end of the meeting, to be told what business was transacted in their absence,[30] although the chairman might think it appropriate to outline what has been decided.

Standing orders

3.20. There is no provision in the model standing orders in respect of the admission or exclusion of the public from local authority meetings;[31] but

---

[29] This (and the corresponding provision in the Public Bodies (Admission to Meetings) Act 1960, s.1(5)) modifies the effect of *De Buse* v. *McCarthy and Stepney BC* [1942] 1 KB 156: see 6.26.

[30] A view expressed at 137 JPN 153 but, of course, the public can always inspect the minutes of the meeting.

[31] But the now wholly outdated model standing order no. 11 was to this effect. 'If any question arises at a meeting of the council (or of a committee thereof to which the Public Bodies (Admission to Meetings) Act 1960 applies by virtue of section 2(1)) as to the appointment, promotion, dismissal, salary, superannuation or conditions of service, or as to the conduct of any person employed by the council, such question shall not be the subject of discussion until the council or committee, as the case may be, has decided whether or not the power of exclusion of the public under section 1(2) of the Public Bodies (Admission to Meetings) Act 1960 shall be exercised.'

there is no reason why standing orders should not be made regulating, within the law, local arrangements. It may be, for example (see 2.11), that the local authority could by standing orders prohibit smoking in the accommodation provided for the public and Press, but whether it could lawfully eject anyone who persisted in smoking is at least open to doubt because once a member of the public is in the council chamber or committee room he is there lawfully and probably cannot be excluded except for disorderly conduct.

3.21. It is not uncommon for local authorities to include in standing orders pro forma motions which may be moved without notice, e.g. motions to exclude the public and Press. Thus in the case of a principal council when exempt information is to be considered:

> That under s.100A(4) of the Local Government Act 1972, the public be excluded from the meeting for the following item(s) of business on the grounds that it (they) involve(s) the likely disclosure of exempt information as defined in paragraph(s) . . . (respectively) of Part I of schedule 12A of the Act.

Or, in the case of, say, a parish or community council:

> That the public be excluded from this meeting during consideration of . . . as publicity would be prejudicial to the public interest because of the confidential nature of the business to be transacted.

Practical considerations

3.22. There is no doubt that the obligation cast upon local authorities to admit the Press and public to committees and subcommittees has created problems. Many authorities object to open committee meetings, not because of any desire to keep secret matters that ought fairly to be public knowledge (indeed, some authorities had formerly permitted the Press to attend on certain conditions), but because of a desire to preserve committees as the workshops of local government where business can be transacted in free and informal discussion with officers. The transaction of business in public is inhibiting: the conditions make it difficult for officers to participate quite so freely in discussion and, inevitably in some instances, council members are prone now and then to indulge in party political debate for the benefit of the Press rather than to address their minds meaningfully to the business before the meeting. (See above (3.3) regarding Widdicombe's proposal for the exclusion of the public and Press from deliberative committees.)

Access to information

Extended access to documents

3.23. The Local Government (Access to Information) Act 1985 considerably extended the right of the public (and the Press) to inspect the documents of principal local authorities and of their committees and subcommittees,[32] and conferred on councillors, as members of those authorities, a statutory right of access to council papers.[33] The rights of the public in this respect are mentioned briefly here because in many ways the rights are closely identified with the right of access to local authority meetings: indeed, in *R. v. Hackney London Borough Council ex-parte Gamper* (1985) (discussed later: see 5.12), it was said that for councillors with a 'need to know' there is no logical distinction between access to documents and attendance at meetings. Public access to documents (agenda and reports) prior to a meeting is dealt with at 6.21 *et seq.* as regards council meetings and at 10.6 as regards committees; and to other documents (minutes and background papers) at 8.37 as regards council meetings and at 12.55 in respect of committees. The statutory right of councillors in this connection is discussed in Chapter 5.

Duty to publish other information

3.24. Each principal council is also required to publish the following information and to keep it available for public inspection:[34]

(a) a register (i) giving the name and address of every member and the ward or division represented, and (ii) the name and address of every member of each committee and subcommittee;

(b) a list specifying (i) the powers exercisable by officers under delegated authority, and (ii) the title of the officer where the power is exercisable for a period of more than six months; and

(c) a document summarising the rights which the law confers[35] upon

---

[32] Access to documents of a limited range of other local authorities, i.e. parish and community councils, the council of the Isles of Scilly and joint boards or joint committees which discharge functions of any of these bodies (or of any of these bodies and a principal council) is still governed by the Local Government Act 1972, s.228 as amended, and is thus exercisable by electors and not members of the public generally.

[33] Local Government Act 1972, s.100F, added by Local Government (Access to Information) Act 1985. The rights are in addition to any common law or other rights. Widdicombe has suggested that these rights should all be contained in statute with no reliance on common law: Widdicombe Report, para.5.71.

[34] Local Government Act 1972, s.100G, added by the Local Government (Access to Information) Act 1985.

[35] This means not only the rights conferred by Pt VA and Pt XI of the Local Government Act 1972 but under 'such other enactments as the Secretary of State by order specifies'.

members of the public to attend local authority meetings and council, committee and subcommittee meetings, and to inspect and copy documents and be furnished with documents.

APPENDIX TO CHAPTER 3

Local Government (Access to Information) Act 1985: Exempt Information

The following schedule 1 of the Local Government (Access to Information) Act 1985, ss.1 and 2, provides for the insertion of a sch.12A into the Local Government Act 1972 in respect of descriptions of *exempt information*.

Part I: Descriptions of Exempt Information

1. Information relating to a particular employee, former employee or applicant to become an employee of, or a particular office-holder, former office-holder or applicant to become an office-holder under, the authority.
2. Information relating to a particular employee, former employee or applicant to become an employee of, or a particular officer, former officer or applicant to become an officer appointed by:
    (*a*) a magistrates' court committee, within the meaning of section 19 of the Justices of the Peace Act 1979; or
    (*b*) a probation committee appointed under paragraph 2 of schedule 3 to the Powers of Criminal Courts Act 1973.
3. Information relating to any particular occupier or former occupier of, or applicant for, accommodation provided by or at the expense of the authority.
4. Information relating to any particular applicant for, or recipient or former recipient of, any service provided by the authority.
5. Information relating to any particular applicant for, or recipient or former recipient of, any financial assistance provided by the authority.
6. Information relating to the adoption, care, fostering or education of any particular child.
7. Information relating to the financial or business affairs of any particular person (other than the authority).
8. The amount of any expenditure proposed to be incurred by the authority under any particular contract for the acquisition of property or the supply of goods or services.

9. Any terms proposed or to be proposed by or to the authority in the course of negotiations for a contract for the acquisition or disposal of property or the supply of goods or services.

10. The identity of the authority (as well as of any other person, by virtue of paragraph 7 above) as the person offering any particular tender for a contract for the supply of goods or services.

11. Information relating to any consultations or negotiations, or contemplated consultations or negotiations, in connection with any labour relations matter arising between the authority or a Minister of the Crown and employees of, or office-holders under, the authority.

12. Any instructions to counsel and any opinion of counsel (whether or not in connection with any proceedings) and any advice received, information obtained or action to be taken in connection with:

    (*a*) any legal proceedings by or against the authority, or

    (*b*) the determination of any matter affecting the authority,

(whether, in either case, proceedings have been commenced or are in contemplation).

13. Information which, if disclosed to the public, would reveal that the authority proposes:

    (*a*) to give under any enactment a notice under or by virtue of which requirements are imposed on a person; or

    (*b*) to make an order or direction under any enactment.

14. Any action taken or to be taken in connection with the prevention, investigation or prosecution of crime.

15. The identity of a protected informant.

Part II: Qualifications

1. Information relating to a person of a description specified in any of paragraphs 1 to 5 of Part I above is not exempt information by virtue of that paragraph unless it relates to an individual of that description in the capacity indicated by the description.

2. Information falling within paragraph 7 of Part I above is not exempt information by virtue of that paragraph if it is required to be registered under:

    (*a*) the Companies Act 1985;

    (*b*) the Friendly Societies Act 1974;

    (*c*) the Industrial and Provident Societies Acts 1965 to 1978;

    (*d*) the Building Societies Act 1962; or

    (*e*) the Charities Act 1960.

3. Information falling within paragraph 8 of Part I above is exempt information if and so long as disclosure to the public of the amount there referred to would be likely to give an advantage to a person entering into, or seeking to enter into, a contract with the authority in respect of the property, goods or services, whether the advantage would arise as against the authority or as against other such persons.

4. Information falling within paragraph 9 of Part I above is exempt information if and so long as disclosure to the public of the terms would prejudice the authority in those or any other negotiations concerning the property or goods or services.

5. Information falling within paragraph 11 of Part I above is exempt information if and so long as disclosure to the public of the information would prejudice the authority in those or any other consultations or negotiations in connection with a labour relations matter arising as mentioned in that paragraph.

6. Information falling within paragraph 13 of Part I above is exempt information if and so long as disclosure to the public might afford an opportunity to a person affected by the notice, order or direction to defeat the purpose or one of the purposes for which the notice, order or direction is to be given or made.

Part III: Interpretation

1 (1) In this schedule:
'child' means a person under the age of eighteen years and any person who has attained that age and:
    (*a*) is registered as a pupil at a school; or
    (*b*) is the subject of a care order, within the meaning of section 20 of the Children and Young Persons Act 1969;
'disposal', in relation to property, includes the granting of an interest in or right over it;
'employee' means a person employed under a contract of service;
'financial or business affairs' includes contemplated, as well as past or current, activities;
'labour relations matter' means:
    (*a*) any of the matters specified in paragraphs (*a*) to (*g*) of section 29(1) of the Trade Union and Labour Relations Act 1974 (matters which may be the subject of a trade dispute, within the meaning of that Act); or
    (*b*) any dispute about a matter falling within paragraph (*a*) above;
    and for the purposes of this definition the enactments mentioned in paragraph (*a*) above, with the necessary modifications, shall apply in relation to office-holders under the authority as they apply in relation to employees of the authority:
'office-holder', in relation to the authority, means the holder of any paid office appointments to which are or may be made or confirmed by the authority or by any joint board on which the authority is represented or by any person who holds any such office or is an employee of the authority;
'protected informant' means a person giving the authority information which tends to show that:
    (*a*) a criminal offence,
    (*b*) a breach of statutory duty,

(*c*) a breach of planning control, as defined in section 87(3) of the Town and Country Planning Act 1971, or

(*d*) a nuisance,

has been, is being or is about to be committed;

'tender for a contract' includes a written statement prepared by the authority in pursuance of section 9(2) of the Local Government, Planning and Land Act 1980 (estimated cost of carrying out functional work by direct labour).

(2) Any reference in this schedule to 'the authority' is a reference to the principal council or, as the case may be, the committee or subcommittee in relation to whose proceedings or documents the question whether information is exempt or not falls to be determined and includes a reference:

(*a*) in the case of a principal council, to any committee or subcommittee of the council; and

(*b*) in the case of a committee, to:

(i) any constituent principal council;

(ii) any other principal council by which appointments are made to the committee or whose functions the committee discharges; and

(iii) any other committee or subcommittee of a principal council falling within subparagraph (i) or (ii) above; and

(*c*) in the case of a subcommittee, to:

(i) the committee, or any of the committees, of which it is a subcommittee; and

(ii) any principal council which falls within paragraph (*b*) above in relation to that committee.

4

CHANGING PRACTICES

Impact of politicisation

Traditional dispatch of council business

4.1. For many years past the traditional way in which local authorities conducted their business was through 'the appropriate channels',[1] which meant that:

> Each matter – irrespective of character or importance or lack of it – that arises for consideration from an external source (a complaint from an individual or a petition from a group of aggrieved electors, representations from a local pressure group, the circulars and directions and guidance that issue forth from Government departments) is ordinarily routed by way of a departmental head to the appropriate committee for consideration and report to the council sitting in full assembly and then back to the departmental head for any necessary executive action. So, too, projects which originate internally (proposals, for example, formulated by departmental heads of their own initiative): these follow through the same channels.

This basic procedure is still discernible but it has become overlaid, as it were, by an authority's political organisation. Yet the law does not recognise that politics is now a main determining factor in many decisions of most local authorities.

Party organisation

4.2. The political organisation and greater political intensity of local government in recent years have had a profound effect on the conduct of local authority business. It is often said that councillors are more assertive now than formerly, though this may only be true to a limited extent, but

---

[1] See Raymond S. B. Knowles, *Modern Management in Local Government*, 2nd edn (1977), p. 16.

policy issues arise for consideration more often nowadays from the initiative of councillors through the majority party group than from officers. After a local election, members of the political party which has secured the largest number of seats will 'form an administration' to run the authority politically, appoint committee chairmen, dominate the policy committee, and significantly discuss and often virtually make the more important decisions in group meetings. Control of the authority means that the group decisions can be carried through the formal meetings procedure and translated lawfully into effective action. Members of minority parties will also hold group meetings and, either in concert or separately, will provide a focus of 'opposition' in the council chamber if not in committees. Where an election has resulted in a hung – or balanced – council, then the parties may seek to arrive at some accommodation between themselves. One party group will 'form an administration' with the support, tacit or otherwise, of another; committee chairmen may in these circumstances be reduced to merely presiding over committee meetings, with a political spokesman who in practice receives the pre-committee briefing which in other circumstances would be provided by officers to committee chairmen. There is no one pattern of political organisation common to all hung councils. Sometimes the committee chairmanships rotate on a meeting-by-meeting basis between the groups. In other authorities a chairman is appointed each time the committee meets. Effective member control is sometimes operated through a representative panel of group spokesmen who meet informally before meetings for a pre-committee briefing. Devices such as these prove helpful to officers in seeking inter-party views and act as a sounding board for the chief executive's management team. Proposals have been put forward (see 3.3) which would bring group meetings within the statutory framework of local government.

Conduct of business

4.3. The ways in which local authorities conduct their business, i.e. through the traditional processes of democratic machinery, have been the subject of several important inquiries over the past quarter-century or so. The 1960s saw publication of the twin reports of Maud on *The Management of Local Government* and Mallaby on *Staffing of Local Government*. Later, prior to the reorganisation of local government outside Greater London in the 1970s, there was the Bains report on *The New Local Authorities: Management and Structure* and the complementary Patterson report *The New Scottish Local Authorities: Organisation and Management Structures*. Finally, there was the Widdicombe report on *The Conduct of Local Authority Business* in 1986, already referred to (see 1.52). These reports were concerned with wider issues than those which relate to local authority meetings, but many of their observations, conclusions and recommendations impinge on the decision-making process.

Decision-making process

General approach

4.4. The purist view of local democracy is that it is the elected members and the elected members alone who should make decisions. Until comparatively recently[2] this principle was supported by the law, which did not permit a local authority to delegate any of its decision-making functions except to a committee or subcommittee of councillors. As the Maud report observed,[3] it was 'the generality of members who are involved in the process of deciding what should be done, how it should be done, and checking whether it has been done'. And the only way in which councillors could lawfully and effectively do this was by discussion and decision at a formal meeting of the full assembly or of a properly constituted committee or subcommittee meeting. As Widdicombe put it: 'The main distinguishing feature of the current local government model is that decisions are taken corporately by, or on behalf of, the whole council';[4] there is no source of executive authority other than the council itself.

4.5. Before considering the structure and the process of decision-making at member level and the changes which have taken place in both in recent years, it is appropriate here to discuss briefly the role of officers in decision-making.

Officer role

4.6. The traditional approach to decision-making has meant that the role of officers was limited to the giving of professional advice and procedural guidance although, in the one-time 'secrecy' of committee deliberations, officers could exercise considerable influence up to the point at which a decision was made. Indeed, it was often said that the officers were the non-voting partners in the conduct of local authority business. How effective in practice this input from officers was depended largely on the relationship

---

[2] The Town and Country Planning Act 1968, s.64, first permitted the delegation of decision-making to officers. The Local Government Act 1972, s.101, now provides general powers in this respect.

[3] Maud Report, vol. 1, para.93.

[4] Widdicombe Report, para.5.2.

between councillors and their chief officers; but where, as was not uncommon, there was real partnership in the sense of mutual trust and confidence, the influence of officers often meant that councillors accepted – sometimes perhaps too unquestioningly – what the officers proposed.

4.7. Two important changes have taken place in comparatively recent times. The more significant is that local authorities now have express statutory power to delegate decision-making to officers on the same terms and subject to the same limitations as in the case of delegation to committees and subcommittees. The other is that the practical effect of opening committees and subcommittees to the public has meant that – as formerly and still so in the case of meetings of the full assembly – officers are more inhibited in making a contribution to member deliberations. On the other hand, it could be argued that the present-day role of the chief executive as the council's principal policy adviser enables him to take a larger share in decision-making at top level in his contact with the leader of the council.

Delegation to officers

4.8. The delegation of functions to an officer may be either to an individual officer by name or, preferably, to a post-holder (see 3.24 as to the obligation of the local authority to publicise officer delegations of more than six months' duration). Delegation in this sense means conferring authority on an officer to make decisions within the parameters of the delegation arrangements; hence the officer cannot pass on the decision-making authority to a subordinate, for otherwise the dictum *delegatus non potest delegare* would be infringed. A distinction needs to be made, however, between real delegation, which connotes the exercise of discretion, and mere executive[5] tasks which officers can perform without formal delegation. The delegation must not be fettered in such a way that, in effect, the decision in a particular instance is really made by an individual councillor; as explained later (see 5.71), this would be unlawful. Action taken under

[5] There are several cases where the courts have considered the implications of, for example, unauthorised action by an officer: *Warwick Rural District Council* v. *Miller-Mead* [1962] 1 All ER 212, where it was held that a local authority can regularise the action by subsequent ratification; *Lever Finance Ltd* v. *Westminster (City) London Borough Council* [1971] 1 QB 222, where it was held that an authority may be bound by the doctrine of estoppel when it is not prepared to ratify what has been done by an officer. In *Lever*, Lord Denning MR said at p. 231: 'An applicant cannot himself know, of course, whether such a delegation has taken place: that is a matter for the "indoor management" of the planning authority. It depends on the internal resolutions which it has made. Any person dealing with it is entitled to assume that all necessary resolutions have been passed'. Now, of course, an applicant could inspect the authority's statutory list of delegations to officers: Local Government Act 1972, s.100G(2), added by the Local Government (Access to Information) Act 1985; and see 3.24.

delegated powers does not have to be confirmed: it is immediately effective.

Can there be delegation to a group of officers?

4.9. The statutory provisions governing the carrying out of functions by officers clearly refer to 'an officer';[6] and although the general rule of interpretation is that 'words in the singular include the plural and words in the plural include the singular', it is submitted that delegation is not permissible to a group of officers. The matter is a practical one rather than one of legality. An individual can be made accountable for what he does under delegated authority, but if a group of officers were collectively entrusted with the discharge of functions, both the powers so delegated and accountability would be diffused. Who in a group would decide what course to pursue if there was disagreement? If, for the sake of argument, the decision were to be settled by majority vote, this would make the position of the chief executive impossible.

Committee system

4.10. For reasons which may be self-evident (considered later in Chapter 9), the council in full assembly could not possibly deal with the totality of business that falls to be discharged by a local authority. Hence, because the law has compelled authorities to appoint certain committees, and the volume and pressure of business has in any event made it unavoidable, authorities conduct their business through committees.[7] The committee system has immense advantages and has served local government well; but it has disadvantages also, and the expansion of local authority business and the demands for more effective and efficient administration have in recent years highlighted the weaknesses of the committee system, particularly its fragmentation of an authority's organisation. Further adjustments are now necessary, in Widdicombe's view, to reflect the reality of political organisation. Some of these matters will be discussed later in their specific relation to committees, but the defects, in the words of Maud, are:[8]

> due to the survival, in the great majority of local authorities, both large and small, of a 19th century tradition that council members must themelves be concerned with the actual details of day-to-day administration;

[6] Local Government Act 1972, s.101(1).
[7] See Tim Mobbs, *Local Government Policy-Making Handbook* (Inlogov, 1983), showing how local authorities have constructed their committee systems in the post-Bains era.
[8] Maud Report, vol. 1, p. ix.

and in consequence even large authorities:

> still rely on an elaborate system of committees and sub-committees, ill-adapted to the mass of business . . . now requiring co-ordinated long-term action . . .

4.11. The expensiveness of this committee activity was recognised:[9]

> . . . committees were costly to maintain in terms of clerical and administrative support, in use of members' and officers' time in attendance at meetings, in terms of the speed at which decisions could be taken (it slowed decision-making), and in the misuse of officers' skills, because of an inadequate framework of delegation.

Management board concept

4.12. Maud urged local authorities to review their internal organisation with a number of points in mind.[10] Subsequent events have overtaken some of them, but several remain valid matters for consideration:

(a) There should be a clearer division of labour between councillors and officers.

(b) Councillors must exercise sovereign power within the authority and accept responsibility for everything done in the authority's name. But having settled the policy they must delegate to officers the making of all but the most important decisions.

(c) Committees should cease to be executive or administrative bodies, save for some exceptional purposes. Their main functions should be deliberative. Widdicombe, too, favours some committees being deliberative only (see 3.3).

(d) There should be as few committees as possible, perhaps not more than half a dozen even in large authorities. Each committee should concern itself with a group of subjects; for example, child care, personal health and welfare might be the concern of a single 'social work' committee.[11]

(e) There should be as few subcommittees as possible.

(f) All but the smallest authorities should appoint a management board of

---

[9] See R. Greenwood, M. A. Lomer, C. R. Hinings and S. Ranson, *The Organization of Local Authorities in England and Wales 1967–75* (Inlogov Discussion Paper Series L, no. 5 (1975)). In 1975 Norfolk County Council estimated that each of its council meetings cost nearly £2,000 and a meeting of its policy and resources committee almost £500: 140 *Local Government Review* (1976) 797.

[10] Maud Report, vol. 1, p. x, where there is a summary of the main recommendations on internal organisation.

[11] Subsequently the Local Authority Social Services Act 1970, s.2, required the setting up of a statutory social services committee: see 9.32.

between five and nine council members, and delegate wide powers to it.

(g) This board should be the sole channel through which business done in the committees reaches the council. It would itself formulate and present proposals requiring council approval. It would also propose the establishment and disestablishment of committees. It would serve as the focal point for management of the authority's affairs and supervise the work of the authority as a whole.

(h) If the council is organised on party political lines, the minority party should be offered representation on the management board; thus knowledge of council business would be shared, and the experience gained by minority-party members would prove valuable if, after an election, their party secured a majority of council seats.

(i) A council should be free to pay the members of its management board a part-time salary (say, £1,000 a year in the largest authorities), additional to any allowances payable to ordinary council members.

Widdicombe wants to see a flat-rate allowance payable to all councillors as an annual sum, with special responsibility allowances continuing: see 5.26.

4.13. The foregoing points dealt with the authority's organisation at member level. Maud also recommended that each authority should appoint a clerk as undisputed head of the whole paid service of the council, not necessarily a qualified lawyer but chosen for qualities of leadership and managerial ability, who would be chief officer to the management board. The other principal officers would form a team under the clerk's leadership and report to the council through him.[12]

4.14. The most significant of Maud's proposals for the reform of internal organisation was that recommending the setting up of a *management board* which would function so long as it retained the confidence of at least a majority of council members. If the management board members lost that confidence they would resign and the council would appoint a new board. It was envisaged that the board's function[13] would be:

(a) To formulate the principal objectives of the authority and to present them, together with plans to attain them, to the council for consideration and decision;

(b) To review progress and assess results on behalf of the council;

(c) To maintain, on behalf of the council, an overall supervision of the organisation of the authority and its co-ordination and integration;

(d) To make decisions on behalf of the council which exceed the authority

[12] Maud Report, vol. 1, paras. 170–82.
[13] Maud Report, vol. 1, para. 162.

of the principal officers, and to recommend decisions to the council where authority has not been delegated to the management board;

(e) To be responsible for the presentation of business to the council subject always to the rights of members under standing orders.

Widdicombe reviewed Maud's management board concept along with other decision-making models but recommended that the system of decision-making in local government should continue to be one in which (a) the council is a corporate body; (b) decisions are made by, or on behalf of, the whole council, without any separate source of executive authority; and (c) officers serve the council as a whole.

Policy committee as alternative

4.15. For a variety of reasons which need not concern us in this work, the management board concept did not commend itself to local authorities. Most preferred the alternative favoured by one of the members of Maud, Sir Andrew Wheatley, who in his note of dissent said:[14]

> I would retain standing committees, investing them with executive powers to manage the services for which they were responsible (but not to authorize every item involving revenue expenditure), with the duty to report to the council on the discharge of their functions; but on any major issue of policy or new scheme involving capital expenditure they should first report to the management board. It would be the responsibility of the management board to ensure that any new proposal of this sort did not conflict with the activities of the council in other directions. No doubt a standing committee, before reporting to the council, would consider any views that might be expressed by the management board, but I see no reason why, in the last resort, if agreement were not reached, both the standing committee and the management board should not report to the council, each expressing their own views on the proposal, and explaining their reasons, leaving it to the council to come to a conclusion and take the decision on which view should prevail.

4.16. Some authorities had appointed a policy committee long before Maud reported;[15] those which subsequently pursued much else of Maud's proposals established a policy committee on Sir Andrew's model[16] No authority called its policy committee by the title of management board, and none gave the committee the executive power to manage which Maud had envisaged. Five years after Maud, Bains recommended the setting up of a

[14] *Ibid.* pp. 154–57.
[15] One such was the former Basildon UDC, where an executive committee was the only one reporting direct to the full council.
[16] 'The policy committee had become an established feature of local government before reorganization': *The Organization of Local Authorities in England and Wales 1967–75* (Inlogov Discussion Paper, Series L, no. 5).

policy and resources committee. If this owed much to the Maud idea of a management board, it nevertheless had more in common with the policy committees set up after Maud. What is worth commenting on is that neither Maud, nor later Bains, really took any serious account of the politicisation which was developing and intensifying in local government. This was left to Widdicombe to do.

Deliberative committees

4.17. Maud envisaged, as already indicated, that the management board would be the sole executive body within the authority at member level. All other committees would be *deliberative and representative bodies* in the sense that they would:[17]

    (a) make recommendations to the management board on the major objectives of the authority and study and recommend the means to attain these objectives and examine new ideas which they and other organizations had formulated;

    (b) have a duty to review progress on plans and programmes and on the operation of individual services as the management board would do for the whole range of services;

    (c) consider the interests, reactions and criticisms of the public and convey them to the officers and if necessary to the management board;

    (d) consider any matters raised by their own members or referred to them by the management board.

4.18. Local authorities swept aside the idea of deliberative committees at that time along with their rejection of the management board concept – which was not surprising because the two things hung together. However, there is now express statutory power enabling an authority to appoint a committee 'to advise the appointing authority . . . on any matter relating to the discharge of their functions'[18] and such a committee may consist wholly of persons who are not members of the authority.

4.19. Widdicombe returned to the idea of deliberative committees but for somewhat different reasons.[19] After recommending that local authorities should be required to include provisions in standing orders governing committees exercising delegated powers for the composition of such committees and subcommittees to reflect as far as practicable the composition of the council as a whole (except in so far as individual parties or

---

[17] Maud Report, vol. 1, para.166.
[18] Local Government Act 1972, s.102(4); and see 9.43.
[19] Widdicombe Report, paras.5.55–5.60.

councillors might waive their rights in this respect),[20] it went on to say that it did *not* propose that the requirement for party balance on committees should apply to committees which are purely deliberative and have no powers to make decisions. It had found from its research that a significant number of local authorities (some 11 per cent) had a one-party policy and resources committee which was purely deliberative:

> If the political reality is that the general policy of the council is formulated by the majority party, we see no reason why this should not be recognised by the creation of a single party policy and resources committee within the formal structure of the council and with full access to officer advice.

If then the public were denied access to deliberative committees – which Widdicombe did not think unreasonable – it would discourage, indeed make unnecessary, policy formulation being forced out of the formal committee system 'into groupings of indeterminate status'. What is more, of course, it would then be permissible for the majority group meeting in a one-party policy committee to have the benefit automatically of officer advice.

Corporate management

4.20. It would be wrong to take the view in the perspective of time that Maud had no influence at all with regard to the decision-making processes. Much of the experimentation undertaken by local authorities prior to reorganisation had been encouraged by Maud: indeed, the Maud Report did much to persuade authorities to take a corporate view of their management function; so much so that Bains later was able to say:[21]

> We believe that the need for a corporate approach is beyond dispute if local government is to be efficient and effective. We recognize that there are widely differing views on how it can be achieved, but it will not be sufficient merely for this principle to be recognized. A framework must be built into the organization of the various public services within which the idea can take root and develop.

---

[20] Statutory provision for party balance on joint authorities in metropolitan counties was introduced by the Local Government Act 1985, s.33: 'Each constituent council shall, so far as practicable, exercise its power to make or terminate appointments to a joint authority so as to ensure that the balance of parties for the time being prevailing in that council is reflected in the persons who are for the time being members of the authority and for whose appointment the council is responsible.'

[21] Bains Report, para.2.12. Bains does not define *corporate management* but *The New Scottish Local Authorities: Organisation and Management Structures* (the Paterson report) explains the corporate management process: see 4.31 *et seq*.

The concept of corporate management which has developed in local government is an expansive, outward-looking process geared to community needs rather than a matter of domestic organisation:

> This corporate approach should be displayed not only within the authority itself but also in its relations with other spheres of local government and with public bodies such as the ... Area Health Boards and Regional Water Authorities.

Policy and resources committee

4.21. Central to the Bains concept of the management structure of local authorities was the policy and resources committee[22] to aid in the setting of objectives and priorities and, once major policy decisions had been made, instrumental in co-ordinating and controlling the implementation of those decisions. It was envisaged that it would have ultimate responsibility under the council for the major resources of the authority: finance, manpower and land (including buildings).

Resources subcommittees

4.22. In each of these areas of finance, manpower and land Bains thought it important:[23]

> that the policy and resources committee should deal only with matters of major importance, not, for example, with trivial questions of expenditure. The more routine matters requiring member participation should be dealt with by three resource sub-committees each dealing respectively with one of the three main resources.

The precise division of responsibility between the parent committee and its subcommittees:[24]

> is a matter which will have to be decided by each local authority, but in making that decision we would urge authorities to bear in mind that the parent committee has a vital strategic role to play. Unless there is strict control over its agenda it will be swamped with a mass of detailed items which will leave insufficient time for realistic debate and decision on the major issues.

---

[22] Bains Report, para.2.11. 'The impact of reorganization has been such that now almost all authorities have a central, co-ordinating policy committee ... now the hub of the committee structure. This contrasts with the position ten years ago when they were virtually unknown': *The Organization of Local Authorities in England and Wales 1967–75* (Inlogov Discussion Paper, Series L, no.5).

[23] *Ibid.* paras.4.14, 4.15.

[24] *Ibid.* paras.4.16–4.19.

Bains envisaged that the subcommittees would comprise 'back-bench' members not necessarily on the parent committee 'to counter any suggestion that all power is concentrated in the hands of the policy and resources committee' and the major political party.[24]

4.23. The question has been debated, both before and since Bains, whether the policy committee should in fact be responsible for both policy *and* resource co-ordination. Many authorities which set up a policy committee before reorganisation retained a separate finance committee. Bains evidently persuaded authorities to reverse the pre-organisation position because a greater number of authorities now have a single policy and resources committee.[25] If there was a potential danger in this, i.e. that the policy and resources committee would be swamped by matters of financial management, it has not materialised. Yet the risk at one time seemed real:

> ... finance is an important issue, but there are other considerations that should exercise the policy committee: one danger is that it will be unable to retain a balance between its financial responsibilities, and its non-financial responsibilities because of the sheer volume of financial business that could be brought before the full committee. Moreover, members are probably more familiar with the language of financial planning and financial control than they are with that of strategic or corporate planning and control. The revenue estimates are a familiar form of budgeting: the performance or output budget is not. Members (and officers) may well seek out financial style documents because of their familiarity. That is, a policy and resources committee may find it easier to become a finance committee than to strike out and develop the less well understood role of a policy committee.

Membership of policy and resources committee

4.24. Bains favoured on balance minority-party representation on the policy and resources committee even though it recognised the disadvantages (that, for example, many of the decisions would be taken within the party group before the committee meets):[26]

> We believe that participation by the minority in the policy debates and decisions serves to ensure that different points of view are heard and more informed decisions arrived at. It also seems likely to lead to less of the sort of mistrust ... and in so doing avoid some of the more violent reversals of policy which can occur following changes of power.

[25] *The Organization of Local Authorities in England and Wales 1967–75* (Inlogov Discussion Paper, Series L, no.5).

[26] Bains Report, para.4.27.

The greater number of local authorities[27] have felt it unwise to deny representation to minority parties; and – something which Bains accepted as inevitable – the leader of the majority party is often chairman of the policy and resources committee.[28]

4.25. Traditionally, membership of central policy and finance committees has been reserved for the chairmen of the service committees plus, in some cases, a few other senior members. Bains accepted that:[29]

> chairmen of major committees must sit on the policy and resources committee; indeed the evidence which we have received indicates that such a committee without committee chairmen has proved ineffective.

Widdicombe wants a change in the policy and resources committee, stating that it should be deliberative only (see 3.3) (and in any case the committees responsible for individual services still often make the real decisions); and by holding its meetings in private it could become a one-party committee and so make it easier for political decisions to take place within the statutory framework of local authority meetings.

Monitoring and review

4.26. In Bains's view the regular monitoring and review of programmes against defined objectives is a responsibility which must rest primarily with members of the committees responsible for the main activities of the authority – the programme area committees, as Bains called them. It thought, however, that some form of independent review process should also be considered:[30]

> What we have in mind is a body of members within each authority rather like the public accounts committee. We believe that a watchdog body of this sort, with the standing and formal authority to make detailed investigation into any project, department, or area of activity would provide an extremely useful service to management. In our view that standing and authority is most likely to be derived from a close link with the policy and resources committee. The role of such a body, as we see it, is very much complementary to those of the resource sub-committees . . . and we suggest that it should in fact be a fourth sub-committee of that committee.

Many authorities now seek a different approach, concentrating on economy, efficiency and effectiveness, and value for money.

---

[27] *The Organization of Local Authorities in England and Wales 1967–75* (Inlogov Discussion Paper, Series L, no. 5).

[28] Bains Report, para.4.31.

[29] *Ibid.* para.4.28.

[30] *Ibid.* para.4.20.

Committees under corporate management

4.27. Bains commented on the reduction in the overall number of committees achieved by many authorities in the years which had elapsed since Maud:[31]

> Some have done so in order to slim the administration and encourage coordination, some to reduce calls on officers' time, some to help break down departmentalism and others, we fear, merely because it was felt to be fashionable to do so.

Bains recognised the problems of co-ordination encouraged by a large number of committees but said it did not subscribe to the view that of itself a reduction in the number of committees would cure the ills of an ineffective management structure 'any more than will the purchase of the latest gift-wrapped management package'.[31] It could find no evidence to support the popular belief that members wish to spend less time in committee, believed that only a structure which provides each member with a seat on at least one committee stands any chance of success, and felt there is no 'best buy' when it comes to deciding the number of committees which a particular authority requires.

4.28. Among the observations made by Bains about committees (in addition to those referred to elsewhere) are the following:

(a) *Grouping services and functions.*[32] Despite wide variations there are certain groups which have frequently emerged. One such is the merging of the various amenity services under either an amenity services or recreation/ leisure committee; another is the creation of a combined highways/ planning committee. Prima facie these groupings seem logical and reasonable and reduce the problem of co-ordination but some groupings have been on a rather superficial basis.

(b) *Area committees.* There is no substantial body of evidence supporting the creation of area committees operating within a particular area under specific delegated powers from the council: 'a number of authorities have in fact abandoned this concept and we can see no advantage from the management or administration viewpoint'.

(c) *Sub-committees.*[33] A standing sub-committee should be created only where there is a permanent job to be done and if created it should be given specific delegated powers within which to perform its task.

---

[31] Bains Report, para.4.32.
[32] *Ibid.* para.4.40.
[33] *Ibid.* para.4.47.

(d) *Functions of committees.*[34] In advocating the adoption of a programme basis for committee structure one of the objectives was 'the breaking down of the departmentalism which thrives on the one-committee–one-department tradition of much of local government'. Programme committees which are serviced by several departments and disciplines will reduce the areas of friction and disagreement between committees evident in the departmental approach: 'there will inevitably remain, however, some matters which will cross committee boundaries and provision should therefore be made for joint working groups representative of all relevant committees to be set up as and when needed'.[35]

(e) *Role of the chairman.*[36] Though the law does not permit the delegation of functions to chairmen of committees 'it would be unrealistic not to recognize that despite this many decisions have been and will continue to be effectively taken by chairmen'. It is, however, his role as 'a link man with the policy and resources committee' that is most important because 'it is through him that the essential lines of communication must flow'.

Community approach

4.29. Bains quoted with favour this view by the former Basildon UDC on the organisation of the new county councils:[37]

> ... if the community is to benefit from local government reorganization, then the closest co-operation must be maintained at all levels within the county organization and between the county and district councils. It is vital that at the 'grass roots' there should be a complete understanding of the reasons for policy decisions and also a means of testing reaction to those decisions and constantly assessing needs.

And in order to encourage this concept of community interest Bains recommended that there should be a district joint committee of county and district members for each district within the county to co-ordinate the interaction of *all* county and district functions and policies for the locality. As an alternative it was considered whether there should be district joint committees in respect of each major function or service but this was rejected on the grounds that:[37]

> such committees might lead to the development of a narrow functional attitude inconsistent with the broad corporate and community approaches to which we attach such importance.

---

[34] *Ibid.* para.4.51.

[35] *Ibid.* para.4.51; and see 9.49–9.50.

[36] *Ibid.* paras.4.52–4.53; and see 5.66 *et seq.* concerning the law relating to chairman's action and Widdicombe's proposals for change.

[37] *Ibid.* para.8.3: *The New Counties – The Same or Different* (Basildon UDC, May 1972).

4.30. In several areas neighbourhood councils are being set up – non-statutory bodies, based on a neighbourhood of around 10,000 people, although the range is from under 3,000 to over 20,000. There is an Association for Neighbourhood Councils, a pressure group founded in 1970, with the principal object of encouraging the introduction of neighbourhood councils on a statutory basis in order to give them stability and the credibility of status. Their size, finance, form and purposes vary considerably, but everywhere – like parish and community councils – they provide a voice for the neighbourhood.

Practice of corporate management

Redefinition

4.31. The approach to corporate management has varied widely. Some local authorities immediately attempted to embrace without compromise the concept of corporate management in its entirety, adopting both a new committee and departmental structure and new management procedures at both officer and member level. Others have moved gradually in that direction. Others still sought to introduce a rudimentary structure of corporate management as a super-overlay on top of the traditional system – not without the cost of some confusion and no little elaboration of both structure and process. Although we are not concerned here with the technique of corporate planning but with its effect upon the structure of committees and the procedure and practice affecting meetings, it may be appropriate at this stage to provide a definition of corporate planning as it has manifested itself in local government generally.

4.32. There are many definitions. Paterson, for example, describes the ultimate objective of corporate management as being:[38]

> to achieve a situation where the needs of a community are viewed comprehensively and the activities of the local authority are planned, directed and controlled in a unified manner to satisfy those needs to the maximum extent consistent with available resources.

Most definitions embrace within the concept these three categories of the management process:[39]

(a) *Strategic planning:* the process of deciding objectives, on changes in these objectives, on the resources used to attain the objectives, and on

[38] Paterson report on *The New Scottish Authorities: Organisation and Management Structures,* para.5.3.
[39] R. N. Anthony in *Planning and Control Systems: a Framework for Analysis* (1965) divides the management process into these three categories.

the policies that are to govern the acquisition, use and disposition of the resources.

(b) *Management control:* the process by which managers assure that resources are obtained and used effectively and efficiently in the attainment of the objectives.

(c) *Operational control:* the process of ensuring that specific tasks are carried out effectively and efficiently.

Many people use the term corporate planning in a sense corresponding to strategic planning, but this is too broad a definition and does not satisfactorily explain the process as it is being pursued in local government today. It seems more profitable to 'give up the attempt to define corporate planning directly and search instead for all the characteristics that distinguish it from conventional management processes' and so produce 'a set of necessary and sufficient conditions for corporate planning'.[40] Thus, it has been suggested, a system of planning is defined as *corporate* if, and only if, it satisfies all of the following five conditions:

(a) It is *outward looking,* in that it puts needs in the community before the internal needs of the organisation or of its members.

(b) It is *anticipatory,* in the sense that it ensures that present decisions are made not only in the light of what is happening now or of what has happened in the past, but also with regard to anticipated future consequences in relation to anticipated future needs.

(c) It is *systematic,* in that it explicitly recognises that the problems to be tackled and decisions to be made are highly interconnected, related to each other by complex interweaving chains running in a variety of directions.

(d) It is *flexible,* in that it continually adapts decisions to take account of the uncertainty that surrounds the decision-making process – of the fact that problems and decision outcomes normally develop in a way which cannot be accurately foreseen at any specific time.

(e) It is *integrated,* in the sense that it brings all the authority's activities together (both vertically and horizontally) at top level, to help determine the organisation's overall objectives and to ensure that adequate progress is made in achieving them.

Committee structure

4.33. It is impossible to find one pattern of committee structure which is fairly typical of that favoured by the majority of present-day authorities.

---

[40] See Alexander Grey, 'Organizing for Corporate Planning', 3 *Local Government Studies* 10.

Even the broadly drawn diagrams in the Bains Report were not intended to be adopted slavishly by all authorities irrespective of local circumstances.[41] As one example, however, the London Borough of Hammersmith and Fulham – which restructured its committee system on the programme structure of an interim corporate plan – now has three levels of committee: a strategic resources committee (which is the authority's policy committee); the executive or service committees based on programme areas; and review subcommittees (made up of members from a number of executive committees which are required to select areas of policy and to review performance and study policy alternatives in depth). Initially, fewer than half the new authorities had a performance review subcommittee:[42]

> Partly this is explained by the belief that such responsibilities more properly belong to the programme committee. On the other hand it may reflect the deeper emphasis, and understanding in local government, of *resources* co-ordination than upon policy co-ordination.

Working parties

Devolution of decision-making

4.34. A development of the devolution of decision-making from the council in full assembly (which has become increasingly a forum for the discussion and determination of significant policy issues) has been a markedly increased use of small groups of council members or officers or both to make decisions on non-policy questions. The Bains working group favoured the setting up of such working groups, without the constraints of formal subcommittees, in order to provide members with the opportunity to identify themselves with areas of activity in which they have a particular interest and to provide officers with an immediate point of reference to opinion of elected members.

4.35. Working parties elsewhere are usually of a more conventional character, each set up by and required to report back to the committee which established it. In many cases there is a standing order regulating their constitution and proceedings: one such is to this effect:[43]

> (a) Any committee or sub-committee may, within its powers, set up a working party of members and officers for the detailed study of any matter referred to it but such working party shall report to the body from which it

---

[41] Bains Report, paras.9.1–9.40.

[42] See *The Organization of Local Authorities in England and Wales 1967–75* (Inlogov Discussion Paper, Series L, no. 5).

[43] Standing Order no. 64 of the then London Borough of Hammersmith, 1974.

was formed and shall not have power to exercise on behalf on the council any authority nor to incur expenditure without prior authority of the committee or relevant sub-committee, nor to issue instructions to any officer likely, in the opinion of the officer or chief executive to incur expense or to use excessive time without prior authority of the committee or relevant sub-committee. The meeting of any such working party shall be convened and minuted by the director of operations and the terms of reference of such a working party shall include a definition of the objects of the working party, the manner and times at which it shall report back and shall require it to define matters of policy.

(b) A working party may set up from among its members a study group or groups which shall be similarly convened and minuted for the purpose of detailed work and such study group or groups shall report back to the working party.

(c) The chairman and vice-chairman of a working party or study group shall be appointed by the body establishing the working party or study group, but in their absence at a meeting the party or group as the case may be shall appoint a member then present to act as chairman, and a chairman shall have a second or casting vote as necessary.

Committee practice

Minutes and reports

4.36. Apart from structural and procedural changes, most local authorities – initially through the influence of measures proposed by O. & M. stemming from the recommendations of the Local Government Manpower Committee in the post-war years[44] and later of the Maud Report[45] – have sought to reduce the paperwork associated with committee meetings. The trend towards greater delegation to officers and a marked distinction nowadays between policy matters (the concern primarily of council members) and administration (the concern of officers) ought to have eliminated the triviality dealt with in committee: but this does not seem to be so to any substantial degree.[46] There has been more extensive adoption of the report system (see 12.38 *et seq.*) as the vehicle through which committee proceedings are brought to the attention of the full assembly, but this has meant also that two documents always have to be prepared after each committee meeting: the committee report and the minutes. Various devices have been employed to avoid too much duplica-

---

[44] The Local Government Manpower Committee was set up by the Government in 1949, to review arrangements for ensuring economic use of manpower in local government. See particularly, *Second Report of the Local Government Manpower Committee* (1951), Cmnd 8421.

[45] Maud Report, vol. 1: see para.121.

[46] *Ibid.* paras.113–14.

tion of this sort, and in many instances the chore of writing up the minutes after a report has been prepared has been eased either by incorporating by reference much of the material provided in agenda which is bound into the minute book or by reference to the report to the full assembly. These methods are not good practice but undoubtedly save time in preparation (though not necessarily the time of any reader who may in later years seek to unravel the minute book).

White papers

4.37. Although committee reports are usually more informative and intelligible than committee minutes, neither as a rule is wholly suitable for disseminating information to the community. Maud suggested that authorities 'should set out major proposals or issues in council papers as public documents on the analogy of "White Papers", with a wide circulation and well in advance of debate in the council'.[47]

Quality of written material

4.38. The quality of material in committee agenda, minutes and reports is largely dependent on the ability of the committee clerks, whose role is discussed below (see 4.41).

The proper officer

4.39. Prior to the reorganisation of local government in the 1970s, the business of summoning members to meetings, the preparation of agenda and its dispatch, and the subsequent compiling of the minutes of proceedings were virtually everywhere the responsibility of the town clerk or clerk of the council. Nowhere were the duties of this officer prescribed by statute – at least in respect of committee work – although certain statutes laid down specific tasks upon the holder of the office. The duty of undertaking committee work was set out in the officer's contract of employment and generally regulated by standing orders. Since reorganisation, however, and the emergence of the office of chief executive with duties differing substantially from those of the former clerk, greater variations exist between authorities in the distribution of top-level duties. An authority's committee work is now more often than not entrusted to the county, borough or district secretary or director of administration, embracing

---

[47] Maud Report, vol. 1, para.439.

responsibility for certain statutory requirements imposed upon 'the proper officer'.[48]

4.40. 'The proper officer' must be appointed by every local authority. Section 270(3) of the Local Government Act 1972 provides that:

> Any reference in this Act to a proper officer and any reference which by virtue of this Act is to be construed as such a reference shall, in relation to any purpose and any local authority or other body or any area, be construed as a reference to an officer appointed for that purpose by that body or for that area, as the case may be.

The choice of proper officer is entirely at the discretion of the local authority and obviously depends upon local circumstances. And it would be prudent for an authority to appoint another officer to act as such in the event of the incapacity of the proper officer to act or in a vacancy in the office.

Committee clerks

Functions

4.41. The officers primarily concerned with committee practice are the committee clerks whose functions, duties and responsibilities differ considerably between authorities. All will be concerned with the preparation of agenda and drawing up minutes and reports, and many will be entrusted with more responsible duties such as advising the committee (either on procedural matters or acting wholly as the chief executive or secretary's representative) and taking limited or full responsibility for overseeing executive action on a committee's decisions.

4.42. The status of committee clerks has depended in the past upon the ability of individual officers and the inclination or disinclination of the town clerk/clerk of the council to entrust them with effective tasks. Often, too, the role of committee clerks has varied according to the size of the authority and the extent to which their work has been dominated by legal rather than administrative considerations. Thus, for example, Herbert Morrison felt able to say of the largest local authority (the old London County Council):[49]

---

[48] The duties of the proper officer in the sphere of committee work have been substantially enlarged by the obligations on principal councils imposed as a consequence of the Local Government (Access to Information) Act 1985. Widdicombe has recommended that certain functions ascribed to the proper officer should be made the statutory function of the chief executive in an extended role as guardian of the propriety of council business: Widdicombe Report, para. 6.151.

[49] Herbert Morrison, *How Greater London is Governed* (1932).

There is an important officer attached to committees called the committee clerk. . . . These men are of high standing, and they have substantial salaries. They are the eyes and ears of the chief officers concerned.

And, flatteringly, in a manual published some years ago under the auspices of the former Society of Clerks of Urban District Councils:[50]

The perfect committee clerk requires to possess the foresight of Old Moore; the accuracy of an adding machine; the judgment of Solomon; the patience of Job; the memory of an elephant; the coolness and tact of a high ranking diplomat; and the literary skill of Bernard Shaw!

4.43. Until recently, however, the committee clerk was a subordinate officer – sometimes no more than a minuting clerk – with predominantly clerical duties whose principal accomplishment was that of an efficient shorthand-writer, with the ability to draft 'agendas, minutes and reports in a clear, well-written, grammatically correct style':[51] he was rarely permitted to act effectively in a secretarial role because the clerk's principal representative at a meeting was usually an assistant solicitor, and in many cases where the smallness of the authority enabled the clerk personally to concern himself with the drafting of minutes, the committee clerk was demoralised by having his work 'continually returned, covered with blue marks, arrows and scratches'[52] by an over-meticulous legal mind. Any attempt in the past to improve the status of the committee clerk and to give him a more influential and personally rewarding role was curtly dismissed.[53]

4.44. There has, however, been a notable improvement of status in the case of some of the larger authorities – encouraged, it is suspected, by the difficulty nowadays in retaining on committee work officers of requisite ability. Posts have been accorded better designations (*committee officer, committee administrator*, even *assistant town clerk* or *chief executive*) and entrusted with real responsibility for handling the work of a major committee or a group of related smaller ones. Regrettably, the move has not always been accompanied by any marked improvement in the competence of some of the officers.

---

[50] *The Clerk of the Council and his Department* (1951), p. 23.

[51] T. E. Headrick, *The Town Clerk in English Local Government* (1962), p. 137.

[52] *Ibid.* p. 135.

[53] This is evident from the general tenor of the writing in Headrick's book, *The Town Clerk in English Local Government*, an excellent and scholarly work marred by the American author's undue influence by the lawyer–clerks whom he consulted: see, e.g. his reference in a footnote on p. 138 to an article by the author, 'Back Room Boys of Local Government' (1949), 57 *Municipal Journal* 677, which Headrick dismissed as 'a vastly exaggerated account' of duties and qualifications now commonplace.

Career prospects

4.45. Committee administration was once the best grounding for advancement on the administrative side of local government. But career prospects were restricted and at best the able committee clerk could expect to aspire to an administrative post of assistant town clerk, embracing responsibility also for general office management of the clerk's department, election work and members' business. With the emergence of a better understanding of the importance of the administrative and managerial side of local authority work, new avenues of promotion have opened up for the able administrator. In the first place there was establishment (now personnel) work, to which was added O. & M. and then a wide range of management services and techniques (work study, network analysis, project co-ordination and corporate planning); this has meant that committee work has become comparatively less attractive than formerly for the able generalist, who now sees better prospects in these other directions.

4.46. Today responsibility for committees often rests with the county (or borough or district) secretary or director of administration, who has inherited most of the duties of clerkship relinquished by the chief executive without departmental ties. This may in some cases mean that the ablest committee clerks can aspire to the post of secretary, but these appointments are still frequently held by former lawyer clerks who have not become chief executives or by lawyers who have responsibility also for legal work.

Training

4.47. Remarkably little attention has been given to the training of staff for committee work. Most attain their knowledge and expertise by sitting next to Nellie and thus their competence depends on the ability of the mentor. Deserving of special mention, however, are the courses in committee administration run for many years by NALGO's Education Department: held usually over a period of a week or ten days on a residential basis at Downing College, Cambridge, they represented the first attempt at systematic instruction geared to the practical needs of students of varying levels of experience.

4.48. The late Sir George Mallaby, in an article in one of the local government periodicals some time ago,[54] advocated the abolition of

[54] George Mallaby, 'Creating a Corporate Staff', *Surveyor: Public Authority Technology* (16 August 1974), pp. 2–3.

committee clerks as such. He could not see why committees need to be serviced by an exclusive corps of committee clerks:

> The varied experience of local government work which committee clerks must naturally acquire ought to be more widely spread and more actively exercised.

Sir George wanted to see an end to the career committee clerks and in their place 'bright young men' – around 30 years of age – drawn from every department in the authority and seconded for this particular service for a two-year stint. The constant *roulement* of these young officers from their own departments to what is in effect the authority's secretariat and then back to their own departments would widen the horizons of the officers themselves:

> In time it would also disseminate throughout all ranks of the authority a knowledge and awareness of the multitude and complexity of its problems.

Qualifications

4.49. Local authorities, in advertising committee clerk posts, rarely specify any particular qualifications, even though today the public service stream examinations of the Institute of Chartered Secretaries and Administrators provide the recognised professional qualification for administrative staff in local government. Some authorities, indeed, still refer to the discontinued Diploma in Municipal Administration or some lesser current qualification or, in a few instances, demand a degree.

5

MEMBERSHIP

Election of councillors

General considerations

5.1. Members of a local authority are those persons who have been elected in accordance with the statutory rules relating to local elections[1] to serve for the requisite term of office in a representative capacity on one of the authorities referred to earlier (see 1.5): indeed, sometimes on more than one for a person may be a member both of the county council and of a district council within the administrative county. When submitting himself for nomination for election and, if elected, then throughout his membership, the person must be of full age and a British subject and possess certain qualifications linking him with the area of the authority. In addition, he must be free from a number of disqualifications. So long as a councillor remains qualified he cannot be removed from office, though he may resign voluntarily at any time. The whole process of election and the detailed rules relating to qualification and disqualification are for the most part matters outside the scope of this work.

5.2. Some reference needs to be made in general terms, however, to the position of persons who may act as councillors though strictly disqualified from office and of the consequences of their attendance at meetings of the council and committees and subcommittees. In this respect s.82 of the Local Government Act 1972 is important; it provides that:

> The acts and proceedings of any person elected to an office under this Act and acting in that office shall, notwithstanding his disqualification, be as valid and effective as if he had been qualified.

'Office' means the office of councillor or chairman or vice-chairman of the

---

[1] Widdicombe has recommended a simplification of the electoral system to provide for single-member wards or divisions and a uniform period of office of four years: Widdicombe Report, paras.7.15–7.30.

council but not membership or the chairmanship or vice-chairmanship of a committee or subcommittee, none of which is of itself an 'office'. Nevertheless, there is a presumption elsewhere in the Act, in sch.12, para.41(3), applied to committees and subcommittees by s.99, that a local authority meeting has been properly constituted:

> Until the contrary is proved, a meeting of a local authority a minute of whose proceedings have been made and signed in accordance with this paragraph shall be deemed to have been duly convened and held, and all the members present at the meeting shall be deemed to have been qualified.

5.3. The vacation of office by councillors who do not secure re-election and the coming into office of new councillors can pose administrative and procedural difficulties for local authorities. Standing orders as a rule provide for the transitionary period between the day of election and the annual meeting and the appointment of newly constituted committees (see Chapter 9). Most authorities avoid holding meetings during this period but sometimes, of course, urgent business demands that decisions must be made by councillors. The normal practice that appointments to committees are made for the council year, i.e. until the start of the next annual meeting, is necessarily conditioned by the rule that persons not re-elected at the end of their term of office cease to be councillors 'on the fourth day after the ordinary day of election' and that newly elected councillors 'shall come into office on the day on which their predecessors retire'.[2] This means that councillors not re-elected may lawfully attend meetings of committees and subcommittees and meetings of outside bodies on which they represent the council on the second and third day after the date of election.[3] A councillor not re-elected may, as committee chairman, for example, properly act as such during this period. But a newly elected councillor cannot in practice attend to any council business until the annual meeting following his election, when committee membership is decided, and in any case cannot act as a councillor until he has made a declaration of acceptance of office in these terms:[4]

> I . . ., having been elected to the office of councillor . . . hereby declare that I

---

[2] Local Government Act 1972, s.26(1) and (7)(b).

[3] Unless a contrary intention appears, a provision of an Act comes into force at the beginning of the day in question: see Interpretation Act 1978, s.4(a). Thus a person not re-elected at an election held on a Thursday goes out of office at the moment after midnight on the Monday following, i.e. at the start of the fourth day after the Thursday, and must cease to act as a councillor not later than during the Sunday.

[4] Local Elections (Principal Areas) Rules 1973, sch.3. Widdicombe considered that the declaration should be made in solemn form, i.e. on oath or by affirmation, as 'an outward demonstration of the fact that election to the council involves assumption of an executive office carrying with it a public duty' (Widdicombe Report, para.6.21).

take the said office upon myself, and will duly and faithfully fulfil the duties thereof according to the best of my judgement and ability.

Rights, duties and obligations

Introduction

5.4. It is appropriate to consider briefly the rights, duties and obligations assumed by councillors following election because these are significant in relation to local authority meetings. If, for example, councillors *en bloc* ceased to attend meetings then the business of the local authority could not continue for very long: how long would depend upon a number of factors. Supposing the members failed to attend the first meeting of the council after their election so that the council's annual meeting could not take place: the council would not be properly constituted because it would not have a chairman.[5] On the other hand, if the members duly met in annual meeting, elected a chairman, conducted such other business as the law required and passed resolutions delegating considerable executive power to their officers,[6] it is conceivable that the authority could function effectively and legally for some time: until no doubt some specific act required the council's formal resolution. In the absolute extremity, i.e. if through the failure of members to attend meetings it became impossible for local government to be carried on, the government would invoke the default powers available.[7]

5.5. The councillor's role is not solely that of attending meetings and helping thereat to make decisions. Maud said:[8]

> It is perhaps true that councillors normally think in terms of a very general and indefinite responsibility: they make contributions where they see an opportunity and rarely attempt to analyse and define their responsibilities *vis-à-vis* the officers and in other respects.

Few members seem to see themselves as policy-makers[9] even though they

---

[5] Section 2, Local Government Act 1972, provides that for every county and every district there shall be a council consisting of a chairman and councillors; s.3 provides that the chairman of a principal council shall be elected annually; and s.4 that the chairman's election shall be the first business transacted at the annual meeting of a principal council.

[6] A local authority may properly arrange for the discharge of its functions by an officer: Local Government Act 1972, s.101.

[7] The power of the central government to act in default is related to particular statutory functions. There is no legislative power to replace the local authority in its entirety.

[8] Maud Report, vol. 1, p. 40.

[9] This conclusion in the Maud Report, *ibid.*, is a widely held view: see Raymond S. B. Knowles, *Modern Management in Local Government*, p. 62.

recognise that this is what they often do in council and committee: many think of themselves as watchdogs 'to ensure that the officers did not go astray or spend public monies extravagantly' and there is no doubt that most attach importance to their constituency role in being accessible to electors and pursuing their complaints and grievances.[10] If, therefore, this chapter may appear to give a distorted view of the councillor's rights, duties and obligations, it is because we are concerned solely with part only of the totality of the machinery through which local authorities operate.

Rights and duties generally

5.6. A councillor when elected to office possesses certain rights conferred upon him by law, e.g. he is entitled to attend council meetings without hindrance; and, if he can show a 'need to know' in relation to a particular item of business, he can claim a common law right to attend the meeting of the committee or subcommittee concerned (see 5.12). He has only a limited right, however, as an individual councillor (see generally Chapter 5); and model standing order no. 27, for example, provides that:

> Unless specifically authorised to do so by the council or a committee, a member of the council shall not issue any order respecting any works which are being carried out by or on behalf of the council or claim by virtue of his membership of the council any right to inspect or to enter upon any lands or premises which the council has the power or duty to inspect or enter.

And the councillor assumes certain obligations on gaining office, e.g. he must disclose any interest he has in a contract or other matter coming before a meeting at which he is present (see 5.27) and may conceivably have some personal responsibility for maladministration (see 5.44); but he does not incur any general legal duty to attend to his voluntarily imposed tasks, e.g. he is not bound to attend meetings, although it could be argued that in making his declaration of acceptance of office a councillor undertakes to discharge his duties, and there are instances (see 7.111) where he may incur liability if he fails to attend a meeting which he ought to attend. If, however, a councillor fails to attend meetings over a prescribed period he forfeits his office as councillor (see 5.76). A councillor's common law right to information – now clarified and given statutory backing – is discussed below: see 5.14 *et seq.*

---

[10] Under the Local Government Act 1974, Pt III, an ombudsman service has been set up for local government (including joint boards of constituent local authorities, police and water authorities), providing in s.26 for complaints of maladministration to be channelled through a member of the authority concerned.

National code of conduct

5.7. The Redcliffe–Maud Committee on Local Government Rules of Conduct, whose report (Cmnd 5636) was published in 1974, recommended that existing rules relating to the conduct of councillors embodied in statutes and standing orders should be supplemented by a nationally agreed code of conduct. Such a code, Redcliffe–Maud said, should include those principles already governing the best practice among members: it should give authoritative guidance to all councillors and provide an explicit public standard by which local government can be measured by those outside it. As a consequence a code of conduct, agreed between central government departments, the local authority associations in England and Wales and the Convention of Scottish Local Authorities, was promulgated to all local authorities in 1975.[11] The code is set out in the appendix to this chapter.

5.8. Widdicombe has recommended that the code should be prescribed statutorily by the Secretary of State following consultation with the local authority associations, and that it should be amended to make clear that councillors hold office by virtue of the law and must act within the law and that sectional loyalties as well as private gain may create conflicts with councillors' public duty. And, furthermore, that all local authorities and their members should be required to have regard to the code and observe its prescriptions: that breach of the code should prima facie constitute maladministration.[12]

Right to attend meetings

5.9. A councillor has an absolute right throughout his term of office to attend every council meeting of the local authority to which he has been elected. Nowhere is this right expressly so stated but an authority would be acting unlawfully if it sought to exclude a member from a meeting of the full assembly, e.g. either by failing to summon him to the meeting or by denying him admission; even the exclusion of a councillor for disorderly conduct or other misbehaviour can only be for a strictly limited period: see 7.123. But a parish or community councillor, if not on the electoral roll for the parish or community concerned, has no right to attend and take part in the proceedings of a parish or community meeting.[13]

---

[11] Under cover of a joint circular of 2 October 1975: D.o.E. circular 94/75; SDD circular 95/75; WO circular 166/75.

[12] Widdicombe Report, paras.6.15–6.21.

[13] This arises because a person, though not on the electoral register, is qualified to be a parish or community councillor if, for example, he lives outside the parish or community but within three miles of it (Local Government Act 1972, s.79). The National Association of

5.10. Where, however, a member:

(a) ceases to be qualified for membership of the authority;[14] or

(b) becomes disqualified for membership of the authority;[15] or

(c) ceases to be a member of the authority by reason of failure to attend meetings (see 5.76);

and the authority has, where necessary, declared the member's office to be vacant, the authority could properly deny him admission as a member – though he could, of course, attend as a member of the public.

5.11. The right of a councillor to attend committee meetings is, however, a qualified one. In the first place he need not serve on any committee at all: he cannot be appointed to a committee if he is unwilling to serve,[16] nor can he dispute the council's decision if it does not appoint him to any committee or, having appointed him, deprives him even arbitrarily of his committee membership.[17] So long, nevertheless, that he remains a member of a committee, he is entitled to attend all the committee's meetings for the duration of his local authority membership.[18] As to a councillor's right to attend meetings of committees to which he has not been appointed, e.g. where he claims a 'need to know': see 5.12.

see 5.12.

5.12. A councillor who has not been appointed to a particular committee can claim a right to attend a meeting of the committee, but not to vote, if he can show a 'need to know'. This appears to be a result of *R. v. Hackney London Borough Council ex-parte Gamper* (1985),[19] where the court applied the principle enunciated in *R. v. Birmingham City District Council ex-parte O* (1983) (see 5.17) which related to a councillor's entitlement to informa-

---

[13] cont.

Local Councils regards this as an absurdity because it means, for example, that a councillor who may have taken a leading part in a parish or community council's decision has no right to explain or defend it at an electors' meeting (although he may be invited to attend and address the electors present), nor may he vote. The law does, however, permit a parish or community council chairman to take part in the proceedings and, indeed, he must preside if present; and although he cannot vote with the body of electors he has a casting vote (*Ibid.* sch.12, para.16).

[14] See Local Government Act 1972, s.79, as to qualification for election and holding office as a councillor.

[15] *Ibid.* s.80, as to disqualification for office.

[16] *R. v. Sunderland Corporation* [1911] 2 KB 458, in which it was held that a person who is appointed to serve on a committee may lawfully resign against the will of the council.

[17] *Manton v. Brighton Corporation* [1951] 2 KB 393; [1951] 2 All ER 101; but the local authority must be scrupulous in observing its standing orders in this respect: *R. v. Rushmore Borough Council ex-parte Crawford* (1981); see 9.61.

[18] This, impliedly, is the effect of Local Government Act 1972, s.102(5).

[19] (1985) 1 WLR 1229. See also *R. v. Sheffield City Council ex-parte Chadwick* (*The Times*, 19 December 1985) and *R. v. Hyndburn Borough Council ex-parte Strak*, 17 December 1985 (unreported). All three cases had been brought by Alliance councillors who had been excluded from committees.

tion. It has always been open to a local authority (in circumstances usually prescribed by standing orders) to permit a councillor to attend meetings of committees of which he is not a member, but until recently it was thought that no councillor could claim a right to attend – except in so far as he could be present in the public gallery as a member of the public. In *Hackney*, however, the court took the view that there was really no logical distinction between access to documents and access to meetings, i.e. the common law was the same if access was necessary in order to enable the councillor to perform his duties as a councillor.

Right with others to call meetings

5.13. A councillor has no right, as an individual member, to demand a meeting of the full assembly. He can, however, join with others in requisitioning a council meeting (see 6.5). Any right he may possess of calling a meeting of a committee is dependent on standing orders (see 10.16).

Access to information

5.14. It has long been recognised that a councillor has a common law right to be provided with or to inspect council documents which it is reasonably necessary for him to see in order to carry out his duties as a councillor. That common law right has now been restated in important respects (see 5.16 *et seq.*); and in 1986, for the first time, the councillor if a member of a principal council was given a statutory right of access to prescribed categories of document (see 5.15). A councillor has always, of course, been able to exercise the same power of inspection of documents that members of the public or electors possess (see 3.23).

5.15. A councillor's *statutory* right of access to documents is provided by s.100F of the Local Government Act 1972, added by the Local Government (Access to Information) Act 1985, which came into effect on 1 April 1986. Thereunder 'any document which is in the possession or under the control of a principal council and contains material relating to any business to be transacted at a meeting of the council or a committee or sub-committee' must be open to inspection by any member of the principal council. This means that a councillor's statutory right of access is limited to documents concerned with business about to be transacted at a meeting. He cannot thereunder, for example, demand to see a document which relates to business not yet due to come before a meeting; and it is submitted that if he wishes to delve into a matter which has been dealt with in the past he must resort to the right of access available to the public generally or to his common law entitlement (see 5.19). Indeed, it is expressly stated that the statutory rights are in addition to any other rights which a councillor might have.[20]

5.16. A councillor's *common law* right of access to council documents is dependent (and always has been though not expressed in precisely the same terms) upon his 'need to know' in order to enable him properly to perform his duties as a councillor: *R. v. Barnes Borough Council ex-parte Conlan* (1938).[21] But it has never been an absolute right. Humphreys J said in *Barnes* it could not extend to all documents 'since in the case of a large local authority [and he quoted the then London County Council as an example] it would be an impossible burden to become acquainted with all the council's business'. And there is no right to 'a roving commission to go and examine the books or documents of a corporation'.[22] Mere curiosity or desire to see and inspect documents is not sufficient.[23] Nor can a councillor properly exercise the right for some indirect motive, e.g. to assist someone in litigation with the council.[24]

5.17. The foregoing principles were upheld by the House of Lords in *R. v. Birmingham City District Council ex-parte O* (1983).[25] In that case a member of the city council's housing committee had asked to see the papers of the social services committee concerning the adoption proceedings of a child in the council's care. The councillor, as a member of the housing committee, had become aware that the prospective adoptive parents had a bad record of rent arrears and that the husband had previously served a prison sentence, and the councillor believed that to allow the adoption proceedings to continue could constitute a serious error of judgement by the social services committee. The councillor's request for access to the social services committee's papers was not opposed by the council but by the prospective adoptive parents, who sought judicial intervention through an order of *prohibition* to prevent disclosure. The House of Lords ruled that the councillor was entitled to see the confidential files in the social services department in connection with the adoption. Lord Brightman said that in the case of a committee of which the councillor was a member he would normally *ex hypothesi* have good reason for access to *all* the committee's written material:

> . . . a councillor is entitled by virtue of his office to have access to all written

---

[20] Local Government Act 1972, s.100F(5), added by Local Government (Access to Information) Act 1985.

[21] *R. v. Barnes Borough Council ex-parte Conlan* [1938] 3 All ER 226.

[22] *Supra.*

[23] *R. v. Southwold Corporation* (1907) 5 LGR 888.

[24] *R. v. Hampstead Borough Council* (1917) 15 LGR 309.

[25] [1983] 1 All ER 497.

material in the possession of the local authority of which he is a member providing he has a good reason for such access.

But in the case of other committees, different considerations applied. The 'outside' councillor had no automatic right of access to documentary material; a need to know had to be demonstrated:

The decision whether an outside councillor has a good reason for access to the information is ultimately one to be taken by the council themselves sitting in council. But the council may expressly or by implication delegate to others the right to decide[26] . . . subject to resort to a meeting of the council if the decision of the delegate is challenged.

Lord Brightman also stressed that:

The court has no jurisdiction to substitute its own opinion. The decision of the council is the final word, subject only to an application for judicial review . . . on *Wednesbury* principles . . .[27]

5.18. Some doubt must remain as to the precise meaning of the dictum that a councillor is entitled to see *all* the papers in a local authority's possession when, in relation to the particular matter, he has shown a 'need to know'. The view must be taken that their lordships in the *Birmingham* case, *supra*, meant literally what they said – even though it was declared that the principle followed was that in *Barnes, supra,* in which it was said that the common law right did not extend to all documents. Lord Brightman said there 'is no room . . . for secrecy between a social worker and a member of the social services committee'; and the obligation now on principal councils to make 'background papers' available for inspection might seem to reinforce the principle of open government to which reference was made in Chapter 3. Nevertheless, there must surely still be a measure of proper confidentiality in informal memoranda passed between chief officers or in opinions scribbled by subordinate staff in the margin of papers – but this is no doubt an issue for decision by local authorities, at least in the first instance, and perhaps regulated by a code of practice.[28]

5.19. There remains to be considered the situation where a newly elected councillor wishes to have access to documents relating to a decision made in the past before the statutory rights of access conferred as a consequence of the coming into effect on 1 April 1986 of the provisions of the Local

---

[26] The delegation could be, of course, to an officer and in the light of the Local Government (Access to Information) Act 1985, ordinarily in practice no doubt to the proper officer.

[27] As to the *Wednesbury* principles: see 1.39.

[28] 'Information' is defined as including *an expression of opinion* as well as any recommendations and any decision taken: Local Government Act 1972, s.100K, added by Local Government (Access to Information) Act 1985.

Government (Access to Information) Act 1985. In *R.* v. *Clerk to Lancashire Police Committee ex-parte Hook* (1980)[29] the question arose as to whether a councillor elected after a highly confidential report had been considered and acted upon had a right to see the document to enable him to perform his duties as a councillor. The Court of Appeal (Lord Denning MR dissenting) upheld the decision of the divisional court refusing to grant an order directing the clerk of the police authority to provide an unabridged copy of the report to the new councillor. The report was the result of an inquiry conducted by the chief constable of Hampshire. It disclosed serious shortcomings in the Lancashire police force and leading counsel had advised the police authority that, as the report contained defamatory statements, publication might endanger the privilege that would otherwise attach to it and that the safest course would be to refuse new members access to it. The report was leaked, however, and a police officer was awarded substantial damages for libel. The new councillor in good faith sought through the courts to compel the clerk to supply him with an unabridged copy of the report. Waller LJ, citing *Stuart* v. *Bell* and *Adam* v. *Ward*,[30] held that the committee had not decided on improper advice and said the final decision must in the last resort be that of the committee, which could take into consideration possible adverse effects on innocent people of allowing the inspection of documents. It was not reasonably necessary for the new councillor to have access to matters not disclosed to enable him to carry out his duties: he was not concerned with the daily management of the police force. Lord Denning dissented. He said the new councillor simply wanted to be better informed at any subsequent consideration of the matter. A member has a right to see all a committee's documents and this included a new member.

Possible changes in law on access

5.20. Widdicombe believed that changes in the law were needed as regards the rights of councillors to inspect documents and attend meetings. First, in line with its view that there should be no public right of access to committees that are purely deliberative (see 4.19), Widdicombe said:[31]

> It is not right that a member of one party should be legally entitled to attend, or inspect the documents of, a committee in which another party are formulating their policy on matters coming before the council. Again this will merely drive discussion underground. The important safeguard, which we propose should

[29] [1980] 2 All ER 353.
[30] (1917) AC 309; [1916–17] All ER 157.
[31] Widdicombe Report, para.5.68.

be maintained, is that all councillors should have the right to attend, and inspect the documents of, the council and of committees that take decisions.

There were two relatively minor respects in which Widdicombe also proposed amendment of the law:[32]

> First, there needs to be a simple neutral procedure for deciding whether councillors have a need to inspect a document or attend a meeting in order to carry out their duties. At present this is governed by common law rather than statute, and it is for the council itself to determine whether such a need arises. This effectively places the decision with the majority party. By contrast the provisions introduced by the Local Government (Access to Information) Act 1985 place similar responsibilities in respect of public rights of access on the proper officer. We [propose] that proper officer functions of this kind should be vested in the chief executive. We consider that the chief executive should . . . be given the function of deciding whether a councillor has a need to inspect a document or attend a meeting. In order to achieve this it would be necessary to place the current common law provisions on a statutory footing. This would have the incidental advantage of simplifying the law on councillors' access, which is at present part in common law and part in statute.

Then, secondly:[33]

> An anomaly has been created by the Local Government (Access to Information) Act 1985, whereby councillors are entitled to inspect documents containing certain categories of exempt information (i.e. information not open to the public) even though they may have a pecuniary interest in the matter. The effect is that, for example, councillors may inspect the tenders of firms for council contracts even where they are proposing to tender in a private capacity. This is clearly wrong. Councillors should never be entitled to inspect documents in which they have a pecuniary interest, unless they are open to the public.

Obligations generally

5.21. The obligations of a councillor at a meeting are the same whether the meeting is that of the full assembly or a committee or subcommittee. He must avoid doing anything which might encourage a charge of maladministration against the council and is expected:

(a) to comply with standing orders;

(b) to behave in an orderly manner;

(c) to disclose any interest he may have in a contract or other matter which is the subject of consideration;

---

[32] *Ibid.* para.5.69.
[33] *Ibid.* para.5.70.

(d) to refrain from taking part in the consideration or discussion and voting on any contract or other matter in which he has a pecuniary interest or in respect of which he is otherwise prohibited from voting; and, necessarily,

(e) to observe the law, e.g. if he votes in favour of illegal expenditure he becomes liable to surcharge.

Compliance with standing orders

5.22. If a councillor fails to comply with standing orders he should be:

(a) called to order by the person presiding if the omission to comply is a breach of the order of debate at a meeting;

(b) interviewed by the chairman of the council, or the leader, and asked to comply if the offending member is in breach of some other standing order.

A councillor intent on flouting standing orders cannot easily be made to mend his ways. If he behaves in a disorderly manner at a meeting the chairman can, with the acquiescence of the meeting, order him to leave temporarily; and in an extreme case of persistent disregard the council could show its displeasure by depriving the member of all committee membership: see 5.11. It could not properly, however, deny him a right to be present at any committee or subcommittee meeting if he can show a 'need to know': see 5.12.

Confidentiality of council papers

5.23. Councillors are also expected to treat as confidential all papers which they receive in the course of council business unless they are made public by law or by the authority's express or implied consent. Model standing order no. 29 provides (and its provisions are still relevant) that:

> All agenda, reports and other documents and all proceedings of committees and subcommittees shall be treated as confidential unless and until they become public in the ordinary course of the council's business.

5.24. Model standing order no. 26 is to this effect, though its terms would now need to be amended appropriately if intended to be adopted:

> (1) A member of the council may, for purposes of his duty as such member but not otherwise, on application to the town clerk/clerk of the council inspect any document which has been considered by a committee or by the council, and if copies are available shall on request be supplied for the like purposes with a copy of such a document.

Provided that a member shall not knowingly inspect and shall not call for a copy of any document relating to a matter in which he is professionally interested or in which he has directly or indirectly any pecuniary interest within the meaning of s.76 of the Local Government Act 1933 and that this standing order shall not preclude the town clerk/clerk of the council or the solicitor to the council from declining to allow inspection of any document which is or in the event of legal proceedings would be protected by privilege arising from the relationship of solicitor and client.

(2) All reports made or minutes kept by any committee shall, as soon as the committee has concluded action on the matter to which such reports or minutes relate, be open for the inspection of any member of the council.

Payment of allowances

5.25. Apart from travelling and subsistence allowances, councillors are entitled to 'remuneration' on a threefold system: an attendance allowance,[34] or a financial loss allowance,[35] and, additionally, a special responsibility allowance if the local authority so decides:[36]

(a) Attendance allowance – not available to co-opted members of committees or to parish or community councillors for approved duty within the parish or community – is paid for the performance of 'approved duty'[37] defined as:

   (i) attendance at a meeting of the council or of any of its committees or subcommittees;

   (ii) the doing of any other thing approved by the council or anything of a class so approved, for the purpose of, or in connection with, the discharge of the functions of the council, or of any of its committees or subcommittees;

   (iii) where, in pursuance of a duty imposed on or a power granted to the council by any enactment or instrument (including a Royal Charter), he has been appointed by or on the nomination of the council to be a member of some other body prescribed . . . the doing of anything as a member of that body for the purpose of, or in connection with, the discharge of the functions of that other body;

subject to a daily maximum prescribed by the Secretary of State;

---

[34] Local Government Act 1972, s.173. A county council cannot pay an attendance allowance to a member of its national park committee who is not a county councillor even though that member is a district councillor: *Hopson* v. *Devon County Council* (1977) LGR 721.

[35] *Ibid.* s.173A.

[36] *Ibid.* s.177A.

[37] *Ibid.* s.177(2).

(b) Financial loss allowance is payable, if a councillor so wishes, instead of an attendance allowance, but the recipient (who may be a co-opted member) must show that he has suffered actual financial loss, and again it is subject to a daily maximum prescribed by the Secretary of State;

(c) Special responsibility allowance is payable at the discretion of a local authority to 'key' members, such as the leader of the council and committee chairmen, and within a maximum (both in total and to an individual councillor) prescribed by the Secretary of State.

The foregoing is based, though departing substantially in many respects, on recommendations made in 1977 by the Robinson *Report of the Committee on the Remuneration of Councillors* (Cmnd 7010).

5.26. There is a widely held view that these present arrangements are unsatisfactory, but little agreement as to what system of remuneration for councillors should be substituted. The most recent review was undertaken as part of Widdicombe's inquiry into the conduct of local authority business and, in summary,[38] it recommended:

(a) Attendance allowance and financial loss allowance should be replaced by a basic flat-rate allowance payable to all councillors as an annual sum;

(b) The levels of basic flat-rate allowance should be banded according to the type of council and its population;

(c) The initial rates of basic flat-rate allowance should be £4,000 per annum in the largest authority and £1,500 in the smallest, and should be regularly reviewed;

(d) The special responsibility allowance arrangements should continue, but each local authority should be statutorily required to draw up a scheme for disbursing the allowance on the following basis:
   (i) the scheme should specify amounts payable for particular posts in such a way that the total payable equates to the maximum prescribed for the authority by the Secretary of State;
   (ii) all councillors in posts specified by the scheme shall be entitled to the amounts specified;

(e) No councillor should be entitled to more than one special responsibility allowance;

(f) The special responsibility allowance maxima currently prescribed for classes of authority and for individual councillors within each class should be doubled and subsequently kept under regular review.

[38] Widdicombe Report, paras.6.85–6.117.

General duty to disclose pecuniary interest

5.27. Probably the most important obligation imposed upon a councillor by law is that which requires him to disclose his pecuniary interest in a matter which is before a meeting at which he is present and to refrain from participating in the discussion thereon and from voting. The provisions of s.94(1) of the Local Government Act 1972, following the wording of earlier enactment, are to this effect:

> Subject to the provisions of s.97 below,[39] if a member of a local authority has any pecuniary interest, direct or indirect,[40] in any contract, proposed contract or other matter,[41] and is present at a meeting of the local authority at which the contract or other matter is the subject of consideration,[42] he shall at the meeting and as soon as practicable after its commencement disclose the fact and shall not take part in the consideration or discussion of the contract or other matter or vote on any question with respect to it.[43]

5.28. This duty of disclosure applies also by s.105 to co-opted members of a committee with a pecuniary interest, who must refrain from discussion and voting at a meeting of the committee. Breach of this duty exposes a member to criminal proceedings[44] (which may only be instituted by or on behalf of the Director of Public Prosecutions).[45] On summary conviction the member is liable to a fine not exceeding £200 unless he proves that he did not know that the contract, proposed contract or other matter in which he had a pecuniary interest was the subject of consideration at that meeting.[46]

5.29. Widdicombe believes that the statutory definition of pecuniary interest should be widened so that it clearly includes those who are employed or contracted to promote the pecuniary interest of others (see 5.27).[47] It instances the case of a councillor who is employed as a full-time

---

[39] This provides for the removal or exclusion of the disability: see 5.37.

[40] As to what is a 'pecuniary interest', see s.95. There have been many cases under the former statutory provisions. Pecuniary interest means, for example, more than pecuniary advantage, and voting in a matter which is to the financial disadvantage of a member is therefore illegal: *Brown* v. *Director of Public Prosecutions* [1956] 2 QB 369. And see *England* v. *Inglis* [1920] 2 KB 636, p. 639.

[41] The words 'or other matter' are to be interpreted in a very general way: per Lord Parker C J [1959] 1 QB 204, p. 212. *Rands* v. *Oldroyd* [1959] 1 QB 204.

[42] If a member is not present at the meeting he does not need to disclose.

[43] A member may give general notice: Local Government Act 1972, s.96; and see 5.34.

[44] As to breach of this duty see Local Government Act 1972, s.94(2). As to the validity of votes cast by interested persons, see 7.102.

[45] There is no precise ruling as to where responsibility lies for bringing alleged infringements to the notice of the Director of Public Prosecutions: it could be the council as a whole or the chief executive or the chairman or mayor who might well report to the chief constable. See *Report of the Bognor Regis Inquiry* (1965).

[46] Local Government Act 1972, s.94(4).

[47] Widdicombe Report, para.6.50.

officer of a trade union which represents the employees of the local authority: though he or she would not stand to gain financially through benefits won for the union's members, he is engaged in the promotion of the interests of those who do. The other example instanced is that of someone who is acting as a consultant to a developer seeking planning permission: although the developer, if a councillor, would be caught by the present definition, it is not clear whether the consultant would be since he would not necessarily gain financially from the decision.

Exclusion of interested member

5.30. A local authority may by standing orders provide for the exclusion of a member from a meeting while any contract, proposed contract or other matter in which he has a pecuniary interest, direct or indirect, is under consideration. Such a standing order could provide that, if a majority of those present so decide, a member may nevertheless remain.

5.31. Model standing order no. 18 is to the following effect:

> If any member of the council has any pecuniary interest direct or indirect within the meaning of [s.76 of the Local Government Act 1933 (other than an indirect interest described in subs.2A thereof)[48]] in any contract, proposed contract, or other matter, that member shall withdraw from the meeting while the contract, proposed contract, or other matter, is under consideration by the council unless:
>   (i) the disability to discuss that matter imposed upon him by the section has been removed by [the Minister of Housing and Local Government[49]] under subs.(8) thereof; or
>   (ii) the contract, proposed contract, or other matter, is under consideration by the council as part of the report of a committee and is not itself the subject of debate; or
>   (iii) the council invite him to remain.

What does 'exclusion' mean?

5.32. What does 'exclusion from the meeting' mean? Does it mean that the councillor excluded must withdraw from the *meeting room* or, in the words of the statute,[50] merely from the *meeting*? What if the councillor

---

[48] Now, of course, Local Government Act 1972, s.94.
[49] Secretary for the Environment or a district council as respects a member of a parish or community council: *ibid.* s.97, and see 5.37.
[50] See the discussion of this question in *Local Government Review* (1981) 145, pp. 765–66 and (1982) 146, p. 30. In the course of that discussion T. I. McLeod says: 'Even where standing orders are not specific as to whether withdrawal from the room is required, an interpretation which is based on their purpose would tend to suggest that such withdrawal should

excluded chooses to sit with the public in that part of the council chamber or committee room reserved for the public? The preferred legal interpretation appears to be that it is sufficient for the councillor to withdraw from that part of the council chamber or committee room where the council or committee members are seated; and, further, that any insistence on the part of the council or committee that the councillor should leave the room altogether might be unlawful as going beyond what is permitted by statute (see 2.8). Nevertheless, in practice it might be wise for the councillor to leave the room in such circumstances so as to avoid any question as to whether or not he is at the meeting. Of course not all meetings are held in rooms. There are such things as site meetings and visits of inspection where members, after gathering at a specified place, may proceed from one location to another. A meeting occurs or is held at a *place*, wherever it may be. In circumstances where a meeting is held other than in the confines of a room, law and prudent practice surely come together: the member who is excluded or decides of his own volition to withdraw should remove his physical presence from the meeting, i.e. he can best do this by moving well away from the gathering.

5.33. Widdicombe addressed itself to this matter. 'At present', it observed, 'there is no statutory requirement for someone who has declared an interest at a meeting to withdraw from the room', and this 'we believe is wrong':[51]

> By staying in the room, even though he or she may not speak or vote, a councillor might still influence the decision or might gather information which would help in the furtherance of his or her interest. The Redcliffe–Maud and Salmon Reports both recommended that the councillor should be statutorily required to withdraw, but this was not implemented by the Government. Recent research[52] shows that about 50 per cent of local authorities in England and Wales require withdrawal under their own standing orders, and a further 20 per cent require withdrawal unless the councillor is specifically invited to stay. We propose that there should be a statutory requirement for councillors in all such instances to withdraw. Withdrawal should be from the room, not just to the space set aside for the public. There should be no option to invite councillors to stay, which could place their colleagues in an invidious position.

50 cont.

take place. . . Additional support for this conclusion can be derived from a consideration of the Public Bodies (Admission to Meetings) Act 1960 which provides that certain meetings "shall be open to the public" . . . in other words a member of the public who attends is present at the meeting even though he is not part of it. It would follow that a councillor who merely withdraws to the public gallery is still present at the meeting and cannot be said to have "withdrawn from the meeting".'

51 Widdicombe Report, para.6.51.

52 Alan Parker, Aidan Rose and John Taylor, *The Administration of Standards of Conduct in Local Government* (Charles Knight, 1986).

Declaration of interest

5.34. A councillor may declare his interest in two ways. He may give a general notice of some interest to the proper officer or he may give particular notice as the occasion arises. A general or particular notice must be recorded[53] and the book in which the record is kept must be open for inspection by members of the authority.[54] Where a general notice has been made, further disclosure of the existence of the interest(s), unless withdrawn, is not required.[55]

Non-statutory disclosure of interest

5.35. As a result of the Redcliffe–Maud report on *Local Government Rules of Conduct* in May 1974,[56] many local authorities adopted additional standing orders encouraging members to disclose interests beyond those which they were bound to declare under the statutory provisions relating to pecuniary interests. According to Widdicombe's research[57] about 50 per cent of authorities in England and Wales have introduced a register of interests – in some instances in the form of questionnaires asking all councillors to state whether they have certain specified interests. Where this type of register is adopted completion of the register is often made a pre-condition of membership of committees, a practice which was held to be lawful in *R. v. Newham London Borough Council ex-parte Haggerty* (1986) (see 9.55).

5.36. Widdicombe has recommended that local authorities should be statutorily required to keep a public register of both pecuniary and non-pecuniary interests of councillors on the following basis:[58]

(a) The register should include any interest which could reasonably be regarded as likely to affect councillors' conduct or influence their actions, speeches or votes;

(b) The register should specifically require entry of land and property owned by councillors in the authority's area, paid employments, and interests in companies above a specified minimum; but otherwise it should be for individual councillors to decide what interests fall within the criteria in (a) above;

(c) Councillors with no relevant interests should be required to state this;

(d) The chief executive should be the registrar, with a statutory duty to maintain the register;

---

[53] Local Government Act 1972, s.96(1).
[54] *Ibid.* s.94.
[55] *Ibid.* s.96(2).
[56] See also Department of the Environment circ. no. 106/74.
[57] Widdicombe Report, para.6.45.
[58] *Ibid.* paras.6.46–6.49.

(e) Completion of the register should not alter the requirement to declare interests orally at meetings as and when they arise. Failure to complete the proposed statutory register should be an offence, but local authorities should be statutorily prohibited from imposing other disabilities for non-completion of registers.

Widdicombe also wanted to see changes in the National Code of Local Government Conduct in respect of non-pecuniary interests (see the appendix to this chapter).

Removal of disabilities

5.37. The Secretary of State is empowered[59] to remove the disability imposed on members where the number of members disabled at any one time is so great as to impede the transaction of business or where it appears to him that it is in the interests of the inhabitants of the area that the disability be removed. In the case of parish or community councils it is the district council which may exercise this dispensing power.[60] The disability of interested members is twofold: they may not take part in the consideration or discussion of the matter and they are precluded from voting. The Secretary of State or district council in granting a dispensation may choose to remove only the first disability, enabling a member to give his view but not his vote.[61]

5.38. The Secretary of State is empowered to remove a disability upon learning the facts from any source. Until the enactment of the Local Government Act 1972 it was questionable whether councillors could properly discuss and vote on a proposition that the dispensation should be sought.

5.39. Councillors who are tenants of council housing accommodation have been given a general dispensation to speak and vote on matters affecting council housing and indeed on any matters in respect of which a disability is imposed by ss.94 or 105 of the Act arising in the right of a tenancy (whether contractual or statutory) of a dwelling let unfurnished. This dispensation is in these terms:

1. The Secretary of State for the Environment as respects England and the Secretary of State for Wales as respects Wales, in exercise of their respective powers under s.97(1) and 105 of the Local Government Act 1972 hereby remove, to the extent specified below, any disability which is imposed by s.94 or 105 of that Act on any member of a local authority or of a committee, joint committee, or subcommittee described in the said s.105 and which

[59] Local Government Act 1972, s.97, which lists certain exemptions.
[60] *Ibid.* s.97.
[61] *Ibid.* s.97(2). See also Department of the Environment circ. no.40/72, app.II, paras.4, 5.

results solely from a pecuniary interest arising in the right of a tenancy (whether contractual or statutory) of a dwelling let unfurnished.

2. This dispensation extends to the consideration and discussion of, and to voting on any question with respect to, any matter of general housing policy (as defined in para.3 below) at any meeting of the local authority, committee, joint committee or subcommittee.

3. In this dispensation 'matter of general housing policy' means a matter relating to the exercise by the body concerned of any housing function as it affects the whole or any part of their area; and it does not include the detailed application of any policy solely to the dwelling in relation to which the pecuniary interest arises.

5.40. An application to the Secretary of State for a dispensation to vote and/or speak may be made either by an individual member or jointly by a group of members – conveniently, as a rule, through the chief executive. *Permission to speak* will normally be given for any matter in which a member has a pecuniary interest so long as it is not an interest which is peculiar to himself. *Permission to vote* will not normally be given unless:

(a) the number of members disabled would be at least half of the whole council or committee; or

(b) the number of members disabled and their distribution among the parties or groups in the council or committee is such that if they did not vote, policies might be adopted to which the majority of members were opposed.

Personal liability

5.41. Responsibility for decisions made in council or committee meetings is, politically at least, a *collective responsibility*: the responsibility is that indivisibly of the members as a whole and the decision made is taken in the name of the local authority. There are, however, circumstances in which a council member incurs personal liability at law. It has been seen that a member who votes on a contract or other matter in which he has a pecuniary interest incurs liability for a penalty (see 5.28). There is also a personal liability upon a member present at a meeting, shared equally with those who act similarly, who votes in favour of or acquiesces in expenditure which is contrary to law or of a proposition which results in a loss or deficiency by wilful misconduct:[62] he is liable to what was formerly 'surcharge' by the district auditor[63] and, if the expenditure involved exceeds £2,000, he may be disqualified from membership of an auth-

---

[62] Local Government Act 1972, s.161.
[63] An account of the powers of the district auditor and the courts would be outside the scope

ority.[64] It is not enough for the member to show that he remained silent on such an occasion because abstention from voting means acquiescence in the decision: he must have voted against the proposition.[65]

5.42. This means that the request of any council member to have his vote *against* a motion recorded should be acceded to (whether or not the request is made following a requisition for the whole voting to be recorded (see 7.109)): the record may well save him from unjustified personal liability. If, however, the minutes do not disclose who voted for and against a proposition it is open to a member to prove that he voted against. Thus in *Attorney-General* v. *Tottenham Local Board* (1872)[66] a member who proved he had opposed a scheme was held not liable personally for illegal expenditure even though he was present when the payment was authorised.

5.43. It is unquestionably the function of an authority's advisers to alert members to any possible illegality of a course which the council or committee wishes to pursue:[67] and if, nevertheless, the council or committee proceeds to act against advice, the committee clerk would be well advised to ensure that the advice tendered and the name of the officer giving it are recorded in the minutes, for this may save the responsible officer from personal liability.[68] Where an authority persists in pursuing what the officers believe may be an unlawful course of action it behoves the officers to do what they properly can to protect the interests of the authority and its individual members. Because expenditure on items which are lawful in themselves can be so excessive and unreasonable in amount as to render the expenditure unlawful,[69] the committee clerk

---

63 cont.

of this work. Where, however, the district auditor considers that any person has failed to bring into account any sum which should have been accounted for and the failure has not been sanctioned by the Secretary of State or that a loss has been incurred or deficiency caused by the wilful conduct of any person, the district auditor is required to certify that the sum or, as the case may be, the amount of the loss or deficiency is due from the person named and may recover that sum or amount for the benefit of the local authority: *ibid.*

[64] *Ibid.* s.161(2)(b).

[65] This appears to be the consequence of several cases: see, e.g. *Roberts* v. *Hopwood* [1925] AC 578; *Re Magrath* [1934] 2 KB 415.

[66] (1872) 27 LTNS 44.

[67] In *R.* v. *Browne* [1907] 2 IR 505, and *Davies* v. *Cowperthwaite* [1938] 2 All ER 685; 102 JP 405, it was held that it was not necessarily misconduct for a councillor to ignore the advice of the town clerk if he honestly believed the advice erroneous.

[68] The auditor's power applies equally to officers: not, of course, as regards decisions taken by members but for loss or deficiency through wilful misconduct by officers.

[69] Where a local authority made payments to its employees which in the opinion of the auditor were, having regard to market wages, so unreasonable as to amount to gratuities in addition to wages, and such excess was surcharged by the auditor, the court upheld the surcharge: *Roberts* v. *Hopwood, supra.*

should ensure that the grounds for the decision and the reasoning are fully recorded;[70] and it may be useful to include a phrase to this effect:

> . . . and the council/committee therefore considered it reasonable in all the circumstances [to take the action decided upon].

Responsibility for maladministration

5.44. The view has been expressed that 'the acts of individual members . . . may become the subject of maladministration':[71]

> This is a revolutionary doctrine in local government where it has been consistently accepted that a council can act only through its officers and the individual member has no power as such. Even chairmen of committees taking decisions on urgent matters must seek subsequent ratification. But a commitment entered into by a member of the council, particularly if he has been held out by the council as having authority, e.g. by a public surgery advertised by the council, could well give rise to a finding of maladministration if the obligation is not honoured. The failure of one committee member to disclose a non-financial interest, as defined by the code of conduct, might constitute maladministration by the local authority itself.

Widdicombe, indeed, has proposed that breach of the National Code of Local Government Conduct should be prima facie maladministration so far as the code comes within the ombudsman's ambit.[72]

Co-opted members

General power of co-option

5.45. Local authorities have a general power[73] to co-opt[74] persons from outside their membership to any committee, other than a finance committee, set up under the Local Government Act 1972.[75] It is a power, not a duty, exercisable by the council in full assembly[76] and not by commit-

---

[70] The court may relieve a person from surcharge if satisfied that the person acted reasonably or in the belief that the expenditure was authorised by law: Local Government Act 1972, s.161(3).

[71] R. G. Brooke and R. Greenwood, 'The Procedures of the Local Commissioners' (1978) 4 *Local Government Studies* 13.

[72] Widdicombe Report, para.6.19.

[73] Local Government Act 1972, s.102(3).

[74] The law does not use the word 'co-opt' or its derivatives: the expression in s.102 of the 1972 Act is 'persons who are not members of the appointing authority'.

[75] I.e. under s.102(1), *ibid.*, but not under any other enactment requiring or permitting the setting up of a committee.

[76] There is no obligation to appoint co-opted members to committees set up under s.102(1), *ibid.*, nor (see 5.47) as a rule to statutory committees.

tees.[77] There is no power to co-opt to the full council.[78] Co-option needs to be distinguished from the non-council members who may be appointed to membership of an *advisory committee* under s.102(4) of the Local Government Act 1972: indeed, such a committee can be comprised wholly of non-council members.

Eligibility for co-option

5.46. Co-opted members appointed under this general enabling power:

(a)   must not exceed in number one-third of the membership of a committee[79] (although there is no restriction on numbers in the case of a subcommittee);

(b)   must not be disqualified from membership of the appointing council[80] but do not need to be positively qualified to be a member of the authority.[81]

But a person is not, by reason of his being a teacher in, or being otherwise employed in, any school, college or other educational institution maintained or assisted by a local education authority, disqualified from a membership of any committee for purposes of education or connected with the execution of the Public Libraries and Museums Act 1964.[82]

Specific powers of co-option

5.47. In the case of certain statutory committees the Act concerned expressly provides for co-option; thus:

---

[77] Committees cannot determine their own constitution but a committee could be empowered by the council to make its own choice of co-opted members to fill the number of co-opted members' seats provided for in the committee's constitution.

[78] The former office of alderman could be filled from outside the council's membership from persons qualified to be members: this was a form of co-option.

[79] Local Government Act 1972, s.102(3). A subcommittee of a committee set up under s.102(1) of the 1972 Act need not include any members of the local authority.

[80] *Ibid.* s.104(1). The learned authors of *Lumley's Public Health,* 12th edn (1974), vol. XIV, p. 334, point out a difficulty by reason of the decision in *Bishop v. Deakin* [1936] Ch. 409; [1936] All ER 255; 100 JP 201. The decision shows that a person may be disqualified for being a member of the council and yet retain his seat; and consequently a disqualified person may be holding office as a councillor. Thus the question whether such a person can be a member of a committee must remain a matter of doubt so long as this case remains law. It would seem, however, nonsensical for a person to be a councillor but unable to serve on any committee and the author agrees with the learned authors of *Lumley* that s.104(1) cannot be intended to exclude a councillor from membership of a committee.

[81] The law is in fact silent as to the qualification of persons for co-option. In practice local authorities which, for example, invite voluntary bodies to appoint a representative to serve on a committee as a co-opted member do not ask (although, of course, they could do) whether the representative is of full age or a British subject or fulfils the requirements as to residential qualification.

[82] Local Government Act 1972, s.104(2).

(a) an *education committee* 'shall include persons of experience in education and persons acquainted with the educational conditions prevailing in the area for which the committee acts'[83] (but this obligation does not necessarily mean that the local education committee *must* co-opt from outside: the elected members could provide the necessary experience and knowledge); at least a majority of the committee must be members of the authority;[84]

(b) a *social services committee* 'may' include persons who are not members of the local authority;[85] and, again, at least a majority of the committee must be members of the authority.[86]

Co-opted members of a social services committee must not be disqualified for membership of the authority[87] but this prohibition does not apply to co-opted members of an education committee.[88]

Rights and obligations

5.48. A co-opted member:

(a) has the same rights as any other member of the committee to which he is appointed (except that he cannot claim an 'attendance allowance' as can a council member): see 5.25;

(b) is under the same obligations as members of the council which appoints him;[89]

(c) possesses no rights or privileges in respect of any other committee of the council, nor may he attend council meetings (other than in the capacity of a member of the public).[90]

5.49. The view expressed in the foregoing paragraph that a co-opted member has the same rights as any other member of the committee to which he is appointed[91] means that the co-opted member has the same

---

[83] Education Act 1944, sch.I, Pt II, para.5.

[84] *Ibid.* para.6: in the case of a joint education committee it is sufficient if more than half of the committee consists of persons who are members of any of the authorities for which the committee is established.

[85] Local Authority Social Services Act 1970, s.5(1).

[86] *Ibid.* s.5(3).

[87] *Ibid.* s.5(1).

[88] The Education Act 1944 is silent on this point.

[89] Thus a co-opted member is under the same obligation as elected members in regard to disclosure of interest in contracts: Local Government Act 1972, ss.94–98, as applied by s.105. See 5.27.

[90] Standing orders could confer upon co-opted members a right to attend other committees (except a finance committee: see 5.45) in much the same way as council members may be permitted to attend committees to which they have not been appointed.

[91] This is a widely held view: see, e.g. Paul Graham, 'Beware of the "advantages" of co-opted members' (1979) *Local Government Chronicle* 320.

general voting powers as a councillor member.[92] True this is implied rather than specifically stated, but why otherwise is there statutory restriction on the proportion of non-councillors on a committee? And why otherwise in the case of the former children's regional planning committee was there express statutory power enabling nominated members to determine the rights of co-opted members to attend, speak and vote (see 9.37). Some local authorities do, however, restrict the powers of co-opted members[93] and there would seem to be no reason why they should not do so,[94] although such a course might be thought to negate the purpose of co-option. If a local authority deems it expedient to deny a co-opted member the right to vote upon particular matters within the committee's terms of reference, it might more seemly refer those matters to a subcommittee with delegated powers on which the co-opted member does not serve or to appoint the co-opted member to a subcommittee rather than the full committee.

5.50. If a co-opted member is denied a right to vote he may in certain circumstances still be liable to surcharge. There is no authority on the point specifically but it may be that a co-opted member could incur liability on the principle – for which there is authority – that a member of a committee who merely abstains from voting rather than voting against illegal expenditure can become subject to surcharge. A court might hold that a co-opted member so denied the right to influence decisions could not be said to have abstained or concurred, but perhaps the co-opted member should, in such circumstances, be advised to declare and have minuted his opposition to what was proposed.

5.51. Widdicombe has suggested that co-option should be discontinued because, in the case of decision-making committees, this would clarify accountability;[95] and that *advisers* could be appointed to attend on a regular

---

[92] Maud clearly assumed that co-opted members had voting rights. One of its conclusions about the use of co-option was that 'co-opted members should continue to have the right to vote': Maud Report, vol. 1, para.366.

[93] Walsall Metropolitan Borough Council evidently appoints co-opted members (for the most part nominees of the political parties) to its area planning committees, which exercise delegated powers, but the co-opted members are denied the right to vote – apparently on the grounds that they are not answerable to the electorate: see T. J. Phillips, 'Area Planning Committees in Walsall' (1979) 5 *Local Government Studies* 32.

[94] Widdicombe expresses the interesting view that 'Where there is a statutory requirement to co-opt, co-opted members are full members of the committee with voting rights. Where co-option is discretionary it is for the local authority to decide whether those concerned should have full membership with voting rights or should have some lesser status': Widdicombe Report, para.5.88. This view could be explained by Widdicombe's belief – which is surely in error – that magistrates are co-opted members of a police committee: Widdicombe Report, para.5.82; as to which see 9.30.

[95] Widdicombe Report, para.5.99. Widdicombe found no great support for co-option but the written evidence to Maud favoured it: Maud Report, vol. 1, paras.357–58.

basis or for particular meetings with no right to vote.[96] The names of the advisers should be made publicly known together with the terms of their attendance at meetings.[97]

Co-opted member as committee chairman

5.52. It follows (see 5.48) that a co-opted member may be elected as chairman of the committee on which he serves. His effective role in such a capacity would, however, be limited to presiding at meetings of the committee. Because he cannot as such attend council meetings he could not pilot his committee's proposals through the full assembly, nor answer questions put to him there, nor represent his committee on, say, the finance committee if it comprises all chairmen of committees.[98]

Removal of co-opted member

5.53. It would seem that a local authority can always, at its absolute discretion, remove from committee membership any person whom it has co-opted to a committee on the analogy of *Manton v. Brighton Corporation*: see 5.11. As it has power to remove a council member from one of its own committees (or a joint committee to which it is a party), then it must be presumed to have similar power over a co-opted member. This view is reinforced, it is submitted, by the decision in *R. v. Peak Planning Board exparte Jackson* (see 5.57), in which a distinction is made between nomination and appointment. If the outside body upon whose nomination the person has been co-opted notifies the local authority that it wishes to replace its nominee then, always assuming that the co-opted person has not become disqualified,[99] the local authority alone can determine whether to accede to the nominating body's request.

Representation on other local authorities and public bodies

General considerations

5.54. Local authorities are often invited, in some instances have a right, to be represented on other bodies, both statutory and voluntary. For

---

[96] *Ibid.* para.5.101.

[97] *Ibid.* para.5.107.

[98] A council member vice-chairman could, however, deputise for him for such purposes. Note the somewhat analogous situation where the chairman of the police committee is a magistrate: see 9.31.

[99] Co-opted persons do not have to be qualified for local authority membership but they must not be disqualified: see 5.46.

example, so far as public bodies are concerned, a district health authority must include members *appointed* by local authorities;[100] and county councils may invite district councils within their area to *nominate* representatives to serve on county committees (although in these cases the arrangement is virtually one of co-option). The role to be exercised by the representatives on these other bodies depends upon the terms of their appointment: sometimes there is an unequivocable duty to represent the collective view of the nominating local authority or other body, in effect to obey instructions; but in other cases more likely to act according to individual judgement much in the manner in which a council member is expected to take account of the interests of residents in the whole local authority area rather than those only of the electors who voted him into office.

5.55. The appointment or nomination of representatives on other bodies is ordinarily reserved to the full council and dealt with at the annual meeting. Model standing order no. 16 regulates the voting on appointments in this manner:

> Where there are more than two persons nominated for any position to be filled by the council, and of the votes given there is not a majority in favour of one person, the name of the person having the least number of votes shall be struck off the list and a fresh vote shall be taken, and so on until a majority of votes is given in favour of one person.

There is another system, however: see 7.106 as to Medina Borough Council's use of the single transferable vote in the selection of nominees.

Nomination or appointment?

5.56. It is a matter dependent upon the circumstances of each particular case whether the representative is an appointee or a mere nominee. In all cases of co-option, as we have already seen (see 5.45), the submission of a person's name is mere nomination and it is the local authority on whose committee the person is to serve that makes the actual appointment. In such a case the nominating body cannot recall the nominee or revoke the appointment: his continuation in office is solely for the appointing local authority to decide. In other cases (but see the next paragraph) where the local authority or other body itself appoints its representatives on another local authority or other public body, the local authority can always revoke the appointment and substitute another representative at any time.

---

[100] National Health Service Reorganisation Act 1973, s.5, sch.1, para.2(1) (a); and see Chapter 14.

5.57. The circumstances in which a local authority is represented on a joint planning board appear to be unique. Thus in *R. v. Peak Park Planning Board ex-parte Jackson* (1976)[101] the divisional court held that a member of a county council appointed to serve on a joint planning board held a statutory office and could not be removed until his term of office expired or he voluntarily resigned. The facts were as follows. The Derbyshire County Council, which had appointed 12 members to the Peak Park joint planning board, wanted to replace two of those members, with whom a difference had arisen, by two other persons and it so decided by resolution and notified the board accordingly. One of the two challenged before the court the county council's right to replace him. The Lord Chief Justice said it was wrong to give to the word 'representation' the significance attached to it by the county council: it was an unhappy word to choose and the court would not give it its literal meaning. The statutory instrument under which appointments to the board were made provided, said His Lordship, that s.80 and other sections of the Local Government Act 1972 which related to the circumstances in which members of a local authority could be removed applied to members of the board. If members of the board were merely representatives of the council there was no reason why the complex machinery for the removal of a member of a local authority should be included. Once members were appointed retention of office depended upon the statutory instrument. The court granted the applicant an order for *certiorari*, quashing his purported removal by Derbyshire County Council from the Peak Park joint planning board.

Defamatory statements in council and committee

General principle

5.58. Statements in council and committee meetings are subject to the general principles of law relating to defamation:[102] that is to say, a person who makes a defamatory statement (one exposing a person to hatred, ridicule or contempt, or which causes him to be shunned or avoided, or which has a tendency to injure him in his office, profession or trade) commits a tort and is liable for the consequences which flow from such an act.

Privilege

5.59. It is a general defence in an action for defamation for the defendant

---

[101] 140 *Local Government Review* (1976) 278.
[102] See, e.g. *Clark & Lindsell on Torts*.

to show that the statement was made on a privileged occasion. There are two kinds of privileged occasion: absolute and qualified. Where the privilege is *absolute* – and this does not apply to local authority meetings of any kind but to certain judicial and Parliamentary proceedings[103] – it is a complete bar against an action for defamation.

5.60. *Qualified* privilege attaches to:

> an occasion where the person who makes a communication has an interest or a duty, legal, social or moral, to make it to the person to whom it is made, and the person to whom it is so made has a corresponding interest or duty to receive it.[104]

Thus qualified privilege will attach to statements made in council and committee.[105] Where pleaded in an action for defamation the author of the defamatory statement must prove (a) a duty to make the statement, and (b) an interest on the part of the recipient to receive it: but the plaintiff may still succeed if he can prove malice on the defendant's part because an essential feature of qualified privilege is the absence of malice. Reckless disregard as to whether what is said is true or not will also destroy qualified privilege.[106]

5.61. It seems probable that informal meetings on council business are not occasions to which qualified privilege attaches[107] such as, for example, a party caucus meeting, and meetings of officers. Nor would protection extend to remarks made in a council chamber or committee room after the chairman has closed the meeting.

---

[103] Local authorities do not enjoy absolute privilege even when acting judicially: see *Royal Aquarium and Summer and Winter Gardens Society* v. *Parkinson* 56 JP [1892] QB 431.

[104] Per Lord Atkinson, *Adam* v. *Ward* (1917) AC 309, p. 334.

[105] In *Horrocks* v. *Lowe* (1972) 138 LGR 131, Lord Denning said that qualified privilege applied to meetings in the council chamber 'or meetings which concerned the council'. And see *Horrocks* v. *Lowe* [1975] AC 135.

[106] It was held in *Horrocks* v. *Lowe, supra*, affirmed by the House of Lords [1975] AC 135, that where an alderman honestly believed in the truth of his assertions but had no reasonable grounds or was hasty in jumping to conclusions or was irrational or prejudiced, this did not destroy his privilege. Lord Denning said: 'It is of the first importance that the members of a local authority should be able to speak their minds freely on a matter of interest in the locality. So long as they honestly believe what they say to be true, they are not to be made liable for defamation. They may be prejudiced and unreasonable. They may not get their facts right. They may give much offence to others. But so long as they are honest, they go clear. No councillor should be hampered in his criticisms by fear of an action for slander. He is not to be forever looking over his shoulder to see if what he says is defamatory. He must be allowed to give his point of view, even if it is hotly disputed by others. This is essential to free discussion'. In *Royal Aquarium and Summer and Winter Garden Society* v. *Parkinson, supra*, Lord Esher MR described a statement made by a county councillor at a meeting to which privilege attached as made by one 'utterly regardless of the truth, or of any personal injury he might be inflicting, perfectly reckless whether what he was saying was true or false'.

[107] See Professor Harry Street, 'Defamation and Local Authorities – Some Recent Developments' (1973) 5527 *Local Government Chronicle* 153.

Other defences

5.62. There are certain other defences. Justification can be pleaded if the words are true and justification provides a complete answer. It is also a good defence to show that what was said was fair comment on a matter of public interest, honestly believed to be true, relevant and not inspired by malicious motive, and that the statements of fact on which the comment was based were materially true.[108]

Committee chairmanship

5.63. The most significant change in a council member's role occurs when he becomes chairman of the council or chairman of a committee or – not of importance so far as meetings are concerned – leader of the council or leader of the opposition.[109] The duties and responsibilities of a council chairman or mayor are discussed later (see 7.28 *et seq.*); our concern here is to examine *the role of a member as chairman of a committee.*

Differing conceptions

5.64. The role adopted by a committee chairman is influenced partly by his own conception of what it should be both in committee and outside the committee room and by the degree of authority ordinarily bestowed upon the chairmanship by local custom. Nowhere today does a committee chairman restrict himself solely to presiding at meetings of his committee and to acting as spokesman at council meetings. Yet, legally, this is the extent of his formal power and authority, for a council member has no effective independent power as an individual: see 5.67. Even within a narrow concept of his role varying attitudes are adopted: some members see their task as chairman as a mere interpreter of the committee's collective will; but others think it proper that they should influence and guide the committee in the decisions it makes. Where it is the authority's practice to re-elect the same committee chairman year after year as long as he is willing to serve there is greater likelihood of his becoming the moulder rather than the interpreter of his committee's views, and some become despotic.[110]

5.65. The choice of committee chairmen lies in the gift of the majority

---

[108] Fair and accurate reports of meetings of local authorities and their committees are privileged unless the publication is proved to be made with malice: Defamation Act 1952, s.7. See 3.16 as to privilege attaching to local authority agenda and reports.

[109] There are, of course, other political offices apart from that of leader: each party will ordinarily appoint a number of whips.

[110] See Finer, *English Local Government*, 4th edn, p. 244.

party on the council but in some authorities the parties arrive at an understanding to share the chairmanships in rough proportion to their strength on the council – although very often the minority party will not allow any of its members to accept a committee chairmanship 'so as to keep clear its opposition role and clear itself of any responsibility in the application of the policy of the dominant group'.[111]

Chairman's action

5.66. In practice a committee chairman is invested with considerable power and influence. But the authority with which he is endowed and the power he exercises are based on convention: 'probably the only example in local government of a convention analogous to the constitutional convention'.[112] The practice of chairman's action – recently challenged in the courts: see 5.67 – began as a convenient arrangement whereby officers in circumstances of urgency between meetings sought authority from the committee chairman before taking this, that, or some other course of action. It avoided delay and was a convenient, workable arrangement which facilitated the dispatch of business but rested solely on mutual trust and confidence and good faith. It was purportedly clothed with legality by ensuring that, at the next ensuing meeting of the committee, the chairman's action was confirmed. Strictly speaking, an individual council member could not be empowered to make decisions because it was unlawful for the committee to purport to empower its chairman to act in advance.

5.67. The practice of chairman's action was examined judicially in *R. v. Secretary of State for the Environment ex-parte Hillingdon London Borough Council* (1986).[113] That case put one question beyond doubt (indeed there was probably little doubt anyhow) but left at least another unsettled. The question settled is that there can be no valid delegation to an individual councillor because s.101 of the Local Government Act 1972, while it permits delegation to a committee, subcommittee, officer or another local authority, does not empower a committee chairman to act alone – even if purportedly comprising a committee of one (see next paragraph). It is open to doubt, however, whether the *Hillingdon* case wholly outlawed chairman's action.

---

[111] J. H. Warren, *Municipal Administration*, 2nd edn, p. 184.
[112] See Knowles, *Modern Management in Local Government*, p. 56.
[113] [1986] 1 All ER 810. The practice was also examined – and the view was the same – in *R. v. Secretary of State for Education and Science ex-parte Birmingham District Council and Another: The Times*, 18 July 1984.

5.68. *Hillingdon* was decided on circumstances that may not ordinarily arise. The local authority had sought judicial review of the Secretary of State's refusal to determine appeals against enforcement notices issued by the council on the authority alone of its planning committee chairman. The council had purportedly clothed the committee chairman with delegated powers to give 'instructions regarding the institution or defence of legal proceedings or the representation of the council in any matters referred to him by the director of law and administration' and expressly to make decisions on a number of matters including enforcement procedure under the Town and Country Planning Act. In other words, the chairman was not merely as a matter of administrative practice required to be consulted in circumstances of urgency and to approve a course of action which an officer wished to take, but was purportedly empowered to make decisions on a continuing basis in a specific sphere of the local authority's functions. Furthermore, the council had sought to justify its standing orders provision on the argument that it had fixed at one the membership of a committee to which it had delegated decision-making powers. The standing orders did not provide for ratification of the committee chairman's action and in the particular circumstances which gave rise to the court proceedings there had been no ratification.

5.69. What, then, are the implications of *Hillingdon* on the practice of chairman's action? It could be argued that the judgement does not rule out chairman's action provided its operation is well-regulated and any decision made by a committee chairman is subsequently confirmed by resolution of the council or committee or subcommittee with delegated powers. Woolf J in *Hillingdon* said:

> There may be difficulties in overcoming the problem by a duly authorised committee . . . ratifying the *ultra vires* action of the chairman retrospectively. As to this, I need to express no conclusive view because there was no ratification in this case.

That there was no ratification was understandable. On the authority's contention that the delegation was lawful it followed logically that there was no requirement for confirmation because any decision, properly made under valid delegated authority, becomes effective from the time it is made. That said, however, there is authority for the view that there can be no effective ratification of action which is in itself unlawful. As to that, in relation to chairman's action, the law remains unclear and, as Widdicombe has pointed out, 'unsatisfactory': (see 5.74).

5.70. It may be that, so long as a committee chairman is not asked to make a decision which affects or prejudices third party interests, it is not unlawful for officers to continue to seek a committee chairman's concurrence with a projected course of action in circumstances of urgency, where it would be impracticable within the time available to call together the full committee or subcommittee. The court in *Hillingdon* appears to have recognised that this might be perfectly lawful within limits. Referring to *R. v. Brent Health Authority ex-parte Francis* (1985)[114] (in which the chairman of the health authority had made a decision about the exclusion of the public from its meetings), Woolf J said:

> In this case . . . urgent action was subsequently ratified by the authority when the meeting was held. . . However, this decision relates to the internal procedures of the authority and I can see a very real distinction between a chairman acting alone in exercising this sort of function in relation to its own proceedings and a chairman purporting to take a decision which legislation such as the Town and Country Planning Act requires to be taken by the authority before enforcement proceedings are commenced . . .

5.71. Difficulties of the kind discussed here can be overcome, as the learned judge in *Hillingdon* himself observed, by delegating the necessary authority to an officer:[115]

> I . . . accept that it would be difficult to fault a procedure where the decisions are taken by a fully authorised officer pursuant to s.101 in consultation with the elected chairman . . . this would be a simple way of dealing with these urgent matters which could not go before an elected committee or sub-committee but for which it is undesirable for a single officer to take sole responsibility . . .

There could well be contentious matters or issues of political sensitivity where a local authority would be reluctant to allow an officer complete freedom to act though willing to make the delegation conditional upon consultation with the appropriate councillor. It is submitted, however, that it is important that *consultation* alone is envisaged and *not prior approval* for that, surely, would be indistinguishable from purportedly conferring delegated authority upon an individual member.[116]

5.72. It is obviously important, in view of the foregoing, that if an authority is to continue the practice of chairman's action – and it needs to

---

[114] [1985] QB 869: and see 7.128.

[115] As to delegation to an officer: see 4.8. A local authority can in certain circumstances be bound by the act of an officer within his ostensible authority but beyond the scope of his delegated authority.

[116] In 'How Small Can Committees Be?' in *Local Government Chronicle* (1979) at p. 350, Harry Sales said: 'For authorities . . . wishing to arm, for example, chairmen with powers to deal with routine, emergency or particular cases, the advice would be to follow the established practice of authorising the appropriate officer, under s.101(1), to act but to require that, in appropriate cases, he shall first consult the chairman or other member'.

be acknowledged that many authorities now think it unnecessary – it should be codified so that the system is properly understood, individual committee chairmen know the limitations upon their authority, and there is no scope for abuse or illegality. The following general principles are suggested:

(a) that a committee chairman's authority to take action should be stated in standing orders or elsewhere in terms which clearly indicate the circumstances in which he may act: these should relate to matters of urgency only (because routine business can and ought to be delegated to officers) within the competence of his committee;

(b) that requests for a committee chairman's action should always be made in writing, preferably in prescribed form, with all the relevant facts upon which a decision can fairly be taken;

(c) that the procedure for seeking chairman's action should be laid down, e.g. it should ideally be made in each case through the chief executive or the county/borough/district secretary (or in a case where another officer ordinarily has to vet the originating officer's proposal, i.e. in financial or staffing matters, through the treasurer or personnel officer) whose responsibility it must be first to be satisfied:

  (i) that the business relates to a matter in which the chairman has competence to act; and

  (ii) that all relevant facts are available; and to record the decision made by the chairman and ensure that it is reported for ratification at the next meeting.

There is an understandable view that codification on the lines of the foregoing provides 'dangerous' encouragement of an unlawful practice.[117]

5.73. It seems reasonable to take the view in any case that a committee chairman can have no greater power than his committee possesses. This implies that he may only properly authorise action within his committee's terms of reference and then, strictly speaking, only if the committee possesses delegated power to deal with the particular issue. A matter beyond the committee's power is also beyond the committee chairman's power. Thus if a matter of urgency arises for decision which is beyond his committee's powers the chairman may act, and only be asked to act by officers, with the concurrence of, for example, the chairman of the policy committee if the matter is one of important principle or of the chairman of the finance committee (where there is no policy committee exercising financial control) if the matter involves expenditure beyond that which the committee may incur. There may well be matters, of course, perhaps of a

[117] See *Local Government Review* (1978), p. 710.

politically contentious character, where the leader of the council and the leader of the opposition may need to be consulted[118] and the chairman of the council/mayor's approval also sought.

5.74. It is hardly surprising that Widdicombe has taken the view that the position as regards chairman's action is 'unsatisfactory'[119] and sought to devise a solution which 'is consistent with the corporate framework of local government and at the same time is consistent with sensible administrative practice'.[120] It concluded:[121]

> We believe . . . that the law should allow the possibility of delegation of decisions to chairmen themselves . . . Such delegation should not be at large: it should not become a device for avoiding decision-taking by committees, not a means of chairmen adopting a ministerial style of administration. The legislation should set clear limits on the scope of delegation to chairmen. It should be permissible only where a decision is required because of urgency. In other circumstances the legislation should state that any decision of the chairman is unlawful, irrespective of whether the council or committee purport to ratify it retrospectively. This should remove the legal doubt about ratification . . . The chief executive either directly or by delegation to one of his chief officers, should be required to agree in each case that the matter is urgent before any decision can be taken . . . We propose furthermore that the decision taken under delegated powers should be reported to the next meeting of the committee or sub-committee in question, that the provisions introduced by the Local Government (Access to Information) Act 1985 should apply to the report and other documents on which the decision is based, and that the chairman should not be able to take a decision where he or she has a pecuniary interest in the matter.

Implied authority

5.75. It must be apparent from all that has been said in the foregoing paragraphs that a committee chairman must be careful not to overreach his implied authority. If the scope of that authority is codified (as suggested in 5.72) there is less risk:

> It is generally recognized, but again only as a convention, that a committee chairman may, by virtue of his office, make suggestions – even, perhaps, in

---

[118] The former Peterborough Borough Council described its special system for political clearance of urgent matters in its own memorandum of evidence to the Maud Committee: 'Chairmen's decisions are there notified to the leader of the opposition or his committee nominee by the town clerk so that the opposition, if it wishes, may enforce a stop on action until the matter is decided by council': Maud Report, vol. 5, pp. 165–66.

[119] Widdicombe Report, para.5.74.

[120] *Ibid.* paras.5.75–5.76.

[121] *Ibid.* para.5.77.

exceptional circumstances, give directions – to an officer. It is also recognized that, by virtue of his chairmanship, he may enjoy a certain limited freedom of access to property under the control of his committee on the assumption that he is doing what the committee would direct him to do. But legally a committee chairman, like any other individual council member, has no power or authority other than that expressly conferred upon him by resolution and thus can only properly give orders through a decision made at a properly constituted meeting.[122]

Failure to attend meetings

Statutory provisions

5.76. The law expressly provides[123] that where a council member fails throughout a period of six consecutive months[124] from the date of his last attendance[125] to attend any meeting of his authority then, subject to certain exceptions, he ceases to be a member of the authority unless the failure was due to some reason approved by the authority before the expiry of that period: see 5.80.

5.77. *Attendance* is generously defined. Attendance as a member at a meeting of any committee or subcommittee of the authority, or at a meeting of any joint committee, joint board or other body by which for the time being any of the functions of the authority are being discharged, or which was appointed to advise the authority on any matter relating to the discharge of those functions, and attendance as representative of the authority at a meeting of any body of persons, is deemed to be attendance at a meeting of the authority. It does not matter how informal the meeting so long as an attendance is recorded.

5.78. A member of any branch of the naval, military or air forces when employed during war or any emergency on any naval, military or air force service, and a person whose employment in the service of the Queen in connection with war or any emergency is such as, in the opinion of the Secretary for the Environment, to entitle him to relief from disqualification

---

[122] See Knowles, *Modern Management in Local Government*, p. 56.

[123] Local Government Act 1972, s.85.

[124] I.e. calendar months: see Interpretation Act 1889, s.3.

[125] The words 'from the date of his last attendance' did not appear in the Local Government Act 1933, s.63. Its inclusion in the 1972 Act negatives in effect the decision in *Kershaw* v. *Shoreditch Corporation* [1906] 70 JP 190: in that case – decided under the Local Government Act 1894, s.46(6) repealed – it was held that absence should be reckoned from the date of the first meeting at which the member was absent. Differing opinions were held on the question whether, under the slightly modified form of the 1933 Act, s.63, the period would run from the date of the last meeting which the member attended but there was considerable support for the view that it still ran from the date of the first absence.

on account of absence, does not cease to be a member of the authority by reason only of a failure to attend meetings of the authority if the failure is due to that employment.[126]

Practical considerations

5.79. There is some argument as to whether it is the chief executive's duty to direct attention to any failure of a councillor to attend meetings over a period that will involve disqualification. Clearly the chief executive must sooner or later direct the authority's attention to the failure and it would seem to be an act of courtesy on the officer's part to warn the member concerned of the near approach of the expiry of the six months' period. But ought the chief executive to assume that a member is going to default? It may be that a member, instead of being grateful for the chief executive's kindly warning, would take exception to what he might regard as precipitous action on the officer's part. And just when should the chief executive bring the matter to the authority's attention? At the same time as he approached the member? That hardly seems appropriate, for no question can yet arise of disqualification. Does the authority then need to be informed at all unless and until the member defaults and so disqualifies himself? These questions suggest that there should be a locally acceptable code of practice which can be put into effect automatically.

5.80. It seems clear now that an authority cannot retrospectively approve an excuse for failure to attend meetings after the six months' period has expired. This was thought permissible formerly because s.63 of the 1933 Act did not contain the words 'before the expiry of that period' – provided the authority acted before declaring the office vacant. If a member once loses his office through failure to attend for the six months' period the disqualification cannot be overcome by his subsequently resuming attendance.[127] Nevertheless, the office becomes vacant only when the authority declares it to be vacant[128] and a casual vacancy arises.[129]

Political group meetings

Their increasing importance

5.81. There has been earlier reference (see Chapter 4) to the significant politicisation of local authorities and the consequent removal of effective

---

[126] Local Government Act 1972, s.85(3).
[127] *R. v. Hunton ex-parte Hodgson* (1911), 75 JP 335.
[128] Which the authority *must* do under the Local Government Act 1972, s.86.
[129] *Ibid.* s.87(1).

decision-making to majority group councillors meeting away from public gaze in the party caucus. This means that many important decisions on policy are first made by the majority group of a local authority and afterwards translated into effective and lawful action through the formal committee machinery and so clothed with legal propriety. It has been said:[130]

> The effect ... has been most marked. With decisions settled by a political process beforehand, the purpose of the committee has changed from one of decision-making to a debating forum where the minority parties and the public can be informed of the decisions of the majority party. The opposition can use the meetings to challenge the policies of the majority party and to seek information from officers. The recommendations before committees will be defended politically by the chairmen and other members and not by officers, whose role will be confined to presentation and interpretation of the facts and the submission of professional judgments.

Such a situation – extreme in many eyes – is not true of every local authority, but in most instances nevertheless 'the majority party feels that it must have articulated its policies'[131] before it goes into what is now the public forum of the committee or subcommittee meeting. Minority group councillors likewise hold group meetings to organise if they can a cohesive approach in opposition to the majority group policies.

5.82. Political group meetings are not local authority meetings and are thus in a sense outside the purview of this book for several reasons (but see 5.86 *et seq*). The decisions taken in group meetings cannot bind the authority; strictly speaking, no officer can be called upon to attend and/or advise such meetings; and in practice they are often wholly informal in character and the decisions, even when not disputed as frequently they are, cannot bind any of the party members. Until recently, little information was available about the practice and procedure of these meetings although their existence has long been accepted and increasingly recognised:

> It is not unusual, for example, for councillors to ask in committee for a decision to be deferred, stating quite openly that this is a matter which must be settled by their party groups, although in some authorities councillors in a similar situation still play for time by asking for a report giving 'further information' to be made at the next committee meeting.[132]

[130] See R. G. Brooke, 'Modern Approach to Committee Practice' (1979) *Local Government Review* 3.

[131] *Ibid.*

[132] Maud Report, vol. 5, p. 103: and see, generally, ch. 5 thereof, pp. 97–118, 'Some Effects of the Presence or Absence of Party Politics on the Operation of Local Authorities'. The most up–to–date account is provided by Widdicombe in Research Volume 1: *The Political Organisation of Local Authorities* (Cmnd 9798).

5.83. The members of each political party on the local authority hold a group meeting as a rule before each council meeting to discuss business on the council meeting agenda, decide upon the party line to be pursued on at least the more important items, and apportion out responsibility for speaking in support or opposition as the case may be. The efficiency and effectiveness with which party business is conducted 'behind the scenes' appears to depend, first, upon the strength of the particular party within the authority (a party with an overwhelming majority tends not to be over-meticulous in its organisation; but where the parties are narrowly balanced each plans its tactics with considerable care); and, secondly, upon the personal qualities of the party whips and other party officials.

5.84. The proprieties ought to be and generally are observed. The activities of the party groups are restricted to determining the course of action to be taken at formal meetings of the authority: no group, even when comprised of all the council members of the majority party on the council, can by decision in the group meeting legally bind the local authority. Where, however, members of the majority party on a particular committee or subcommittee decide to defer action pending discussion 'in another place' there is always the possibility, inadvertently rather than by design, that officers may find themselves under pressure to take action following a political decision in a group meeting or, more rarely (but it can happen), for officers to be asked to accept instructions from the leader of the council rather than, say, the appropriate committee chairman. Officers must, of course, act with tact and discretion in such circumstances: they must be realists and recognise that the leader individually or the group collectively has or can secure the support of the majority of councillors, but at the same time the officers must require compliance with due formality and insist – in practice invariably through the chief executive – that any political decision so made shall be properly reported to and confirmed by the appropriate committee or the council and so clothed with due legality.

5.85. What can never properly be done, of course, is for a majority party group to purport to rescind or to override a decision already made by a committee or subcommittee and expect the officers to take executive action on the group's purported rescission or to seek to undo what may properly have been done in pursuance of the committee or subcommittee's decision.

Regularisation of party control

5.86. Widdicombe addressed itself to political activity of this character. Its recommendation for *pro rata* representation on committees (see 4.19) and the consequent need for statutory recognition of the existence of political groups on local authorities would, it believed, 'help remove any sense that such groups are somehow improper or alien to local government'[133] – a point made to it in written evidence:[134]

> We believe the political parties should also do more themselves to remove any sense of mystery surrounding party groups. We would certainly not wish to suggest that party groups should meet in public ... nor that their minutes should be open to public inspection. Where, however, they are discussing issues which will come before the council or its committees for decision, we believe that they should be prepared to make public a list of all those attending including non-councillors. The list should be deposited with the chief executive of the authority. Although the point does not strictly relate to party groups, we also believe that the local party organisation should publish the names of those on their executive committee.

5.87. Widdicombe expressed the view:[135]

(a) that there needs to be greater openness about groups and their proceedings so that unnecessary suspicions are avoided: party groups should not meet in a hole-and-corner atmosphere;

(b) that the formulation of decisions in party groups outside the formal local government system should not be allowed to undermine the statutory safeguards that apply within the system; and

(c) that there should be adequate access to the advice of officers so that the policy of the majority group does not become predetermined without full knowledge of the facts and law.

On this last point Widdicombe said that officers' terms and conditions of service should be amended so that no special inhibition is placed on the attendance of officers at party groups (see 5.97 below).

5.88. It is impossible here to recite in full all that Widdicombe had to say about the incursion and operation of party politics in local government. In summary, however, it proposed that the national political parties (and local parties and groups) should take steps:[136]

(a) to ensure that party groups keep a publicly available list of those attending their meetings;

(b) to ensure observance of their model standing orders in so far as they limit the number of non-councillors attending meetings of party groups, preclude non-councillors from voting at such meetings and prevent non-councillors from determining the policy to be followed by the party group on matters before the council for decision;

---

[133] Widdicombe Report, para.6.64.
[134] *Ibid.* para.6.65.
[135] Widdicombe Report, para.6.62.
[136] *Ibid.* paras.6.65, 6.73, 6.74 and 7.78.

(c) to debar from attendance at party group meetings persons disqualified from council membership following surcharge proceedings by the auditor;

(d) to ensure that the National Code of Local Government Conduct is implemented in respect of conflicts of interests arising at meetings of party groups and to amend their model standing orders accordingly.

Group meetings not 'committees'

5.89. The distinction between caucus meetings and formal meetings of the local authority and its committees and subcommittees is important. Usually this is clear but not always. Thus in *R. v. Hyndburn Borough Council* (1985)[137] a decision of a group leaders' meeting (comprising the leader and deputy leader of the Conservative Group and the leader and deputy leader of the Labour Group on a local authority) not to allow SDP/Alliance Group councillors to attend was held to be lawful on the grounds that the meetings, designed for purposes of informal consultation between the political parties and chief officers, formed no part of the formal committee machinery of the council: 'Any decision which it was felt goes beyond this category, whether as a matter of political prudence or to avoid any doubt about legalities, is referred to committee for ratification', acknowledged Woolf J.

5.90. Political group meetings of the kind discussed here, because they are not local authority meetings, are not obliged to be open to the public.

Officers at meetings

General

5.91. Officers are not, of course, part of the membership of the local authority;[138] and thus they cannot be a party to the decisions made in the full assembly or in committee or subcommittee–even though, outside the council chamber or committee room, they may well be invested with delegated power (see 4.8) enabling them to make decisions of often greater significance than those made by members collectively in council or committee. Nevertheless, officers do participate in discussion at committee and subcommittee meetings and may influence the decisions made by

---

[137] (1985) Unreported but see 150 *Local Government Review* 57.

[138] For this reason it is not good practice to include the names of officers among those recorded as present at a council, committee or subcommittee meeting. Nevertheless, a record might usefully be made that a named officer, having declared an interest, withdrew from the meeting.

reason of the facts which they lay before the members or of the advice which they tender. In many authorities the relationship between members and officers is one of mutual trust and confidence and in these cases the officers act virtually as non-voting partners in the business of local government. In other words, the officers join in the debate whenever they think fit, speak more than once if need be, sway members deliberately towards one course of action rather than another until the point when a decision is about to be made, when they must hold their silence – and, of course, accept unquestioningly the decision when it is made, whether it is to their liking or not.

Council meetings

5.92. At council meetings, however, it is the tradition that officers shall not speak unless, exceptionally, any one of them may be called upon to do so. The chief executive will necessarily have announcements to make and will advise the chairman quietly as occasion may demand on procedure; but it is requisite that in the full assembly the council members should be seen to be the decision-makers.

Committees

5.93. If it is acceptable locally that an officer may join freely in discussion in committee[139], the officer should be scrupulous in ensuring, particularly if he wishes to influence the council members to take the course he favours, that all the relevant facts are before the committee including the pros and cons of alternative courses of action. He must take care, too, not to dominate the committee so that he virtually imposes his will upon the members – particularly nowadays with members of the public present – and if he finds in the course of debate that the majority of members are against him he must not then press his view unduly.[140]

5.94. If, on the other hand, officers are discouraged from speaking at

---

[139] Lord Morrison of Lambeth thought this undesirable. At a summer school in Cambridge in July 1956, before his elevation to the peerage, he said: 'I think it best that the officer should not talk too much in committee – and often not at all – thereby planting responsibility for the decisions on the committee members'.

[140] When an officer is speaking in council or committee he must take care to ensure that he can be heard and understood by everyone in the room. Roland Freeman in *Becoming a Councillor* (2nd edn, 1975), p. 85, tells the story of a new member of a small district council who rose somewhat nervously after a meeting had been in progress for an hour to say 'On a point of order, I can't hear what the clerk is saying and could he possibly speak up a little'. As the new councillor sat down an older member leant across to him and said: 'I'm so glad you did that. I haven't heard a word he's said for the past seven and a half years!'

meetings then they must rely on the written material prepared for the committee. *There are times, however, when it is the duty of an officer to speak out even if forbidden to do so.* No officer should sit silently by and allow his committee to embark on a course of action which is *ultra vires* or may have consequences which the members have clearly overlooked. As the author has said elsewhere:[141]

> It is often a matter of judgment, not easy to exercise in practice, when discursive discussion in committee takes an unexpected turn, whether the officer should speak or hold his tongue. He must be careful to distinguish between, for example, errors of fact and errors of judgment. The officer ought to stand up – and persist in standing up and speaking even if ordered to sit down – if he sees his committee about to make a decision of consequence on a misunderstanding of fact. To remain silent would be a gross dereliction of duty. But it may be wise for him to remain unmoved and unspeaking if the committee in full possession of the facts is about to make a decision which is wayward, capricious, imprudent or manifestly wrong.

5.95. There is a widely held view among many council members that nowadays the information provided – probably processed through a computer – is so impeccable and incapable of challenge, and the alternative courses of action so calculated and the probabilities so meticulously assessed by the chief executive and his management team, that the only option open is self-evident before discussion begins on the issue. Where on major questions the committee has been provided with a comprehensive report and the decision to be taken is one of major policy, the chief executive (through whom, increasingly, major recommendations are submitted) may deem it prudent to remain silent beyond proffering a word or two of explanation or clarification. It is on other matters where professional expertise could be decisive that the officer may have to judge whether or not to intervene.

5.96. It needs to be borne in mind that some officers will not be regular participants in committee business: many 'back-room boys' may attend only very exceptionally, perhaps merely to listen to discussion on a particular issue (when they might conveniently sit in the seats reserved for the public) or to advise on a matter which they have been handling personally or to support their chief officer if detailed information is asked for. For such officers committee attendance will be an unusual experience and they may need to be briefed to ensure they understand the conventions of committee procedure, know where to sit, when to speak (and whether to stand or remain seated when speaking), when to leave, and so on. Such briefings should be part of the routine of pre-committee work.

[141] Knowles, *Modern Management in Local Government*, p. 68.

There is, however, much to commend the practice of some local authorities in arranging periodical training sessions – for no more than a day or half a day – to advise officers who may not be regular committee attenders on committee procedure and practice.[142]

Attendance at party groups

5.97. The ability of officers to act as effective advisers to councillors will in some local authorities depend on whether they attend, or are prepared to attend, meetings of the party groups. Widdicombe's research[143] showed that attendance at present is the exception rather than the rule, possibly because of this specific clause in officers' terms and conditions of service:

> The officer should not be called upon to advise any political group of the employing authority either as to the work of the group or as to the work of the authority, neither shall he or she be required to attend any meeting of any political group.

In the case of chief executives, chief and deputy chief officers there is this additional sentence:

> This shall be without prejudice to any arrangements to the contrary which may be made in agreement with the officer and which includes adequate safeguards to preserve the political neutrality of the officer in relation to the affairs of the council.

Widdicombe felt that this makes unnecessarily 'heavy weather' of the subject.[144] It recommended that no special inhibition should be placed on attendance at party groups subject to the following safeguards:

(a) All requests for attendance should be addressed to the chief executive who should decide which officers should attend; and

(b) The chief executive should notify the other parties and offer a similar facility.

These safeguards, it was said, should be included in the list of conventions which Widdicombe recommended that all local authorities should prepare.[145]

---

[142] See Ivan Brown,'Officers Newly into Committee' (1975) 139 *Local Government Review* 359.
[143] Widdicombe Report, para.6.173.
[144] *Ibid.* paras.6.175–6.176.
[145] *Ibid.* para.6.178.

APPENDIX TO CHAPTER 5
National Code of Local Government Conduct

This code was promulgated under cover of joint circular 94/75 of the Department of the Environment (Scottish Development Department 95/75; Welsh Office 166/75) in October 1975 as a guide for all councillors elected or co-opted[a] to local authorities in England, Wales and Scotland. It supplements both the law enacted by Parliament and the standing orders made by local authorities. It has been agreed by the associations representing local authorities in all three countries and by the Government.

1. Law, standing orders and national code
Make sure that you fully understand the rules of conduct which the law,[b] standing orders and the national code require you to follow. It is your personal responsibility to apply their requirements on every relevant occasion. Seek any advice about them that you need from your council's appropriate senior officer or from your own legal adviser.[c]

2. Public duty and private interest
(i) Your over-riding duty as a councillor is to the whole local community.
(ii) You have a special duty to your own constituents, including those who did not vote for you.
(iii) Whenever you have a private or personal interest in any question which councillors have to decide, you must not do anything to let that interest influence the decision.
(iv) Do nothing as a councillor which you could not justify to the public.
(v) The reputation of your council, and of your party if you belong to one, depends on your conduct and what the public believes about your conduct.
(vi) It is not enough to avoid actual impropriety; you should at all times avoid any occasion for suspicion or the appearance of improper conduct.[d]

3. Disclosure of pecuniary and other interests
(i) The law makes specific provision requiring you to disclose pecuniary interests, direct and indirect.[e] But interests which are not pecuniary can be just as important.[f] Kinship, friendship, membership of an association, society or trade union, trusteeship and many other kinds of relationship can sometimes

---

[a] Widdicombe has proposed that advisers with no voting powers should replace co-opted members on committees: Widdicombe Report, paras.5.92–5.102; and see 5.51.
[b] Widdicombe has recommended that individual councillors should be required by law to have regard to this code and should also undertake to do so as part of their statutory declaration on acceptance of office: Widdicombe Report, paras.6.19–6.22.
[c] It is no part of an officer's responsibility, for example, to advise a councillor whether in particular circumstances he has an interest which ought to be disclosed.
[d] Widdicombe points out that sectional loyalties as well as private gain may create conflicts with a councillor's public duty: Widdicombe Report, para.6.15.
[e] See 5.27 *et seq.* as to the statutory provisions regarding pecuniary interest.
[f] Many authorities keep a register of the non-pecuniary interests of their members. Widdicombe thinks there should be a statutory duty to keep such a register and to make it available for public inspection: Widdicombe Report, paras.6.46–6.49.

influence your judgment and give the impression that you might be acting for personal motives. A good test is to ask yourself whether others would think that the interest is of a kind to make this possible. If you think they would, or if you are in doubt, disclose the interest and withdraw from the meeting unless under standing orders you are specifically invited to stay.[g]

(ii) The principles about disclosure of interest should be borne in mind in your unofficial relations with other councillors – at party group meetings, or other informal occasions – no less scrupulously than at formal meetings of the council, its committees and sub-committees.

4. Membership and chairmanship of council committees and sub-committees

(i) You, or some firm or body with which you are personally connected, may have professional business or personal interests within the area for which the council is responsible; such interests may be substantial and closely related to the work of one or more of the council's committees or sub-committees, concerned with (say) planning or developing land, council housing, personnel matters or the letting of contracts for supplies, services or works. Before seeking or accepting membership of any such committee or sub-committee, you should seriously consider whether your membership would involve you (a) in disclosing an interest so often that you could be of little value to the committee or sub-committee, or (b) in weakening public confidence in the impartiality of the committee or sub-committee.

(ii) You should not seek or accept the chairmanship of a committee or sub-committee whose business is closely related to a substantial interest or range of interests of yourself or of any body with which you are associated.

5. Councillors and officers

(i) Both councillors and officers are servants of the public, and they are indispensable to one another.[h] But their responsibilities are distinct. Councillors are responsible to the electorate and serve only so long as their term of office lasts. Officers are responsible to the council and are permanently appointed. An officer's job is to give advice to councillors and the council, and to carry out the council's work under the direction and control of the council and its committees.

(ii) Mutual respect between councillors and officers is essential to good local government. Close personal familiarity between individual councillor and officer can damage this relationship and prove embarrassing to other councillors and officers.

(iii) If you are called upon to take part in appointing an officer, the only question you should consider is which candidate would best serve the whole council. You should not let your personal or political preferences influence

---

[g] As to the meaning of 'withdraw from the meeting' see 5.32 and Widdicombe's view that where councillors declare a pecuniary interest at a meeting they should be statutorily required to withdraw from the room: Widdicombe Report, para.6.51.

[h] While breach of the code in other respects is normally regarded by the local ombudsman as maladministration, this is not true of staff matters – which are at present outside the ombudsman's jurisdiction. The ombudsman would not therefore be able to investigate a complaint by a prospective officer that his or her application for a job had not been properly considered: Widdicombe Report, para.6.130.

your judgment. You should not canvass the support of colleagues for any candidate and you should resist any attempt by others to canvass yours.

6. *Use of confidential and private information*

As a councillor you necessarily acquire much information that has not yet been made public and is still confidential. It is a grave betrayal of trust to use confidential information for the personal advantage of yourself or of anyone known to you.[i]

7. *Gifts and hospitality*

Treat with extreme caution any offer or gift, favour or hospitality that is made to you personally. The person or organisation making the offer may be doing or seeking to do business with the council, or may be applying to the council for planning permission or some other kind of decision. Working lunches and other social occasions arranged or authorised by the council or by one of its committees or sub-committees may be a proper way of doing business, provided that no extravagance is involved. Nor can there be any hard and fast rule about acceptance or refusal of tokens of goodwill on special occasions. But you are personally responsible for all such decisions and for avoiding the risk of damage to public confidence in local government. The receipt or offer of gifts should be reported to the chief executive.

8. *Expenses and allowances*

There are rules entitling you to claim expenses and allowances in connection with your duties as a councillor. These rules should be scrupulously observed.

9. *Use of council facilities*

Make sure that any facilities – such as transport, stationery or secretarial services – provided by the council for your use in your duties as a councillor are used strictly for those duties and for no other purpose.

Note: It was disclosed in a research report *The Administration of Standards of Conduct in Local Government* by Alan Parker, Aidan Rose and John Taylor (Charles Knight), published in 1986 at the same time as the Widdicombe Report, that 94 per cent of local authorities had in operation a code substantially based on the National Code of Local Government Conduct with only a marginal number having made changes to that developed in D.o.E. circular 94/75. Many authorities registered the interests of both members and officers but few had identifiable procedures for effective monitoring.

---

[i] As to a councillor's statutory right of access to documents: see 5.14 *et seq*. Although the public now has access to a wide range of council documents there are items which remain confidential: see 5.23.

PART TWO

COUNCIL MEETINGS

6

CONVENTION

Notice and summons

Essential prerequisites

6.1. There are two essential preliminaries to the holding of a council meeting, i.e. the meeting in full assembly of a principal, parish or community council. These are the giving of *notice* and the service of a *summons*: the former is a public intimation, published in prescribed manner, to the community at large, not merely to local government electors; the latter is directed privately to the council members who are entitled to attend. Notice is general while the summons is individual.

6.2. If there is failure to comply with statutory requirements as to notice and summons then the meeting itself may not be properly convened and the business transacted of no effect.[1] In certain circumstances the notice and in every case the summons must specify the business to be transacted. In this sense the *agenda* (a term not used in any of the statutes regulating local authority meetings until introduced by the Local Government (Access to Information) Act 1985: see 6.19) may be said to be part of the notice and summons.

6.3. In the case of parish and community meetings the obligation at law is to give public notice only.[2]

Initiation of a meeting

6.4. As indicated earlier (see 1.18) a council meeting will be held (a) as directed by statute, e.g. the annual meeting; or (b) in accordance with the timetable of meetings fixed by the council, usually at the annual meeting,

---

[1] This is discussed below at 6.18. It is expressly provided that want of service of the summons does not affect the validity of the meeting but there is no such proviso as regards failure to give notice.

[2] Local Government Act 1972, sch.12, paras.15(2), 30(2).

i.e. the cycle of ordinary meetings; or (c) for a special purpose required by statute or on the decision of the council; or (d) upon the requisition of the chairman or the prescribed number of members, i.e. an extraordinary meeting.

Requisitioned meetings

6.5. It is expressly provided[3] that if the chairman of a principal, parish or community council refuses to call an extraordinary meeting after a requisition for that purpose, signed by five members in the case of a principal council or two in the case of a parish or community council, has been presented to him; or if, without so refusing, the chairman does not call the meeting within seven days after the requisition has been presented to him, then, in the case of a principal council any five members, or in the case of a parish or community council any two members, may on that refusal or on the expiration of the seven days, as the case may be, themselves call an extraordinary meeting of the council forthwith.

What is meant by 'presented'?

6.6. The use of the word *presented* in the statute suggests an act more formal than, say, serving the requisition by post or other method of delivery, and it may be that the requisition should be handed personally to the chairman by one of the signatories to the requisition. If, of course, the chairman cannot be contacted through absence from the area and is thus unable to receive the requisition it may be, strictly, that the requisition should be handed physically to the vice-chairman, who is empowered generally to act in the absence of the chairman;[4] but it is submitted that the presenter must make reasonable attempts to present the requisition to the chairman before going to the vice-chairman. Compliance with the requirement to present the requisition is important because if an extraordinary meeting was called on the claim that the chairman had refused or had neglected to call the meeting, the extraordinary meeting subsequently called by individual councillors might be held invalid.[5]

---

[3] Local Government Act 1972, sch.12, paras.3, 9, 25. There is provision also for the calling of a parish and community meeting in similar circumstances but the term *extraordinary* meeting is not used: *Ibid.* paras.15, 30.

[4] The vice-chairman can only act, subject to standing orders, in the absence of the chairman (Local Government Act 1972, s.5(3)), and absence means more than being temporarily unavailable.

[5] The possibility of a successful challenge is probably slight. There is always a presumption that a local authority meeting and the proceedings thereat are valid: Local Government Act 1972, sch.12 generally.

What is meant by 'call a meeting'?

6.7. The obligation on the chairman to call an extraordinary meeting in the foregoing circumstances is to ensure that the notice and summons to the meeting are given within the prescribed seven days. It does not mean that the meeting itself must take place within that period. The requisition could ask that the meeting be held on a particular date but the chairman has discretion and is not bound to comply with such a request. Upon the chairman's refusal or neglect the extraordinary meeting called by the prescribed number of members can be held whenever the members themselves determine:[6] there is no time limit. In exercising discretion as to date, the chairman ought not to delay unduly in calling the meeting.

Notice

6.8. In the case of every meeting of the full assembly, public notice must be given:

(a) three clear days at least[7] before a meeting of a principal council (and of its committees and subcommittees: see 10.6 *et seq.*) and published at the council's offices;[8] or, if the meeting is convened at shorter notice, then at the time it is convened;[9]

(b) three clear days at least before a meeting of a parish or community council, fixed in some conspicuous place[10] in the parish or the community as the case may be;[11]

and in the case of a parish or community meeting public notice must be given:

(c) not less than seven clear days beforehand (14 days in certain cases) by posting the notice in some conspicuous place or places in the parish or the community[12] as the case may be,

---

[6] These do not necessarily have to be the members who signed the requisition.

[7] 'Clear' days means that the time is to be reckoned exclusive both of the day on which the notice is given and of the day of meeting: *R. v. Herefordshire JJ* (1820) 3 B & Ald.581. A Sunday or public holiday may be counted as one of the clear days because s.243 of the Local Government Act 1972 does not require a Sunday or public holiday to be disregarded in reckoning a period of time, and applies only where the day or the last day is a Sunday or public holiday.

[8] A public notice must be given (a) by posting the notice in some conspicuous place or places within the area of the local authority, and (b) in such other manner, if any, as appears to the local authority to be desirable for giving publicity to the notice: *Ibid.* s.232.

[9] Local Government Act 1972, sch.12, para.4(2), and s.100B(3), added by Local Government (Access to Information) Act 1985.

[10] What is a conspicuous place is a question of fact: *West Ham Corporation* v. *Thomas* (1908) 73 JP 65; 6 LGR 1043.

[11] Local Government Act 1972, sch.12, paras.10(2), 26(2).

[12] *Ibid.* sch.12, paras.15(2), 30(2): 14 days' notice must be given of the proposed establishment or dissolution or grouping of a parish or community council.

and, although there is no statutory requirement to such effect, the notice at least of an ordinary or annual meeting is usually signed by the chief executive[13] or the chairman: as to who signs in the case of an extraordinary meeting see 6.11.

6.9. The notice of an ordinary meeting of a principal, parish or community council and of a parish or community meeting *may take any form* so long as it includes the time and place of the intended meeting.[14] The notice must be reasonable and effective with sufficient information to enable an interested person to attend: thus the 'time' must be precise as to date and time and the place of meeting clearly described.[15] The notice must be *prominently* displayed, even in the case of a principal council where the requirement is merely to publish the notice at the council's offices rather than in some conspicuous place: it should, therefore, be displayed near the main entrance to the council's offices (and, if there is more than one town or county hall or council offices in the area – and there may well still be after reorganisation – the notice should, it is suggested, be displayed at each); in the other cases the notice should be conspicuously displayed on official notice boards throughout the parish or community. A model public notice of a council meeting appears in the appendix to this chapter.

6.10. The statutory requirements as to notice are contained in two places in the Local Government Act 1972: first, in sch.12 as originally enacted, and secondly in s.100A(6), which was added by the Local Government (Access to Information) Act 1985. Additional notice is required of meetings at which resolutions are to be considered to promote or oppose a Bill in Parliament: see 7.139.

6.11. In the case of an extraordinary meeting of a principal or parish or community council there are two additional requirements as to form. In addition to the time and place, the notice must specify the business proposed to be transacted thereat and must be signed by the members of the council who have called the meeting.[16] If the chairman of the council calls a meeting of a principal, parish or community council, it is not clear whether he should sign the notice; but in the case of a parish or community

---

[13] The 'proper officer' could sign the notice under s.234 of the 1972 Act; and thereunder 'signature' includes a facsimile of a signature by whatever process reproduced.

[14] Local Government Act 1972, sch.12: Pt I, para.4(2); Pt II, para.10(2); Pt III, para.15(2); Pt IV, para.26(2).

[15] Although there are no decided cases on the point it might be that the courts would construe less stringently the requirements as to *notice* where there is also an obligation to serve a *summons* on members entitled to attend.

[16] This can be in general terms so long as the purport of the business is fairly indicated: see 6.23. In any case the requirement now that an agenda and accompanying reports must be open to public inspection (see 6.21 *et seq.*) reduces the need for the business to be spelt out in detail in the notice.

meeting the notice must be signed by the person or persons convening the meeting.[17]

Summons generally

6.12. A summons to attend a council meeting must be sent to every member of the principal, parish or community council as the case may be:
(a) at least three clear days[18] beforehand in the case of every type of ordinary meeting;[19]
(b) specifying the business to be transacted at the meeting;[20]
(c) signed by the proper officer of the council;[21]
(d) left at[22] or sent by post[23] to the usual place of residence of the member,[24]

and, of course, giving date, time and place of meeting. This means that the document sent to councillors should strictly be phrased literally in the manner of a summons, e.g. *You are hereby summoned to attend a meeting . . .* or words to like effect; and if it seems inappropriate for an officer to address a missive in such peremptory terms to councillors the justification lies in the words of the 1972 Act requiring a *summons* to be sent to members[25] signed by the proper officer.[26] A model summons to a council meeting appears in the appendix to this chapter. There is no similar statutory obligation to summon members to attend committee or subcommittee meetings: see 10.7.

6.13. There is no obligation to summon individual electors to a parish or community meeting: those entitled to attend must rely on the public notice.[27]

---

[17] Local Government Act 1972, sch.12: Pt III, para.15(2); Pt V, para.30(2). See also as to public notice of a parish meeting: s.233(2).
[18] As to the meaning of 'clear days', see 6.8.
[19] This is so whether the meeting is an ordinary, annual or extraordinary one or called for a special purpose, e.g. to consider the promotion or opposition of a Bill in Parliament.
[20] In practice the summons incorporates the agenda for the meeting.
[21] The signature may be a facsimile signature by whatever process reproduced: Local Government Act 1972, s.234.
[22] It is fairly common practice, particularly in the case of district councils, for the summons to be delivered by hand.
[23] Post means ordinary post, i.e. as opposed to registered or recorded delivery, but first-class mailing should be used.
[24] In the case, exceptionally, of a principal council a member may give notice in writing to the proper officer that he desires summonses to be sent to him at some address specified in the notice other than his place of residence and in such a case any summons addressed to him and left at or sent by post to that address is deemed sufficient service of the summons: *ibid.* sch.12, Pt I, para.4(3).
[25] Local Government Act 1972, sch.12: Pt I, para.4(2); Pt II, para.10(2); Pt IV, para.26(2).
[26] This is the officer appointed by the local authority for that purpose: *Ibid.* s.270(3): see 4.39.
[27] The chairman of a parish or community council is specifically entitled to attend a parish or

Signature on the summons

6.14. As indicated above a summons must be signed by the proper officer, i.e. the officer appointed for that purpose by the local authority; and, strictly, any document bearing the signature of an officer not so appointed will be invalid.[28] But a signature purporting to be that of the proper officer may be a facsimile.[29] There may thus seem in practice little need for anyone to sign on behalf of the proper officer *per procurationem* but it may be that such a summons would not be effectively challenged under the analogy of *Tennant* v. *London County Council* (1957),[30] where it was held that this was permissible in respect of the authentication of documents under s.184 of the London Government Act 1939.

6.15. There may be some instances – there is at least one – where, for historical or other reason, the summons will be signed by an officer not needing to do so as the proper officer: thus, for example, in the case of the Corporation of the City of London, where the sword-bearer – an office dating back to 1394 – is still today charged with the duty of summoning members of the Court of Common Council to its meetings.[31]

Members' withdrawal from requisition

6.16. What is the position if a councillor, having signed a requisition for an extraordinary meeting (see 6.5), indicates before the summons is issued that he wishes to withdraw his signature? Does this invalidate the requisi-

---

27 cont.
    community meeting as the case may be (or, where a grouping order is in force, for any meeting of the parishes or communities comprised within the group), whether or not he is an elector for the parish or community (Local Government Act 1972, sch.12, paras.16, 31); and it may be that he should be individually notified.

28 See *West Ham Corporation* v. *Benabo* (1934) 32 LGR 202, and other cases which all concern, however, notices under the Housing Acts.

29 Local Government Act 1972, s.234(2).

30 (1957) 55 LGR 421.

31 Before 1822 responsibility for summoning members to the Court of Common Council of the Corporation of London was shared between the Serjeants of the Chamber and the Yeoman of the Waterside, but on 20 December 1922 the common council decided that:
    the swordbearer, whose duty it is always to be attendant on the Lord Mayor, on obtaining His Lordship's directions for the courts of common council, direct the proper officers to obtain from the respective officers of this city, the accounts of what business is to be inserted in the Summonses, and that upon receiving the same it would be expedient that the swordbearer should cause a fair copy thereof to be made for the inspection and direction of the Lord Mayor, and then send to be printed, and the Officer-in-Waiting, whose duty it is to summon Members of the said Court, should also after his name affix the date on which he issues them from the Mansion House, whereby it will be easily ascertained whether there is at any time any delay in the delivery of the same.
    Today the town clerk prepares the business for the agenda.

tion? The calling of the meeting should surely proceed. Where a course of action is prescribed by statute those who exercise an entitlement to initiate that action cannot, it is submitted, withdraw; and thus the steps laid down ought to be commenced the moment the requisition is presented and thereafter not halted by anything which may intervene before the issue of the summons (and certainly not between the summons and the holding of the meeting because under common law a meeting once convened cannot properly be postponed: see 6.31).

6.17. Of course the statutory provisions do envisage that the chairman of the council might refuse or neglect to call a meeting following the requisition, notwithstanding that he is under a clear duty to call it (see 6.7). The view could therefore be taken that if before the summons is issued a councillor who has signed the requisition withdraws with the result that fewer than the number of councillors prescribed are, in effect, left seeking the meeting, the chairman might be judged to act reasonably if he refused to call the meeting, knowing that there is the fall-back allowing a similar number, though not necessarily the same councillors, to call the meeting themselves.

Want of service

6.18. At common law, failure to serve a summons upon everyone entitled to attend a corporate assembly invalidates the meeting.[32] So far as a meeting of a principal, parish or community council is concerned, however, there is express statutory provision to this important effect,[33] i.e. that:

> Want of service of any . . . summons . . . on any member of the . . . council concerned shall not affect the validity of the meeting.

Nevertheless, care should be taken to ensure there is no defect of service. The courts could be expected to construe this provision strictly and want of service on a substantial number of councillors or wilful failure or neglect to summon members could affect the validity of the meeting. It is recognised as good practice that any request from a member that he does not wish to receive a summons over a specified period (because, for example, of his absence overseas on holiday or business) should be ignored.

---

[32] *Kynaston* v. *Shrewsbury Corporation* (1736) 2 Stra.1051; *sub nom. R.* v. *Shrewsbury Corporation*, Lee *temp.* Hard 147; *Smyth* v. *Darley* (1849), 2 HL Cas.789; even though dispensed with by a particular member: *R.* v. *Langhorn* (1836) 4 Ad. & El. 538; 6 Nev. & MKB 203; see also *Staple of England (Mayor, etc. of Merchants of)* v. *Bank of England* (1887) 21 QBD160, 52 JP 580.

[33] Local Government Act 1972, sch.12, paras.4(4), 10(3), 26(3).

Council meeting agenda

Business must be specified

6.19. The agenda[34] for a meeting is the list of items of business to be transacted. There has always been a statutory prohibition against the transaction of business not on an agenda in the case of principal councils,[35] although the statutory provisions were at one time differently worded in this respect for no apparent reason: 'a strange discrepancy' Vaisey J called it in *Ayles* v. *Romsey and Stockbridge RDC* (1944).[36] The position is now clear beyond doubt.

6.20. The prohibition against the transaction of business not specified in the agenda is now reinforced by the following provision in s.100B(4) of the Local Government Act 1972, which was added by the Local Government (Access to Information) Act 1985:

> An item of business may not be considered at a meeting of a principal council[37] unless either:
> (a) a copy of the agenda including the item (or a copy of the item) is open to inspection by members of the public . . . for at least three clear days before the meeting or, where the meeting is convened at shorter notice, from the time the meeting is convened; or
> (b) by reason of special circumstances, which shall be specified in the minutes, the chairman of the meeting is of the opinion that the item should be considered as a matter of urgency.

The obligation to make the agenda available for public inspection is dealt with below (see 6.21 *et seq.*). The power conferred upon the chairman of the meeting represents an unusual, if not unique, statutory provision and it raises the question whether it remains wholly wrong, as it was until recently, to include in any council agenda a concluding item: *Any other business*[38] – at least unconditionally; it would not seem improper now to

---

[34] The term *agenda* is used in regard to local authority meetings for the first time, but without definition, in the Local Government (Access to Information) Act 1985. The term, though in form plural, is used throughout this work in the now widely accepted singular. 'Nobody would say "the agenda for Monday's meeting *have* not yet reached me". If a word is needed for one of the components of the agenda, say "item No. so-and-so of the agenda", not "agendum No. so-and-so", which would be the extreme of pedantry.': Sir Ernest Gowers, *The Complete Plain Words.* ' "Agenda" as a singular has become almost universally acclimatised and even pedants and purists, too craven to say "agenda are . . ." take refuge in circumlocutions such as "agenda paper" to keep the word's plural flag flying.': *Words* by John Silverlight of the *Observer*.

[35] Local Government Act 1972, sch.12, para.4(5).

[36] (1944) 108 JPN 175, p. 179.

[37] Or at a committee or subcommittee meeting: Local Government Act 1972, s.100E, which applies s.100B(4) to such meetings.

[38] Business required to be transacted by law at an annual council meeting could presumably still be dealt with even though not specified on the agenda.

provide for: *Any other business which the chairman decides is urgent.* The discretion given to the chairman probably could not be challenged – though it might, presumably, if the chairman exercised this power on so regular a basis that the justification becomes suspect.[39]

Public access to agenda

6.21. There is now an obligation upon principal local authorities,[40] but not others, to make copies of the agenda for a meeting and copies of any report for the meeting open to inspection by members of the public for three clear days before the date of the meeting[41] except that:

(a) where the meeting is convened at shorter notice then the documents must be open to inspection from the time the meeting is convened; and

(b) where an item is added to an agenda afterwards, copies of any report relating to the item must be available for inspection from the time the item is added to the agenda;

but there is no obligation to make the documents available for public inspection until copies are available to councillors.[42] Unless the foregoing requirement is complied with the business concerned cannot lawfully be dealt with at the meeting (see 6.20; and 10.6 as regards business at committee meetings).

6.22. There may be excluded from the copies of reports the whole or any part which relates only to items during which, in the opinion of the proper officer, the meeting is not likely to be open to the public. In such cases the copy or the relevant part of it must be marked *Not for publication* and a statement put thereon indicating, in the prescribed terms, the list of 'exempt information' by virtue of which the council is likely to exclude the public during the item to which the report relates.[43]

With what detail should business be specified?

6.23. It is not necessary that the items for consideration at a meeting should be set out in absolute detail so long as the business is fairly stated.

---

[39] It may be thought prudent for the chairman's consent to the transaction of urgent business to be put into writing and signed with the reason why the business is regarded by the chairman as urgent. There is nothing to stop the chairman consulting whomsoever he wishes in arriving at his decision.

[40] Local Government Act 1972, s.100B, added by Local Government (Access to Information) Act 1985.

[41] The terms of the statute are 'shall be . . . open at least three clear days before the meeting' but this must mean throughout the whole of the period of three days preceding the meeting during which the council's offices are open.

[42] *Ibid.* s.100B(3).

[43] *Ibid.* s.100B(2) and (5).

This means that those who are summoned to the meeting or are entitled to be present can judge whether the business warrants their attendance or not: it is especially important that the business to be transacted should be specifically stated if it is important and not merely a matter of routine or common occurrence and where the meeting has been specially convened. For example, in *R.* v. *The Corporation of Dublin* (1911)[44] a special meeting of the corporation was summoned on a requisition of seven ratepayers to consider the question of unemployment in the city and ways and means of alleviating it. At the meeting a resolution was passed authorising the city treasurer to arrange payment of £10,000 on useful works for the alleviation of unemployment. It was held that the notice of the meeting was insufficient to enable the meeting to pass a resolution. In a later case, Peterson J said:[45]

> It may be that a very important question is going to be considered at the meeting; it may be on the other hand that the only business is purely formal, paying some tradesman or something of that description. In the one case the members would attend in force and in the other case it was a mere matter of form, the members would not attend beyond the necessary quorum. Accordingly, in my view, I think these regulations do require that the notice convening the meeting should contain sufficient description of the important business which the meeting is to transact, and that the meeting cannot in ordinary circumstances go outside the business mentioned in that notice.

The position as regards oral reporting by officers or of indicating that a report will be laid on the table is more appropriately dealt with in Chapter 10.

6.24. It is thus not sufficient (except in circumstances of urgency: see 6.20) to include an item on the agenda which, for example, says in effect: *To receive the report of . . . committee* unless the report itself is circulated to councillors and made available for public inspection for the three days preceding the meeting; nor an item: *The chief executive will report* unless the subject-matter and the purport of the oral report are fairly summarised.

Defamatory matter in documents

6.25. There is now statutory protection as regards defamatory matter in published documents which are required to be accessible to members of the public. It is expressly provided by s.100H(5) of the 1972 Act that where any such document:

(a) is supplied to, or open to inspection by, a member of the public; or

---

[44] [1911] 2 Ir. R.245; and see *R.* v. *M'Donald* [1913] 2 IR 55.
[45] *Longfield Parish Council* v. *Wright* (1918) 88 LJ Ch. 119.

(b) is supplied for the benefit of any newspaper under s.100B(7);

the publication thereby of any defamatory matter contained in the document is privileged unless the publication is proved to be made with malice.

6.26. The foregoing overrules *De Buse* v. *McCarthy* (1942)[46] in which it was held that certain defamatory information disclosed in a notice of a council meeting and accompanying agenda reports, circulated to public libraries by the town clerk, was not privileged because, under the law as it then was, there was no necessity to make the documents public.

Order of business on agenda

6.27. The agenda will not only specify the business to be transacted but will also determine the order in which that business is dealt with at the meeting. Usually this order, so far as it is not determined by statute,[47] will be prescribed in standing orders, and the standing orders will invariably provide that the council may on grounds of urgency, possibly of convenience, vary that order on particular occasions.[48] What may be termed the traditional order of business is thus listed in model standing order no. 5:

(a) To choose a person to preside if the chairman and vice-chairman be absent.

This will not appear as an item on the agenda unless it is known in advance that both chairman and vice-chairman will be absent. In the case of an annual meeting the first item must be:

(i) To elect[49] a chairman for the ensuing year;

and later, usually after an item (ii) relating to the confirmation of minutes:

(iii) To elect a vice-chairman for the ensuing year.

(b) To deal with any business required by statute to be done before any other business.

The election of chairman must be the first item of business at the annual meeting of a principal, parish and community council.

(c) To approve as a correct record and sign the minutes of the last meeting of the council.[50]

The minutes will usually be circulated with the agenda but this is not necessary. There is no reason why the minute book should not be laid on the table before the meeting for any council member to inspect if he may so wish.

[46] [1942] 1 KB 156; [1942] 1 All ER 19; 106 JP 73.
[47] Local Government Act 1972, ss.4(1), 23(1), 15(2), 34(2).
[48] Model standing order no.5(2); see 6.28.
[49] The Local Government Act 1972, ss.5(1), 15(6), 24(1), 34(6), continues an unexplainable distinction in earlier statutes and refers to the 'appointment' of a vice-chairman but the 'election' of a chairman.
[50] Although these are the precise words of the model standing order, the phrase is not well expressed: the council will be expected to approve but not sign the minutes, which is the task of the person presiding, and 'the previous meeting' is to be preferred to 'the last meeting', which could mean something quite different.

(d) To deal with any business expressly required by statute to be done.
It is convenient to despatch at an early stage of the proceedings any formal business which it may be necessary to clothe with the requisite legality: unless the matter arises on a committee's report when it might more conveniently be dealt with when the report is being considered.

(e) Chairman's announcements.
This item is often couched in different terms, e.g. to receive such communications as the chairman may desire to lay before the council.

(f) To dispose of business (if any) remaining from the last meeting.

(g) To receive and consider reports, minutes and recommendations of committees.
This item is more usually dealt with after the one shown next in the model standing order.

(h) To answer questions asked under standing order 8.
Again fault could be found with the terms of this item: the respective committee chairman, not the full council, will answer the questions.

(i) To authorize the sealing of documents.
Nowadays the authority to seal documents is often delegated to committees.

(j) To consider motions in the order in which notice has been received.
Even though the motions may be listed together under this item, each is often taken immediately after the report of the committee to whose business it relates.

(k) Other business, if any, specified in the summons.[51]

There is other business often dealt with at the annual meeting, e.g. where the political organisation is well regulated there may appear an item to this effect:

To receive a report as to the appointment of leader of the council and leader of the opposition, chief whip and opposition chief whip, and their deputies as necessary.

And invariably:

To appoint committees;
To appoint representatives on other bodies and authorities where the power to appoint or nominate is reserved to the council.

Sometimes also:

To fix dates of council meetings and the hour of such meetings for the coming year and the dates of meetings of standing committees.

Varying the order of business

6.28. Model standing order no. 5(2) is to this effect:

Business falling under items (a), (b), or (c), of [6.27 above] shall not be

[51] As to 'Any other business', see 6.20.

displaced, but subject thereto the foregoing order of business may be varied:
(a) by the mayor/chairman at his discretion;
(b) by a resolution passed on a motion (which need not be in writing) duly
    moved and seconded, which shall be moved and put without discussion.

Notification of questions

6.29. Although questions proposed to be asked by members are not usually specified in the agenda, there have to be arrangements to ensure that prior notice is given in order that answers can be prepared in advance of the meeting. Model standing order no. 8(2) is to the following effect in this respect:

A member of the council may:
(a) if . . . clear days' notice in writing has been given to the town clerk/clerk of
    the council ask the chairman/mayor or the chairman of any committee
    any question on any matter in relation to which the council have powers
    or duties or which affects the . . .
(b) With the permission of the mayor/chairman, put to him or the chairman
    of any committee any question relating to urgent business, of which such
    notice has not been given; but a copy of any such question shall, if possible,
    be delivered to the town clerk/clerk of the council not later than . . .
    o'clock in the morning of the day of the meeting.

Question time at council meetings is dealt with in the next chapter at 7.37 *et seq.*

6.30. As in practice officers will provide committee chairmen with the basic facts and material for answering questions it is probably better that members should not seek the aid of officers in drawing up their questions (but see 7.40 on the matter of editing questions). It is surely preferable that some questions should be unduly lengthy, even near unintelligible, than that officers should assist and consciously or unconsciously so frame them to enable a committee chairman in answering to score a point or evade the issue. Questions are not always asked to elicit information: many are put merely as a device to make a political point. Those asked of committee chairmen are less likely to be outside the scope of the local authority's functions than any put to the chairman of the council; but the comments on relevance in the case of original motions apply equally to questions.

Postponement and adjournment

Postponement

6.31. It is doubtful whether a council meeting, once convened, may properly be postponed in any circumstances.[52] It is unquestionably bad practice to cancel or abandon or postpone any meeting once it has been validly convened – and unlawful in any case to purport to postpone an annual council meeting to a date outside the prescribed statutory period for its convention. If circumstances make it impossible for the meeting to be held as convened (as, presumably, in the event of a last-minute destruction of the council chamber or other meeting-place), the proper course would seem to be to hold the meeting as nearly as possible in accordance with the notice and summons and then to adjourn it.

6.32. The purported postponement of a meeting is to be distinguished from failure to make a meeting.

Failure to make a meeting

6.33. Until a quorum is present no council meeting can commence. In practice it is usual to wait a reasonable time to allow latecomers to assemble but, strictly, if a quorum does not exist at the time fixed for the commencement of the meeting, the meeting fails and those present are not competent to resolve upon its adjournment. It is therefore desirable (though in practice rare) for there to be a standing order to the effect that if a quorum is not present within, say, half an hour from the time appointed for the meeting, it shall stand adjourned. Alternatively, the meeting must be reconvened.

Effect of adjournment on convention

6.34. An adjourned meeting is part of the original meeting which it continues.[53] It is not essential for notice of an adjourned meeting to be given[54] but there is advantage in doing so. Nothing can be transacted at the adjourned meeting except the unfinished business of the original meeting.[55]

---

[52] See *Smith* v. *Paringa Mines Ltd* [1906] 2 Ch. 193, in which it was held that the postponement of a general meeting of shareholders was inoperative without special power to postpone being given by the regulations governing the meeting: consequently resolutions passed at a gathering of shareholders held in pursuance of the notice were valid and effective.

[53] *Scadding* v. *Lorant* (1851) 3 HL Cas.418.

[54] *Kerr* v. *Wilkie* (1860) 6 Jur. (NS) 383.

[55] *Reg.* v. *Grimshaw* (1847) 10 QB 747.

APPENDIX TO CHAPTER 6

Model public notice of a council meeting and of the individual summons to members entitled to attend

Public notice

The notice, to be displayed outside the council's offices and/or posted conspicuously throughout the area, should be reproduced on the authority's headed notepaper or a representation of it: see 1.31. 3.5, 6.1, 6.2, 6.8–6.10.

NOTICE IS HEREBY GIVEN that a meeting of . . . . . .[a]

will be held at . . . . . .[b] on . . . . .[c] at . . . . . .[d]

[for the purpose of . . . .][e]

DATED this . . . . . . day of . . . . . . 19 . . .[f]

. . . . . .[g]

A copy of the agenda and other relevant papers will be available for public inspection at . . . . . . from . . . . . . onwards between the hours of . . . . . . and . . . . . .[h]: see 3.5, 6.20–6.22.

---

[a] Here will be indicated the character of the meeting, i.e. of the council of the county, borough, or district council, parish or community council [or of a committee or subcommittee of the principal council concerned] or of a parish or community meeting: see 1.16–1.24.

[b] The place of meeting and the date[c] and time[d] must be clearly stated: see 6.9.

[e] In the case of an extraordinary meeting of a principal council and of a parish or community council the business to be transacted must be specified (in general terms so long as the purport of the meeting is reasonably indicated): see 6.11.

[f] The date on which the notice is posted should be given as evidence that it has been given at least three clear days before the meeting or at such shorter notice as may be (seven clear days in the case of a parish or community meeting): see 6.8.

[g] The notice will ordinarily be signed by the proper officer but it may be signed by the chairman and in the case of an extraordinary meeting by the requisite members: see 6.8, 6.11.

[h] It would seem appropriate in the case of a principal council to provide in the notice an indication of where and when the agenda and other papers may be inspected: see 3.5. In the case of a local authority of a large area, several places of inspection might usefully be indicated.

Individual summons

The summons and the agenda will be reproduced on the council's headed notepaper or a representation of it.

$$\ldots\ldots\text{a}$$

A MEETING/THE ANNUAL MEETING/A SPECIAL MEETING/ AN

EXTRAORDINARY MEETING[b] of the COUNCIL

...... will be held on ...... the ...... 19 .. at ....[c]

to which you are summoned,[d] for the transaction of the

undermentioned business.[e]

$$\ldots\ldots\text{f}$$

To all Members of the
Council.

Party group meetings have been notified as follows:[g]

Conservative .... in Committee Room 1 at ....
Labour .... in Committee Room 2 at ....
SDP/Liberal Alliance .... in Committee Room 3 at ....

AGENDA: see 6.27.

[a] At least three clear days' notice must be given: see 6.1, 6.2, 6.12.
[b] The type of meeting should be indicated: see 1.16–1.24. The example given here is for the meeting of a principal council but the summons for other meetings can easily be adapted.
[c] The three essentials of place, date and time must always be given or the summons might be declared void for uncertainty: see 6.12.
[d] The law requires councillors to be 'summoned' (see 6.12) and therefore it would seem appropriate to use these or words to similar effect.
[e] The business to be transacted must be set out (6.19–6.20); a specimen agenda appears elsewhere: see 6.27.
[f] The summons should be signed by the proper officer (see 6.12) or the chairman of the council or, in the case of an extraordinary meeting, by the members who have called the meeting (see 6.11). The signature(s) may be reproduced by any process of facsimile: see Local Government Act 1972, s.234.
[g] An indication of the pre-council meetings of the party groups may be given but it is important that this information should appear below and so not form part of the formal summons; the order in which the group meetings is listed could reflect party strength on the council or could be alphabetical.

7

CONDUCT

General character of proceedings

Introduction

7.1. Proceedings at a meeting of a principal, parish or community council and the business transacted thereat must:

(a) take place in public except to the extent that the public is required to be excluded (i) in the case of a principal council either during an item of business whenever it is likely that confidential information (see 3.6) would be disclosed in breach of the obligation of confidence or by resolution whenever there would otherwise be disclosure of exempt information (see 3.7); (ii) in the case of any other authority when the council by resolution excludes the public because publicity would be prejudicial to the public interest (see 3.4);

(b) follow any order prescribed by statute and standing orders or as set out in the agenda;[1]

(c) have been set out in the notice where the meeting has been convened by councillors (see 6.11) and in every case in the summons and in the case of principal councils in the agenda and accompanying reports (see 6.20);[2]

(d) be *intra vires*, i.e. within the scope of the authority's powers and duties.[3]

In addition, the meeting itself must be properly constituted, i.e. it must

---

[1] The order of business is regulated by statute only in the case of the annual meeting of a principal council which prescribes that the election of chairman must be the first item: see 6.27.

[2] The transaction of business which is outside the scope of a notice convening a meeting will not render the whole meeting irregular: *Re British Sugar Refining Co.* (1857) 3 K. & J. 408.

[3] In practice local authorities sometimes pass resolutions on matters over which they have no jurisdiction but in which the local community may have an interest. There is no reason why they should not do so but a resolution to act in defiance of the law is clearly *ultra vires*.

have been lawfully convened by public notice and individual summons to councillors entitled to attend, the proper person must be in the chair, and a quorum must be present.

Insignia

7.2. The mayor in the case of a borough will wear the robes and chain of office at a council meeting, and the chairman in other cases a badge of office. Robes may also be worn by the deputy mayor, and ex-mayor's badges by councillors who have held the mayoralty; but in comparatively few boroughs now do councillors wear robes. Most important of the insignia at council meetings is the *mace*, which is the emblem of power and dignity of the mayor and the symbol of authority. All boroughs, except 'new' boroughs created under the Local Government Act 1972, have at least one mace and many have two or more; and in every case the mace (or maces) is (or are) carried by the mace-bearer on the slope into the council chamber preceding the mayor and placed in position horizontally before the mayor (with the crown to his right or in the more important direction) to remain there while the council is in session,[4] and then carried in procession in front of the mayor as he leaves. The deputy mayor, when acting on the mayor's behalf at council meetings (but no one else), is entitled to have the mace precede him.

Opening ceremony

7.3. Most local authorities 'open' proceedings in the full assembly with a modicum of ceremony, adding 'to the dignity of council proceedings'.[5] In the case of a borough it is usual, after council members have assembled, for the mayor and town clerk/chief executive – preceded by the mace-bearer – to enter the council chamber in procession; and for the members and public to stand on their entry either as a matter of course or upon the announcement of the mace-bearer: 'Ladies and gentlemen: Be upstanding for His Worship the Mayor'.[6] In many instances the meeting is closed in somewhat similar manner.

---

[4] For more information see G. N. Waldram, *Civic Ceremonial: A Handbook of Practice and Procedure*, 3rd edn (1979); and *The Manual of the Mace* (Guild of Mace Bearers), extracts from which are quoted in *Civic Ceremonial*.

[5] *The Clerk of the Council and His Department* (1950), p. 34.

[6] Some authorities have a standing order to the simple effect: 'The entrance of the mayor shall be announced on each occasion and all members shall stand'.

Prayers

7.4. In some authorities it is the custom for proceedings to begin with prayers. The practice is tending to fall into disuse for a number of reasons which it would be inappropriate to discuss in this work.[7] Where the practice is followed prayers are usually led by the mayor or chairman's chaplain (ordinarily an honorary post to which an appointment is made personally by the mayor or chairman) or in some cases by local preachers or as custom may dictate: in Durham, for example, the Dean of the Cathedral is ex officio the chaplain to the council.

Business generally

7.5. The nature of the proceedings will vary according to the purpose of the meeting. Thus an annual meeting, apart from essential business (such as the election of a chairman and the appointment of committees for the ensuing year), is largely of a ceremonial character (particularly in the case of mayor-making); and an extraordinary meeting will be concerned as a rule with one item of business alone. Ordinary meetings will follow a fairly uniform pattern and the greater part of the business will be the consideration of committee reports. So long, however, as an authority observes statutory requirements and does not violate the common law rules governing meetings procedure (including its own standing orders), the conduct of proceedings is for each authority to decide.

7.6. Business is ordinarily conducted in a formal manner and this means that for the greater part discussion takes place upon a motion before the assembly. It is a convention that officers do not participate in any way (although the chief executive may be called upon to advise on procedure or he or any other chief officer may exceptionally be invited to speak). This means, as a general rule, that the officers' influence over proceedings and the efficient and effective dispatch of business is limited to preparatory work beforehand, i.e. in the preparation of council papers, the careful briefing of the chairman and of committee chairmen, the stage-managing of procedure, and attention to the several matters relating to the physical conditions of the council chamber or other accommodation in which the meeting is to be held: see, e.g. 10.48.

---

[7] See, however, Ivan Brown, 'Prayers at Council Meetings' (1974) 138 *Local Government Review* 653.

Confirmation of minutes

7.7. The confirmation of the minutes of the previous meeting is always placed as an early item on the agenda: see more particularly 6.27. Model standing order no. 9 is to this effect:

> (1) The mayor/chairman shall put the question that the minutes of the meeting of the council held on the . . . day of . . . be approved as a correct record.
>
> (2) No discussion shall take place upon the minutes, except upon their accuracy, and any question of their accuracy shall be raised by motion. If no such question is raised, or if it is raised then as soon as it has been disposed of, the mayor/chairman shall sign the minutes.

Behaviour of members

7.8. Although there are some forms of behaviour which are not expected of members present at a council meeting, e.g. conduct which is so disorderly as to interrupt business (as to which see later: 7.123), there are no widely accepted conventions otherwise governing councillors' behaviour (although often members are expected to make obeisance to the chair when entering or leaving the council chamber) and few other instances where behaviour is regulated by standing orders. One reason for this may be that it would be difficult to secure compliance because in the final resort there is no power to exclude a councillor – probably not even temporarily: see 7.121 – from a council meeting at which he is lawfully entitled to be present.

7.9. The standing orders of the House of Commons do contain several restrictions on the conduct of Members of Parliament in the House and the Speaker is endowed with formidable authority to secure compliance.[8] Members are required to keep in their places and not rove around the chamber; they must not read any book, newspaper or letter in their places except in connection with the business of the House; they are not permitted to wear decorations or uniforms and it is the custom for Members to wear jackets and ties; they may not smoke during any of the proceedings of the House, nor may refreshments be brought into or consumed in the chamber. It may seem strange, in view of the noisy behaviour often heard when proceedings in the Commons are broadcast, that members are expected to maintain silence or converse only in undertones, that members must not disturb a member who is speaking by hissing or interruption and that cries of 'shame' are strongly condemned. The Lords are directed by standing orders to keep their dignity and order.[9]

[8] Erskine May on *Parliamentary Practice*, 12th edn (1983), pp. 440–42.
[9] *Ibid.* p. 487.

Addressing the chair

7.10. Councillors should be expected (and standing orders will often so provide) to stand when speaking at a council meeting and always to address the chair. Whether the term *Sir* or *Mr Chairman* – or, commonly nowadays, merely *Chairman* – is employed is a matter of local custom (but *Mr Mayor* can never properly be shortened to *Mayor*). The manner of addressing a woman chairman varies. The form most favoured appears to be *Mr Chairman* rather than *Madam Chairman* but often *Madam* rather than *Sir*. When the former London County Council first had a woman chairman it was her personal wish that she should be addressed as *Mr Chairman* and *Sir* – on the ground that 'it is the chair which is being addressed and not the sex of its occupant'.[10] Some 35 years later, when the Greater London Council first elected a woman chairman, Dame Evelyn Denington said on being installed that she had rejected the appellation of *Mr Chairman* at the insistence of 'women's libbers', disliked *Madam Chairman* and *Chairperson*, and wanted to be known as *Chairman*. Shortly after the Sex Discrimination Act 1975 came into effect the term *Chairperson* was favoured in some quarters but has not been widely adopted, if at all. The practice has grown up in some local authorities, especially in Greater London, of referring to a committee chairman as *'chair'*.

The chairman

Election of chairman of the council

7.11. The chairman of a principal, parish or community council must be elected annually from among the councillors[11] and the election must be the first business transacted at the council's annual meeting.[12] Anyone so elected cannot act in the office until he has made the prescribed declaration of acceptance of office,[13] and this he does, if present, immediately after his election.

---

[10] See *The Times*, 15 March 1939.

[11] Local Government Act 1972, ss.3(1), 8(sch.2, paras.2(1), 15(1), 22(1), 34(1)). The former provision in the Local Government Act 1933 enabling a local authority to appoint a chairman from outside the council's membership no longer applies. It is sufficient qualification for election to be a member of the council and no restriction, it is submitted, can be placed upon such a member's eligibility by the council: certainly it would be an offence for a local authority to decide that a woman could not be elected as chairman.

[12] Local Government Act 1972, ss.4(1), 8(sch.2, paras. 3(1), 15(2), 23(1), 34(2)). It was decided in *R.* v. *McGowan* (1840) 11 A. & I. 869, that any business carried out before the election of the chairman – in that case the election of aldermen – was void but the election of the chairman was valid: see also *R.* v. *Parkyns* (1828) B. & Ad.668.

[13] Local Government Act 1972, s.83.

Procedure on election

7.12. No procedure for the election is prescribed by statute and it is rare for standing orders to do so. In practice councillors often agree upon a nominee beforehand (in the party caucus where the authority is run on party political lines) so that at the annual meeting there is usually only one nomination proposed and seconded: a prior arrangement of this kind enables someone other than the nominee to preside at his election: see 7.18. Where, however, more than one nomination is made various methods can be adopted to determine where the preponderance of favour lies: a direct vote is convenient where there are only two nominees; an elimination vote can be used where there is a larger number (which does not often occur), a succession of votes being taken, on each of which the nominee receiving the least votes is excluded from the next vote. If more than one nomination is anticipated there is virtue in making the appointment by ballot.

7.13. Voting at the election proceeds in the normal way, i.e. the election is decided by a majority of the councillors present and voting: but see 7.105. The person presiding at the meeting *must* give a casting vote in the case of an equality of votes;[14] but otherwise he may not vote unless he is the retiring chairman or the vice-chairman still in office.[15]

Failure to elect

7.14. If a council fails to elect a chairman the council is not properly constituted[16] and (except in the case of the chairmanship of a parish or community council or meeting) the High Court may direct the election to be held at a time fixed by the Court.[17] Despite the mandatory terms of the law as to election annually it would not seem improper for a council to elect a chairman pro tem but the term of office should be clearly stated.

Adjournment of election

7.15. A council may for a specific reason wish to adjourn the election for a short period, either until later in the proceedings (because, perhaps, of the absence of a particular councillor who is a candidate or the proposer of a candidate) or to a later meeting (e.g. for political reasons). It would seem,

---

[14] Local Government Act 1972, ss.4(3), 8(sch.2, para.3(3)), 23(3).

[15] *Ibid.* s.4(2), 8(sch.2, para.3(2)), 15(3), 23(2).

[16] *Ibid.* ss.2(1), 14(1), 8(sch.2, para.1), 21(1), 33(1).

[17] *Ibid.* s.44(2). No rules of procedure have been prescribed for the application to the High Court in this respect.

on a strict interpretation of the terms of the statute, that this cannot be done: the election must be the first item of business (see 7.11). It may be, however, that an adjournment of the meeting could meet the circumstances although other difficulties could thereby be created.

7.16. On the other hand, it might be argued that the law does not require that someone shall necessarily be elected but only that the first business shall be the election. Thus, so long as the question of election is considered as the first item of business, the decision on that consideration could be to adjourn the election. This is probably not a persuasive argument: indeed, the fact that the person presiding at the election is compelled to give a second or casting vote in the event of an equality of votes (see 7.13) seems additional support for the view that Parliament's intention was that the election must take place so that the council can be properly constituted.

Election of disqualified councillor

7.17. If the person elected as chairman is disqualified from being a councillor it would seem that the election is nevertheless valid by the terms of s.82 of the Local Government Act 1972, which provides that:

> The acts and proceedings of any person elected to an office under this Act and acting in that office shall, notwithstanding his disqualification or want of qualification, be as valid and effectual as if he had been qualified.

In *Forrester* v. *Norton* (1911)[18] it was held that since the election of the councillor had not been challenged by an election petition, he was a councillor *de facto* whose election as chairman was rendered valid by s.73 of the Municipal Corporations Act 1882 (now s.82 of the 1972 Act).

Presiding at one's own election

7.18. It is well established that a person who presides at an election is disqualified from being a candidate. Thus, in *R.* v. *Owens* (1858)[19] the mayor of a borough had presided over the election of councillors and, as returning officer, had returned himself as one of the persons elected: the validity of this election was successfully impeached. Local practice, no matter how long established, cannot justify disregard of this rule.[20]

[18] [1911] 2 KB 953.
[19] (1858) 28 LJQB 316.
[20] *R.* v. *Reynolds* (1896) LGC 900.

Vacation of chair before election

7.19. If, however, an outgoing chairman wishes to be re-elected he can provide a substitute to perform his functions temporarily.[21] This in practice is what is ordinarily done though it means that a person must be proposed as a candidate *before* the election: if, while presiding, his name is put forward as a candidate, he cannot then vacate the chair because the proposal made while he occupies the chair would be void. It means also that an outgoing chairman wishing to be re-elected must not only not preside but must not be in the meeting because if he is present he must preside:[22] see further 7.24.

Failure to give notice of election

7.20. There is authority for the view that the election of a chairman at a meeting for which notice has not been given is invalid. Thus, in *R. v. Langborn* (1836),[23] in an action impeaching the validity of a mayoral election, the jury found that one of the burgesses (all of whom were entitled to vote) had not been served with a notice of the meeting at which the mayor was elected, and it was held that he was not duly elected. The statutory provision which now stipulates that want of service of a summons on any member shall not affect the validity of a meeting of a principal, parish or community council would nowadays seem to avoid challenge on these grounds.[24] It might be, however, that the election of a chairman of a parish or community meeting would be held invalid if the requisite notices of such a meeting were not given.[25]

Vice-chairman

Appointment

7.21. A principal council *must*[26] and a parish and community council *may*[27] appoint a member of the council to be vice-chairman of the council.

---

[21] *R. v. White* (1867) LR 2 QB 557.
[22] Local Government Act 1972, ss.3(2), 15(4), 22(2), which provide that the chairman shall continue in office until his successor becomes entitled to act as chairman; and sch.12, paras.5(1), 11(1), 27(1), which provide that the chairman, if present, shall preside.
[23] (1836) 4 Ad. & El.538.
[24] Local Government Act 1972, sch.12, paras.4(4), 10(3), 26(3).
[25] *Ibid.* sch.12 paras.15(2), 30(2).
[26] Local Government Act 1972, s.5(1).
[27] *Ibid.* ss.15(6), 34(6). Where a parish or community council decides always to have a vice-chairman it may be convenient to adopt model standing order no. 2 which is to the effect that 'The council shall at the annual meeting appoint a vice-chairman'.

The Local Government Act 1972 follows the wording of the former 1933 Act and refers to the *appointment* and not the *election* of a vice-chairman, but the difference in term is of no significance. The vice-chairman, unless he resigns or becomes disqualified, holds office until immediately after the election of a chairman at the next annual meeting.[28] During that time he continues to be a member of the council notwithstanding the statutory provisions relating to the retirement of councillors.[29]

7.22. What has been said earlier about the procedure for the election of a chairman (see 7.11 *et seq.*) applies equally to the election of a vice-chairman.

Powers

7.23. Subject to standing orders anything authorised or required to be done by, to or before the chairman may be done by, to or before the vice-chairman.[30] Standing orders can place such restrictions upon the vice-chairman's powers as the council thinks appropriate – except that it would not be lawful for standing orders to prohibit the vice-chairman from presiding at a meeting of the full assembly in the absence of the chairman because the law expressly requires him if present to take the chair: see 7.25. Model standing order no. 3 is to the following effect:

> Any power or duty of the mayor/chairman in relation to the conduct of a meeting may be exercised by the person presiding at the meeting.

Who presides?

Principal councils

7.24. The chairman of the council (or the mayor) if present at a meeting of the full assembly of a principal council must preside.[31] If, for any reason, he vacates the chair, he must leave the meeting (as to whether he need leave the council chamber altogether: see 5.32) so as not to contravene this specific statutory direction that he must preside if present. In *Re Wolverhampton Borough Council's Aldermanic Election* (1961),[32] which concerned an election of aldermen for which the mayor was a candidate, the

---

[28] *Ibid.* ss.5(2), 15(7), 34(7). Strictly interpreted this provision might seem to deny a vice-chairman, unless he resigns first, the opportunity of being elected as chairman in the event of a vacancy in the office of chairman before the next annual meeting!

[29] *Ibid.* ss.5(2), 15(8), 34(8), and sch.2, para.4(2).

[30] *Ibid.* ss.5(3), 15(9), 34(9), and sch.2, para.4(3).

[31] Local Government Act 1972, sch.12, para.5(1).

[32] [1961] 3 All ER 446.

mayor vacated the chair just before the council proceeded to the election of aldermen but he delivered a voting paper and remained in the council chamber. Glyn-Jones J said:

> In my opinion it was Parliament's intention that at a meeting of the council the mayor's place, and his only place, should be in the chair. Seated in the mayoral chair he can exercise all his one and indivisible functions . . . When he is not in the mayoral chair . . . then, since his functions are one and indivisible, he has lost his right to exercise any of them so far as taking part in the meeting is concerned.

7.25. If the chairman is absent from the meeting then:[33]

(a) except in Greater London, the vice-chairman of the council if present must preside;

(b) in the case of a London borough council, the deputy mayor, if at that time he remains a councillor and is chosen for that purpose, must preside.

If:

(a) in the case of a principal council outside Greater London both the chairman and vice-chairman of the council are absent from a meeting of the council;

(b) in the case of a London borough council the mayor and deputy mayor are so absent or the deputy mayor being present is not chosen;

another member of the council chosen by the members of the council present must preside.[34]

Parish and community councils

7.26. The chairman of the council must preside at a meeting of a parish council or a community council as the case may be if present at the meeting.[35] If the chairman is absent from the meeting the vice-chairman if present must preside.[36] If both the chairman and the vice-chairman are absent from the meeting then such councillor as the members of the council present shall choose must preside.[37]

Parish and community meetings

7.27. In a parish having a separate parish council the chairman of the

[33] Local Government Act 1972, sch.12, para.5(2), as amended by Local Government Act 1985, s.102, sch.17.
[34] *Ibid.* para.5(3).
[35] Local Government Act 1972, sch.12, paras.11(1), 27(1).
[36] *Ibid.* sch.12, paras.11(2), 27(2).
[37] *Ibid.* sch.12, paras.11(3), 27(3).

parish council if present must preside at a parish meeting; and if he is absent the vice-chairman if any must if present preside.[38] In a parish which does not have a separate parish council the chairman chosen for the year in question must if present preside.[39] If the chairman and the vice-chairman of the parish council or the chairman of the parish meeting, as the case may be, is absent from an assembly of the parish meeting, the parish meeting may appoint a person to take the chair and that person has, for the purposes of that meeting, the powers and authority of the chairman.[40] In a community for which there is a community council the chairman of the council if present must preside at the community meeting.[41] In any other case a community meeting must appoint a person to be chairman at that meeting.[42]

Powers and duties of person presiding

Generally

7.28. Upon taking the chair at a meeting the chairman (or whoever may be presiding) becomes invested with authority to regulate and control proceedings for purposes of the meeting.[43] The powers and duties of the chairman are not prescribed by statute (except in certain limited respects: he has conferred upon him, for example, the power to give a second or casting vote in the case of an equality of votes: see 7.114) but derive from standing orders and common law. He 'collects his authority from the meeting'.[44]

7.29. So long as the chairman acts *bona fide* and remains in the chair he has virtually absolute rule: admittedly the full assembly could by majority decision dislodge the person presiding[45] but not if he is the chairman of the council or the vice-chairman of the council because the duly elected chairman of a principal or parish or community council remains in office until he resigns of his own accord, or becomes disqualified, and if present at a council meeting must preside as must a vice-chairman if present in the absence of the chairman.[46] While acting in good faith the chairman's

---

[38] *Ibid.* sch.12, para.17(1).
[39] *Ibid.* sch.12, para.17(2).
[40] *Ibid.* sch.12, para.17(3).
[41] *Ibid.* sch.12, para.33(1).
[42] *Ibid.* sch.12, para.33(2).
[43] *Taylor* v. *Nesfield* (1855), *Wills on Vestries*, p. 29n.; those who put someone in the chair devolve upon him by agreement the conduct of the meeting and 'attorn to him, as it were, and give him the whole power of regulating themselves'.
[44] *Taylor* v. *Nesfield*, *supra*.
[45] *Booth* v. *Arnold* [1895] 1 QB 571.
[46] The Local Government Act 1972, ss.3(2), 15(4), 34(1), also provides that the duly elected chairman shall continue in office unless he resigns or becomes disqualified until his successor becomes entitled to act.

decisions, even if not strictly correct, will be upheld by the court provided no substantial injustice has arisen therefrom.[47] If, however, the chairman acts improperly or *mala fide* his decisions are not binding and in a proper case the court will intervene. The proper course for anyone who considers that a ruling of a chairman is erroneous is to seek an order of the court compelling the chairman to convene a fresh meeting: the court will not ordinarily interfere unless the complaint of irregularity comes from a representative majority of the meeting, but if a specific individual right is infringed action could be taken by the party aggrieved.[47]

Specific functions

7.30. From judicial decisions there has emerged a widely recognised catalogue of the powers and duties of a chairman: it is the duty of the chairman and his function:[48]

> to preserve order, and to take care that the proceedings are conducted in a proper manner, and that the sense of the meeting is properly ascertained with regard to any question which is properly before the meeting.

More specifically it is the chairman's responsibility:

- (a) to determine that the meeting is properly constituted and that a quorum is present;
- (b) to inform himself as to the business and objects of the meeting;
- (c) to preserve order in the conduct of those present;
- (d) to confine discussion within the scope of the meeting and reasonable limits of time;
- (e) to decide whether proposed motions and amendments are in order;
- (f) to formulate for discussion and decision questions which have been moved for the consideration of the meeting;
- (g) to decide points of order and other incidental questions which require decision at the time;[49]
- (h) to ascertain the sense of the meeting by:
  putting relevant questions to the meeting and taking a vote thereon (and if so minded giving a casting vote[50]);

---

[47] *Breay* v. *Brown* (1896) 41 *Sol. Jo.*159. It strengthens a chairman's hands if a local authority adopts a standing order on the lines of model standing order no. 42 which is to this effect: 'The ruling of the mayor/chairman as to the construction or application of any of these standing orders, or as to any proceedings of the council, shall not be challenged at any meeting of the council.'

[48] *National Dwellings Society* v. *Sykes* [1894] 3 Ch. 159, p. 162, per Chitty J.

[49] In *Re Indian Zoedone Co.* (1884) 26 Ch. D.70.

[50] There is no casting vote at common law. In local government the power is conferred by statute: see 7.114.

declaring the result;
causing a ballot to be taken if duly demanded;
(i) to approve the draft of the minutes or other record of proceedings;
(j) to adjourn the meeting when circumstances justify or require that course;
(k) to declare the meeting closed when its business has been completed.

The chairman's responsibility under (j) to adjourn the meeting must not be taken to mean that the power of adjournment vests solely in the chairman. A chairman cannot adjourn a meeting without the consent, express or implied, of those present. There could be implied consent in exceptional circumstances when, for example, a member may have collapsed and died in the course of proceedings. The right of adjournment is vested in the assembly but in practice, of course, only the person presiding can declare the assembly's decision to adjourn. As to the effect of an improper adjournment by a chairman: see 7.80.

Quorum

General considerations

7.31. A quorum[51] is the minimum number of members whose presence is necessary at a meeting for the valid transaction of business.[52] In the absence of special custom or particular regulation, by statute or otherwise, a majority of the members of a body must be present at a duly convened assembly in order that an effective meeting should exist.[53] In the case of local authorities a quorum is prescribed by statute for meetings of a principal, parish and community council[54] but not for meetings of committees and subcommittees: see 11.16.

7.32. If a quorum is not present at a council meeting any business transacted is, generally speaking, invalid; and the mere fortuitous assembly of the requisite minimum number of councillors can never constitute a meeting for the purpose of transacting valid business for there must be an intention to meet known to all members entitled to attend, i.e. there are, as already indicated, statutory formalities in regard to notice and summons which must be observed before a meeting may properly be held: see 1.31.

---

[51] *Quorum* is Latin for 'of whom' and derives from the wording of commissions by which persons were, from at least the fifteenth century, designated as members of a body by the words: *quorum vos . . . unum esse volumus,* i.e. 'of whom it is our wish that you . . . shall be one': Ian Shearman, *Shackleton on the Law and Practice of Meetings,* 7th edn (1983).

[52] The quorum needs to be distinguished from the minimum number of persons who can form a meeting: see 1.7.

[53] *Mayor, Constables and Company of Merchants of the Staple of England* v. *Governor and Company of the Bank of England* (1887) 21 QBD 160, 165.

[54] Local Government Act 1972, sch.12, paras.6, 12, 28.

Statutory regulation

7.33. Subject to what is said below in 7.35 no business may be transacted at a meeting of:

(a) a principal council unless at least one-quarter of the whole number of members of the council are present;[55]

(b) a parish or community council unless at least one-third of the whole number of members of the council are present but in no case is the quorum to be less than three.[56]

Calculation of quorum

7.34. The quorum is ordinarily calculated in relation to 'the whole number of members of the council'; and this means the total number of seats.[57] If, however, more than one-third of the members of the authority become disqualified at the same time, then – until the number of members in office is increased to not less than two-thirds of the whole number of members of the authority, i.e. seats – the quorum must be determined by reference to the number of members remaining qualified instead of by reference to the whole number of members.[58] This provision is intended to meet the situation where a considerable number of members, i.e. more than one-third, are *disqualified*: it applies if seats are vacant for other reasons (e.g. by reason of death or resignation) but members who have died or resigned clearly must not be counted with members who are disqualified.

Duration of quorum

7.35. Is it necessary, once a meeting has commenced with the requisite quorum present,[59] for that quorum to be present throughout the meeting or at least present at the time a vote is taken? There seems to be widespread practice to support the contention that at least until attention is drawn to

[55] Local Government Act 1972, sch.12, para.6.
[56] *Ibid.* paras.12, 28.
[57] *Newhaven Local Board* v. *Newhaven School Board* (1885) 30 Ch. D.350; 53 LT 571.
[58] Local Government Act 1972, sch.12, para.45.
[59] It was held in *Re Hartley Baird Ltd* [1955] 1 Ch. 143, that where a company's articles provide, *inter alia*, that no business shall be transacted at any general meeting unless a quorum is present 'when the meeting proceeds to business' and there is in fact a quorum at that time, the subsequent departure of a member thereby reducing the number below the quorum does not invalidate the proceedings after his departure. This cannot apply to a local authority council meeting because the quorum prescribed by statute is not in those terms.

the absence of a quorum the proceedings should continue.[60] This may seem a reasonable and practical course to adopt – particularly in the case of large assemblies where the absence of a quorum may not be immediately apparent – but in law any business transacted at a council meeting in the absence of a quorum is invalid.

7.36. Model standing order no. 4 provides that:

> If during any meeting of the council the mayor/chairman after counting the number of members present declares that there is not a quorum present the meeting shall stand adjourned. The consideration of any business not transacted shall be adjourned to a time fixed by the mayor/chairman at the time the meeting is adjourned, or, if he does not fix a time, to the next ordinary meeting of the council.

Some authorities provide, in a standing order to the following effect, for a short interval to elapse between the formal recognition that a quorum is not present and the decision to end the meeting:

> If the chairman finds that a quorum is wanting, the bell shall be rung for three minutes. If a quorum is then wanting, the meeting shall end and the remaining business carried forward.

Question time

Types of question

7.37. Many local authorities now devote an allotted time to questions at every council meeting;[61] but some still permit questions to be asked only upon reports of committees actually before the council. Widdicombe attached importance to question time 'as a means by which minority parties and "backbench" councillors can not only obtain information but also call the majority party to account'.[62] There are, therefore, in effect two types of question: the *spontaneous* question, which may be asked at any time without notice; and the *deliberate* question which, because of its character and the need usually for some research or verification of facts before an answer can be prepared, requires advance written notice.

---

[60] Parliamentary procedure provides a general exception to the rule. Business transacted in the House of Commons is valid notwithstanding the absence of a quorum until that fact is brought to the notice of the Speaker or chairman as the case may be and there is a 'count-out'.

[61] For a discussion of 'Question Time in the Council Chamber' see an article by the author in 115 *Justice of the Peace* (1951) 423.

[62] Widdicombe Report, para. 5.117.

Questions are not, as a rule, set out in the agenda though many authorities record both questions and answers in council minutes.

Spontaneous questions

7.38. Model standing order no. 8 provides, in part, that:

> A member of the council may ask the chairman of a committee any question upon an item of the report of a committee when that item is under consideration by the council.

Whether or not the committee chairman answers will depend upon the question. If need be the chairman can always ask the member concerned to give notice or offer to provide the answer later.

Deliberate questions

7.39. Model standing order no. 8 also provides that:

> A member of the council may:
> (a) if . . . clear days' notice in writing has been given to the clerk/town clerk, ask the mayor/chairman or the chairman of any committee any question on any matter in relation to which the council have powers or duties or which affects the [county] [borough] [district] [parish].
> (b) With the permission of the mayor/chairman, put to him or the chairman of any committee any question relating to urgent business, of which such notice has not been given; but a copy of any such question shall, if possible, be delivered to the clerk/town clerk not later than . . . o'clock in the morning of the day of the meeting.
> Every question shall be put and answered without discussion, but the person to whom a question has been put may decline to answer.
> An answer may take the form of:
> (a) a direct oral answer; or
> (b) where the desired information is contained in a publication of the council, a reference to that publication; or
> (c) where the reply to the question cannot conveniently be given orally, a written answer circulated to members of the council.

7.40. Several local authorities have adopted standing orders which further regulate the business of asking questions, e.g. in limiting the duration of question time or the number of questions which may be asked:

> . . . there shall be a question time for a period of not more than thirty minutes, which period is called 'question time';
> The number of questions which may be asked by any one member at any one meeting shall be limited to three;

or:

> Questions shall be edited,[63] if necessary, by the clerk/chief executive, both to bring them into proper form and to secure reasonable brevity, and any which, in the opinion of the chairman/mayor, are unsuitable in form, frivolous or derogatory to the dignity of the council, shall be disallowed by him. Questions as to letters or other communications received by the council and/or action proposed thereon shall not normally be allowed until a fortnight has elapsed from the date of their receipt.

7.41. There are many ways, of course, in which question time could be further regulated. If the authority sets a time limit for question time then it might permit members to ballot for a specified number to be answered orally and the remainder dealt with by written answer – much in the manner of Parliamentary procedure. It is also a matter for consideration whether a councillor's question should be answered if he is absent when the question is called; or, alternatively, provision made by standing orders that:

> If a member who has submitted a question is not present when the question is called, the question may, with the consent of the council, be asked by any other member.

Widdicombe proposed that it should be obligatory on all local authorities to provide for question time at council meetings. 'The precise form of the requirement', it said, 'would need further consideration but it should be limited to questions from councillors as opposed to questions from the public gallery', and the arrangement should provide for:[64]

(a) a reasonable time limit (at least 30 minutes);
(b) questions to be handed to the chief executive and addressed to the leader or the chairman of the responsible committee;
(c) a reply to be given unless there is good reason to the contrary (e.g. confidentiality);
(d) a right to at least one supplementary question, with the questioner having priority.

This substantially reflects common practice.

Petitions

7.42. Petitions submitted to a local authority by a body of its citizens are usually presented to the full council by one of the council members. This

---

[63] As to whether it is appropriate for officers to do more than edit questions, see 6.30, and motions, see 7.54.
[64] Widdicombe Report, para.5.118.

procedure is followed so that the council as a whole may have cognisance of the petition and the petitioners assured that it has been received by the council. Practice varies but as a rule no speech or debate is permitted on the petition which, either on the motion of the member presenting it or of the chairman or automatically under standing orders, is referred to the appropriate committee for consideration.

7.43. A typical standing order is to this effect:

> Petitions may be presented by any member of the council, but shall not be accompanied by any speech or comment, and every petition shall (without discussion) stand referred to the committee within whose reference it falls, which shall be decided by the chairman/mayor, and such a committee shall report thereon to the council.

Deputations

7.44. It is rare for a local authority to receive a deputation in full assembly but there is no reason why it should not do so if the issue is thought sufficiently important to justify that course rather than referring the deputation to the appropriate committee. Some local authorities have regulated the procedure for receiving deputations by appropriate provision in standing orders.[65]

[65] Thus, for example, this provision in the standing orders of the London Borough of Hammersmith and Fulham:

Deputation to furnish request
29. A deputation may request the council or a committee of the council to receive that deputation and the mayor or chairman of that committee as appropriate shall determine whether or not the deputation shall be received; in the case of a request to appear before the council the mayor may decide that the deputation should appear before an appropriate committee.

Procedure
30. (a) A request from a deputation shall be in writing and signed by at least ten local government electors in the borough having a legitimate and *bona fide* interest in the objects of the deputation and shall be delivered to the chief executive not later than 10 clear days before the date on which the deputation wishes to be received stating clearly the purposes of the deputation. In case of doubt the mayor or the chairman of the committee concerned may refer the question as to whether or not the deputation should be received to the council or the committee as appropriate.

(b) The persons signing the request for the reception of a deputation shall each furnish a short statement of their interest in the subject which shall also state their address.

Receiving the deputation
31. A member of the council may move that a deputation be not received, or shall be received by a committee or sub-committee, and on being seconded it shall be debated in accordance with standing orders.

Constitution of deputation
32. A deputation shall consist of not less than three persons other than members of the council and not more than 10 persons. The members of the deputation shall be persons

Minority party business

7.45. A comparatively new development within some local authorities has been a procedure under which minority party councillors are able to get issues of their choice debated at council and committee meetings. Widdicombe commended the arrangement, particularly if appropriately controlled in some such manner as that provided by Westminster City Council in a standing order to this effect:

> *Minority party business at council meetings*
> (1) At each ordinary meeting of the council, the largest minority party shall after the completion of the report of the policy and resources committee, be entitled to use up to 40 minutes excluding any time taken by a chairman or his nominee in reply to the debate for discussion on one topic of their choice being an item on the agenda for that council meeting other than a motion of which written notice has been given in accordance with standing order . . .
> (2) The leader of the opposition shall notify the chief executive at least seven days (excluding Saturdays and Sundays) prior to the date of the relevant meeting of the council of the choice of item.
> (3) Debate on any item brought forward in accordance with this standing order shall not exceed 40 minutes excluding any time taken by a chairman or his nominee in reply to the debate.
> (4) Not later than the expiration of 40 minutes from the commencement of minority party business the person presiding shall call upon the appropriate chairman or his nominee to exercise his right of reply. If at the expiration of 40 minutes a person other than the chairman or his nominee is speaking he shall resume his seat immediately.
> (5) For the avoidance of doubt the rules as to the conduct of debate shall apply during minority party business, subject to the modifications required by this standing order.

Widdicombe proposed that all local authorities should be required to include in their standing orders provision of this kind, with a minimum allotment of time (say 30 minutes).[66] Where there are several minority parties the right should not be limited to the largest but should rotate between them pro rata to their strength on the council.[67]

---

65 cont.

who signed the request but they may appoint another person to act as their spokesman. Only one member thereof shall be at liberty to address the council or committee, and the speech of such member of the deputation shall be limited to 15 minutes. The council or committee may agree to questions from members of the council or committee being answered by any member of the deputation. The matter shall not be further considered by the council or committee until the deputation shall have withdrawn.

Limitation of deputation
33. No deputation shall appear before the council or any committee within three months after a deputation has appeared before it with the same or like object.

[66] Widdicombe Report, para.5.119.
[67] *Ibid.* para.5.120.

Motions

Discussion out of order otherwise

7.46. Discussion and debate at a council meeting will ordinarily only be permitted on a motion properly before the assembly: that is to say any matter before the meeting for consideration must be expressed as a motion in positive terms to adopt a certain course of action or to do some act or declare a particular attitude. When passed – by a majority of the members present and voting – with or without amendment, the *motion* becomes a *resolution*.

Types of motion

7.47. Motions are broadly of two types: *original and procedural*. The first, defined more explicitly below in the local government context, is one propounding a substantial issue for consideration and action; a procedural motion (see 7.69), sometimes called a *formal motion*, and which includes a *dilatory motion*, is one affecting matters of procedure or form. Sometimes amendments are termed *amending motions* but this is a fairly uncommon phrase, although an amendment is by its character a motion to amend the main proposition before the meeting.

Original motions

7.48. An original motion may not be moved at a council meeting unless prior notice thereof has been given so that its terms may be included in the agenda. This is necessary so as to comply with the statutory requirement that the summons to attend (and, sometimes, the notice of) the meeting must specify the business to be transacted. The procedure for the giving of notice and the consequential steps are usually prescribed in standing orders.

7.49. Model standing order no. 6 provides that:

> (1) Notice of every motion other than a motion which under standing order 7 may be moved without notice shall be given in writing, signed by the member or members of the council giving the notice, and delivered [at least . . . clear days/not later than the (Friday)] before the next meeting of the council, at the office of the clerk/town clerk, by whom it shall be dated, numbered in the order in which it is received, and entered in a book which shall be open to the inspection of every member of the council.
>
> (2) The clerk/town clerk shall set out in the summons for every meeting of the council all motions of which notice has been duly given in the order in which they have been received, unless the member giving such a notice intimated in

writing, when giving it, that he proposed to move it at some later meeting, or has since withdrawn it in writing.

(3) If a motion thus set out in the summons be not moved either by a member who gave notice thereof or by some other member on his behalf it shall, unless postponed by consent of the council, be treated as withdrawn and shall not be moved without fresh notice.

(4) If the subject matter of any motion of which notice has been duly given comes within the province of any committee or committees it shall, upon being moved and seconded, stand referred without discussion to such committee or committees, or to such other committee or committees as the council may determine, for consideration and report.

Provided that the mayor/chairman may, if he considers it convenient and conducive to the despatch of business, allow the motion to be dealt with at the meeting at which it is brought forward.

(5) Every motion shall be relevant to some matter in relation to which the council have powers or duties or which affects the [county] [borough] [district] [parish].

There are in practice countless variations of the foregoing in use but the general effect is much the same in every case.

Motions that stand referred

7.50. Where, under model standing order no. 6(4), a motion stands referred without discussion to a committee when proposed and seconded, the proposer has no right to a speech, introductory or otherwise.[68] The term *without discussion* means precisely that. No one may speak and there can be no discussion unless the chairman allows the motion to be dealt with at the meeting at which it is brought forward, i.e. it does not stand referred. Nor, if it stands referred, is any amendment permissible. This is because the council, in referring the motion to a committee for consideration and report, is neither accepting nor rejecting it. If a councillor wishes to make a point germane to the motion he can do so in one or both of two ways: he can ask to be allowed to attend and speak at the committee meeting at which the motion is to be considered (indeed he may be so entitled under standing orders); and he will in any case ultimately have an opportunity of participating in the debate when the committee's report comes before the full assembly.

Rejected notices of motion

7.51. The proper officer must consider whether the motion of which notice has been given is one which may properly be accepted. If it is and

[68] It is submitted that the proposer could, under standing orders, with the consent of the council and without his seeking to explain the reason, alter the wording of the motion.

notice has been given in time then he must proceed to place it on the agenda for the next council meeting. If he considers the terms of the motion out of order, illegal, irregular or improper, he should consult the chairman and/or the leader or take such other action as may be laid down in standing orders. In any case if a motion is rejected the member giving notice should be so advised. A standing order covering these matters might be framed in these words:

> If notice be given of any original motion which, in the opinion of the proper officer is out of order, illegal, irregular or improper, the proper officer shall forthwith submit such notice to the chairman and it shall not be accepted and placed on the agenda without his sanction. In the event of non-acceptance the proper officer shall so inform the member giving notice.

7.52. A motion which seeks to require the local authority to do something which it patently cannot do would be out of order and one which sought action which was *ultra vires* or otherwise illegal would similarly be out of order. One which was defamatory or might offend against public propriety or the scruples of members could be ruled out as improper. But a motion ought not to be rejected merely because it refers to matters which are not within the scope of the authority's powers and duties: what may be relevant for the council's consideration is a difficult question to determine. It has been said:[69]

> A motion of congratulation to the Queen on her accession may be deemed to be relevant, since a local authority is legally in the position of a subject of the Crown and is certainly a public body owing allegiance. A motion protesting against the raising of railway fares may be considered relevant, in that it may affect the council's housing tenants or employees and have in consequence an effect on staff recruitment or the letting of houses. There are some topics of general interest to the local citizens on behalf of whom the council may deem itself the proper representative body to express opinion; but there are limits to this. Expression of opinion on foreign affairs, for example, or on aspects of national policy which are not the concern of local government, are not appropriate for debate by a local council.

Nowadays local authorities are less inhibited: many think that, as the representative voice of the community, they have a duty to express a view on contentious issues of national and international affairs.

7.53. A motion which is rejected must nevertheless be recorded in the book kept for that purpose and a note made to the effect that it was rejected.

7.54. A motion may also be rejected on the grounds that it is vague and

---

[69] W. Eric Jackson, *The Secretarial Practice of Local Authorities* (1953), p. 79.

equivocal in its terms: and in such circumstances it may properly be returned to the member with an indication to that effect and need not, it is submitted, be recorded in any way until it has been resubmitted in acceptable form. Whether a motion which is ungrammatical or otherwise imperfectly expressed but whose purport is clear should be corrected by the officers is a matter of judgement: if the grammatical error is a simple one it might be corrected but if the changes that ought to be made are extensive it would be wise for the officers tactfully to seek the member's prior approval before making corrections.

Debate on a motion

7.55. The meeting is not bound to pursue consideration of a motion in the form in which it is originally proposed or to come to any decision upon it at all. Original motions may be passed with or without amendment or may be thrown out, and the debate may at any time be interrupted either by the moving of a procedural (or dilatory) motion (see 7.69) or by a member raising a point of order: see 7.81.

Need a motion be seconded?

7.56. Notwithstanding that notice of motion has been duly given the motion must still be moved at the meeting. At common law it is not necessary that a motion should be seconded: in *Re Horbury Bridge Coal, Iron and Wagon Co.* (1879) James LJ said:[70]

> There is no law of the land which says that a motion cannot be put without a seconder and the objection that the amendment was not seconded cannot prevail.

In practice most local authorities require by standing orders that all motions – whether one of which notice has been given or otherwise – shall be seconded as a prerequisite to their being open to discussion. Where standing orders require a seconder and a motion is moved but not seconded it drops as a matter of course and the next business can be proceeded with.

7.57. Model standing order no. 10 (which deals fairly comprehensively with the rules of debate at council meetings) includes the following provision:

> (1) A motion or amendment shall not be discussed unless it has been proposed

---

[70] (1879) 11 Ch. D.109.

and seconded, and unless notice has already been given in accordance with standing order 6 it shall, if required by the mayor/chairman, be put into writing and handed to the mayor/chairman before it is further discussed or put to the meeting.

(2) A member when seconding a motion or amendment may, if he then declare his intention to do so, reserve his speech until a later period of the debate.

Alteration of motion

7.58. In the course of discussion on a motion – or even before discussion commences – the proposer may wish to make an alteration which he thinks might make the motion more acceptable to members. Model standing order no. 10 provides that:

> (9) A member may with the consent of the council signified without discussion:
> (a) alter a motion of which he has given notice; or
> (b) with the further consent of his seconder alter a motion which he has moved
>
> if (in either case) the alteration is one which could be made as an amendment thereto.

Withdrawal of motion

7.59. Model standing order no. 10, giving effect to the common law rule, provides for the withdrawal of a motion in these terms:

> (10) A motion or amendment may be withdrawn by the mover with the consent of his seconder and of the council, which shall be signified without discussion, and no member may speak upon it after the mover has asked permission for its withdrawal, unless such permission shall have been refused.

Amendments

Definition

7.60. An amendment is a formal proposal to vary the terms of a motion before the latter is adopted by the meeting. The motion in its original form, before amendment, is termed – as already indicated – the *original motion*. The original motion, altered by the incorporation therein of the amendments so far passed, is known as the main motion or *substantive motion*; and this substantive motion may be further amended.

Motions and amendments which may be moved without notice

7.61. It is appropriate at this stage to refer together both to motions and to amendments which may be moved without notice. Model standing order no. 7 is to the following effect:

> The following motions and amendments may be moved without notice:
> (1) Appointment of a chairman of the meeting at which the motion is made.
> (2) Motions relating to the accuracy of the minutes.
> (3) That an item of business specified in the summons have precedence.
> (4) Remission to a committee.
> (5) Appointment of a committee or members thereof, occasioned by an item mentioned in the summons to the meeting.
> (6) Adoption of reports and recommendations of committees or officers and any consequent resolutions.
> (7) That leave be given to withdraw a motion.
> (8) Extending the time limit for speeches.
> (9) Amendments to motions.
> (10) That the council proceed to the next business.
> (11) That the question be now put.
> (12) That the debate be now adjourned.
> (13) That the council do now adjourn.
> (14) Authorizing the sealing of documents.
> (15) Suspending standing orders, in accordance with standing order 40.
> (16) Motion under s.1(2) of the Public Bodies (Admission to Meetings) Act 1960 to exclude the public.
> (17) That a member named under standing order 12 be not further heard or do leave the meeting.
> (18) Inviting a member to remain under standing order 18 (pecuniary interest).
> (19) Giving consent of the council where the consent of the council is required by these standing orders.

Amendment to motions

7.62. There are well established rules governing amendments and these are well summarised in model standing order no. 10:

> (6) An amendment shall be relevant to the motion and shall be either:
> (a) to refer a subject of debate to a committee for consideration or reconsideration;
> (b) to leave out words;
> (c) to leave out words and insert or add others;
> (d) to insert or add words;
> but such omission, insertion or addition of words shall not have the effect of negativing the motion before the council.

(7) Only one amendment may be moved and discussed at a time and no further amendment shall be moved until the amendment under discussion has been disposed of.

[Provided that the mayor/chairman may permit two or more amendments to be discussed (but not voted on) together if circumstances suggest that this course would facilitate the proper conduct of the council's business.]

(8) If an amendment be lost, other amendments may be moved on the original motion. If an amendment be carried, the motion as amended shall take the place of the original motion and shall become the motion upon which any further amendment may be moved.

7.63. Not only must an amendment *not negative* the motion which it seeks to alter (because the same effect can be secured by voting against the motion) but it must be *pertinent and relevant* to the original motion (or otherwise a question may be brought before the council of which the requisite notice has not been given: see 7.48) and must be within the scope of the meeting (for the same reason).

7.64. There are circumstances during the discussion of contentious business when the chairman may have difficulty in interpreting the rules governing amendments. For example, an amendment may be moved which, otherwise consistent with the rules outlined above, virtually displaces the original motion. It is a matter of judgement whether such an amendment is acceptable (one local authority is known to accept amendments of this character provided the amendment is prefaced with the words *that the original motion be not approved and that . . .*). The chairman would probably be wise to allow rather than disallow amendments if thereby the sense of the meeting can finally be determined on the issue before it.

Amendments must be put to meeting

7.65. The chairman must put an amendment which has been moved (and, if standing orders so require, seconded)[71] unless it is:

(a) *ultra vires*, i.e. it is outside the scope of the meeting or beyond the council's powers;

(b) *irrelevant*, where it bears no relation to the original motion or subject-matter;

(c) *inconsistent*, where it is incompatible with a decision previously taken at the same meeting;

(d) *vexatious* and intended only to impede the transaction of business;

---

[71] An improper refusal to put an amendment will vitiate the decision to which the proposed amendment relates: *Henderson* v. *Bank of Australasia* (1890) 45 Ch. D.330.

or

(e) in *bona fide* exercise of his discretion as chairman he has grounds for excluding it by standing orders or resolution of the meeting itself.

Series of amendments

7.66. Each amendment must be voted separately. There can be no amendment of an amendment and if notice is given of several amendments these should be taken in due succession: the chairman should examine the amendments and determine the order in which they should be put to the meeting. No amendment can be considered which is inconsistent with an amendment already adopted or which reproduces an amendment previously rejected. There are circumstances when a motion cannot be amended, e.g. in the case of a special meeting of the council to pass a resolution in specific form to meet statutory requirements.

Order of debate

General considerations

7.67. Having now discussed the transaction of business by motions and amendments, it is necessary to deal with a miscellany of procedural matters which is often referred to collectively as the *order of debate*. Model standing order no. 10, for example, in the paragraphs not so far considered, provides as follows:

Only one member to stand at a time
(3) A member when speaking shall stand and address the mayor/chairman. If two or more members rise, the mayor/chairman shall call on one to speak; the other or others shall then sit. While a member is speaking the other members shall remain seated, unless rising to a point of order or in personal explanation.

Content and length of speeches
(4) A member shall direct his speech to the question under discussion or to a personal explanation or to a point of order. No speech shall exceed . . . minutes except by consent of the council.

When a member may speak again
(5) A member who has spoken on any motion shall not speak again whilst it is the subject of debate, except:
    (a) to speak once on an amendment moved by another member;
    (b) if the motion has been amended since he last spoke, to move a further amendment;
    (c) if his first speech was on an amendment moved by another member, to speak on the main issue, whether or not the amendment on which he spoke was carried;

(d) in exercise of a right of reply given by para. (11) or (13) of this standing order;

(e) on a point of order;

(f) by way of personal explanation.

Right of reply

(11) The mover of a motion has a right to reply at the close of the debate on the motion, immediately before it is put to the vote. If an amendment is moved, the mover of the original motion shall also have a right of reply at the close of the debate on the amendment, and shall not otherwise speak on the amendment. The mover of the amendment shall have no right of reply to the debate on his amendment.

Motions which may be moved during debate

(12) When a motion is under debate no other motion shall be moved except the following:

(a) to amend the motion;

(b) to adjourn the meeting;

(c) to adjourn the debate;

(d) to proceed to the next business;

(e) that the question be now put;

(f) that a member be not further heard;

(g) by the mayor/chairman under standing order 12(2) that a member do leave the meeting;

(h) a motion under s.1(2) of the Public Bodies (Admission to Meetings) Act 1960 to exclude the public.

Closure motions

(13) A member may move without comment at the conclusion of a speech of another member 'That the council proceed to the next business', 'That the question be now put', 'That the debate be now adjourned', or 'That the council do now adjourn', on the seconding of which the mayor/chairman shall proceed as follows:

(a) *on a motion to proceed to next business:* unless in his opinion the matter before the meeting has been insufficiently discussed, he shall first give the mover of the original motion a right of reply, and then put to the vote the motion to proceed to next business;

(b) *on a motion that the question be now put:* unless in his opinion the matter before the meeting has been insufficiently discussed, he shall first put to the vote the motion that the question be now put, and if it is passed then give the mover of the original motion his right of reply under para.11 of this standing order before putting his motion to the vote;

(c) *on a motion to adjourn the debate or the meeting:* if in his opinion the matter before the meeting has not been sufficiently discussed and cannot reasonably be sufficiently discussed on that occasion he shall put the adjournment motion to the vote without giving the mover of the original motion his right of reply on that occasion.

Points of order

(14) A member may rise on a point of order or in personal explanation, and shall be entitled to be heard forthwith. A point of order shall relate only to an alleged breach of a standing order or statutory provision and the member shall specify the standing order or statutory provision and the way in which he considers it has been broken. A personal explanation shall be confined to some material part of a former speech by him which may appear to have been misunderstood in the present debate.

(15) The ruling of the mayor/chairman on a point of order or on the admissibility of a personal explanation shall not be open to discussion.

Respect for chair

(16) Whenever the mayor/chairman rises during a debate a member then standing shall resume his seat and the council shall be silent.

As to content of speeches: see next paragraph; and as to points of order: see 7.81.

Content of speeches

7.68. The power vested in a chairman by common law to regulate the conduct of a meeting (see 7.30) and to preserve order (see 7.122) may be assumed to include power to direct a councillor to cease making unseemly remarks in the course of a speech. It could be helpful, however, if there is a standing order to such effect:

> The chairman shall check a member for irrelevance, tedious repetition, failure to address the chair, unbecoming language, or reflections of a personal character on another member. If the member disregards the chairman, the chairman may order him to end his speech and, if he considers it necessary, following a resolution of the council or on his own initiative, order his removal from the meeting.

When a standing order in these or like terms applies and a councillor makes a defamatory statement unchecked the chairman would not appear to incur liability for allowing the defamatory statement because (a) until the statement is made the chairman could hardly be expected to anticipate it, and (b) even if checked or unchecked further defamatory statements are made by a councillor the act of defamation is a personal liability upon the defamer. As to defamatory statements: see 5.58 *et seq.*

Procedural motions

7.69. Procedural or formal motions are designed to close the debate, either by forcing an immediate vote on the motion or amendment before the meeting or by postponing a decision on the motion or amendment: hence they are sometimes termed *closure* (as in model standing order no. 7: see 7.61), *dilatory*,[72] or *interruptive* motions. They cannot be moved by anyone who has moved or seconded or spoken on the original motion being debated; and no person may intervene in discussion on a particular motion by moving more than one formal motion.

7.70. The procedural motions include the following:

(a) the motion *to proceed to next business;*	referred to in
(b) the motion *'that the question be now put'*;	model
(c) the motion *to adjourn the debate;*	standing
(d) the motion *to adjourn the meeting;*	order no.7

and a variety of *suspensive motions*, i.e. those that suspend debate, including the motion *'that the question lie on the table'* but, most particularly within the local government context, the motion *'that the matter be referred back to committee'*.

The previous question

7.71. The *previous question* may be moved – usually in the form *'That the council proceed to the next business'* (or *'That the motion be not now put'*; or, simply, *'I move the previous question'*) – by any member who has not spoken on the original motion and provided no one else is speaking at the time. It derives its name from the fact that it proposes an independent issue which must be decided previously to the main issue. If properly seconded it may be discussed but cannot be amended; and if carried the original question is removed from the scope of the meeting and can only be revived by a motion at a subsequent meeting. If, however, the motion is lost then the implication is that the meeting desires the substantive question to be put to the vote forthwith and thus further discussion cannot be permitted. The mover of the previous question has no right of comment on the reply of the mover of the original motion.

'That the question be now put'

7.72. This motion, which is a form of closure, must be voted upon without debate after it has been moved and seconded – unless the chairman refuses to accept it on grounds that the matter before the meeting has been insufficiently discussed. If carried the main question must be put immedi-

---

[72] The term *dilatory* motion is best used to describe a motion which obstructs or frustrates the transaction of business.

ately after the mover of the original motion has been given his right of reply. If the matter under discussion is an amendment the closure affects only that amendment.

7.73. There is nothing to prevent the chairman himself applying the closure, with the consent of the meeting, if he is of the opinion that the views of the minority have been reasonably heard.[73] This he can do simply by calling on the mover of the motion to reply to the debate.

Adjournment of debate

7.74. This motion, which may seek to delay discussion on the question before the meeting either for a specified time or indefinitely, may be moved by any member other than the mover or seconder of the main question or the mover or seconder of any amendment or formal motion in reference thereto. No amendment is possible except as regards the period of suspension or the time to which discussion is to be postponed or the place to which adjournment is proposed: if the motion is not explicit as to this, then, depending on standing orders, the discussion on the main question will ordinarily be resumed at the next meeting of the council. Such a standing order may be to this effect:

> When a motion that the debate be now adjourned is carried the discussion shall be resumed at the next meeting of the council, when the member who moved its adjournment shall be entitled to speak first.

If the motion is rejected a second motion for adjournment may be moved during the same meeting after the lapse of a reasonable time or such period as may be prescribed in standing orders.

Adjournment of meeting

7.75. A motion to adjourn the meeting (a suspensive motion) is a more drastic proposition than any of the procedural motions so far considered, for it operates if carried to bring about a suspension of the entire proceedings either for a particular period or indefinitely.[74] An adjournment may be:

(a) *sine die*, i.e. for an unspecified period of indefinite duration; or

(b) for an *unspecified period* not exceeding a given maximum; or

---

[73] *Wall* v. *Exchange & Northern Assets Corpn* [1898] 2 Ch. 469.

[74] There is no statutory power to adjourn a council meeting but at common law an assembly is deemed to be invested with the power to adjourn its proceedings of its own volition: *Stoughton* v. *Reynolds* (1737) Fortescue's Rep. 168.

(c) until *a date specified*, or for *a fixed interval of time*; or

(d) to *another place*; or

(e) for *a given time and to a named place.*

7.76. It seems that, even where certain matters must be transacted on a particular day, a local authority has an implied power to adjourn so as to enable business which could not be finished for lack of time on the day fixed to be brought to its conclusion;[75] and this inherent power exists also where it is not possible to transact the whole of the business for which a meeting has been called.[76]

7.77. The motion to adjourn may be proposed at the close of any speech but cannot be moved by a person who has already spoken on the question then before the meeting or who has moved or seconded an amendment or formal motion in relation to it. When moved and seconded the motion creates an independent question for the *immediate* consideration of the meeting, and discussion on the substantive question (and on the previous question if it has been moved) must give way to the motion to adjourn the meeting.

7.78. Discussion on the motion is governed by the ordinary rules of debate (except in so far as they may be altered by standing orders) but:

(a) the mover has no right of reply nor has the owner of the original motion;

(b) no amendment is permissible other than alteration of the time or place of adjournment (or both);

(c) subject to standing orders the motion to adjourn may be renewed after the lapse of a reasonable time in the course of the same meeting.

Standing orders sometimes limit the effect of the motion, e.g.:

> When a motion 'that the council do now adjourn' is carried, the council, before adjourning, may take the remaining business on the agenda which is unopposed, and the question under debate, if any, shall stand adjourned to the next meeting.

In cases where such a standing order applies, the chairman after the motion has been carried should seek the view of the meeting as to the unopposed business.

Adjournment by chairman

7.79. The power of adjournment vests in the full assembly: it arises from 'the common right, which is in the whole assembly, where all are upon an

---

[75] *Rex* v. *Carmarthen Corpn.* (1813) 1 M.&S.697.
[76] *Kerr* v. *Wilkie* (1860) 6 Jur. (NS) 383.

equal foot'.[77] This means that only in exceptional circumstances, e.g. in the case of persistent disorder, can the chairman order an adjournment: see 7.122.

7.80. If a chairman illegally declares a meeting to be adjourned, e.g. in circumstances where it is patently not the wish of the majority of those present, then after the chairman has left the members may elect someone to preside over the transaction of the remainder of the business, and their act and the business transacted are valid.[78] In *National Dwellings Society* v. *Sykes, supra,* Chitty J said:

> ... in my opinion, the power which has been contended for is not within the scope of the authority of the chairman: namely, to stop the meeting at his own will and pleasure. The meeting is called for the particular purposes ... According to the constitution ... a certain officer has to preside. He presides with reference to the business which is then to be transacted. In my opinion, he cannot say, after that business has been opened, 'I will have no more to do with it; I will not let this meeting proceed; I will stop it; I declare the meeting dissolved and I leave the chair'. In my opinion, that is not within his power. The meeting by itself can resolve to go on with the business which the other chairman forgetful of his duty or violating his duty, has tried to stop because the proceedings have taken a turn which he himself does not like.

What if the chairman of the council, who must preside if present at the council meeting (see 7.24), having improperly declared the meeting adjourned, remains in the council chamber? If he does remain he cannot be deemed to be 'in the meeting' and the council could elect someone else to preside: see 5.32.

Points of order

7.81. A point of order is an objection submitted to the chairman for decision respecting any irregularity in the constitution or conduct of the meeting. The more usual irregularities include:

(a) the use of irrelevant or improper language;

(b) that a quorum is not present;

(c) that an amendment is a simple negative of the motion before the meeting;

(d) that the motion is *ultra vires* or not within the scope of the notice given;

(e) that no question is before the meeting, e.g. where a motion has not been seconded (if this is required by standing orders);

(f) any non-compliance with standing orders.

---

[77] *Stoughton* v. *Reynolds* (1736) 2 Strange 1044.
[78] *R.* v. *Doris* (1908) 45 ILT 267.

7.82. A member may raise a point of order at any time without notice. It must, however, be raised immediately the alleged irregularity or impropriety becomes apparent. The member who is speaking must stop, sit down, and allow the chairman to make a decision; and the chairman's decision is conclusive and final. Ordinarily no debate is permitted on a point of order; but some authorities consider that 'a terse discussion of the point raised may be allowed'.[79]

7.83. A point of order relates to procedure: it is not concerned with the arguments or the principles or the political views put forward in debate or with the truth or falsehood, correctness or incorrectness of statements made in the course of debate. A difference of opinion is not a point of order. Nor may a member making a point of order abuse it by making a speech.

7.84. A useful standing order is as follows:

> On any member indicating a desire to raise a point of order he shall state at the outset the standing order or rule of debate considered to have been infringed. Every point of order shall be decided by the chairman before the debate proceeds and his decision shall be final and cannot be discussed.

Personal explanation

7.85. A member may find that he has made a mis-statement which is being quoted by a later speaker or that the latter has misunderstood him or misquoted him. In such circumstances the member is allowed to rise on a point of explanation and to interrupt the speaker for a few moments while he (the member) makes the desired correction. This prevents the speaker developing his argument on wrong facts or figures or a misunderstanding and so wasting the time of the meeting. The concession is one which must be carefully controlled by the chairman.

Consideration of committee reports
General approach

7.86. The consideration of committee reports is ordinarily the main item of business of the full assembly. These reports – whose style will depend upon local practice – (a) record matters dealt with by committees under delegated powers and submitted to the council for information, and (b) submit recommendations for the council's approval with or without amendment or rejection or reference back. It is the practice of some local authorities to require the submission of the full minutes of committees, or

---

[79] Shaw & Smith, *The Law of Meetings*, 4th edn (1974), p. 75.

an edited version or a selection of those minutes containing recommendations for the council's consideration. This gives rise to procedural problems because the *minutes* of committee proceedings are a record of business already transacted and thus cannot be altered in the full assembly. For this, and other persuasive reasons discussed later (see 12.38), most authorities today make use of the report system, which requires committees to submit a *report* on their proceedings, with any necessary recommendations, instead of the minutes.

Procedure

7.87. The practice in dealing with committee business (whether submitted by way of reports or minutes) varies between authorities. Some prescribe by standing orders the order in which each committee's report will be taken. Others may vary the order from meeting to meeting if an alteration is thought likely to facilitate the transaction of business. Some consider and debate as the meeting thinks appropriate each report in turn. Others require the chairman to call over all the reports first to ascertain which items are agreed and which may be opposed: if any member raises objection to any item, that paragraph is put aside to be dealt with after all unopposed committee business has been disposed of.[80]

Reception of reports

7.88. Although some local authorities regard a reference to a committee's report on the agenda as sufficient presentation, in which case the chairman calls over the report paragraph by paragraph, most first require each committee chairman in turn (or someone on his behalf in each case) when invited so to do by the chairman to bring the report formally before the council for consideration by moving *'That the report of the . . . committee be received'*. The motion is regarded as a procedural one, not requiring a seconder and one not to be debated; indeed, if the motion were voted upon and rejected the effect would be that the report had not been received which, it has been said, 'is absurd since the council has already had it and

---

[80] The Maud Committee in its report, vol. 5, para.21, commented thus: 'In a very large proportion of authorities there is no spotlighting of items from the committees for special discussion. Each committee chairman presents the whole of his committee's minutes and has to be prepared for questions and discussion on any matter dealt with in them. In certain council meetings we attended the mayor or chairman or the committee chairman concerned read out the number of every minute, or of every page of the minutes, to give members a chance to come in at an appropriate point. This was usually done so rapidly that members had to be very fast to seize an opportunity, and in some cases when they spoke on a matter with reference to the wrong minute had obviously lost their place.'

debated it!'[81] In any case if a report is not received, what happens to it? It cannot dissolve into the air! To avoid such a nonsense arising, standing orders can make provision to the effect that:

> No amendment to the motion for the reception of a report shall be in order, except that consideration of the report be postponed or that the report be referred back to the committee for further consideration.

Motion 'That the report be received'

7.89. The motion *'That the report be received'* is wholly appropriate and can be resolved upon in those terms where the whole of the report records action taken in pursuance of delegated powers or otherwise contains no recommendations calling for action by the council. The use of the word 'received' indicates that the council has had the report before it but does not necessarily approve or disapprove it. There are variants, useful in distinguishing the 'reception' of the report for procedural purposes and its 'reception' in another sense: thus the motion could be *'That the report be accepted'* or *'That the report be noted'*.

Amendments by leave of the council

7.90. If the committee chairman, or someone on his behalf, wishes to make an amendment to the report (which, strictly, may only be done with the leave of the council) or proposes to speak himself in explanation or elaboration of a particular paragraph in the report, it is usual for an indication to that effect to be given in moving the reception of the report. Thus the committee chairman may say *'I move the reception of the report and'* – as the case may be – *'with the leave of the council wish to make a correction on paragraph . . .'* or *'I would like to say something on paragraph . . .'* The committee chairman will then make his correction or statement when the paragraph concerned is called from the chair.

Adoption of report

7.91. Where a committee report contains recommendations on which there is no dissent, the motion at the conclusion of the call-over of the report, moved either by the committee chairman or the chairman of the meeting, is to the effect *'That the report be approved and adopted'*. If any recommendation is amended in the course of the report's consideration

[81] W. Eric Jackson, *The Secretarial Practice of Local Authorities* (1953), p. 85.

then the motion at the conclusion of the call-over is to the effect *'That the report, as amended, be approved and adopted'*.

Reference back

7.92. It is in order, upon the reception of a committee report or later in the course of debate, for a *motion* (not an *amendment*, for the motion for reception is procedural only) to be moved *'That the report be referred back to the committee'* either *'for further information'* or *'for further consideration'* or with an instruction that some specified action be taken. Or, of course, there can be a reference back of a paragraph of a report. (The term *reference back* may seem tautologous to the purist: indeed, in *Usage and Abusage* Eric Partridge includes 'refer back' in his 'shortlist of very common tautological expressions'. It can be justified in meetings procedure, however, on the grounds that the subject-matter in a reference back is not merely being referred to a committee – for it was so referred in the first place – but is being referred again, i.e. referred back to the committee for review or further consideration or whatever it may be.)

Withdrawal of report

7.93. Alternatively, the committee chairman might decide, with the leave of the council, to withdraw a report or a paragraph therein – either in the light of the debate which has taken place or because circumstances have arisen since the committee's meeting which make such a course desirable. The withdrawal of a report or one of its paragraphs should be regarded as exceptional: it may be a tactical move politically to avoid defeat on a proposal of importance but, as a general rule, committee proceedings placed before the full assembly with the object patently of being acted upon should not ordinarily be withdrawn.

Regulation by standing orders

7.94. The particular procedure favoured by a local authority in dealing with committee reports at a council meeting should be laid down in standing orders. The following example is from the standing orders of the London Borough of Hammersmith and Fulham:[82]

---

[82] In this case it is the practice for the local authority to require the report of each committee to be in two parts: part I dealing with referred matters upon which recommendations are included for the council's consideration; and part II containing a report on matters dealt with by the committee under delegated powers.

Manner of dealing with committee reports at council meetings

(a) The report of a committee shall be presented to the council and its reception moved by the chairman of the meeting at which the report arose, or may in his absence be presented by some other member who was present at that meeting or who shall have been deputed by the chairman of the committee or called upon by the mayor so to move.

(b) The mover of the report shall move 'that the report of the . . . committee held on . . . be received, approved and adopted'. When moving the report the mover may briefly address the council. No seconder shall be required for this motion and the mover may, with the consent of the council signified by a show of hands, amend the report or withdraw an item. Thereafter the order of proceedings shall be as follows:

(i) The mayor shall ascertain whether any member wishes to reserve any item of the report for question or discussion (known as 'reserved items'). When so ascertained the remaining items shall without further formality be taken as received, approved and adopted in the terms of the motion.

(ii) The mayor shall then take each reserved item in numerical order and the member reserving the item and any other member may ask the mover one question and one supplementary question, unless the mayor determines that sufficient questions have been asked having regard to the replies being given, the time taken or the complexity of the subject matter. The mover may decline to answer an oral question, and shall decline to answer when the matter is a question of administrative detail or where written notice under standing order 18 would have been appropriate.

(iii) When the questions on each reserved item have been taken, the mayor shall ask for comments and any member may then speak on an item for not more than five minutes and may move reference back or an amendment of any part I item with or without an instruction. Such reference back or an amendment shall be seconded and debated in accordance with standing orders.

(iv) In respect of a part II item no reference back shall be moved, but a member may move in respect of an individual item any one of the following motions:

(A) That it be an instruction to the committee to submit a report giving further information regarding the matter reported in paragraph . . .

(B) That the council regret the decision arrived at by the committee as reported in paragraph . . .

(C) That it be an instruction to the committee . . . and any such motion shall be moved and seconded but no amendments shall be allowed in relation to motions (A) and (B) above. Motion (C) shall be limited to an instruction to the committee concerned as to the action to be followed by it or as to consideration to be borne in mind in future cases of a like kind and shall be in writing. Subject as above standing orders shall have effect in relation to these motions and, if applicable, to amendments. Any such motion shall be seconded and may be debated and amended in accordance with standing order 25.

Rescission of resolutions

Not at meeting at which passed

7.95. It is a widely accepted rule – and a matter of common sense also – that a resolution cannot be rescinded at the meeting at which it is passed or adopted, even though all present are prepared to consent to such a proposition. Different considerations might apply in the case of a committee meeting: see 11.34.

If passed at earlier meeting

7.96. A resolution passed at one meeting may be rescinded at a subsequent meeting provided there are no practical obstacles, e.g. where action taken under the original resolution would make its rescission a nullity or the rights of third parties who have acted on the earlier decision need to be taken into account and safeguarded. A proposal to rescind a resolution must be treated as an original motion[83] unless it arises out of a committee report. Local authorities normally make provision in standing orders to control the rescission of resolutions (and to restrict the frequency with which unsuccessful motions can be revived). Model standing order no. 14 is to this effect:

> No motion to rescind any resolution passed within the preceding six months, and no motion or amendment to the same effect as one which has been rejected within the preceding six months, shall be proposed unless the notice thereof given in pursuance of standing order 6[84] bears the names of at least . . . members of the council.[85] When any such motion or amendment has been disposed of by the council, it shall not be open to any member to propose a similar motion within a further period of six months.
>
> Provided that this standing order shall not apply to motions moved in pursuance of a recommendation of a committee.

The kind of decisions which can be rescinded are, generally speaking, those which have determined the authority's policy or which otherwise are of continuing effect. And there is a category of decisions which can be rescinded only in special circumstances – *revoked* is a more appropriate term – which include, e.g. the revocation of planning permission with consequent liability to pay compensation.

---

[83] See *Mayer v. Burslem Local Board, ante.*
[84] This is a reference to the standing order regulating the giving of notice of original motions: see 7.49.
[85] A footnote to standing order no. 14 says: 'This figure might be the same as the quorum.'

Rescission of a rescission

7.97. Where a resolution is rescinded and later the rescinding resolution is itself rescinded then, in the absence of any clear indication to contrary effect, the original resolution is revived.[86] As to whether a resolution dismissing an officer is a resolution rescinding the resolution by which he was appointed is a matter for speculation:[87] as a general rule the purported rescission of a resolution is of no effect if executive action has been taken under the original resolution and the intention is to invalidate what has properly been done thereunder.

Voting

General considerations

7.98. As indicated earlier (see 1.35), in all ordinary instances questions coming or arising before a local authority are required to be decided by a majority of the members present and voting thereon at a properly constituted meeting of the authority.[88] In the case of principal councils the method of voting is not prescribed by statute; in the case of parish and community councils the voting is by show of hands unless standing orders otherwise provide;[89] and any member may 'on requisition' require that the voting shall be recorded so as to show whether each member present and voting gave his vote for or against the question.[90] In the case of parish and community meetings a question is similarly decided as a rule by show of hands in the first instance (although the statute does not expressly so stipulate), and the decision of the person presiding as to the result of the voting is final 'unless a poll is demanded'.[91]

7.99. Model standing order no. 15 is as follows:

> *County councils and borough councils*
> The mode of voting at meetings of the council shall be by show of hands and on the requisition of any member of the council made before the vote is taken [and supported by . . . other members who signify their support by rising in their places], the voting on any question shall be recorded so as to show

---

[86] See *Weir* v. *Fermanagh County Council* [1913] 1 IR 63, 193; and see also as to rescission *R.* v. *Tralee* UDC [1913] 2 IR 59.

[87] See *Ex-parte Richards* (1878) 3 QBD 368; *sub. nom. R.* v. *Jones*, 42 JP 614.

[88] Local Government Act 1972, sch.12, para.49(1).

[89] *Ibid.* sch.12, paras.13(1), 29(1).

[90] *Ibid.* sch.12, paras.13(2), 29(2).

[91] *Ibid.* sch.12, paras.34(2), 18(2). It is expressly provided that each elector eligible to attend may give one vote and no more on any question, whether at a meeting or at a poll consequent thereon: paras.18(1), 34(1).

whether each member present gave his vote for or against that question or abstained from voting.

or

The mode of voting at meetings of the council shall be by show of hands: Provided that on the requisition of any member of the council made before the vote is taken [and supported by . . . other members who signify their support by rising in their places], the voting on any question shall be by roll-call and shall be recorded so as to show how each member present and voting gave his vote. The name of any member present and not voting shall also be recorded.

Urban and rural district councils and parish councils
If on the requisition of a member of the council the voting on any question is recorded, there shall also be recorded the name of any member then present who abstained from voting.

Meaning of 'present and voting'

7.100. Members present at a meeting who do not vote[92] or are prohibited from voting on the particular question before the meeting are nevertheless present for purposes of forming the necessary quorum; and a bare majority of those who in fact vote is sufficient to pass a resolution even if that number is less than the quorum. If, however, members under a disability are excluded from the meeting by standing orders (see 5.30) or themselves voluntarily leave the council chamber until the particular matter is disposed of, they are not 'present'; and it may be that a member who has declared himself disabled from taking part, but who has not actually been excluded, must be regarded as technically not present until that business has been disposed of.[93]

Who may vote

7.101. Council members at a council meeting, if 'present' in the sense just referred to, i.e. are under no legal disability from voting, are entitled to vote. It has been held that persons who are *de facto* councillors may vote until such time as they are in fact unseated.[94]

---

[92] Members who are present and do not vote may, in certain circumstances, be regarded as having acquiesced in the decision taken: see 5.41. 'There are circumstances in which a council member may well wish his abstention to be recorded: where, for example, the motion is to the effect that an officer shall be reprimanded and the individual member feels he cannot vote against it because he regards the reprimand as totally inadequate and does not want his name recorded against the only sanction likely and so leave a false impression on the record': see Ivan Brown, 'Abstention from Voting' (1975) 39 *Local Government Review* 762.

[93] This view is taken by the learned editors of *Lumley's Public Health*, 12th edn, vol. XIV, p. 547.

[94] *Holden* v. *Southwark Corpn* [1921] 1 Ch. 550; 85 JP 126.

7.102. It may be that a member who is clearly under a disability persists in speaking and voting. As indicated above, such a member is probably technically not present and therefore the chairman of the meeting would be justified in refusing to count his vote 'for the "vote" has been cast illegally and . . . can be said not to be a vote at all'.[95]

Methods of voting

7.103. Despite differences in the words of the statute most local authorities proceed by taking most votes by show of hands and the chairman will ordinarily make his decision on the evidence of the show of hands without taking a count. There is no reason, however (at least in the case of principal councils) why a vote should not be taken in some other way, e.g. by voice or by conduct (such as nodding the head): and it is well established that there can be an implied vote in favour by silent assent.[96]

7.104. In some authorities mechanical devices have been installed in order to expedite the taking of votes; but these would not be permissible in the case of parish and community meetings.

7.105. There are circumstances where it is impracticable to reach what might be termed a fairly representative decision by simple majority vote, e.g. in the case of the election of persons to various offices where there are several nominations, or in the selection of an individual from a shortlist of candidates for a staff appointment when the interviewing panel cannot agree. Local authorities as a rule adopt some kind of balloting system which provides for the choice of nominee who secures the greatest number of individual votes, but this can be an imperfect mechanism because it can produce a perverse result, e.g. the choice may fall on someone with fewer votes than the aggregate of votes for other candidates. Model standing order no. 16 makes this provision:

> Where there are more than two persons nominated for any position to be filled by the council, and of the votes given there is not a majority in favour of one person, the name of the person having the least number of votes shall be struck off the list and a fresh vote shall be taken, and so on until a majority of votes is given in favour of one person.

[95] This view is taken by C. A. Cross, *Principles of Local Government Law*, 5th edn, p. 56, who quotes in support *Nell v. Longbottom* [1894] 1 QB 767, in which the mayor-elect of Louth voted for himself, and it was held that his vote was invalid and could not therefore be regarded as having been cast.

[96] Where an interested person was present at a meeting at which a resolution was carried unanimously and so entered on the minutes and the defendant did not dissent or abstain from voting though he did not expressly indicate assent, it was held that he had voted for the resolution: *Everett v. Griffiths* [1924] 1 KB 941; 88 JP 93.

7.106. At least one local authority – Medina Borough Council – uses the single transferable vote system[97] where there are more nominees than places available on the election of the mayor, committee chairmen and vice-chairmen, and in choosing councillors to serve on committees, sub-committees, and as representatives on outside bodies. Its standing order provides:

> . . . If the number of nominations exceeds the number of vacancies there shall be a secret ballot of the members present at the meeting in which each member of the council shall vote for as many candidates as there are vacancies to be filled. Vacancies shall thereupon be filled using the single transferable vote system. Any ballot shall be conducted by the secretary whose return shall be final and conclusive.

No other local authority in this country, as far as is known, has adopted the single transferable vote system for internal elections but if Widdicombe's proposals for proportionality on local authority committees (see 9.59) were to be pursued it is likely that the system would receive greater attention. The Electoral Reform Society (whose principal object is to promote the adoption of proportional representation for elections in the British Isles and elsewhere) points out, however, that it is inconsistent to argue for proportionality on council committees if the council itself is 'distorted or lopsided in its political composition due to the workings of the first-past-the-post system rather than the way in which the electors actually voted'.

Challenge to chairman's ruling

7.107. Any challenge to a chairman's ruling, including his decision on a vote on a show of hands, must be made promptly at the time.[98] A show of hands, convenient though it is at both council and committee meetings, is 'only a rude and imperfect declaration of . . . sentiments'. Where it is believed that the chairman's declaration of the result of a show of hands is in error the proper course is to call for the voting to be determined more

---

[97] The single transferable vote system has long been used in Northern Ireland. In the Electoral Law (Northern Ireland) Order 1972 it is defined thus: 'transferable vote' means a vote (a) capable of being given so as to indicate the voter's preference for the candidates in order; and (b) capable of being transferred to the next choice when the vote is not required to give a prior choice the necessary quota of votes or when, owing to the deficiency in the number of votes given for a prior choice, that choice is eliminated from the list of candidates. For an explanation of how the system works see the several publications of the Electoral Reform Society, including particularly Robert A. Newland and Frank S. Britton, *How to Conduct an Election by the Single Transferable Vote.*

[98] *Anthony* v. *Seger* (1789) 1 Hag. Con. 9.

accurately in some such manner as described in the foregoing paragraphs.[99]

Taking a poll

7.108. Exceptionally in the case of parish and community meetings there is provision in law for the taking of a poll in certain circumstances.[100] A poll may be demanded before the conclusion of a meeting on any question arising thereat and must be taken if the person presiding consents or the poll is demanded by not less than 10, or one-third, of the electors present at the meeting, whichever is the less. A poll so demanded is a poll of the local government electors and is conducted substantially as for the election of parish or community councillors as the case may be.[101]

Abstention

7.109. It may be convenient here to discuss more fully a point referred to earlier: see 5.41. There is a presumption that councillors, and co-opted members of committees, who merely abstain from voting thereby assent to the resolution and where no formal vote is taken all those present are presumed to have assented; and this is important in determining personal liability for surcharge:[102] see 5.42. Without this presumption there would be endless argument over whether an individual should or should not be held liable where he did not actively vote against unlawful expenditure. Nevertheless, other evidence of opposition may suffice for exemption from personal surcharge.

7.110. The principles involved are drawn from common law – mostly in cases which concern appeals against surcharge by the district auditor. If a councillor votes against a proposal and his vote is not recorded in the minutes, other evidence may protect him.[103] And in the classic case of *Roberts* v. *Hopwood* (1925)[104] four councillors who had initially been surcharged were able to show to the satisfaction of the court that they

---

[99] *Cornwall* v. *Woods* (1846) 4 Notes of Cases 555, where the court refused to upset a decision of a meeting of parishioners at which a rate was fixed because, if the chairman was in error, the correct procedure should have been to call for a division or a poll.

[100] Local Government Act 1972, sch.12, paras.18, 34.

[101] *Question* in *ibid.* paras.18(4) and 34(4) refers to the same sort of question as in paras.18(2) and 34(2): therefore a poll can be demanded only on a question which has been the subject of a vote at the parish or community meeting: see *Bennett* v. *Chappell* [1966] Ch. 391; [1965] 3 All ER 130 CA, Winn LJ *dubitante.*

[102] A record of abstentions from voting has the advantage of accounting for all members present at the time the vote was taken.

[103] *Attorney-General* v. *Tottenham Local Board* (1872) 27 LT 440.

[104] [1925] AC 578; [1925] All ER 24; 89 JP 105.

dissented from the motion to incur unlawful expenditure. In another case Devlin J said:[105]

> No one should suppose that the mere failure to vote against an illegal resolution necessarily entails the consequences which have followed in this case.

The principle that abstention may amount to acquiescence is at least partly based on the duty which a councillor undertakes in making his declaration of acceptance of office.[106]

7.111. What if a councillor absents himself from a council or committee meeting knowing that a proposal to incur unlawful expenditure is to be put forward at the meeting? Is he not in breach of his duty? Regard must be had to all the surrounding circumstances. An absentee for good reason is not likely to incur personal liability; but inability to attend a meeting at which a matter is finally decided does not absolve a councillor from doing what he can to oppose the illegality.[107] An eminent former district auditor and inspector of audit has said this of an unreported case (*Barnes* v. *District Auditor for No. 11 District* (1976)) in which Watkins J declared that liability could arise 'by either action or inaction':[108]

> Special consideration was given to the position of certain individual members. Two members of the old council had not been present at council meetings at which resolutions had been passed authorising expenditure held to be illegal. They had been present at earlier committee meetings when the proposals had been discussed and officers had advised of their illegality. The district auditor found that they were aware that the proposals were to be considered by the council at the meetings from which they were absent, and that they knew or ought to have known that the proposals were illegal. He held that they were therefore under a duty to attend the council meetings and to oppose the proposals or, if they were unable to attend the council meetings, to take such steps as they would to make known their opposition. Since they failed in this duty he held that they shared responsibility for authorising or incurring the expenditure and also that loss was caused by their negligence and misconduct.

One man, one vote

7.112. The practice of voting by show of hands means that each person present at a meeting shall put up one hand only and so record one vote. It is,

---

[105] *Rothnie* v. *Dearne UDC* (1951) LGR 123.
[106] *Asher* v. *Secretary of State* [1974] Ch. 208. As to acceptance of office: see 5.3.
[107] See Raymond S. B. Knowles, 'Abstain from all intentional wrongdoing . . .' (1982) 146 *Local Government Review* 107.
[108] Reginald Jones in *Local Government Audit Law*, 1981.

in any case, a common law rule that every person voting at a meeting is reckoned as one vote:[109] that each voter is accorded one vote unless there exists, in some form, a specific provision to the contrary[110] – as in the case, of course, of a chairman's second or casting vote (dealt with in 7.114).

7.113. The principle of *one man, one vote* means that on each issue on which a vote is taken a person may vote once only, either for or against. He cannot properly vote both for and against even though this could be said to have the same effect as an abstention because the vote for and the vote against cancel each other out; nor even, it would seem, to correct an error he made in voting in the first place[111] (see 7.120) or to suggest by the record that a quorum was present when it was not.[112]

Chairman's casting vote

7.114. Although at common law the person presiding at a meeting has no casting vote,[113] the chairman of every local authority meeting, i.e. a council or committee or subcommittee or like meeting, has a second or casting vote which he may exercise where there is an equality of votes.[114]

7.115. What the term *a second or casting vote* means – and the meaning might have been clearer if the term had been 'a second or *a* casting vote' – is that the chairman has a second vote if he has already voted as a member, i.e. with the body of the meeting, or a casting vote if he has not already voted as a member and does not vote in his capacity as a member. In other words, if there is an equality of votes, whether or not the voting includes a vote by the chairman, the chairman may 'break the deadlock' by then using his casting vote. If the chairman does not elect to use his second or casting vote in this way the proposition falls to the ground, i.e. it is not carried. In the case of a controversial question or in other instances where an affirmative vote is not required as a matter of urgency, the chairman may choose not to exercise his second or casting vote on the grounds

---

[109] *Rex* v. *Rector of Birmingham* (1837) 1 A.& E.254 pp. 259, 260.

[110] *Re Horbury Bridge Coal, Iron & Waggon Co.* (1879) 11 Ch. D.109.

[111] No authoritative decision exists as to whether an error on the part of a voter in giving his vote can be corrected. When the result has been declared the voting is regarded as closed: before the declaration the chairman could presumably exercise a discretion to allow a voter to correct an error.

[112] In July 1975 in the House of Commons three MPs cast their vote twice, i.e. both for and against a motion in an attempt, unsuccessfully as it happened, and not seriously it was said, to achieve a quorum on the record and so enable a resolution to be passed to which it was known the majority was not opposed. The ruse was discovered and the Whips concerned had to apologise.

[113] *Nell* v. *Longbottom* [1894] 1 QB 767.

[114] Local Government Act 1972, sch.12, para.39(2).

(though he is not bound to explain his action[115]) that in his impartial capacity as chairman he ought not to determine an issue on which opinion is equally divided or where the matter can be raised again at a later date.[116]

7.116. Examples may help clarify what a chairman may or may not do. Suppose, after a motion has been moved and seconded and the chairman asks those present to signify, first those in favour and three members so signify, and then those against and three members so signify, the chairman may use his casting vote. If, however, when the proposition has been put, three members, including the chairman, vote in favour and three members vote against, the chairman may use his second vote in favour. The preferred opinion seems to be (although there is some doubt as to whether it could be sustained) that the chairman cannot withhold his ordinary vote and then purport to give two votes when it is evident how the voting is going, i.e. he cannot properly say when there are, for example, two votes for and three against a proposition: 'I'm in favour of the motion so it's a tie and I'll use my casting or second vote to carry the motion'. He can, however, give a contingent casting vote in certain circumstances: see next paragraph.

Contingent casting vote

7.117. A casting vote may be given contingently in circumstances where the chairman has good reason for believing that one of the votes cast may be invalid. Thus in *Bland* v. *Buchanan* (1901)[117] both petitioner and respondent were candidates for the office of mayor of a borough. The mayor in office presided at the election. Sixteen votes, including the mayor's first vote, were cast for the respondent and 15 for the petitioner. The mayor, with good reason for believing that one of the votes cast for the respondent might be impeached, purported to give a casting vote for the respondent. The casting vote was held valid in these circumstances.

---

[115] 'The chairman does not have to explain or justify his choice – though perhaps some might think it only fair that he should say why he has taken one view rather than another. Nor need he, indeed, take a reasoned decision. He can, like the chairman recently of the North Cornwall District Council, toss a coin to settle the matter – though the chairman concerned did explain his otherwise seemingly capricious action by saying he did not believe that planning decisions should be up to one man alone . . . By flipping a coin . . . he seems to have incurred criticism of behaving flippantly. But why? . . . in any case a returning officer decides an election by the drawing of lots if two candidates secure the same number of votes. Why not a committee chairman when faced with much the same sort of decision?': Editorial in 141 *Local Government Review* (1977) 622.

[116] Of course a chairman may not regard his role as impartial where he has been put into the chair by the ruling party group or where there is a hung council.

[117] [1901] 2 KB 75.

The moment of decision

7.118. We have considered earlier when a resolution becomes effective (see 1.46). But when, precisely, does a meeting commit itself to a decision on a vote? Suppose, after a show of hands on a motion but before a requisition, i.e. a recording of the vote, is demanded (either under standing orders or, in the case of a parish or community council, under statutory provisions), a late-arriving member turns up and demands to be included in the voting. Is this permissible or is the requisition a clarification of the voting already under way, i.e. merely machinery for ascertaining accurately what the sense of the meeting was on the discussion which has preceded it?

7.119. The answer is that a member present at a meeting is entitled to vote at any time before the chairman declares the outcome of the voting *in a final way*. Thus, where a requisition is demanded after a show of hands (and, as indicated above, it must be demanded immediately: see 7.107), a decision has not yet been made and there is nothing to stop a member who was not present at the show of hands from voting on the requisition or to prevent a member who voted one way at the show of hands changing his mind and voting differently. Just when a vote has finally been settled is a question of fact which must rest with the chairman. See also the discussion at 11.34 on when a committee decision has been finalised.

Voting under misapprehension

7.120. It is not good practice to allow a member to alter his vote after he has cast it. Except, therefore, where a member changes his mind before the final declaration by the chairman of the outcome of the vote (see the foregoing paragraph), a member who has voted under a misapprehension ought not to be allowed subsequently to alter his vote.[118]

Preservation of order
Chairman's powers and duties

7.121. The chairman of a meeting is entitled to call upon any disorderly person, whether councillor or stranger, to behave properly. If that person continues to misbehave then, if the person is a stranger (i.e. a member of the public or, conceivably, an officer) he should be asked to withdraw from

---

[118] This is Parliamentary practice. 'A member who has voted under a misapprehension will be allowed to alter his vote provided that he makes his request before the numbers have been declared from the chair': Erskine May, *Parliamentary Practice*, 20th edn, p. 675.

the meeting; and if he refuses the chairman may direct his removal by such force as may be reasonably necessary for the disorderly person's expulsion.[119] If the person is a councillor he should be asked to withdraw voluntarily; and if he refuses, the chairman's most practical course is to suspend or adjourn the meeting temporarily: see 7.124. The distinction is important because a stranger is present by licence on what are private premises (and this is the case even though there is a statutory right for the public to have access to local authority meetings), whereas a councillor is present by right of his office and cannot be excluded from attending.[120]

7.122. Where there is unruly behaviour by several persons, whether councillors or strangers or both, so that the continued transaction of business is impracticable, the chairman may (and in practice ought to) suspend the meeting temporarily until order can be restored: *suspend* is a more appropriate term than *adjourn* in such circumstances, although the terms are interchangeable. Thus, in *John v. Rees* (1969),[121] Megarry J said this (and the learned judge's views merit quoting at length now that, regrettably, violent disorder at council meetings has become common):

> The first duty of the chairman of a meeting is to keep order if he can. If there is disorder his duty, I think, is to make earnest and sustained efforts to restore order, and for this purpose to summon to his aid any officers or others whose assistance is available. If all his efforts are in vain, he should endeavour to put into operation whatever provisions for adjournment there are in the rules, as by obtaining a resolution to adjourn. If this proves impossible, he should exercise his inherent power to adjourn the meeting for a short time, such as 15 minutes, taking due steps to ensure so far as possible that all present know of this adjournment. If instead of mere disorder there is violence, I think that he should take similar steps, save that the greater the violence the less prolonged should be his efforts to restore order before adjourning. In my judgment, he has not merely a power but a duty to adjourn in this way, in the interests of those who fear for their safety. I am not suggesting that there is a power and a duty to adjourn if the violence consists of no more than a few technical assaults and batteries. Mere pushing and jostling is one thing; it is another when people are put in fear, where there is heavy punching, or the knives are out, so that blood may flow, and there are prospects, or more, of grievous bodily harm. In the latter case the sooner the chairman adjourns the meeting the better. At meetings, as elsewhere, the Queen's Peace must be kept.
>
> If, then, the chairman has this inherent power and duty, what limitations, if

---

[119] The public's right of access to meetings is without prejudice to any power of exclusion to suppress or prevent disorderly conduct or other misbehaviour: Local Government Act 1972, s.100A, added by Local Government (Access to Information) Act 1985, and Public Bodies (Admission to Meetings) Act 1960.

[120] See *Marshall* v. *Tinnelly* (1937) 81 SJ 902, as to ejection of a disorderly councillor from the meeting of an urban district council.

[121] [1969] 2 WLR 1294, at 1317.

any, are there upon its exercise? First, I think that the power and duty must be exercised *bona fide* for the purpose of forwarding and facilitating the meeting, and not for the purpose of interruption or procrastination. Second, I think that the adjournment must be for no longer than the necessities appear to dictate. If the adjournment is merely for such period as the chairman considers to be reasonably necessary for the restoration of order, it would be within his power and his duty; a longer adjournment would not. One must remember that to attend a meeting may for some mean travelling far and giving up much leisure. An adjournment to another day when a mere 15 minutes might suffice to restore order may well impose an unjustifiable burden on many; for they must either once more travel far and give up their leisure, or else remain away and lose their chance to speak and vote at the meeting.

Disorderly conduct by members

7.123. Standing orders will usually prescribe a procedure seeking first to restrain the individual member from disorderly conduct, and if reason does not prevail for the temporary suspension of the sitting. Model standing order no. 12 is to this effect:

(1) If at a meeting any member of the council, in the opinion of the mayor/ chairman notified to the council, misconduct himself by persistently disregarding the ruling of the chair, or by behaving irregularly, improperly, or offensively, or by wilfully obstructing the business of the council, the mayor/chairman or any other member may move 'That the member named be not further heard', and the motion if seconded shall be put and determined without discussion.

(2) If the member named continue his misconduct after a motion under the foregoing paragraph has been carried the mayor/chairman shall – EITHER move 'That the member named do leave the meeting' (in which case the motion shall be put and determined without seconding or discussion); OR adjourn the meeting of the council for such period as he in his discretion shall consider expedient.

(3) In the event of general disturbance which in the opinion of the mayor/ chairman renders the due and orderly dispatch of business impossible, the mayor/chairman in addition to any other power vested in him may, without question put, adjourn the meeting of the council for such period as he in his discretion shall consider expedient.[122]

7.124. The terms of this standing order would not preclude the chairman himself from calling the offending councillor to order because of the chairman's common law duty to preserve order (see 7.122); but the chairman would be wise – because of the member's statutory right to be

---

[122] See *R. v. St. Mary's, Lambeth* (1832) 1 A. & E. 346 as to adjournment of a meeting by the chairman of his own volition when general uproar arose.

present in the council chamber – not to ask the councillor to leave, even temporarily, without positive assurance that it is the wish of the meeting. There is no power (as in the case of Parliament) to suspend a member. The power of the House of Commons to expel a Member of Parliament derives from the ancient usages of Parliament. The Speaker is nowadays armed by standing orders with precisely defined powers. The Commons can, if so minded, expel an MP for any reason whatsoever – even though, in so doing, it effectively disenfranchises the electors who voted the member into office. This extreme power is rarely exercised in full measure: what is more usual is for a Member of Parliament, having been named by the Speaker for, say, gross disorderly conduct, to be suspended under the Commons standing order no. 25 for five sitting days of the House including the day of suspension and then escorted from the precincts of the House by the serjeant at arms using such force as may be necessary. It is interesting that the local authority model standing order no. 12 does not provide for a councillor's removal by force.

Disorderly conduct by public

7.125. Disorderly conduct by an individual other than a councillor is best dealt with if practicable by his removal after he has been given the opportunity, and refuses, of leaving quietly of his own accord. If the disorder is committed by a number of persons the suspension of the sitting is preferable either to give the offending persons the opportunity of behaving properly or to facilitate their removal from the meeting. No more force should be used than is reasonably necessary for the purpose of securing the offenders' removal:[123] the removal should be carried out by, say, a hall attendant employed by the council. If unnecessary violence is used in ejecting a person, damages may be awarded against the chairman.[124]

7.126. If a person expelled by order of the chairman resists his removal and lays hand on the chairman or other person who is removing him, it is an unjustifiable assault amounting to a breach of the peace. Such resistance would justify his being given or taken into custody. But mere disorderly conduct short of a breach of the peace, though it may justify ejection, would not justify a person's being given into custody.[125]

---

[123] See *Hawkins* v. *Muff* (1911), 2 *Glen's Local Government Case Law* 151.

[124] *Doyle* v. *Falconer* (1866) LR 1 PC 328; but only if the chairman authorised the removal beforehand or subsequently ratified the ejection (*Lucas* v. *Mason* (1875) LR 10 Ex.251).

[125] See *Wooding* v. *Oxley* (1839), 9 C.&P.1.

7.127. Model standing order no. 13 is to the following effect:

> If a member of the public interrupts the proceedings at any meeting the mayor/chairman shall warn him. If he continues the interruption the mayor/chairman shall order his removal from the council chamber. In case of general disturbance in any part of the chamber open to the public the mayor/chairman shall order that part to be cleared.

A standing order on these lines could now, of course, be applied to proceedings at committee meetings. Widdicombe felt it was important that there should be this express duty on a chairman to bring disturbance to a halt because of 'suspicion of connivance by the chair' in recent disorder at council meetings.[126]

Anticipation of disorder

7.128. It appears that a local authority could properly on reasonable grounds anticipate the probability of disorder and so exclude the public in advance. In *R. v. Brent Health Authority ex-parte Francis and Another* (1985)[127] it was held that it was lawful for a body to which at that time the Public Bodies (Admission to Meetings) Act applied to exclude members of the public from attending a meeting in view of the likelihood that members of the public would disrupt proceedings. Forbes J said: 'Exclusion did not only have the meaning of excluding people already at a meeting but also . . . of preventing people coming at all.'

Mass demonstrations

7.129. Mass lobbying of councillors attending council meetings and the presence of large numbers of demonstrators in the public gallery are ever-present possibilities that need to be anticipated and appropriately regulated so as to permit orderly and effective representations without disruption of council proceedings and breach of public order. It will rarely be practicable to accommodate all those who may wish to enter the council chamber (and there is no obligation on the local authority to go beyond making reasonable provision in this respect: see 3.11) but much can be done to avoid trouble and misunderstandings if simple precautionary measures are taken in advance, e.g.:

(a) When the presence of large numbers of demonstrators is expected, invite the organisers to attend beforehand for a discussion as to how best to meet their reasonable and lawful wishes.

[126] Widdicombe Report, paras.5.121–5.122.
[127] [1985] QB 869.

(b) Offer to provide assembly points for demonstrators outside the town or county hall or council offices, an opportunity for their leaders to meet the chairman or leader of the council before the meeting begins, and the reservation of an agreed number of seats in the public gallery for representatives of the demonstrators. It may be thought desirable to publicise the likelihood of an abnormal attendance and explain that the general public will be admitted up to the limit of accommodation on a 'first come first served' basis.[128]

(c) Review security measures to prevent unauthorised access to the council's offices and restrict entry to the public gallery by one door only.

(d) Alert the police and enlist their help and co-operation: see next paragraph.

Powers of the police

7.130. The police have no power to enter upon council premises, except by leave of the council or its officers, unless they have 'reason to believe that a breach of the peace is being committed'[129] or they have 'reasonable grounds for believing that an offence is imminent or is likely to be committed'.[130] It is a wise precaution therefore for the local authority to ask police constables to be present when disorder is anticipated.

7.131. Where the police are so employed they should not be called upon to intervene unless there is a breach of the peace or a breach is imminent. The chairman should ask any disorderly person to leave and if this proves ineffectual the chairman should direct the council's own employees (usually the hall attendants in practice) to eject the offending person in the first place and only if he violently resists would the police be justified in intervening. The police, indeed, must intervene if there is breach of the peace and may arrest without warrant anyone they believe responsible for such breach.

---

[128] In November 1979 Derbyshire County Council's headquarters at Matlock were invaded through several entrances by some 600 to 700 people taking part in a demonstration by the Derbyshire Co-Ordinating Committee Against Cuts, causing disruption of the council meeting and chaos in offices although there was no damage to property or personal injury. According to an official press release few demonstrators had really wished to come into the building – the organisers had apparently lost control of the situation – and they would have been satisfied if there had been arrangements to allocate 30 to 40 seats in the council chamber and for a delegation to meet the chairman of the county council.

[129] What is a breach of the peace depends upon circumstances. The Queen's Peace in society is its normal state and anything that tends to disturb the peace and order of a civilised community is a breach.

[130] *Thomas v. Sawkins* [1935] 2 KB 249.

Duration of council meeting

7.132. Unless standing orders provide to the contrary or the members at a meeting decide otherwise proceedings must continue until all business on the agenda has been dealt with. Many authorities, however, provide by standing orders for a break in proceedings after a specified period of time: either for purposes of luncheon:

> Unless the council at any meeting resolves to the contrary the sitting shall be suspended for three-quarters of an hour at such time between one and one-thirty o'clock in the afternoon as the chairman in his discretion may decide.

or to ensure that an evening meeting does not go on beyond the patience and attentiveness of those present:

> In the event that the council meets in the evening there shall be a first adjournment as soon as is convenient at the discretion of the mayor after one and a half hours for 20 minutes; and thereafter provided the business lasts so long when one hour has elapsed as soon as is convenient and at the discretion of the mayor thereafter there shall be a second adjournment of 15 minutes. In the event that the council meeting continues beyond the second adjournment further adjournment shall be at the discretion of the meeting whose views shall be taken on a show of hands without discussion.

> A meeting of the council shall (unless then otherwise determined by show of hands on a proposal by any member) adjourn at 12 midnight and the matter then under discussion and all other business yet to be considered shall be adjourned to a further meeting of the council at a date to be fixed or to the next ordinary meeting of the council.

Transaction of special business
Honorary aldermen and freemen

7.133. A principal council may, by resolution passed by not less than two-thirds of the members[131] voting thereon at a meeting of the council specially convened for the purpose,[132] with notice of the object,[133] confer the title of honorary alderman on persons who have, in the opinion of the council, rendered eminent services to the council as past members of that council but who are not then councillors of the council.[134]

---

[131] I.e. more than the normal majority of those present and voting: see 1.36.

[132] No other business can be transacted at such a meeting, but the specially convened meeting could either precede or follow an annual or ordinary or extraordinary meeting of the council.

[133] Notice would need to be given in accordance with Local Government Act 1972, sch.12, para.4(2), apart from the specific obligation in this case.

[134] Services rendered to the council of one of the old county, county borough, borough or urban or rural district councils wholly or partly included in a new county or district may be treated for the purpose as services rendered to the council of the new county or district as the case may be: *ibid.* s.249(3).

7.134. An honorary alderman may attend and take part in such civic ceremonies as the council may from time to time decide but, as such, has no right (a) to attend meetings of the council or a committee (including a joint committee upon which the council is represented), or (b) to receive any of the allowances or other payments to which councillors are entitled.[135]

7.135. Only the council of a London borough or a district which has the status of a city, borough or royal borough[136] may spend such reasonable sum as it thinks fit for the purpose of presenting an address or a casket containing an address to a person upon whom it has conferred the title.[137]

7.136. The council of a London borough or a district having the status of a city, borough or royal borough[138] may, by resolution passed by not less than two-thirds of the members voting thereon at a meeting of the council specially convened for the purpose with notice of the object, admit to be honorary freemen of the city, borough or royal borough, persons of distinction and persons who have, in the council's opinion, rendered eminent services to the city, borough or royal borough, but the admission of a person to be an honorary freeman does not confer on him the rights granted to an honorary alderman.[139] The council may spend such reasonable sum as it thinks fit for the same purposes as in the case of an honorary alderman.

7.137. In most cases the proposal to confer the title of honorary alderman or to admit a person to be an honorary freeman will be submitted to the specially convened meeting of the council as a recommendation from one of the council's committees. Appropriate recommendations would be:

That
(1) In pursuance of s.249 of the Local Government Act 1972 . . be admitted as an honorary alderman/freeman of the . . . in recognition of [the eminent services which he has rendered to . . .] [his distinguished . . .] [and that his name be enrolled on the freemen's roll].
(2) That the common seal of the council be affixed to the [enrolment of . . . on the said freemen's roll and to the certificate to be presented to him on his admission as an honorary freeman of . . .] [certificate conferring upon . . . the title of honorary alderman].
(3) That an estimated expenditure of . . . be approved for purposes associated therewith and that the chairman of the . . . committee be authorised to agree any consequential matters.

---

[135] *Ibid.* s.249(1).
[136] *Ibid.* s.249(4).
[137] *Ibid.* s.249(6).
[138] As to such status, see Local Government Act 1972, s.245.
[139] *Ibid.* s.249(5).

Promoting or opposing a Bill in Parliament

7.138. A local authority, other than a parish or community council – if satisfied that it is expedient so to do – may promote a local or personal Bill in Parliament; and *any* local authority – again if satisfied that it is expedient so to do – may oppose any local or personal Bill.[140] In either case, however, it may only do so in accordance with the procedure laid down.[141]

7.139. This procedure requires that a resolution of the council to promote or oppose a Bill shall be:[142]

   (a) passed by a majority of the whole number of the members of the authority at a meeting of the authority held after the requisite notice of the meeting and of its purpose has been given by advertisement in one or more local newspapers circulating in the area of the authority, such notice being given in addition to the ordinary notice required to be given for the convening of a meeting of the authority; and
   (b) in the case of the promotion of a Bill, confirmed by a like majority at a further meeting convened in accordance with paragraph (a) above and held as soon as may be after the expiration of 14 days after the Bill has been deposited in Parliament and, if the resolution is not confirmed, the local authority shall take all necessary steps to withdraw the Bill.

For this purpose the requisite notice is 30 clear days' notice in the case of promotion of a Bill and ten clear days' notice in the case of opposition to a Bill.

7.140. This procedure thus overrules that by which questions before the local authority are ordinarily decided, i.e. by a majority of the members merely present and voting at a meeting, and, further, requires additional notice;[143] exceptionally, too, in the case of the promotion of a Bill there has to be a confirmatory resolution at a further meeting convened after special additional notice. The terms of the statute imply though they do not expressly state that the meeting must be specially convened and exclusively for the purpose.

Political organisation of council business
Acknowledgement in standing orders

7.141. Something has already been said in Chapter 5 about political group meetings – briefly, because they are regarded as outside the scope of this book. It may be appropriate, however, to refer here to some of the

---

[140] Local Government Act 1972, s.239(1).
[141] *Ibid.* s.239(2). Note the restriction in *ibid.* s.70.
[142] *Ibid.* s.239(3).
[143] As to this notice, see Local Government Act 1972, sch.12, paras.4(2), 10(2), 26(2), *post.*

consequences which flow from the political organisation of local authority business, particularly where it is well developed: indeed, it is increasingly the practice for authorities to acknowledge the existence and the role of party politics in the provision made in standing orders.[144] There is much to commend this: for example, the chief executive will ordinarily now turn to the *leader of the council*, i.e. the leader of the majority political group on the council (nowadays often chairman of the policy and resources committee)[145] rather than as in the past to the chairman of the council or the mayor when wishing in circumstances of urgency to take the council's collective view of a matter; and, as circumstances may dictate, consult also the *leader of the opposition* group. The major parties invariably appoint *whips* for the organisation of group business, and certain nominal duties associated with the membership of the council may well devolve upon them: settling, for example, the seating arrangements in the council chamber.

Party group business

7.142. There is, it is submitted, council territory into which party political organisation should not encroach. Standing orders may properly be drawn up to require the party groups to notify certain information to the council officially, to place nominal duties of a political nature upon the party whips, and such like; but standing orders must not, for example, by taking cognisance of political decisions in the party groups, purport to supersede the formal decision-making procedure prescribed by law; for that, as indicated in Chapter 2, would be *ultra vires*. See 9.59 as regards party balance in committee membership.

Standing orders

7.143. The following examples are from standing orders of the London Borough of Hammersmith and Fulham. As regards the *leader of the council* and the *leader of the opposition* standing orders might provide that:

Two members of the council selected from time to time one as leader by the

---

[144] The GLC made attendance at party group meetings an 'approved duty'.

[145] 'The complexity of local government makes it difficult for one man to be the boss of his authority': G. W. Jones and Alan Norton (eds.), *Political Leadership in Local Authorities*, (Inlogov, 1978). There is no common pattern. In some authorities one man is clearly the leader, dominating the working of the council (but still falling short of being undisputed boss, for leadership in local government is leadership by consent); in others although a particular member may have the title of leader he seems powerless; in others the functions of leadership are shared among a small inner group; and in others the functions are so dispersed among members of the council and others that there is no apparent leader.

members forming the party in office on the council and one by those forming the largest party in opposition on the council respectively shall be known as the leader of the council and the leader of the opposition respectively. The leaders may have such deputies as may from time to time be appointed. All the names when so appointed shall be notified to the chief executive for report to the council.

The leader of the council shall be entitled to reply to questions asked by members at meetings of the council upon matters of policy or the general business of the council including such matters as have not been considered by a committee and in any event may act as a spokesman for the council whenever appropriate.

The expression 'whenever appropriate' no doubt implies matters of policy, particularly if controversial: formal statements on behalf of the local authority would remain the responsibility of the chairman of the council or mayor.

7.144. With regard to *whips*, standing orders might provide that:

Two members of the council elected from time to time as whips by the members forming the party in office on the council and by those forming the largest party in opposition on the council respectively shall be known as the chief whip and opposition whip respectively.

The whips shall, as far as possible, jointly and in consultation with the chief executive, consider as necessary the despatch of the business at meetings of the council and its committees and the appointment to membership of committees and other bodies.

The party in office on the council may appoint junior whips.

It should be noted particularly that the whips are charged with the task of considering but not deciding matters of council business: the decisions remain properly to be made by the council, albeit on the recommendation of the whips.

7.145. Certain other consequential matters may need to be included in standing orders, e.g. in the standing order dealing with the order of business at the annual meeting, the following item:

To receive a report as to the appointment of leader of the council and leader of the opposition, chief whip and opposition whip, and their deputies as necessary.

and perhaps one to this effect elsewhere:

The seating positions of members in the council chamber shall be such as may be agreed from time to time by the chief whip and opposition whip.

8

COUNCIL MINUTES

General considerations

Introduction

8.1. This chapter is concerned with the law and practice relating to the keeping of local authority minutes of proceedings and their authentication,[1] and the obligation to make them available for public inspection.[2] Much of the statutory provisions apply also to minutes of committees and subcommittees:[3] where there are differences these will be referred to later in Chapter 12. Also considered here is the form which council minutes take, invariably differing from that adopted for committee and subcommittee minutes.[4] For reasons which largely defy logical explanation the formality of meetings of the full assembly is generally reflected in a corresponding formality of style in minuting the proceedings.

What are minutes?

8.2. Minutes, in the sense commonly understood, are brief notes of the proceedings at a meeting which in particular record the decisions made thereat. There is, however, no statutory definition of 'minutes';[5] and at common law, indeed, no obligation that a permanent or any written record

---

[1] Local Government Act 1972, sch.12, para.41.
[2] *Ibid.* ss.100C, 228.
[3] *Ibid.* sch.12, para.44.
[4] The general principles which should be observed in drawing up minutes of any meeting are more appropriately discussed later: see Chapter 12.
[5] The term 'minutes' appears to have originated in the sixteenth century, when it was applied to Treasury memoranda. Records of the proceedings in the House of Lords are known to have been kept as early as 1461 and known as *journals*; in the House of Commons the records of proceedings known as *votes and proceedings* were first published in 1680 though no doubt kept earlier.

of matters transacted at a meeting should be kept. Clearly it is expedient and convenient, apart from any legal requirement, that minutes should be kept in some permanent form. If, however, the record is to have greater weight than mere recollection, the minutes must be made within a reasonable time after the meeting to which they relate.[6] Even where, as in the case of local authority minutes, the law requires that minutes shall be kept,[1] the minute book may be written up from rough notes taken at the time of the meeting.[7]

8.3. There is justification for the view that minutes can mean two things: the narrative record of all business transacted at a meeting, and a copy of the resolutions passed by those present. The law permits evidence to explain the *narrative*, e.g. to show reasons for a decision and the basis upon which it was taken;[8] but not to explain a *resolution*,[9] and thus has arisen the view that resolutions must be framed so as to be self-explanatory, wholly intelligible without reference to any other document or evidence.[10] Evidence has been held to be admissible to show that a resolution not recorded had in fact been passed.[11]

The minute book

Keeping the minutes

8.4. The law requires that the minutes of proceedings of council and committee (and subcommittee) meetings, when drawn up, shall be 'entered in a book kept for that purpose'.[12] This requirement, formerly enacted in the Local Government Act 1933 and earlier legislation, was

---

[6] *Toms* v. *Cinema Trust* (1915) WN 29.

[7] *Re Jennings* (1851) I 1. Ch. Rep.236.

[8] Evidence was allowed to explain minutes, as distinct from resolutions, in *Westminster Corporation* v. *London and North Western Rail Co.* [1905] AC 426; 69 JP 425, where a chairman of the works committee was allowed to prove that the primary object of a committee in providing certain conveniences was for sanitary purposes and not as an underground passage from one side of a street to the other, that being the point of substance in the case and one on which the recorded resolution was silent; and in *Clanricarde (Marquess)* v. *Congested Districts Board for Ireland* (1914) 79 JP 481; 31 TLR 120, where the resolution was definitely ambiguous, even if – as was disputed – it amounted to a resolution at all.

[9] 'Such a body as a county council necessarily acts by the resolution of a majority of the members present at a particular time, and in my view evidence is not admissible to show that some of the persons present and voting took a particular view of the resolution which they concurred in passing', *per* Maugham LJ in *Re Magrath* [1934] 2 KB 415, at p. 434; *sub nom. Lee* v. *McGrath*, 50 TLR 518.

[10] But see *Sheffield City Council* v. *Graingers Wines Ltd* (1977) referred to at 1.48.

[11] A resolution duly passed but not recorded in the minutes of a private company may be proved *aliunde*: *Re Fireproof Doors* [1916] 2 Ch. 142; 114 LT 994.

[12] Local Government Act 1972; sch.12, para.41(1).

rigidly construed[13] so that it was the practice of many local authorities at one time to insist that the minutes were written up by hand in the numbered pages of a bound book, later that they were entered in such a book either by typing direct on to the pages (by means of a special typewriter, probably no longer manufactured, called a book-writer) or by pasting in to the book sheets of paper on which the minutes had been typed. Then, more recently, most authorities defied the law and kept their minutes temporarily in a loose-leaf system until there was a sufficiency of sheets to warrant binding.

Loose-leaf minutes

8.5. Minutes may lawfully be 'recorded on loose leaves consecutively numbered' provided each leaf is initialled by the person who signs the minutes to which the leaves relate.[14] This initialling must be done at the time the minutes are signed.

Preservation in perpetuity

8.6. Minutes must be kept in perpetuity. For this reason they must be prepared on durable paper and, if kept initially in loose-leaf form, bound up ultimately for their better preservation. The arrangements should be made the specific responsibility of an identified officer and systematically planned in advance, i.e. it should be decided how frequently the loose-leaves are to be bound together (because this will determine the consecutive numbering of pages and the make-up of the index) and whether documents incorporated by reference are to be bound in the minute book itself as appendices or preserved separately and, if separately, in what manner. Foolscap was for long the most widely used size of paper but this is now being replaced by A4.

Safe custody

8.7. The safe custody of minutes is important: and it is the responsibility of each principal council[15] (without prejudice to the powers of the *custos*

---

[13] In *Hearts of Oak Assurance Co. Ltd* v. *James Flower & Sons* (1935) AE Rep.420, it was held that, under similar provision in the Companies Act 1929, a number of loose leaves fastened together in two covers in such a way that anyone could take a leaf out and substitute another was not a 'book' within the meaning of that Act.

[14] Local Government Act 1972, sch.12, para.41(2).

[15] Local Government Act 1972, s.224.

rotulorum[16] to give directions as to the documents of any county) to make proper arrangements with respect to any documents which belong to or are in the custody of the council or any of its officers.[17] Minutes must be kept under lock and key and ordinarily in fire-resistant safes (although not so inaccessibly stored away as not to be readily available for purposes of inspection): and these precautions are especially needed in the case of minutes kept in a loose-leaf system pending binding.

Form

General

8.8. Council minutes can take whatever form is preferred by the individual authority or draftsman concerned. There are certain general principles governing the drafting of minutes which should be observed (and these are set out later in Chapter 12 in regard to committee minutes) but the principles are flexible and what matters primarily is that the minutes record clearly and concisely all decisions taken at the meeting and so much of the other proceedings as the good sense of the committee clerk or local custom deems necessary. To quote one example only of the wide variations in practice: some authorities meticulously minute all questions asked and the replies given at question time in the council chamber, but most authorities do not.

8.9. It is not considered worth while, therefore, to devote space here to examples of the differing methods employed beyond those of a general character which follow.

General style

8.10. As indicated above (see 8.1), council minutes traditionally reflect the formality of council proceedings and thus in general conform to a style which differs from that adopted in the case of committee minutes. Thus resolutions are usually recorded showing, as a rule,[18] the names of the proposer and seconder, e.g.:

> 00. *Report of Policy Committee*
> Moved (or proposed) by Councillor Jones,

---

[16] The *custos rotulorum* is usually the Lord Lieutenant of the county, whose responsibility includes judicial records. In practice the county council will act for the Lord Lieutenant in this respect.

[17] In practice responsibility for the safe custody of council documents will be placed upon the proper officer (Local Government Act 1972, s.270(3)), who may be the chief executive or the county or district secretary as the council may determine.

[18] Some authorities do not record the names of proposer and seconder: see 8.15.

Seconded by Councillor Robinson, and
Resolved: That the report of the Policy Committee of . . . be approved and
    adopted.

Or, where there have been amendments moved to a committee report
(and irrespective as to whether the amendments were accepted or rejected), the style may be, e.g.:

00. *Report of Policy Committee*
    Moved (or proposed) by Councillor Jones,
    Seconded by Councillor Robinson; and
    Resolved: That the report of the Policy Committee of . . . be received.

    Amendment
    Moved (or proposed) by Councillor Smith,
    Seconded by Councillor Brown:
    That para.A (Corporate Plan) be referred back to the committee for
    reconsideration.

    After debate,
    Amendment put to the vote and declared not carried.

    Further amendment
    Moved (or proposed) by Councillor White,
    Seconded by Councillor Black:
    That para.A (Corporate Plan) be approved in principle only and that the
    committee be instructed to report further on the detailed implemen-
    tation of the corporate plan.

    After debate,
    Amendment put to the vote and declared carried.

    Resolved: That the report of the Policy Committee of . . . be approved and
    adopted as amended.

8.11. It will be evident that there could be almost endless variations in this
style. Of importance, it is suggested, is consistency and uniformity within
each authority so as to avoid the use of different phrases meaning the same
thing, i.e. there should be standardisation of layout and commonly occur-
ring phrases and terms. If, for example, it has been decided that motions
shall be minuted in this manner:

Proposed by Councillor Jones,
Seconded by Councillor Robinson; and
Resolved: That . . .

then variations of the following kind should not be permitted, e.g.:

Proposed by Councillor Jones, seconded by Councillor Robinson,
and
Resolved: That . . .

or, e.g.:

Moved by Councillor Jones, seconded by Councillor Robinson, and
thereupon, *Resolved:* That . . .

or, again, e.g.:

Upon the motion of Councillor Jones, seconded by Councillor Robinson, it was
Resolved: That . . .

and so on!

Recording divisions

8.12. There are occasions, i.e. whenever there is a division or a requisition
to such effect, when the names of members present must be recorded to
show how each voted – for or against – or abstained from voting. No
particular form of minute is required so long as the manner in which each
member voted or abstained from voting is clearly recorded.

Minuting committee reports

8.13. Each local authority has its own practice in the way in which
committee reports submitted to the full assembly are incorporated in the
council minutes and the debate thereon recorded. Some authorities reprint
in council minutes the whole of the text of each committee report; others
'incorporate' the reports by reference; a minority adopt in addition some
expedient way of using the council agenda as a reference document for
day-to-day use: see 8.23.

8.14. The most widely adopted (and the most easily intelligible and
visually tidy) practice is for the committee reports to be incorporated by
reference. Thus, for example, the adoption of a committee report will be
minuted in this manner (and the report itself will have to be sought
elsewhere by those who do not have access to the signed minutes):

Moved by Councillor Jones,
Seconded by Councillor Robinson; and
Resolved: That the report of the Policy Committee of . . . (*set out hereto as
Appendix . . . to these minutes*) be approved and adopted.

Generally the particular report will be identifiable by reference to the
council meeting agenda. Where the recommendation in a report is

amended or there is debate to be recorded the minuting will be as indicated above in 8.10.

8.15. An example of the other kind of practice is that followed by the old Greater London Council. Each committee report is reprinted within the council minutes: against each recommendation there appears, in heavy type, the words 'Agreed' or 'Not carried', and the procedural matters and any debate are recorded at the end of the report. In the case of a report not containing a recommendation which is received without debate there is recorded simply:

> *Resolved:* That the report be received.

If there is debate then the record is:

> The motion was made – That the report be received.
> After debate, the motion was put and agreed to.
> *Resolved:* That the report be received.

Where the report contains a recommendation, accepted without debate, these additional words appear:

> Recommendation 1 was moved, put and agreed to.
> *Resolved* accordingly.

The term 'resolved accordingly' is not, however, regarded as good practice: see 12.34.

Minuting question time

8.16. Some local authorities minute verbatim the questions which are asked at council meetings (see 7.37 *et seq.*), and the answers provided by committee chairmen. On the principle that minutes should record the whole of the proceedings this practice is defensible though rather extravagant in terms of printing and paper cost. Where such a practice is adopted then both question and answer should be recorded: a few authorities (Leeds Metropolitan District Council is evidently one[19]) merely record the question with a note to the effect that the committee chairman replied without specifying what the terms of the answer were.

Authorising use of the common seal
General considerations

8.17. Because the use of the local authority's common seal on a deed binds the authority (and provides unimpeachable authenticity to any other

[19] According to *Local Government Chronicle*, 22 August 1975, p. 784, which criticised the practice as 'a half-hearted sort of public relations'.

document to which it is affixed[20]), the seal must be kept in safe custody and used only in pursuance of a resolution of the council or of a committee to which the council has delegated its power in that respect. The model standing orders deal with both matters.

Safe custody

8.18. Model standing order no. 23 is to this effect:

> The common seal of the council shall be kept in a safe place in the custody of the town clerk/clerk of the council and shall be secured by two different locks, the keys of which shall be kept respectively by the mayor/chairman and the town clerk/clerk of the council.
>
> Provided that the mayor/chairman may entrust his key temporarily to another member of the council, and the town clerk/clerk of the council may entrust his key temporarily to any deputy appointed by the council.

Sealing of documents

8.19. Model standing order no. 24 is to this effect:

(1) The common seal of the council shall not be affixed to any document unless the sealing has been authorized by a resolution of the council or of a committee to which the council have delegated their powers in this behalf, but a resolution of the council (or of a committee where that committee has the power) authorizing the acceptance of any tender, the purchase, sale, letting, or taking of any property, the issue of any stock, the presentation of any petition, memorial, or address, the making of any rate or contract, or the doing of any other thing, shall be a sufficient authority for sealing any document necessary to give effect to the resolution.

(2) The seal shall be attested by the following persons present at the sealing, viz., mayor or deputy mayor/chairman or vice-chairman of the council or other member of the council, and the town clerk/clerk or deputy town clerk/deputy clerk of the council, and an entry of every sealing of a document shall be made and consecutively numbered in a book kept for the purpose and shall be signed by a person who has attested the seal.

8.20. It is nevertheless a wise precaution to provide a 'wrapping-up' resolution which can be passed at the conclusion of each council or committee meeting to provide appropriate authentication for the signature and/or sealing of any document which may be necessary to give effect to the local authority's decisions. Thus, for example, Surrey County Council

[20] Certain documents require by law the affixing of the common seal of the authority, e.g. by-laws for good rule and government: Local Government Act 1972, s.236(3), which, however, in the case of by-laws made by a parish or community council not having a seal, permits the authentication by the hands and seals of two members of the council.

provides as the final item of the agenda of every council and committee meeting this motion:

> The chairman to move:
> That the common seal of the council be affixed to, or the clerk do sign on behalf of the council, where appropriate, any orders, deed or documents necessary to give effect to any of the matters and recommendations contained in [the minutes of this meeting of the . . . committee] [the volume of reports as presented to and approved by the council on . . .]

Date of sealing operative date of document

8.21. A resolution to make, for example, a compulsory purchase order which must be sealed does not itself 'make' the order: the resolution is no more than an expression of intention or instruction to those who have the duty of affixing the seal. A local authority can – subject to exceptions not here relevant – act only by seal and a compulsory purchase order is not 'made' until sealed.[21]

Indexing

Council minutes as reference documents

8.22. Where, as in the case of the GLC earlier referred to, the council minutes set out *in extenso* the committee reports before the assembly, this single document (the minutes for a particular meeting) can be referred to in the confident knowledge that the minutes are wholly self-contained. Where, as in the majority of cases, the committee reports are *not* reprinted direct into the minutes, a reader must necessarily look at two documents: the council minutes and, elsewhere, the committee reports referred to; and although this may not be an onerous task it is often not difficult to misread or misunderstand the purport of a decision in the council minutes.

8.23. An expedient adopted by Surrey County Council has much to commend it. The council meeting agenda is prepared as a booklet, bound within green covers, and known officially, for obvious reasons, as the *Green Book*. On the front of the Green Book appear these words in red type:

> *NOTE:-* This volume must not be regarded as reliable for future reference unless it contains upon page i an inset to the effect that either (a) all the recommendations as set out were adopted, or (b) certain modifications were made by the council. A copy of the inset will be forwarded to members after the county council meeting.

[21] Opinion expressed in (1954) 118 *Justice of the Peace & Local Government Review* 16. See also 1.46.

The inset summarises the decisions of the council on the committee reports and thus the Green Book for each council meeting provides a convenient document for reference purposes.

Indexing

8.24. What is said in Chapter 12 about indexing committee minutes applies substantially to the indexing of council minutes.

Authentication of minutes
Confirmation

8.25. Council minutes, when written up, approved in draft by the chairman (or whoever presided at the meeting concerned) and entered in the minute book, are submitted for confirmation to the next succeeding meeting.[22] This means that minutes, whether of an annual or extraordinary meeting, are properly submitted at the next meeting whatever its character, i.e. the minutes of, say, an annual meeting do not have to wait for confirmation until the next annual meeting. The term *confirmation* is misleading. Minutes do not require confirmation in the ordinary sense of that word: the decisions taken at a meeting are of immediate effect[23] and do not depend upon their first being written up and subsequently approved and signed at the next succeeding meeting. The minutes are merely a record of what has already actually taken place but their confirmation – in the manner referred to below – has important legal consequences.

8.26. The act of confirmation does not require the minutes to be read nor need a copy have been circulated beforehand to members. Minutes of the previous council meeting are nevertheless quite often circulated with the summons and agenda (although this practice is less common in the case of committee minutes). If the unsigned minutes are circulated it makes it difficult for any person to challenge their accuracy after confirmation. If they are not circulated the minute book should be kept available for inspection by any member who may wish to check the minutes before agreeing to their confirmation and, in any case, the minute book should be

---

[22] There was a useful amendment of the 1933 Act, Pt V, para.3(1), by the London Government Act 1963, sch.4, para.44, which permitted the minutes of committee meetings (but not council meetings) to be lawfully confirmed *at any subsequent* meeting, i.e. not necessarily the same or next meeting. This was not carried forward into the present law.

[23] But see what is said at 1.46 about the effective date of decisions which need to be clothed in due legal form.

laid on the table for, say, half an hour before commencement of the meeting at which the minutes are to be confirmed.

8.27. The only question which can properly arise on the confirmation of minutes is that of their accuracy. Model standing order no. 9(2), for example, provides that:

> No discussion shall take place upon the minutes, except upon their accuracy, and any question of their accuracy shall be raised by motion. If no such question is raised, or if it is raised then as soon as it has been disposed of, the mayor/chairman shall sign the minutes.

The occasion is not one for a resumption of debate on items recorded in the minutes[24] nor, strictly, should the minutes be used as the basis for reporting subsequent action. Thus the inclusion on an agenda of an item to this effect:

> 00. Matters arising on the minutes

is bad practice. If any item dealt with at a previous meeting needs to be discussed further a separate item should appear on the agenda.

8.28. Model standing order no. 9 provides that:

> The mayor/chairman shall put the question that the minutes of the council held on the . . . day of . . . be approved as a correct record.

This is a convenient arrangement. The motion to confirm the minutes of the previous meeting can be moved and seconded by members who were not present at that meeting although it is preferable that those who were not present should abstain from voting and comment on the motion. Ordinarily, of course, there will be no formal motion: the chairman, whether or not acting in pursuance of a standing order on the lines of model standing order no. 9, will merely ask whether he may sign the minutes as a correct record and will proceed to place his signature in the minute book upon murmurs of assent. Where, however, a member does vote in favour of the signing of the minutes he votes not for the decisions recorded but only for the accuracy of the record and he does not incur any liability or responsibility for the proceedings at such a meeting if he was not present thereat.[25]

8.29. The chairman who signs the minutes does so in pursuance of the requirement that he must do so:[26] he need not have been present at the meeting of which the minutes are a record. If, however, for any reason, e.g. that the chairman suspects an inaccuracy in the minutes but has no

---

[24] See *Mawley* v. *Barber* (1803) 2 Esp.687; *R.* v. *Mayor of York* (1853) 1 E.&B.594.
[25] *Re Lands Allotment Co.* (1894) 1 Ch. 616, p. 635.
[26] Local Government Act 1972, sch.12, para.41(1).

support for his contention, and he refuses to sign the minutes, the proper course is to record the circumstances by a minute to this effect:

> 00. *Minutes*
> The minutes of the meeting of . . . were confirmed as a correct record of the proceedings thereat but the chairman refused to sign them on the grounds that he believed them to be inaccurate in the following particular . . . but his view was not upheld by the council/committee/subcommittee.

Evidence without further proof

8.30. Minutes which have been drawn up and entered in the minute book and signed at the same or next following meeting by the person presiding thereat, i.e. at the meeting at which confirmation takes place, are prima facie good evidence of the proceedings: the law prescribes that any minute purporting to be so signed 'shall be received in evidence without further proof'.[27] Furthermore, until the contrary is proved, the meeting is deemed to have been duly convened and held and all the members present are deemed to have been duly qualified.[28]

8.31. The effect of the foregoing is that if a responsible officer of the local authority goes into a witness box in court and produces the signed minutes, there is no need to prove that the minutes were actually signed at the meeting or that the signature on them is actually the signature of the person presiding.[29] These provisions do not, however, mean that a signed minute is unchallengeable proof of the events recorded in the minutes. It is open to anyone who wishes to do so, if he can, to try to prove in court that the minutes are not a true record of what took place at the meeting. But the onus of proof to the contrary is on the person challenging the signed minute.[30]

[27] It is a common law rule that where minutes have been properly kept they shall be admissible as evidence. The effect of the provisions in the Local Government Act 1972, sch.12, para.41(1)–(2), is that the minutes are inadmissible unless signed as prescribed.

[28] Local Government Act 1972, sch.12, para.41(3).

[29] Under the Local Government (Miscellaneous Provisions) Act 1976, s.41, a document which (a) purports to be a copy of (i) a resolution, order or report of a local authority or precursor of a local authority, or a committee or subcommittee thereof, *or* (ii) the minutes of the proceedings at a meeting of a local authority or precursor of a local authority, or a committee or subcommittee thereof, *and* (b) bears a certificate purporting to be signed by the proper officer or someone authorised on that behalf by himself or the authority and stating that the resolution was passed or the order or report was made by the authority or precursor or committee or subcommittee thereof on a date specified in accordance with para.41 of sch.12 to the Local Government Act 1972 or the corresponding earlier provisions, is evidence in any proceedings of the matters stated in the certificate and of the terms of the resolution, order, report or minute in question.

[30] See *Re Indian Zoedone Co.* (1884). In this case the chairman made an entry in the minute book that a resolution had been confirmed and the court declined, in the absence of evidence that votes were improperly disallowed, to question the decision of the chairman.

Alteration of minutes

8.32. Once the minutes have been confirmed they must not be altered in any circumstances whatsoever.[31] If, however, when a meeting is being asked to confirm the minutes of the preceding meeting and it is agreed – either on a member's representation or that of the chairman – that there is an inaccuracy which needs to be corrected, it is advisable for the fact to be duly noted in the minute recording the signing of the minutes, e.g.:

> *Resolved:* That the minutes of the meeting of . . . were approved and signed by the chairman subject to correction of . . .

If an inaccuracy is discovered *after* the minutes have been signed then, again, the inaccuracy should be corrected by resolution, e.g.:

> *Resolved:* That the minutes of the meeting on . . ., approved and signed by the chairman at the meeting on . . . be amended in the following respect to correct an inaccuracy subsequently discovered:

The particular minute challenged and agreed to be inaccurate should never be altered although a pencilled note could properly be made against the disputed minute by the proper officer indicating its subsequent correction.

Inspection of minutes

Statutory provisions

8.33. The public right of inspection of council minutes depends on the type of local authority and the date of the council meeting. Prior to the coming into force of the Local Government (Access to Information) Act 1985 on 1 April 1986 the minutes of the proceedings of every local authority in full assembly were required to be open to inspection by any *local government elector* for the area and any such elector was entitled to take a copy or extract from the minutes.[32] That is still the position as regards the minutes of parish and community councils.[33] Now, by virtue of the 1985 Act, the minutes of the council meetings of principal councils are open to inspection by the *public* generally; but, strictly, for a period of six years beginning with the date of the meeting.[34] The position is substantially the

---

[31] *Re Cawley & Co.* (1889) 42 Ch. D.209. In this case the directors at a board meeting passed a resolution making a call on shares, but omitted to state the date of payment. After the minutes had been signed the secretary repaired the omission by adding a date. Esher MR said: 'I trust I shall never again see or hear of the secretary of a company, whether under superior direction or otherwise, altering minutes of meetings, either by striking out anything or adding anything'.

[32] Local Government Act 1972, s.228(1), now amended.

[33] *Ibid.* as amended by Local Government (Access to Information) Act 1985, s.3, sch.2, para.6(2).

[34] *Ibid.* s.100C, added by Local Government (Access to Information) Act 1985: and see 8.38.

same as regards the committee and subcommittee minutes of principal councils: see Chapter 12.

Who may inspect

8.34. The simplification of the law by extending to the public – not just electors alone – the right of inspection of council minutes of principal councils has eliminated some of the problems which had arisen in the past over who may in fact exercise the right to inspect. Nevertheless, as regards the council minutes of a local authority meeting held prior to 1 April 1986 (and still as regards those of parish and community councils and a parish meeting), the right of inspection vests strictly only in electors,[35] although the right can be exercised through an agent.[36]

8.35. A member of every local authority has always possessed, as a councillor, a common law right to production of documents, including council minutes, which he needs to see to carry out his council duties.[37] The statutory right of access to council documents now provided does not extend this common law right as regards council minutes.

8.36. Strictly speaking the officer who has custody of the minutes of a parish or community council or parish or community meeting ought to check upon a person's credentials before making the minute book available for inspection. This may rarely be done in practice either because the council or the meeting makes its minutes freely available (as, e.g. by depositing copies in public libraries in the area) or because it decides that anyone may inspect as a matter of public relations policy.

What may be inspected

8.37. The distinction between council minutes and committee and sub-committee minutes is no longer as important as it was prior to the Local Government (Access to Information) Act 1985 because – at least in the case of principal councils – both must equally be available for public inspection. In the case, however, of the minutes of parish and community councils and of all other council minutes of meetings prior to 1 April 1986, the minutes which must be open to inspection by electors include the minutes of a committee if submitted to the council for approval.[38] Such committee minutes are inseparable from the council minutes because, it has been

---

[35] Local Government Act 1972, s.228(1).

[36] *R.* v. *Gloucestershire CC* [1936] 2 All ER 168.

[37] But not for any other purpose. See *R.* v. *Wimbledon UDC* (1897) 62 JP 84; *Stevens* v. *Berwick-upon-Tweed Corporation* (1835) 4 Dowl.277; but where there is now a public right of inspection the motive of the person inspecting is surely immaterial.

[38] *Williams* v. *Manchester Corporation* (1897) 45 WR 412. Minutes of certain statutory committees were also open to inspection by electors: see 12.55.

held,[39] 'one could not understand the approval without seeing the recommendations'.

8.38. The law now provides that after the council meeting of a principal local authority (and after the meeting of a committee or subcommittee) the following documents must be open to public inspection at the offices of the council until the expiration of a period of six years beginning with the date of the meeting:[40]

(a) the minutes, or a copy of the minutes,[41] of the meeting excluding so much of the minutes of proceedings during which the meeting was not open to the public as discloses exempt information;

(b) where applicable, a summary of the whole or part of the proceedings;

(c) a copy of the agenda for the meeting;[42] and

(d) a copy of so much of any report for the meeting as relates to any item during which the meeting was open to the public.

The summary must be prepared by the proper officer where in consequence of the exclusion of parts of the minutes which disclose exempt information the document open to inspection does not provide the public 'with a reasonably fair and coherent report' of the whole or part of the proceedings without disclosing any exempt information.

Background papers

8.39. In addition,[43] 'if and so long as copies of the whole or part of a report for a meeting of a principal council are required ... to be open to inspection by members of the public' there must be open to inspection at the council's offices for up to four years afterwards beginning with the date of the meeting:

(a) copies of a list,[44] compiled by the proper officer, of the background papers for the report or the part of the report; and

---

[39] Even though in s.228(1) of the Local Government Act 1972, as originally enacted, the term *local authority* minutes, rather than *council* minutes, was used, the minutes of a committee exercising delegated powers were not open to inspection notwithstanding that the decisions of the committee had in all respects the force and validity of decisions of the local authority itself: *Wilson* v. *Evans* [1962] 1 All ER 247.

[40] Local Government Act 1972, s.100C, added by Local Government (Access to Information) Act 1985.

[41] It may be convenient ordinarily to make a copy available so as to make it easier not to disclose excluded minutes.

[42] Except for the statutory requirement to preserve a copy of the agenda it would be common practice, as in the past, to dispose of the agenda because it has no practical or legal significance after a meeting. Presumably the obligation to preserve the agenda or a copy of it for inspection is to enable a member of the public to check that an item of business was or was not transacted and if it was that the item was duly minuted. See 12.19.

[43] Local Government Act 1972, s.100D, added by Local Government (Access to Information) Act 1985.

[44] The fact that a list must be prepared with copies of the documents on the list means that, conveniently, the originals can be retained in the appropriate files.

(b) at least one copy of each of the documents included in that list.

However, there is no obligation to include any document which discloses exempt information or 'any document which, if open to inspection, would disclose confidential information in breach of the obligation of confidence'.[45] A member of the public cannot demand the instant production of the papers.

8.40. Background papers are defined as those documents relating to the subject-matter of the report which:

(a) disclose any facts or matters on which, in the opinion of the proper officer, the report or an important part of the report is based; and

(b) have, in his opinion, been relied on to a material extent in preparing the report;[46]

but do not include any published works.[47]

8.41. There are several questions which arise on the foregoing. Why, for example, was six years fixed as the period for inspection of minutes, agenda and reports when, at least in the case of council minutes, a local authority would ordinarily allow inspection virtually in perpetuity? Does it mean – though no local authority would surely so act – that inspection could be refused to a member of the public who wished to see minutes and other supporting papers more than six years old? And why the difference between the six years for minutes, agenda and reports and four years only for background papers?

When minutes may be inspected

8.42. Documents, including minutes, open to public inspection, must be made available[48] at all reasonable hours[49] and:

(a) in the case of background papers, upon payment of such reasonable fee as may be required for the facility; and

(b) in any other case, i.e. including minutes, without payment.

Where a document is so open to inspection then any person may, subject to what is said below as to copyright:

(i) make copies of or extracts from the document; or

---

[45] Local Government Act 1972, s.100D(4), added by Local Government (Access to Information) Act 1985.

[46] *Ibid.* s.100D(5). It is probable that the proper officer need not list, or otherwise disclose, papers which have been looked at and rejected as not relevant to the issue reported upon.

[47] There is no definition of *published works*, but presumably the term would cover publications of HMSO and therefore most government departmental circulars.

[48] Local Government Act 1972, s.100H(1), added by Local Government (Access to Information) Act 1985.

[49] 'Reasonable hours' is probably fairly interpreted as the hours during which the council's offices where the documents are kept are ordinarily open.

(ii) require the person having custody of the document to supply a
  photocopy of or extracts from the document;
upon payment of such reasonable fee as may be required for the
facility.[50]

Copyright

8.43. There is, however, protection for copyright. Nothing in the foregoing requires or authorises the doing of anything which infringes the
copyright in any work except that, where the owner of the copyright is a
principal council, nothing done in pursuance of the foregoing constitutes
an infringement of copyright.[51] This means that, although members of the
public may inspect copyright documents they must not be allowed to copy
them: thus, for example, deposited plans and drawings for planning and
building regulations approval[52] may not be copied but the application
forms and the usual sort of site plan could be.

Obstruction of the right to inspect

8.44. Anyone having custody of the documents of a principal council
required to be open to public inspection, who without reasonable excuse
(a) intentionally obstructs anyone exercising the right of inspection or of
making a copy of or extracts from the document, or (b) refuses to furnish
copies to any person entitled to obtain them, is liable on summary
conviction to a fine not exceeding level 1 on the standard scale.[53]

8.45. In the case of parish and community councils and parish meetings,
obstruction of the right of inspection and of making a copy of or extract
from documents required to be open to inspection by electors renders the
person with custody of the documents liable on summary conviction to a
fine not exceeding £20.[54] The right to take copies is not a right to be
furnished with copies.[55]

---

[50] Local Government Act 1972, s.100H(2), added by Local Government (Access to Information) Act 1985.
[51] *Ibid.* s.100H(3).
[52] Protected by Copyright Act 1956, ss.3, 48(1).
[53] Local Government Act 1972, s.100H(4), added by Local Government (Access to Information) Act 1985. The absence of the person having custody of the documents is no excuse for
the failure to produce the documents for inspection: see *R.* v. *Andover RDC* (1913) 77 JP
296, 29 TLR 419, where it was said that when the clerk to a council goes away he should
leave some person with authority to produce the minute book to anyone entitled to see it.
[54] Local Government Act 1972, s.228(7), as amended.
[55] *Russell-Walker* v. *Gimblett* (1985) 149 JP 448.

PART THREE

COMMITTEE PRACTICE

9

THE COMMITTEE SYSTEM

What is a committee?

Importance of definition

9.1. There is no statutory definition of a committee for purposes of local government – nor of a subcommittee for that matter. Yet it can be important to be able to say what is a committee or subcommittee and what is not. For example, committee and subcommittee meetings are required to be open to the public, which is not the case of meetings which are not meetings of committees or subcommittees (see 9.2); and only attendance at meetings of the full assembly, a committee or a subcommittee attracts attendance allowance automatically (see 5.25), although an authority can make attendance at some other meetings, e.g. a panel or working party, eligible by designating it 'approved duty'.

9.2. According to the *Concise Oxford Dictionary*, a committee is 'a body of persons appointed for a special function by, and normally out of, a normally larger body'; and in *Chambers Twentieth Century Dictionary* it is defined as 'a portion selected from a more numerous body, or the whole body, to which some special business is committed'. But these definitions are not satisfactory for local government purposes – although it is interesting that they imply a plurality of persons: see 9.3. There are groupings of councillors which might seem to satisfy the dictionary definitions of a committee but which are not local authority committees in a statutory or even common law sense. Thus a working party comprised both of councillors and officers is not a committee or a subcommittee because the inclusion of officers within its constitution takes it out of the definition of a committee or subcommittee (see 9.5): it cannot have functions delegated to it and it does not need to reach decisions on the basis of a majority of those present and voting. For somewhat similar reasons, so-called committees for consultative purposes (e.g. a joint staff committee or a committee for health and safety purposes) are not local authority committees. There are, however, groupings which though not termed committees or subcommittees have most of the characteristics of such, and a local authority cannot evade the requirements of the law merely by calling what is in reality a committee or subcommittee by some other name, e.g. a *panel* of councillors.

Plurality of membership

9.3. For local government purposes a committee or subcommittee must comprise a plurality of persons: there cannot be a committee (or a subcommittee) consisting only of one person – any more, as we have seen, than could there conceivably be a meeting of one person alone: see 1.7. In *R. v. Secretary of State for the Environment ex-parte Hillingdon London Borough Council* (1986), referred to earlier in connection with the practice of committee chairman's action (see 5.67), the local authority had argued unsuccessfully that it could delegate functions to a committee chairman if it had constituted that single councillor as a committee of one person. The court would have none of it. Having dismissed the argument that there could be delegation to an individual councillor under s.101 of the Local Government Act 1972, Woolf J went on to rule that there could not be a committee of one member alone:

> The 1972 Act . . . must, in my view, be taken to use the word 'committee' in the sense that that word is now used [i.e. in ordinary parlance] and if this approach to the interpretation of the section [i.e. s.101] is correct, then the only permissible interpretation is one which involves rejecting the concept of a committee of one . . . had it been the intention that the terms 'committee' and 'sub-committee' in s.101(1) should include a committee or sub-committee of one, it is considered that this would expressly have been provided for.

9.4. It is indeed clear that the Local Government Act 1972 supports plurality of membership in, for example, sch.12, para.39, where it lays down the cardinal principle that all questions coming before the local authority are to be decided by a majority of members present and voting. It would be impossible, of course, to secure a majority in a committee of one. What has been said earlier (see 1.8) about the minimum number of persons who may constitute a meeting for local government purposes applies equally to the minimum number of persons who may constitute a committee or subcommittee.

Definition for local government purposes

9.5. It is possible, by collecting together the several references to committees in the relevant statutes, to build up a definition of a committee or subcommittee for purposes of local government.[1] In this way, it can be said that a local authority committee or subcommittee is a body which the council in the case of a committee, or a committee in the case of a subcommittee, has formally constituted by resolution to act as a unit forming part of the hierarchy of legal power, and:

(a) has functions of the local authority referred or delegated to it;[2]
(b) has a fixed and not a fluctuating membership;[3]
(c) may include persons who are not councillors but the number of such persons must be limited;[4]
(d) has its proceedings regulated by the local authority's standing orders and/or sch.12 of the 1972 Act;
(e) must admit the public and the Press to its meetings;[5]
(f) cannot wholly comprise or include paid officers of the council;[6]
(g) must comprise at least three members (on the basis that there can be no fewer number to constitute a meeting: see 1.8);
(h) has a limited term of office and prescribed area of authority;[7]
(i) can, in the case of a committee, delegate its functions to a subcommittee (which it alone can appoint) or, equally with a subcommittee, to an officer unless the terms of its appointment forbid it;[8]
(j) must reach decisions by a majority of members present and voting in prescribed manner;[9]
(k) must keep formal minutes of its proceedings in prescribed manner;[10]
(l) must report its decisions direct to the council in the case of a committee and to a committee in the case of a subcommittee and not through any intermediary (as standing orders will generally provide);
(m) may exclude from participation in the business of its meetings any person, including councillors (save for the exercise of their common law right to be present on the basis of a 'need to know': see 5.12), who is not among the number of members of the committee appointed by

---

[1] The author is indebted for this concept to Ian McKay, 'A Committee Resolution' (1979) 143 *Local Government Review* 199.
[2] Local Government Act 1972, s.101.
[3] *Ibid.* s.102(2): but see 9.64 as to substitute members.
[4] *Ibid.* s.102(3).
[5] See generally Chapter 3.
[6] Local Government Act 1972, s.80. Thus the adoption panel set up under the Adoption Agencies Regulations 1984, regs. 5, 10, is intended to be a mixture of councillors and officers and is not a subcommittee of the social services committee: Department of Health and Social Security circ. LAC(84) 3, para.11.
[7] Local Government Act 1972, s.102(2).
[8] *Ibid.* s.101.
[9] *Ibid.* sch.12, para.39.
[10] *Ibid.* sch.12, para.41.

the council, or in the case of a subcommittee, appointed by the committee;

and whose members:

(i) are under an obligation to disclose any pecuniary interest in a matter which is before the meeting at which they are present and to refrain from participating in the discussion thereon and from voting;[11]

(ii) are automatically entitled to attendance allowance (see 5.25).

Committee structure

General principles

9.6. Committees are not just separate groupings of councillors each operating in isolation and independently of one another: committees can have no greater powers than those conferred on them by the council and cannot themselves amend their terms of reference or shelve the business committed to them, and can never dissolve themselves. Committees are part of a unified system and are an integral feature of the internal organisation of local authorities in this country. The committee system, it has been said, 'is engrained in English life'[12] and democratic control of local government services would have been impracticable without it; in addition, the law has obliged local authorities from earliest times to set up particular committees for the discharge of specific functions.[13] The committee in English local government exists *to administer* – a function which a committee is peculiarly unsuited to perform. Yet this is what, traditionally, the local authority committee has attempted to do: and against the balance of probability, has performed passably well. It has been the task of committees to administer a number of related services by exercising oversight of the chief officer and department responsible for the executive work, to contribute to policy by making recommendations to the full council for the development of existing and new services, and under delegated authority to make such decisions as may need to be made for the implementation of policy. The close alignment between committees and departments has been largely responsible for the fragmentation of internal machinery and the lack of unity in a local authority in the past. Some committees have performed a co-ordinating role – the finance and the

[11] Local Government Act 1972, s.94. This obligation does not extend to membership of any other groupings of councillors.

[12] Second report of the Local Government Manpower Committee (1951), Cmnd 8421, appendix IX: Report of a Working Party on Statutory Committees, para.4.

[13] See an essay by Professor H. J. Laski in *A Century of Municipal Progress* (1935) for the historical development of the committee system in local government.

establishment committees particularly – and, before the emergence of the concept of corporate management and the setting up of policy committees, these often succeeded in achieving an integrated approach to the authority's functions.

9.7. Because local authority committees must reach decisions in accordance with the cardinal principle referred to earlier, i.e. by a majority of members present and voting (see Chapter 1), there is no scope for minority reports from councillors who may disagree with the majority view. Their objection can be expressed only by voting against a proposition in committee and in the full assembly.

Flexibility

9.8. An important feature of the committee system as an instrument of administration is its flexibility. New committees can be set up permanently or temporarily as need dictates. Existing committees whose tasks have been completed can be dissolved. Committees whose duties have diminished or lost their former importance may be amalgamated with others. There can, in short, be continual arrangement and rearrangement in this way to meet altered circumstances. Standing committees can be increased or reduced in membership to meet changes in the interests to be represented and the subcommittee organisation can be adjusted accordingly. Special *ad hoc* committees can be set up to examine and report upon particular matters of topical concern or special importance. Joint committees may be set up to deal with matters which concern more than one committee or to deliberate or act upon matters of common interest to two or more local authorities. The elasticity of the committee system can be stretched, indeed, to the extreme without the necessity of altering, amending or adapting the parent body. This is true, of course, of the committee system of any association but it is of paramount importance to the modern local authority, which has to resolve into a workable, manageable whole a complexity of related and sometimes unrelated functions, many of a highly specialised nature and all possessing individual technicalities. It is no exaggeration to say that the resilience of the committee system in local government has largely enabled local authorities to absorb more and more tasks – though not always very successfully.[14]

9.9. There are necessarily physical limitations to this flexibility. The size of membership of the authority and to a less extent its resources in revenue and manpower are limiting factors – not of the quality of flexibility but of

[14] See B. J. Ripley, *Administration in Local Authorities* (1970), p. 22.

the stretch of elasticity. Unless there is a limit to the number of committees set up there will not only be disintegration but too heavy a call on members' time and too burdensome a responsibility for imaginative or sustained good work and for the creation of that quasi-specialisation which inevitably emerges from committee experience. For the present it need only be pointed out that the flexibility of the system can be misused either by deploying available resources beyond a certain point or, less common, by not making sufficient use of it. The problems of secretarial work closely bound up with all this will be considered later.

Endurability of the system

9.10. In recent years the disadvantages of the committee system have been thought to outweigh the advantages.[15] It has, however, survived fundamentally unchanged despite plans to change it (by, for example, reducing the functions of committees to those of a consultative rather than executive character[16]) and improvements wrought in the light of experience. Its disintegrating features have been modified by reducing the number of separate committees,[17] by measures to co-ordinate in various ways, by a movement towards corporate management and by counteracting the close alignment of committees with departments. And its effectiveness and efficiency have been increased by delegating to committees wide executive powers within policy guidelines, by defining more precisely the relationship between council and committees, and by reducing the amount of administrative detail with which committees have traditionally been concerned.[18]

Legal basis

9.11. It needs to be said at this juncture that at common law and by statute the power of a local authority to appoint committees to discharge its functions is well recognised. There are wide powers in the Local Government Act 1972 enabling an authority to appoint committees[19] (recognising, too, that the authority is compelled for certain functions to appoint specific committees[20]) and to refer and to delegate functions to them.

9.12. The courts have placed considerable credence on the effectiveness of

[15] Maud Report, vol. 1, para. 128.
[16] *Ibid.* vol. 1, para.166.
[17] *Ibid.* vol. 1, para.167.
[18] *Ibid.* vol. 1, paras.109–14.
[19] See ss.101–102.
[20] See s.101(8)–(9).

committees even where powers have not been expressly delegated. Thus it has been held that action taken by an officer on the direction of a committee before the committee's act was confirmed by the council effectively ratified the officer's action. In *Firth* v. *Staines*[21] a health committee had directed a sanitary inspector to serve notice on an owner to abate a nuisance and after the failure of the owner to comply with it laid an information against him and a summons was issued. After the issue of the summons the committee's acts were confirmed. The court held, applying the principles of the doctrine of ratification, that the acts of the committee became valid as from the time when they were done. In *Firth* v. *Staines*, however, the committee had had specific authority to act subject to subsequent ratification by the vestry: an unusual arrangement. Where there is express delegation there is, of course, no requirement upon the council to confirm or ratify or approve what has been done under delegated powers. Thus an act of the committee in such circumstances is the act of the local authority and what the committee does binds the council.

9.13. It is thus evident that a local authority's committee system is regulated by law, structure and procedure. It must be framed to meet the authority's objectives: the system is not an end in itself but an administrative instrument through which the authority can effectively, efficiently, lawfully and democratically discharge its several functions.

Structural considerations

9.14. The committee system must be so arranged that it contributes to the effective and efficient management of the local authority's affairs: it must ensure that ultimate direction and control lie with councillors; it must enable them to review progress and the performance of the services provided for the community; and it must assist in the identification of the authority's objectives and the formulation of plans to achieve those objectives. There is a persuasive school of thought that only a committee structure based on programme areas can secure this: see 9.51.

9.15. If it is to meet these criteria then there should be no more standing committees than are necessary, the membership of the committees should be small, their terms of reference and order of delegation should be clearly specified, and their relationship to the full assembly and any policy committee defined: each committee should be concerned with matters that can only be dealt with at member level, i.e. there should ordinarily be

---

[21] [1897] 2 QB 70.

no involvement in matters of day-to-day administration that can properly be left in the hands of officers.

Co-ordination

9.16. The absence until recently of any kind of managing body within the organisation was noted in Chapter 4. Maud considered this one of the fundamental weaknesses of the committee system in English local government. Maud recognised that committees had been accepted axiomatically as 'practically essential as a means of conducting business' where executive authority is 'entrusted to a large body'; and it saw the committee system as 'a contrivance for decentralizing the various functions of the council and for creating a number of microcosms of it to meet problems as they arise; it is not a means of establishing responsibilities of individual members or groups of members'.[22]

9.17. This 'disunity in the whole' persuaded Maud to draw up the outline of a management structure based on the following principles:

(a) effective and efficient management under the direction and control of the members;
(b) clear leadership and responsibility among both members and officers;
(c) an organisation which presents to the public an intelligible system of government;
(d) responsiveness to the needs of the public.

Maud felt that the existing committee system made it difficult to identify major issues and to isolate them from routine matters: it considered it necessary to establish more clearly the functions and responsibility of members and officers. To remedy these defects Maud recommended the establishment of a *management board* (see 4.12) – which had little support at the time although it prepared the way for Bains's policy committee.

Organisation

9.18. The organisation which local authorities have adopted traditionally has been to apportion responsibilities to committees according to the main functions of the authority (the vertical system) and to the type or nature of the work to be done (the horizontal system). The application of the *vertical system* means that a committee is set up to deal with such functions as housing, planning, social services, education and so on. The idea behind the current fashion of committees for programme areas is a variant of this: see 9.51. The *horizontal system* implies one where a committee is set up for purposes of finance, central purchasing, personnel and similar functions

[22] Maud Report, vol. 1, paras.93–96.

that relate to the whole of the council's activities. The objection to this conventional distribution of tasks is that it tends to be unnecessarily divisive and encourages the disintegrating influences which have made each local authority in the past a fragmented organisation instead of a corporate one. An authority's principal objectives and the programmes to achieve them matter more than the concurrent pursuit of limited objectives in narrowly defined activities. The horizontal committees have had an important co-ordinative role to perform, and where standing orders have endowed them with substantial powers, they have done a great deal towards achieving a measure of unity which otherwise rested upon unregulated measures (such as common membership between committees) or the imperfect co-ordinating function of the full assembly.

Types of committee

Broad classification

9.19. There are several ways of classifying committees. The broadest classification is between committees with power only to consider and report upon matters within their terms of reference and those with executive power to make the final decision on all or some of the matters within their terms of reference. A committee's terms of reference are its remit: they specify, precisely or broadly (preferably always the former), the matters with which the committee is concerned; and they may go further and specify the executive powers of the committee on matters within the terms of reference.

Statutory and discretionary committees

9.20. Committees may be statutory or discretionary, i.e. there are committees which a local authority is compelled to set up by express statutory enactment, and ones which it is not bound to set up but may do so if it wishes. Committees set up year after year are often referred to as *standing committees*.

Statutory committees

9.21. There are now far fewer statutory committees than there were prior to reorganisation.[23] The Local Government Act 1972, s.101(9), repealed

---

[23] The statutory obligation upon local authorities to set up specific committees has long been criticised: see, e.g. the second report of the Local Government Manpower Committee, 1951, Cmnd 8421, appendix IX; the Maud Report (1967), vol. 1, paras.203–4: '. . . the requirement that a local authority must appoint a specific committee for a specific purpose . . . is an unnecessary interference with local authorities who should be free to develop and experiment with their own schemes of organization'; and the Bains Report (1972), pp. 133–35.

many of the provisions requiring the establishment of committees for specific purposes but continued the following:

(a)   the *education committee*,[24]

(b)   the special education committee known as the *Inner London Education Authority*;[25]

(c)   the *police committee*,[26]

(d)   any *committee established for purposes of sea fisheries*;[27]

(e)   the former *children's regional planning committees*;[28]

(f)   the *social services committee*;[29]

(g)   any committee required to be established for the administration of the *superannuation of persons employed in local government*;[30]

(h)   *national park committees*.[31]

9.22. There are certain features common to several of the statutory committees and others particular to each. In the case, for example, of both the education and the social services committees it is expressly provided that the local authority may not exercise any of its functions within the scope of the committee until it has considered a report from the committee:[32] this is less restrictive than may be thought because it does not mean that the authority must agree necessarily with the committee's recommendation – only that it must consider its report before deciding upon a course of action; and there is a proviso which enables the authority to act without first considering the committee's report in matters of urgency.[33] There is also some similarity between a police committee and a national park committee in that each when set up by more than one county authority becomes virtually the police authority and the national park authority respectively.[34] By and large, however, the statutory committees now have few similarities (indeed, there never was much uniformity in their constitution and regulation even in their heyday): each has characteristics moulded by the particular functions which it is set up to serve.

9.23. When the Bill which became the Local Government Act 1972 was being drafted the Government of the day said it wanted to allow the new

[24]   Education Act 1944, sch. 1, Pt II, paras.1, 3. See 9.24.
[25]   London Government Act 1963, s.30(2): now a directly elected authority: see 1.5.
[26]   Police Act 1964, ss.2, 3. See 9.29.
[27]   Sea Fisheries Regulation Act 1966, s.1, applicable only where sea fisheries districts have been set up under the Act.
[28]   Health and Social Services, etc. Act 1983. s.4.
[29]   Local Authority Social Services Act 1970, s.2. See 9.32.
[30]   Superannuation Act 1972, s.7.
[31]   Local Government Act 1972, sch.17, Pt I. See 9.38.
[32]   Education Act 1944, sch.1, Pt II, para.1; Local Authority Social Services Act 1970, s.4(1).
[33]   *Ibid.* para.7 and s.3(3) respectively.
[34]   Police Act 1964, ss.3, 21; Local Government Act 1972, sch.17, Pt I, para.5.

authorities to set up such committees as each thought most suitable to its needs, but could not immediately remove all existing requirements as to statutory committees. It decided to retain the specific provisions affecting *police and national parks* because:[35]

> these provisions are related to the special nature of the functions rather than to the need to impose any particular management pattern. In both cases the functions involved are of national significance; and in each case statutory provision is made for the committees to include persons appointed from outside.

As regards *social services committees* (see 9.32):

> The requirement to appoint a separate (social services) committee was specifically linked to the need to define guidelines for a newly integrated service and the Government (proposes) that it should be carried forward into the new local government system.

And as regards *education committees* (see next paragraph):

> The arguments in favour of retaining the statutory requirement to establish an education committee are different. The Government sees no need to retain this requirement indefinitely, but consider it would be appropriate initially to carry it over into the new system.

Education committees

9.24. Every local education authority[36] is required to set up, in accordance with arrangements approved by the Minister,[37] such education committees as it thinks expedient for the efficient discharge of its functions with respect to education.[38] Where the Minister thinks it expedient he may by order, after consulting the authorities concerned, require the setting up of a joint education committee for the purpose of exercising some but not all of their education functions;[39] and any such order may provide for

---

[35] Consultative paper issued by the Department of the Environment and Welsh Office, 26 August 1971.

[36] The local education authorities are the county councils and metropolitan district councils outside London (Local Government Act 1972, s.192(1); and the Inner London Education Authority, in respect of the area of the inner London boroughs and the outer London borough councils for their areas in the remainder of Greater London (London Government Act 1963, s.30, as amended by the Local Government Act 1985).

[37] The Minister is the Secretary of State for Education and Science.

[38] The statutory system of education is that prescribed by the Education Act 1944, s.7, organised in three progressive stages known as primary education, secondary education and further education. Most local education authorities appoint at least three main subcommittees of the education committee to deal separately with each, i.e. a primary, secondary, and further education subcommittee.

[39] Education Act 1944, sch.1, Pt II, para.1.

authorising the joint education committee to exercise any of those functions on behalf of the authorities concerned and may include such
incidental and consequential provisions – including provisions with
respect to the setting up and functions of subcommittees – as the Minister
thinks desirable.[40]

9.25. Every education committee must include persons of experience in
education and persons acquainted with education conditions in the area.[41]
Although this implies co-option it is not obligatory so long as the local
education authority is satisfied that its elected members on the committee
fulfil these conditions; where co-opted persons are brought in at least a
majority of every committee must be members of the authority[42] (and in
the case of a joint education committee this requirement is to have effect so
that at least one half of the joint committee are members of any of the
authorities for which the committee is established).

9.26. The local education authority must consider a report from its
education committee before itself exercising any of the functions with
respect to education, although it may dispense with such a report if, in its
opinion, the matter is urgent;[43] and it is not bound necessarily to accept the
committee's recommendations. In *R. v. Brent London Borough Council ex-
parte Gunning* (1985)[44] the local education authority's decision to close a
school was held to be *ultra vires* because, *inter alia*, it had not first considered
a report from its education committee or, alternatively, had not specifically, i.e. by resolution, dispensed with such a report. It seems that the
authority had merely had before it a brief minute of the education
committee's deliberations. Hodgson J said:

> There is argument about what a report consists of. Of course, it is very import-
> ant to decide what a report is. In my view . . . a report from an education

---

[40] *Ibid.* sch.1, Pt II, para.3.
[41] *Ibid.* sch.1, Pt II, para.5. Teachers and other education employees are not necessarily
disqualified from co-option: Local Government Act 1972, s.81(4).
[42] In practice every local education authority co-opts on to its education committee either by
selection or upon the nomination of other bodies. Thus, for example, Surrey County
Council has 18 persons on its education committee: eight selected members (including
persons with experience or knowledge of further education, education not part of the
statutory system, rural pursuits, music, art and physical and recreational facilities activities); and ten members, nominated by London University (1), Diocese Education Committees of Southwark and Guildford (1 each), Free Church Federal Council (1), Roman
Catholic Bishop of Southwark (1), Surrey County Teachers' Association (2), Joint Four
Secondary Associations (1), Surrey Trades Council Federation (1), employers in the
county (1).
[43] Education Act 1944, sch.1, Pt II, para.7. This does not compel the local education authority
to refer to the education committee or one of its subcommittees any matter which by some
other enactment stands referred to some other committee of the authority: *ibid.* sch.1, Pt II,
para.11.
[44] (1985) 84 LGR Pt 2.

committee should either make some recommendation or should at least, if not making a recommendation, set out the arguments for and against a particular course of action. Otherwise I cannot see how the local education authority is to inform itself adequately of the views of the education committee before performing one of its functions.

Procedural flaws are always liable to invalidate a local authority's decision (see, generally, Chapter 1); and as to the advantages of a committee report, as opposed to a committee minute, as the medium through which to advise the full assembly: see 12.38.

9.27. There is power enabling the local education authority to delegate any of its education functions to an education committee except the power to borrow money or to raise a rate.[45] And every education committee may, subject to any restrictions imposed by the authority or the order of the minister by which the committee was established, (a) appoint subcommittees, constituted in such manner as the committee may determine, and (b) authorise any such subcommittee to exercise any of the functions of the committee on its behalf.[46]

9.28. The minutes of proceedings of an education committee must be open to inspection by local government electors for the area and any elector may make a copy thereof or an extract therefrom.[47] The requirement that a fee shall be charged has not been repealed even though minutes open to inspection for the last several years under the general powers of the Local Government Act 1972, s.228, are open to inspection without charge and, since the Local Government (Access to Information) Act 1985, are freely open to public inspection.

Police committee

9.29. The statutory police committee is the police authority for a non-metropolitan county or for a combined force where the constituent authorities have agreed that there shall be a police committee of one of their number on behalf of all.[48] It is the committee which is itself the police

---

[45] Education Act 1944, sch.1, Pt II, para.8. The education committee cannot delegate functions to an officer (*ibid.* para.10): *R. v. Birmingham City Council ex-parte NUPE* (*The Times*, 24 April 1984), though the local education authority can do so: see 4.8. And neither the local education authority nor an education committee may delegate to the committee chairman: *R. v. Liverpool City Council ex-parte Professional Association of Teachers* (1984) 82 LGR 648; *R v. Secretary of State for Education and Science ex-parte Birmingham City Council* (1984) 83 LGR 79.

[46] *Ibid.* sch.1, Pt II, para.10.

[47] *Ibid.* sch.1, Pt II, para.9.

[48] Police Act 1964, ss.3, 21, sch.1, as amended by Local Government Act 1972, s.196(2), sch.30.

authority and the duties imposed on the authority are thus directly imposed on the committee, which is not accountable in any way to the county council[49] (although the county council must approve expenditure from the police fund[50] and it may ask questions concerning police administration: see 9.31). This unique committee does not exist, however, in the special case of the Metropolitan Police,[51] or in the City of London[52] or the metropolitan counties:[53] and in these cases, except in the City of London, the police authority issues a precept upon the constituent authorities. The former watch committee of county borough councils disappeared with the reorganisation of local government in the 1970s.

9.30. The police committee of a non-metropolitan county council consists of county councillors appointed by the council and of magistrates appointed by the magistrates' courts committee: two-thirds of the membership comes from the former and one-third from the latter.[54] All members are full members of the committee: there is no power of co-option to a police committee, nor may any subcommittee of the police committee include co-opted persons.[55]

9.31. Questions on police administration may be asked at meetings of the county council (or constituent councils in the case of a combined police authority) but these may deal only with matters concerning the discharge of the police authority's functions and not matters within the province of the chief constable.[56] For this purpose the police committee is required to appoint one of its county council members (who may or may not, of

---

[49] Accountability both in this sense and in the accountability of a chief constable to elected members is a matter of current controversy: see, e.g. John Harrison *What the Police Committee Member Needs to Know* (1984). Several local authorities have set up their own non-statutory police committee to provide a representative voice on matters of police policy.

[50] Police Act 1964, s.8, as amended by Local Government Act 1972, s.196(2), sch.30, and Local Government Act 1985, sch.11, para.1(5).

[51] Metropolitan Police Acts 1829–1963.

[52] Police Act 1964, s.62, sch.8.

[53] The police authority is the metropolitan county police authority, other than in Tyne and Wear, the Northumbria Police Authority (for Tyne and Wear and Northumberland): Local Government Act 1985, Pt IV.

[54] Police Act 1964, s.21: this same proportion of elected members and magistrates applies in the case of the police authorities constituted for the metropolitan counties under the Local Government Act 1985, Pt IV.

[55] Perversely, it may be thought, Widdicombe assumed that the magistrates *were* co-opted members: it recommended a review of the special rights of magistrates in relation to the police service to see whether any continued role should be purely deliberative or consultative without voting rights: Widdicombe Report, paras.5.103–5.107.

[56] Police Act 1964, s.11, as amended by Local Government Act 1972, sch.30, and Local Government Act 1985, sch.11, para.1(6).

course, be the committee chairman because the chairman could be a magistrate) to answer questions in the council chamber.[57]

Social services committee

9.32. The councils of non-metropolitan counties and of metropolitan districts in England and Wales, the London borough councils and the Common Council of the City of London are required[58] to establish a social services committee[59] to which, much as in the case of local education authorities and their education committees, there must stand referred all matters relating to the discharge of the authority's statutory functions in respect of the social services.[60] Except with the consent of the Secretary of State (which may be given either generally or with respect to a particular authority) or as otherwise provided, no other matter may be referred to or dealt with by the committee.[61] There is express power to delegate to the committee the functions which stand referred to it; and where functions are not so delegated the authority itself must nevertheless not exercise any of those functions (unless the matter is urgent) without considering a report of the committee with respect to the matter in question.[62]

9.33. These provisions do not, however, preclude an authority from referring to a committee other than its social services committee a matter which, although required to be referred to the social services committee, should in the authority's opinion be referred to that other committee on the ground that 'it relates to a general service of the authority'; but before referring any such matter the authority must receive and consider a report of the social services committee with respect to the subject-matter of the proposed reference.[63] This, it is submitted, permits a local authority to refer to, say, a personnel or staffing committee matters relating to the staffing of the social services department, including the appointment of the director of

---

[57] This useful expedient could be used in other instances where, for example, a co-opted member is elected chairman of a committee: the committee could in such circumstances appoint a councillor member to pilot the committee's report through council and also answer questions: see 5.52.

[58] Local Government Act 1972, s.195(1), amending Local Authority Social Services Act 1970, s.1.

[59] Local Authority Social Services Act 1970, s.2(1) as continued in force by Local Government Act 1972, s.101(9).

[60] Local Authority Social Services Act 1970, s.2(1) and sch.1, as amended by Local Government Act 1972, s.195, and sch.23.

[61] Local Authority Social Services Act 1970, s.3(1).

[62] *Ibid.* s.3(3); and see 9.26.

[63] Local Authority Social Services Act 1970, s.3(4).

social services[64] – provided the views of the social services committee are sought before the reference is made.

9.34. Two or more social services authorities may, instead of setting up individual social services committees, concur in establishing a joint social services committee;[65] and in such cases the joint committee stands in relation to the constituent councils in the same way as does the individual social services committee with its parent authority.[66] A social services committee may, subject to any restrictions imposed by the local authority or, as the case may be, the authorities concurring in the establishment of the committee, establish subcommittees and delegate to them any of the functions of the committee.[67] The social services committees of two or more authorities may concur in the establishment of joint subcommittees and may, subject to any restrictions imposed by the local authorities concerned, delegate to them any of the functions of either or any of the committees.

9.35. The membership of an authority's social services committee may include persons who are not members of the authority or, as the case may be, of any authority concurring in the establishment of the committee provided they are not disqualified from being members of that authority or any such authority.[68] Provided at least a majority of its membership comprises members of the authority (or of the constituent authorities in the case of a joint committee)[69] the social services committee may itself,[70] if authorised to do so by its parent authority (or the constituent authorities in the case of a joint committee) and subject to any restrictions imposed by the authority (or those authorities), co-opt persons to serve on the committee – provided they are not disqualified from being members of that authority or any of the said authorities.[71] A subcommittee may similarly include co-opted persons.[72]

9.36. Every subcommittee must include at least one member of the parent authority or, as the case may be, of each of the local authorities con-

---

[64] *Ibid.* s.6(1) and (6).

[65] *Ibid.* s.4(1).

[66] *Ibid.* s.4(2).

[67] *Ibid.* s.4(3).

[68] Local Authority Social Services Act 1970, s.5(1). This follows the general provisions relating to co-opted persons: they do not need to be positively qualified for membership of the authority but must not be disqualified: see s.104, Local Government Act 1972.

[69] Cf. the general rule as to discretionary committees which requires that two-thirds of a committee must be members of the authority: see Local Government Act 1972, s.102(3).

[70] Ordinarily co-option to committees is a function of the council: see 5.45.

[71] Local Authority Social Services Act 1970, s.5(2) and (3).

[72] *Ibid.* s.5(4).

cerned.[73] Every joint subcommittee must include at least one member of each of the constituent authorities.

9.37. The regulations relating to the former children's regional planning committee (set up jointly by the local authorities within the area concerned for purposes of planning provision of community homes for children in care and for the equipment and maintenance of such accommodation[74]) included unusual provisions restricting the rights ordinarily available to co-opted members. It expressly provided that the appointed members of the committee, referred to as nominated members – who had to be in a majority – could determine, subject to any directions given by the constituent authorities, the powers of any co-opted members to attend, speak and vote at meetings. Furthermore, only the nominated members could determine the quorum and procedure of the committee.[75]

National park committees

9.38. For every national park for which there is no joint planning board or special planning board[76] the council or councils of the county or counties in which the park is comprised must set up a national park committee to discharge statutory functions relating to the park under the National Parks and Access to the Countryside Act 1949 and the Countryside Act 1968 as extended by the Local Government Act 1972.[77] The national park committee for a park comprised in two or more counties is to be appointed either by one of the county councils as agreed by the county councils concerned or by the county councils jointly; and where one county council sets up the committee on behalf of another or other counties the expenses must be apportioned by agreement between them.[78] The constitution and membership of a national park committee are regulated by sch.17 of the Local Government Act 1972.

Quasi-statutory committees

9.39. There was formerly within the classification of statutory committees

---

[73] *Ibid.* s.5(5).
[74] These committees were set up under the Child Care Act 1980 ss.31–34 now repealed.
[75] *Ibid.* s.31, sch.1, now repealed.
[76] Joint boards differ from joint committees: see Ch. 13 as to the former and 9.49 as to the latter.
[77] Local Government Act 1972, s.184 and sch.17, para.5.
[78] *Ibid.* para.9.

a small group which local authorities were not bound to set up but if they elected to do so the committees had to be constituted in the manner provided by statute. Within this group were, particularly, the planning committee (regulated formerly by the Town and Country Planning Act 1962, s.2, and sch.2, Pt I) and the fire brigade committee (by the Fire Services Act 1947, s.20). None of the statutory provisions affecting this group now has effect: the Local Government Act 1972, s.101(8) provides that any enactment (except those relating to the statutory committees listed in s.101(9): see 9.21) which contains provisions empowering or requiring local authorities singly, or in collaboration with other authorities, to establish committees, including joint committees, for any purpose, or enabling a minister to make an instrument to such effect shall, to the extent that it makes such provision, cease to have effect. This 'blanket' provision means that any statutory provision (other than, as just indicated, the statutory committees continued in operation by the 1972 Act) in force prior to the coming into effect of the 1972 Act need not be consulted.

Discretionary committees

9.40. The law confers upon local authorities a general power[79] to appoint a committee (or a joint committee in the case of two or more authorities) for purposes of discharging any of their functions (except functions for which a statutory committee must be established). Even without this express statutory power a local authority could conceivably set up any number of discretionary (non-statutory, or permissive) committees so long as the committees' functions were deliberative and not executive, i.e. limited to considering and reporting; the authority would not be able, however – without express statutory power – to delegate to any such committee because of the maxim *delegatus non potest delegare*: see 9.83.
9.41. This general enabling, but not unrestricted, power extends to permit[80] expressly any such discretionary committee to appoint one or more subcommittees and the authority or authorities or, in the case of a subcommittee, the appointing committee to fix the number of members, their term of office, and the area (if restricted) within which the committee (or subcommittee) is to operate.
9.42. The restrictions upon this general enabling power are that:[81]
(a) in the case of a committee for regulating and controlling the finance of the authority, the members must be members of the appointing

---

[79] Local Government Act 1972, s.102(1).
[80] *Ibid.* s.102(2).
[81] *Ibid.* s.102(3).

authority or authorities or, in the case of a subcommittee, of the authority or authorities of which it is a subcommittee (see 9.46);

(b) in the case of other committees the members may include co-opted persons but at least two-thirds of the committee (other than a subcommittee) must be members of the authority or authorities appointing the committee;

(c) in the case of any committee: every member who at the time of his appointment to the committee was a member of the appointing authority or one of the appointing authorities ceases to be a member of the committee when he ceases to be a member of the appointing authority or one of them.

Advisory committees

9.43. An entirely new power conferred by the Local Government Act 1972, s.102(4), empowers an authority either by itself or jointly with another or other authorities to appoint a committee 'to advise the appointing authority or authorities on any matter relating to the discharge of their functions'. An advisory committee may comprise members or non-members of the authority or authorities, appointed for whatever term may be determined; and the committee may appoint one or more subcommittees to advise the committee. Any non-council members are not, it is submitted, properly termed co-opted members. The consultative committees which authorities set up for certain personnel functions are *not* advisory committees under s.102(4): see 13.20.

Special committees

9.44. A special committee is one appointed for a short-term purpose, e.g. to deal with a specific matter which does not fall within the terms of reference of any standing committee or which otherwise is considered to merit particular attention by a committee of members – perhaps selected for their knowledge or experience. Sometimes such a committee is referred to as an *ad hoc* committee, for obvious reasons. The late J. H. Warren considered that a committee 'regularly appointed from time to time for recurring purposes' should be regarded as a special committee:[82]

> Such is the selection committee, appointed to recommend the personnel for standing committees, and often invested with the duty of revising standing orders and the terms of reference to standing committees.

[82] J. H. Warren, *The English Local Government System.*

If, however, an authority's standing orders provide for the appointment of a selection committee, or a committee of this kind is in practice regularly appointed year after year, there is justification for considering it a standing committee, even though, as may be the case, the committee is constituted somewhat differently from other standing committees. A second example from Warren is, perhaps, a better one, i.e. a committee appointed by some local authorities to consider the choice of mayor.

Other classifications

9.45. Some local authorities make a distinction between what they call *service* committees and *machinery* (or, a term first used by the former London County Council, *co-ordinative*) committees. The service committees, as the name implies, are those responsible for an authority's main services, e.g. housing, education, social services, fire brigade and so on: all committees organised on the vertical principle: see 9.18. These committees are largely, but not wholly, subordinate in matters of finance, staffing, supplies, land transactions, etc., to the machinery or co-ordinative committees charged solely with the oversight of these administrative tasks: all committees organised on the horizontal principle: see 9.18.

Finance committee

9.46. Any committee set up specifically for purposes of regulating and controlling the finance of the local authority or of its area or charged with that responsibility as part of other functions must be comprised solely of councillors.[83] Prior to reorganisation all authorities appointed a finance committee (indeed, there was formerly an obligation upon county councils to appoint a statutory finance committee) but nowadays, in line with the Bains report and current practice, financial business is part of the remit of the policy and resources committee, with the main committee concerning itself with financial policy and the finance subcommittee exercising financial control. The former conflicting views as to choice of membership for the finance committee, e.g. should it comprise the chairmen of spending committees, are no longer relevant.

Committees of parish meetings

9.47. A parish meeting in a parish where there is no separate parish council may set up a committee of local government electors for the parish

---

[83] Local Government Act 1972, s.102(3).

to discharge any of the functions of the parish meeting. Express power to do this, conferred by the Local Government Act 1972, s.108, was no doubt thought necessary because a parish meeting is not a local authority and therefore the general powers[84] enabling local authorities to set up committees do not apply: apart from the statutory provision there would appear to be no reason why a parish meeting should not set up a committee of electors for purposes of considering any matter of concern to the parish and reporting back to the parish meeting. Most of the statutory provisions relating to local authority committees apply also to the committees of a parish meeting.[85]

Committees of community meetings

9.48. There is no express statutory power conferred upon a community meeting to establish a committee of local government electors for the community.

Joint committees

9.49. There are two kinds of joint committee:

(a) those set up by a single local authority to consider a matter which falls within the terms of reference of two or more standing committees; and

(b) those set up by two or more local authorities or by a combination of one or more local authorities and another body or bodies for purposes in respect of which they are jointly interested.

The first of these is dealt with in the next paragraph; the other – which is of the character of a committee for a special purpose – is examined in Chapter 13. The term 'joint committee' is also commonly used for committees of council and employee representatives but these are of an entirely different character.

9.50. A joint committee set up by a local authority will be established under its general enabling power[86] to appoint a committee for any purpose it thinks fit. Therefore its membership, term of office, terms of reference and so on can all be determined by the council at its discretion. These joint committees must be distinguished from the statutory joint authorities set up in the metropolitan counties to act as (a) police, (b) fire and civil

---

[84] Local Government Act 1972, s.102.
[85] *Ibid.* s.99, which applies the provisions of sch.12.
[86] Local Government Act 1972, s.102.

defence, and (c) passenger transport authorities; and as the fire and civil defence authority for Greater London.

Programme area committees

9.51. Some authorities have organised their committee system on the basis of programme areas. Such authorities have first determined their main objectives, divided up the totality of their work into spheres of activity, each with its own objectives and programme for meeting those objectives, and then made a committee responsible for each programme and for the allocation of resources within it. Bains, in describing the evidence it received on this issue, reported in these terms:[87]

> The results, of course, differ according to the circumstances of each authority. If we take the library service as an example, several authorities have included this with education in an education (or educational services) committee whilst others are administering libraries through an amenities and recreation committee. Another example is a protection programme area which includes both fire brigade and the consumer protection services (weights and measures, etc.). There is nothing to prevent one committee dealing successfully with these two apparently diverse services if the idea of programme areas is accepted and we think that a more effective allocation of resources will result.

9.52. The advantages of a committee structure built on this basis is claimed to be that it becomes directly linked to the main needs and objectives of the authority. It encourages a corporate rather than a departmental approach 'so that each programme area committee can call upon and be serviced by the skills and experience of a number of different departments'.[88]

Constitution of committees
Appointment to committees

9.53. As indicated in Chapter 6, members are ordinarily selected for committee membership at the annual council meeting. This means that it is necessary to settle in advance of the council meeting the names of those who are to be nominated as members of the various committees. Usually the council members meet in private, either informally as a whole or in their political groups, and settle the names to be recommended at the council meeting. Much will depend upon local practice.[89] The chief

---

[87] Bains Report, p. 32.

[88] *Ibid.* As to the organisation of the committee system for purposes of corporate management: see Chapter 4.

[89] Note the system of proportional representation adopted by Medina Borough Council in the selection of committee membership referred to earlier: see 7.106.

executive may well consult the leaders of the political parties on the council to obtain agreement on the course to be followed: it may be that, as a first step, each member will be asked by letter to indicate his preferences and thereafter for the replies to be submitted to the party leaders, or to a selection committee constituted in some pre-arranged manner. Whatever the arrangement it ought to be possible for the council at its annual meeting to have before it more or less agreed recommendations on committee membership.

9.54. Alternatively, the appointment of committees will have to be dealt with at a later meeting of the council despite the disadvantage that there may be no committees in existence at all for a period of time. Some authorities, however, under a standing order to the following effect, allow formerly existing committees to go on functioning with depleted membership until new committees are constituted:

> Every committee shall hold office until the first meeting of its successor, except in the years in which all councillors go out of office when, subject to . . . the several committees as constituted at the dissolution of the council shall be entitled to continue to act until their successors as provisionally constituted under standing order . . . have met.

Or they may allow provisional committees to meet and act under a standing order to this effect:

> . . . the members of the council who are to be recommended by the selection committee for appointment on the various committees are empowered provisionally to meet and act as members of such committees up to the date of the meeting of the council to which the selection committee is submitting its recommendations, and such provisional committees shall, in the interim, have the same powers respectively (including the power to appoint subcommittees) as they would have had if they had been regularly appointed by resolution of the council.

9.55. Model standing order no. 28 deals with the appointment of committees at the council's annual meeting:

> The council shall at the annual meeting appoint such committees as they are required by or under any statute or under standing order 30 (standing committees) and may at any time appoint such other committees as are necessary to carry out the work of the council but, subject to any statutory provision in that behalf:
>
> (i) shall not appoint any member of a committee so as to hold office later than the next annual meeting of the council;
> (ii) may at any time dissolve a committee or alter its membership.

Even without a standing order in these terms it is clear that an authority may dislodge a member from a committee even though he has been appointed for the ensuing municipal year: in *Manton* v. *Brighton Corporation* (1951)[90] it was held that as the council had power to revoke the authority of a committee as a whole it also had power to revoke the authority of a single member before the end of his prescribed period of office. And in *R.* v. *Newham London Borough Council ex-parte Haggerty* (1986)[91] the local authority was held to be entitled to formulate criteria as to who should be appointed to its committees subject to 'rationality', i.e. compliance with the *Wednesbury* principles of reasonableness (see 1.39). In this case a councillor had unsuccessfully sought through judicial review an injunction against the council for denying him membership of committees because he had refused to provide a range of personal details which standing orders required him to disclose in a declaration.

9.56. Every member of a discretionary committee who at the time of appointment was a member of the appointing authority automatically ceases to be a member of the committee on ceasing to be a member of the authority: but not if he is re-elected a member of the authority not later than the day of retirement.[92]

9.57. Model standing order no. 30 is to the following effect:

> (1) The following committees shall be the standing committees of the council and shall consist of the number of members (exclusive of the mayor/chairman of the council) specified opposite each committee:
>
> . . . .
>
> [Although not set out in the model standing order the practice is to list the committees and the membership under headings such as these:

Name of committee	Members of the Council	Ex officio	Co-opted, Nominated or Selected	Total]

> (2) Except where otherwise provided by statute or a scheme made under statutory authority, the mayor/chairman of the council shall be *ex officio* a member of every standing committee appointed by the council.

As to ex-officio membership of committees and subcommittees: see 9.62–9.63.

Membership

9.58. Except where there is specific statutory provision to the contrary a local authority may appoint whom it likes on its committees, whether or

[90] [1951] 2 KB 393; [1951] 2 All ER 101.
[91] *The Times*, 11 April 1986.
[92] Local Government Act 1972, s.102.

not members of the council,[93] so long as at least two-thirds are members.[94] The committee members who are not councillors are ordinarily known as co-opted members. But a member of a committee who at the time of his appointment was a member of the appointing authority ceases to be a member of the committee upon ceasing to be a member of the appointing authority.[95] Generally, but there are exceptions, co-opted members do not have to have any prescribed qualifications: but they must not be disqualified from membership.[96]

9.59. Widdicombe felt that the discretion enabling a local authority to appoint whomever it likes to its committees (referred to in the foregoing paragraph) should be conditional upon there being an appropriate party balance in membership – at least in the case of committees and subcommittees exercising delegated powers. It recognised that this might lead to problems but not insurmountable ones:[97]

> We would expect that local authorities, in fixing the overall number of councillors on a committee, would have regard to whether this number was readily divisible according to whatever formula was required to achieve proportionality. In some cases this might mean avoidance of very small subcommittees, although we would certainly hope that committees would not become unwieldy simply to ensure precise proportionality. It must be accepted that some difficulties would occur, especially in relation to small parties. In most cases such difficulties would be capable of resolution by negotiation between the party whips (as they commonly are in authorities at present). Slight unrepresentation on one committee could be traded against slightly over-representation on another. However, we believe it unsatisfactory to rely solely on negotiation and believe that a neutral arbiter is required. We believe that this role should be given to the chief executive of the local authority, who often informally performs such a role at present ... The task of chief executives would be to prepare a proposal for committee membership on which they would then consult the political groups. Following consultation their decision would be final.

In summary, Widdicombe recommended that local authorities should be statutorily required to include provision in their standing orders governing the composition of committees and subcommittees with delegated powers to make decisions on behalf of the council so that the committees and subcommittees reflect as far as practicable the composition of the council as a whole, except in so far as individual parties or councillors might waive

---

[93] *Ibid.* s.102(4), but a member is not obliged to serve against his will: see 5.11.
[94] *Ibid.* s.102(3).
[95] *Ibid.* s.102(5).
[96] *Ibid.* s.102(5), and see Chapter 5.
[97] Widdicombe Report, paras.5.46–5.53.

their rights. Different considerations, Widdicombe said, should apply to deliberative committees: see 4.19.

9.60. The one-third ratio of co-opted to local authority members does not apply to subcommittees of discretionary committees[98] (which may consist wholly of co-opted members[99]); nor does a member of the appointing authority lose his place on the subcommittee if he ceases to be a member of the authority unless standing orders so prescribe (as ordinarily they will do to avoid misunderstanding as to the position).

Revocation of committee membership

9.61. We have seen elsewhere that a local authority is fully entitled to put an end to a councillor's membership of a committee even before the expiration of the term for which he had been appointed,[100] but the authority must observe, while they remain in force, any standing orders which would not entitle the council to do so[101] – provided the standing orders in this respect do not go beyond what is reasonable.[102]

Ex-officio members

9.62. Ex-officio members of a committee are those councillors, such as a council chairman or vice-chairman, whose appointment to a committee or subcommittee is by virtue of the office held and not by their selection as individuals. Unless the council determines otherwise, ex-officio members are full members of the committee, able to speak and vote. There appears to be no reason, however, why a local authority should not, if so minded, restrict the right of ex-officio members to that of mere attendance at committees and subcommittees, i.e. with no voting rights; and the view has been expressed that it would equally be in order for the authority to permit an ex-officio member to propose or second a motion but not to vote.[103] Whatever the local arrangement it should, of course, be regulated by formal standing orders.

9.63. Ordinarily the chairman of a committee, and the vice-chairman if

---

[98] Local Government Act 1972, s.102(3).

[99] This is not always so of subcommittees of statutory committees, e.g. subcommittees of the social services committee must include at least one councillor: Local Authority Social Services Act 1970, s.5(4).

[100] *Manton* v. *Brighton Corporation* [1951] 2 KB 392.

[101] *R.* v. *Rushmore Borough Council ex-parte Crawford: The Times,* 28 November 1981: see 2.9.

[102] See *R.* v. *Newham London Borough Council ex-parte Haggerty: supra.*

[103] An opinion expressed in 142 *Local Government Review* 589.

there is one, will be ex officio a member of each of the committee's subcommittees. Model standing order no. 33 is to this effect:

(1) Every committee appointed by the council may appoint sub-committees for purposes to be specified by the committee.

(2) The chairman [and the vice-chairman, if any] of the committee shall be [an] ex officio member[s] of every sub-committee appointed by that committee, unless [he signifies to the committee that he does] [they signify to the committee that they do] not wish to serve.

And thus it is that committees sometimes appoint a *panel*, rather than a subcommittee, in circumstances where the membership is intended to be small: a committee chairman or vice-chairman should not automatically be ex officio a member of the panel.

Substitute members

9.64. A committee has a fixed membership (see 9.5), i.e. the number of members and the individuals appointed to membership are determined by the local authority. The committee itself has no power beyond what may be conferred upon it by the council to vary its membership. A local authority could, exceptionally, permit a committee itself to co-opt non-councillors up to a prescribed number or allow it to substitute another councillor if an appointed councillor is unable to attend on any occasion. This procedure has become popular in the case of hung councils, where the political balance on a committee could be upset by the absence of just one member.

9.65. Whatever the arrangement it is advisable for the practice to be laid down in standing orders and for standing orders to regulate it so that the system can be properly controlled, e.g. to ensure that if a substitute member is present at a meeting and the appointed member turns up during the course of proceedings, the substitute is required to withdraw from further participation. The name of each substitute must be notified in advance to the proper officer so that he can be summoned to a particular meeting or be sent a notice and agenda on every occasion.[104]

9.66. The former Greater London Council had carefully regulated the attendance of substitutes at meetings by a standing order to the following effect, introduced at a time when the Labour administration had only a narrow majority:

(a) Members of an appointing body may attend and speak at meetings of a subsidiary body, but not vote.

---

[104] See Raymond S. B. Knowles, 'Voting by Substitutes' (1981) 145 *Local Government Review* 412.

(b) A member of a subsidiary body may nominate a member of the council to act as his substitute, who in the absence of the member from any meeting of the body (other than the policy co-ordinating committee) shall be entitled to attend, speak and vote at the meeting.

A member may revoke the nomination of a substitute. Where the nominating member is a chairman, vice-chairman or authorised member of a subsidiary body the substitute shall not thereby be entitled to act in that capacity.

The nominating or revocation of a substitute shall be in writing specifying the body or bodies to which it relates and signed by the nominating member, shall be promptly sent to the director-general and clerk to the council, and shall not take effect earlier than 21 days after it is so received.

In the foregoing an 'appointing body' meant the council in relation to its committees, committees in relation to their subcommittees, and subcommittees in relation to any section or panel they appoint. 'Subsidiary body' meant the body so appointed.

9.67. A councillor who attends a meeting as a substitute attends, speaks and votes in his own capacity. He does not relinquish his own personal responsibilities or, as it were, take on the mantle of his nominator. The substitute is personally under the same obligations as any other councillor to disclose his interest in any contract or other matter before the committee or subcommittee and must refrain from speaking or voting if disqualified on that account.

Non-members of a committee

9.68. As to the attendance of non-members of a committee at a meeting of a committee: see Chapter 5.

Size

9.69. The number of members on a committee or subcommittee is a matter to be decided by the local authority or, in the case of a joint committee, the authorities which set it up.[105] Several considerations affect the size of membership. Just as there must be a plurality of persons present to constitute a meeting, so too must there be a plurality of persons present to constitute a committee or subcommittee.[106] There is also a limit to the size of a committee because a committee which consists of all members of the council (or perhaps more than that if co-opted members were brought

---

[105] Local Government Act 1972, s.102(2).
[106] See 1.7. In any case as there is no power to delegate functions to an individual council member there could hardly be said to be power to delegate to a committee of one member.

in) cannot by definition be a committee of the parent body: see 9.2. Nevertheless, for procedural purposes, it was once common practice for local authorities to 'go into committee' to evade the need to conduct business of the full assembly in public, or to constitute a finance and general purposes committee of all members of the council for much the same purpose.[107]

9.70. There are grounds for the view that a local authority committee cannot comprise fewer than three persons. It cannot comprise one member alone for the reason just given, nor should it comprise two only because the power of the person presiding to give a second or casting vote would mean that the committee could become a dictatorship of the chairman. It could be argued also that even a committee of three members gives considerable power to the chairman in so far as he can cast an original vote or a casting vote if the other two are divided in their views to decide any matter in his favour. These are, possibly, theoretical objections: an authority which constitutes a committee of two or three members must be presumed to know what it is doing (and, in any case, the potential danger is not very real even if the committee is entrusted with executive powers because of the authority's freedom to dissolve the committee at any time);[108] and, of course, it is a convention that a committee chairman should not be too freely disposed to exercise his second or casting vote.

9.71. Taking account of the foregoing and of the advantages of a small rather than a large committee, an optimum size could be four or five members including the chairman, preferably four so as to eliminate the possibility of too frequent an equality of votes. A small committee is more likely to reach a decision speedily and is less costly to convene; but it may not be fairly representative of political or other opinion or of electoral wards or divisions, and may need to be increased in size if there is a desire or an obligation to bring in co-opted persons because of the two-thirds rule: see 9.58.

9.72. In practice the membership of committees varies considerably in size. Maud's research report[109] found that over half of county finance committees had between 20 and 29 members, and nearly three-quarters of those of county borough councils had between ten and 19 members. County education committees had at least 40 members but those of county borough councils tended to be smaller (though two cases were cited of a membership of over 50). Housing, children's (now social services) and

---

[107] The Maud Committee's research group found this practice surprisingly widespread: Maud Report, vol. 5, ch. 2, paras.13–18.

[108] See *Manton* v. *Brighton Corporation* [1951] 8 KB 393; [1951] 2 All ER 101.

[109] Maud Report, vol. 1, para.117.

transport committees tended to be smaller. Most local authorities have now reduced the size of committees but this was evidently an unpopular move.[110]

Can there be a committee of the full council?

9.73. If – as indicated above (see 9.5) – there is a minimum number of members which may validly constitute a committee or subcommittee, can there be a maximum number? Or, put another way, can there be a committee of the whole membership of the local authority? As a matter of historical fact, before local authorities were compelled to throw open their committees to the public, councils sometimes resolved to 'go into committee' so as to exclude the public and Press (see 9.69). No one challenged their right to do so. However, there is now no need for the expedient of 'going into committee' – at least to exclude the public, because such a move would be purposeless.

9.74. There seems, nevertheless, no lawful reason why a local authority should still not decide to go into committee if it wishes, or otherwise set up a committee comprised of all members of the council. But there is a contrary opinion, based on the view that a committee which consists of all the councillors cannot by definition be a committee of the parent body. Further, that the terms of the 1972 Act, looked at as a whole, presuppose that a committee will comprise fewer members than the whole council membership, and that in the case of delegation of functions to a committee, which the law permits, it would be nonsense to contemplate the delegating body delegating functions to itself, albeit in another guise.[111] Further still, the statutory arrangements for the discharge of functions by committees can be likened to the relation of principal (the council) and agent (the committees), and for the council to appoint itself as agent for itself is nonsensical.

9.75. What if, irrespective of legal considerations, the local authority does set up a committee of the whole membership? It must mean that the formalities required to be observed in the case of council meetings need not be followed, e.g. the chairman of the council does not automatically take

---

[110] Bains Report, paras.4.35–36.

[111] In s.108 of the Local Government Act 1972, governing committees of parish meetings, the same words are used as in s.101, i.e. 'may arrange for the discharge of any of their functions by a committee of local government electors for the parish'. On this analogy it could be argued that the parish meeting could appoint a committee consisting of the whole of the parish electorate!

the chair (indeed, it would be inappropriate for him to do so[112]) and a committee chairman would need to be elected; and, further, persons from outside the council's membership could be co-opted.

Terms of reference

Definition

9.76. A committee's terms of reference – its remit – specify the functions with which the committee is charged and define the limits of its authority. Precision is important in framing terms of reference so as to avoid doubt about the scope of a committee's tasks. If the terms are narrowly drawn the committee's powers and duties may be unduly restrictive; if widely drawn there is risk that the terms may overlap those of another committee or committees.

9.77. Terms of reference, it has been said,[113] should be 'collectively all-embracing and mutually exclusive'. By this is meant that the terms of reference of all committees should cover the whole of the council's area of operations but should be so drawn that one set of terms does not overlap another. However skilfully the terms are drafted it is impossible to foresee every eventuality and thus most authorities provide for the terms of reference of an appropriate committee, e.g. a general purposes committee, to include responsibility for:

> Any matter not delegated or referred to or coming under the cognisance of any other committee.

Form

9.78. It is common practice but not essential for terms of reference to be framed in imperative words, e.g.:

> To exercise the functions of the council relating to . . .

or:

> To consider and make recommendations to the council upon . . .

Only a little less favoured is the more ponderously phrased:

> There shall be referred to the committee all the powers and duties of the council in relation to . . .

---

[112] If all members of the council were summoned to attend on requisite notice and the chairman of the council presided it might be difficult to contest any submission that the gathering was other than a meeting of the council.

[113] See Knowles, *Modern Management in Local Government*, p. 19.

Distinguished from delegation

9.79. Although the expression *terms of reference* is often used somewhat loosely to include also the extent of delegated powers, it is preferable to distinguish between matters merely referred to a committee, i.e. for consideration and report, and those in respect of which executive powers have been delegated. On the other hand, if a particular authority has chosen to delegate as widely as it can there might be thought no reason why the terms of reference should not reflect this, e.g. in this example of the terms of reference of an amenities committee:

> To exercise the functions of the council relating to public libraries, museums, art galleries, baths, open spaces, parks and other recreational and entertainment and cultural activities.

The following is an example where a distinction is made between the terms of reference and the order of delegation:

Records and Ancient Monuments Committee

Order of Reference

(1) There shall be referred to the committee all the powers and duties of the council in relation to records and ancient monuments (other than current official records).

Delegation

(2) All the powers and duties of the council referred to the committee shall stand delegated to the committee.

Delegation to committees

General power to delegate

9.80. Every local authority has power to delegate, within limitations,[114] any of its functions (other than functions with respect to levying or issuing a precept for a rate or borrowing money[115] – including any functions it may be discharging on behalf of another local authority – to a committee or subcommittee (or, indeed, to an officer).[116]

9.81. The Local Government Act 1972 does not use the term *delegate* as did

---

[114] The limitations are those contained within the Local Government Act 1972 (e.g. the election of chairman of a principal council must be conducted by the full assembly) or by any statute passed subsequently: Local Government Act 1972, s.101.

[115] *Ibid.* s.101(6).

[116] This is entirely new. Except for the power first given in the Town and Country Planning Act 1968, s.64, local authorities have never before been permitted to delegate to an officer. The law still does not permit delegation to an individual council member: see e.g. 5.67.

the Local Government Act 1933.[117] It provides that 'a local authority may arrange for the discharge of any of their functions' and this difference in wording is necessary no doubt because of the wider power now available enabling an authority to arrange for the discharge of functions by any other local authority:[118] and this could not properly be described as delegation because delegation implies the existence of a principal and a subordinate whereas the use of another local authority in this way is a matter between a principal and an agent.

Specific power to delegate

9.82. Specific power is conferred upon local authorities required to set up statutory committees to delegate functions to the statutory committee. Thus, for example, a local education authority may authorise an education committee of the authority to exercise on its behalf any of its functions with respect to education except the power to borrow money or to raise a rate.[119]

9.83. Without express statutory power to do so a local authority would be unable to delegate its decision-making powers because of the common law maxim *delegatus non potest delegare*. Parliament entrusts functions to local authorities as such – not directly to their committees and subcommittees or officers – and any delegatee entrusted with a task cannot lawfully pass that task on to another without the concurrence of the delegator. Indeed, the earliest of the modern local authorities were expressly denied the power to delegate: s.22(2) of the Municipal Corporations Act 1882 read as follows (although, of course, the concluding words were not italicised in the official text):

> The council may from time to time appoint out of their own body such and so many committees, either of a general or special nature and consisting of such number of persons as they think fit for any purposes which, in the opinion of the council, would be better regulated and managed by means of such committees; but *the acts of every such committee shall be submitted to the council for their approval.*

County councils when set up under the Local Government Act 1888 were, however, wholly relieved of this disability. Section 82(2) of the 1888 Act provided:

> Every committee shall report its proceedings to the council by whom it was appointed, but to the extent to which the council so direct, the acts and

[117] See the former Local Government Act 1933, s.85.
[118] Local Government Act 1972, s.101.
[119] Education Act 1944.

proceedings of the committee shall not be required by the provisions of the Municipal Corporations Act 1882, to be submitted to the council for their approval.

Effect of delegation

9.84. A local authority does not denude itself of its responsibility by delegating functions to committees: this was so decided in *Huth* v. *Clarke* (1890)[120] but now, in any case, the Local Government Act 1972 expressly provides in s.101(4) that:

> Any arrangement made by a local authority . . . for the discharge of any functions by a committee, sub-committee (officer or local authority) shall not prevent the authority or committee by whom the arrangements are made from exercising those functions.

This means two things: first, that the local authority remains responsible (and this, of course, is so of any principal who delegates because it is *authority* which is delegated and not responsibility) and the committee when it acts does so for and in the name of the local authority; second, that the council can continue to perform the functions which it has delegated.

9.85. In *Goddard* v. *Minister of Housing and Local Government* (1958)[121] the plaintiff challenged the validity of a compulsory purchase order made by a committee under delegated powers and put forward two contentions: one was that the council itself had never applied its mind to the issue, for the resolutions of the council's committees were merely 'rubber-stamped', whereas the council was obliged by statute to 'satisfy' itself. The court held that the council, acting through its committee, was satisfied.

9.86. The principle that an authority can continue to exercise the functions it has delegated could in practice lead to difficulties and possible confusion. Thus the council must take care not to act in a matter known to be receiving a committee's attention under delegated powers or at least not to act without close consultation with the committee. If it wishes to do so it ought first to withdraw the delegated powers from the committee in respect of the particular matter on which it proposes to act itself. What it cannot properly do is to purport to put an end to delegated powers retrospectively so as to invalidate what a committee has done already in exercise of those powers.[122]

---

[120] (1890) 25 QBD 391.
[121] [1958] 3 All ER 482.
[122] *Battelley* v. *Finsbury Borough Council* (1958) 56 LGR 165.

Method of delegation

9.87. There are two ways in which the terms of delegation can be expressed. An authority can either (a) list the particular matters which a committee is empowered to do without reference to the full assembly, or (b) bestow upon each committee the power to take executive action on everything within its respective terms of reference except those matters specifically excluded. The former is usual where the scope of a committee's delegated power is intended to be limited to a few specific functions and the other where delegation is extensive: the latter is to be preferred because it is easier to put down in writing and interpret in practice and the exclusions highlight the important questions that the full council needs to settle itself.

9.88. Where, therefore, the powers to be delegated are substantially less than the functions referred to the committee, the terms of delegation should be spelt out specifically. Thus, in the case of, say, a law and parliamentary committee whose terms of reference include the task of considering and advising the council upon a wide variety of matters (ranging, perhaps, from Bills which might affect the authority and its area to litigation), the terms of delegation might be so framed:

> The committee shall:
> (1) Conduct on behalf and in the name of the council:
>> (a) All legal proceedings, litigation and arbitrations in which the council may become engaged except such as may from time to time be vested by Parliament in or delegated by standing order or resolution of the council to specified persons or committees of the council.
>> (b) The conveyancing and general legal business of the council including the giving of directions upon all questions relating to or affecting the title to lands, hereditaments and property of the council and the registration of local land charges.
> (2) Prepare, obtain and deposit Bills, plans, books of reference, petitions, orders, objections and representations; employ agents, counsel and witnesses; and take such steps as may be required to comply with the standing orders of Parliament.
> (3) Take such action as may be necessary or expedient to give effect to the resolutions of the council or their committees or pending a meeting of the council as the committee, in consultation (if deemed expedient) with any other committee concerned, may consider desirable or necessary in the interest of the council to give effect to or in connection with any purpose of this standing order.

As an example of the other case, however, the order of delegation could be simply expressed:

> All the powers and duties of the council referred to the committee shall stand delegated to the committee.

Subcommittees

Power to appoint

9.89. A discretionary committee appointed by a local authority individually or by two or more authorities under the Local Government Act 1972[123] may by that same Act appoint 'one or more subcommittees',[124] and so, too, may most of the statutory committees (e.g. the education committee under the Education Act 1944).[125] Just as a local authority could be assumed to be able to appoint committees even without express statutory power, so, too, could a committee appoint subcommittees. No parent body, such as a local authority, can itself appoint a subcommittee.

Constitution

9.90. A committee may determine the number of members of each of its subcommittees, the term of office and the area (if restricted) within which the subcommittee is to exercise its authority;[126] and the subcommittees may include co-opted persons – without, however, the one-third limitation imposed on committees.[127] Most of the statutory provisions relating to committees are applicable also to subcommittees (as to the manner in which decisions shall be made, the casting vote of a chairman, the recording of names of members present, the keeping and signing of minutes, the applicability of standing orders, and the validity of proceedings despite defects in its constitution or in the election or qualification of members).

Delegation to subcommittees

9.91. A local authority has a general power[128] in respect of discretionary committees to delegate any of its functions (except with respect to levying, or issuing a precept for, a rate, or borrowing money) to a subcommittee direct; and a discretionary committee may, unless the authority otherwise directs, itself delegate any of its functions to its subcommittees; and, in turn, a subcommittee may unless otherwise directed delegate any of its

---

[123] Section 102.
[124] Sections 102(1), 102(4).
[125] Schedule 1, Pt II, para.10.
[126] Local Government Act 1972, s.102(2): indeed, in the case of a subcommittee of the statutory social services committee only one of the subcommittee need be a member of the local authority (Local Authority Social Services Act 1970, s.5(4)).
[127] Local Government Act 1972, s.102(3).
[128] *Ibid.* s.101(2): but note that the phrase 'may arrange for the discharge' of any of its functions is used instead of the word *delegate*.

functions to an officer.[129] No longer is a committee bound by the maxim *delegatus non potest delegare* in delegating to subcommittees as was formerly the case.[130] Statutory committees in most cases are permitted to delegate any of their functions to subcommittees.[131]

9.92. Where an authority has made arrangements for another authority to discharge the functions of the former then, subject to the terms of the arrangements, that other authority may delegate in the same way as an authority in respect of its own functions.[132]

9.93. For reasons explained earlier it is not permissible for a committee to constitute one member as a subcommittee, any more than it is permissible for an authority to constitute a committee of one: see 5.67.

Advantages and disadvantages of subcommittees

9.94. Subcommittees should not be set up unless such a course is unavoidable. Professor K. C. Wheare has said:[133]

> Difficulties are avoided, decisions postponed, discussion shortened or prevented by the use of sub-committees. And the process of referring matters to smaller and smaller bodies seems at times to have no limits – sub-committees have their sections, sections their sub-sections; there are panels and working parties and informal groups and drafting sectors and segments. There is a sort of law of gravity in committee work by which things are referred farther and farther back and down. Along with this tendency there goes the tendency for each small group to feel a sense of its own importance and to conspire against the body to which it is nominally subordinate.

Subcommittees can, however, assist positively in advancing the work of a committee: a smaller group of council members can often more effectively examine a matter requiring detailed consideration, or more efficiently and effectively constitute a staff selection board or panel; and there is the

---

[129] The council will itself, in most instances, regulate the delegation of functions to officers.

[130] The former Local Government Act 1933 made no provision for the delegation of functions by a committee to a subcommittee. Some local authorities, however, had obtained such power by private Act. And there was a unique provision in the Local Government (Records) Act 1962, s.3, of no effect since the Local Government Act 1972, which permitted any committee – appointed under the general enabling powers of the 1933 Act, s.85 – which had functions relating to records, to appoint a subcommittee and (this was its distinctive feature) to delegate any of those functions to the subcommittee *unless fewer than two-thirds of the members of the subcommittee were members of the authority* in which case the subcommittee could only act in an advisory capacity.

[131] See, e.g. Education Act 1944, sch.1, Pt I, para.10. The quasi-statutory planning committee is not, however, given statutory power to delegate functions to subcommittees; indeed, the Town and Country Planning Act 1962, sch.2, Pt I, contains no specific reference to the constitution of subcommittees.

[132] Local Government Act 1972, s.101(3).

[133] *Government by Committee* (1955), p. 194.

advantage that a small number of members can be called together more easily than the membership of a full committee. Subcommittees should never be set up, as Professor Wheare implies, to postpone an unpalatable decision or as a device to shelve an item of business. Ideally a committee should decide at the outset of its term of office whether there is need for any standing subcommittees and to accept as a near immutable principle that it shall not set up any *ad hoc* subcommittees during the council year. If the disadvantages of subcommittees are recognised there is less risk of appointing them needlessly or of misusing those which are unavoidable.

9.95. Nevertheless, it is preferable for a local authority to allow a committee with substantial responsibilities to appoint subcommittees for each identifiably different part of its totality of functions rather than for the authority to divide the responsibilities between two or more committees. It is sometimes thought to be nonsensical to amalgamate, say, two committees and then for the combined committee to appoint two subcommittees each to deal respectively with the functions of the former two committees. It is, however, demonstrably easier for a committee to co-ordinate and control the work of two subcommittees than for the full assembly (or a policy committee) to co-ordinate and control an additional committee.

Co-ordination

Its predominantly negative character

9.96. Co-ordination of committee work has been secured in the past by measures that were part informal – to describe the process charitably – and part formal: by, for example, specific provision for that purpose in standing orders. The informal measures included the expectation that council members serving on more than one committee and committee clerks generally would recognise in the course of deliberations in one committee that an item impinged on the concern of another. Formal measures included the requirement in standing orders that policy matters had to be submitted to the full assembly for decision and that certain matters (finance, staffing, land transactions, etc.) must be submitted to committees charged with co-ordinative responsibility in those areas: see 9.18. In many authorities there was also what is now usually termed the chief executive's management team which exercised a co-ordinative role in the more important of the authority's activities.

9.97. Maud considered all these co-ordinative arrangements as formal ones:[134]

---

[134] Maud Report, vol. 5, pp. 197–98.

. . . intentional cross-membership, joint committees to provide for the smoothing out of conflict at an early stage and 'horizontal' committees such as the general purposes, finance and establishment committees to reconcile the policies of the service committees with each other and with the limited means available.

It recognised that:

The full council itself is, of course, the ultimate co-ordinator in this sense since it can settle by means of a vote any differences which cannot be reconciled at committee level.

And went on to describe the whole process as a negative approach to co-ordination:

a realistic acceptance of the centrifugal tendencies of the committee system and the establishment of machinery to keep them in check.

Co-ordination by standing orders

9.98. The following is an example of a standing order designed to secure appropriate co-ordination of a county authority's activities (where there is no policy committee) by excepting from committee delegation those matters which had to be dealt with by the full assembly by reason of statute or for purposes of administrative convenience or in order to ensure that matters of importance are brought to the council for decision:

Except as hereinafter provided in these standing orders, the delegation to or exercise of functions by any of the committees of the council (and in the case of a statutory committee within the terms of the statute) is subject:
(a) to the statutory exclusion of the power of raising a rate or borrowing money;
(b) to compliance with the standing orders of the council as to:
 [*Here follows a list of matters within the province of machinery or co-ordinative committees*]
(c) to the reservation to the council of:
 (i) the making, variation and revocation of the statutory schemes, development plans, reports of surveys, proposals, by-laws, and other general administrative arrangements required to be submitted from time to time for ministerial sanction;
 (ii) the exercise of any power relating to the delegation of county functions to the several [county] district authorities;
 (iii) any matter arising in the exercise of a committee's delegated functions which involves new policy of major importance or the substantial variation or extension of existing policy.
The responsibility of deciding which matters shall be reserved to the council under sub-paragraph (iii) shall rest upon the chairman of the council.

Positive approach to co-ordination

9.99. Present-day approach to co-ordination is more positive in character: the view is taken:[135]

> that policy should as far as possible be a unity, that co-ordination should start from a coherent set of objectives for the council as a whole and that the part of the committees is to work within this general policy.

And thus it is that many authorities require their policy committee to exercise a co-ordinating role – albeit as a task subordinate to its main function of helping formulate and carry out an overall plan for the community, to set objectives and priorities, to control the implementation of those objectives and to monitor and review performance.

9.100. The role of a policy and resources committee has already been discussed (see 4.21) but it may be appropriate here to quote the following example of a standing order applicable in circumstances where such a committee is *primus inter pares* and operates largely as a co-ordinator:[136]

> All committee reports shall, before being submitted to the council, be submitted for the consideration of the policy and resources committee and that committee may:
> (a) recommend to the council that any recommendation or proposal contained in a report:
>   (i) be not approved; or
>   (ii) be varied; or
>   (iii) be referred back to the committee by whom the report was submitted for further consideration by that committee, with or without any direction or instruction from the council as to the matter concerned; in which event they shall also submit to the council a report on the matter, such report to incorporate the relevant part of the committee report concerned; or
> (b) require that a specified item contained in a report be deleted and be further considered by the committee by which the report was submitted.
> Provided that a committee report may be submitted to the council before it is submitted to the policy and resources committee in any case where the urgency of the situation so requires.

And, as a precautionary measure to avoid risk of different recommendations being approved by the full assembly, this 'catch-all' provision might be made:

> Where any committee make to the council any recommendation which is contrary to or inconsistent with any recommendation to the council made by

---

[135] Maud Report, vol. 5, p. 198.
[136] See R. G. Brooke and K. P. Bounds, 'The Bains Report and Standing Orders' (1974) 137 *Local Government Review* 506.

the policy and resources committee at the same meeting of the council and both such recommendations are approved, then, unless the council resolve to the contrary in any particular case, the recommendation of the policy and resources committee shall prevail and the approval of the council to the recommendation of the other committee shall, to the extent that it is contrary to or inconsistent with the approval of the recommendation of the policy and resources committee, be of no effect.

10

WORK BEFORE MEETINGS

General considerations

Timetable of meetings

10.1. Most local authorities fix their timetable of committee meetings for a period of one year in advance (at or about the time of the annual council meeting), compiled as a rule by an updating of the programme for the previous year. There is much to commend this widely adopted practice: councillors and officers can enter the dates in their diaries before other commitments arise and it sets the pattern for the organisation and transaction of council business at member level.

10.2. Considerations to be borne in mind in drawing up the timetable include the following:

(a) There should be no greater frequency of meetings than the volume of business demands: not all committees need meet in each cycle but some may need to meet more than once.

(b) The actual dates of meetings should be related to the dates of council meetings, particularly where recommendations may need to be submitted to the full assembly.

(c) The order of meetings within the cycle should be related to the character of committee business: thus committees which regularly or periodically have to consider the recommendations of other committees must meet at the end of the cycle but in sufficient time before the council meeting to enable reports to be prepared and incorporated within the council agenda.

(d) Administrative considerations must not be overlooked: time needs to be allowed for the drafting of items, an agenda planning discussion, and the final preparation and dispatch of the summons and agenda (often when typing and ancillary services are fully stretched to cope).

Indeed, the timetable of meetings can form the basis of a committee programme for administrative purposes showing the various deadlines that committee clerks will need to observe, including, for example, the last date for the receipt of items for an agenda: see 10.18.

10.3. In particular cases it may not be practicable to prepare a programme for a committee (because, for example, of an irregular and unpredictable flow of business). Even then, however, it is desirable at each meeting to fix the date and time of the next meeting (which can be cancelled if need be) rather than wait until sufficiency of business warrants the calling together of members.

10.4. A pre-arranged timetable of meetings does not obviate the necessity of giving separate notice of each meeting at the requisite time: indeed, notification of a committee meeting merely by means of the circulation annually of a timetable is unlikely to be held to be proper notice because at common law a summons must be served upon members with an agenda of the business to be transacted thereat. Many authorities prepare a weekly bulletin of meetings which is circulated for the information of members generally and this serves, not only as a reminder to members of particular committee meetings in advance of the summons and agenda, but as notification to members who may wish to attend committees of which they are not members.

Time of meeting

10.5. The time at which committee meetings are held must be related to the convenience and availability of members. Generally county councils arrange committee meetings during the day (according to Maud the large majority before 2 p.m. and the remaining in the afternoon), not because the members of county authorities are composed largely of retired people or others of independent means, as often they are, but because of the distance many have to travel and the consequent difficulty of returning home after a late evening meeting. Some other principal councils may be influenced by similar considerations: rural district councils used to favour daytime meetings (according to Maud, about evenly divided between morning and afternoon meetings). Most district councils opt in the main for evening meetings: again, according to Maud twice as many larger councils arranged their committee meetings in the evening as in the morning; urban districts and the smaller non-county boroughs had comparatively few daytime meetings and even in the larger non-county boroughs only about a third of the committee meetings were held during the day; and of all the committees in London boroughs only one authority regularly had meetings during the day. It may be that the pattern of timing is being materially affected now by the payments available to members.

Convening committee meetings
Notice, summons and agenda

10.6. There is now less difference than formerly between the legal requirements as to the notice and the summons in the case of committees and subcommittees of principal councils and the requirements as to the notice and the summons relating to principal council meetings. Public notice of the meeting of every committee and subcommittee of a principal council must be given and the agenda and accompanying reports (excluding any reports or parts of reports for items of business during which the meeting is likely to be closed to the public) made available for public inspection at least three days before a meeting or, if the meeting is convened at shorter notice, then as soon as it is convened.[1] Business not specified on the agenda may not be considered unless the chairman agrees that it is urgent.[2] In short all that has been said earlier (Chapter 6) about the giving of public notice of a council meeting and its agenda and the making available of agenda papers and reports applies equally to committees and subcommittees of principal councils.

10.7. In the case, however, of the meetings of committees and subcommittees of parish and community councils the rules governing the summons and agenda will be those set out in the standing orders of the council concerned or, where standing orders are silent, then as prescribed by common law. Public notice of committee meetings must nevertheless be given.[3]

10.8. There is no common form of summons or agenda for a committee or subcommittee meeting. Many authorities omit any formal words of summons, i.e. an agenda is dispatched to those entitled to attend headed merely with the name of the committee or subcommittee and the date, time and place of meeting.

10.9. The agenda may also need to be sent to certain councillors other than those appointed to the committee or subcommittee according to local practice, e.g. to members with a constituency interest in certain of the items on the agenda or to substitute members (see 9.64) or to councillors

---

[1] Local Government Act 1972, s.100E, added by Local Government (Access to Information) Act 1985.

[2] *Ibid.* s.100B. This means that a non-urgent report for consideration cannot properly 'be laid on the table' at a meeting – unless it merely updates an item already on the agenda and does not introduce wholly new business.

[3] Public Bodies (Admission to Meetings) Act 1960.

claiming a 'need to know' (see 5.12). If sent in error to someone not entitled to attend that person cannot thereby claim a right to be present on that score, e.g. if there is a mistake on the part of a dispatch clerk and a councillor is summoned because his surname is the same as another member entitled to be present. Where, nevertheless, the wrong councillor does attend a meeting which he is not entitled to attend and actually votes, his vote is invalid (see 7.102). Errors in service of the summons do not affect the validity of proceedings for it could be argued that an erroneous summons is less heinous than want of a summons altogether, and that is covered by statutory provisions.[4]

Notice of meetings one after the other

10.10. It is not unusual – particularly in the case of smaller authorities – for committee meetings to follow one another on the same day or evening: each to begin upon the conclusion of another. It is never satisfactory – because a notice must be clear, explicit and unconditional[5] – for a committee (or any other body for that matter) to be convened to meet at an indeterminate time 'immediately upon the rising' of an earlier committee: even though it may be felt to be justified in circumstances where the two committees comprise the same membership. For certainty an estimate of the likely starting time should be made and the summons can then clearly state, e.g. that the meeting will commence:

. . . at 7 p.m. or upon the rising of the . . . committee whichever is the later.

Notice to officers and others

10.11. Care must be taken not to overlook the notification of committee meetings to officers expected to be present – especially, of course, where an officer not usually in attendance (or, indeed, an outside adviser) is being invited to attend for a particular item of business. Such an officer, or other person, may well need to be briefed in certain respects before the actual meeting: see 10.47.

Who may convene

10.12. The proper officer will normally convene committee meetings in accordance with the pre-arranged timetable and, in consultation with the

---

[4] Local Government Act 1972, sch.12, paras.4(4), 10(3), 26(3).
[5] In *Alexander* v. *Simpson* (1889) 43 Ch. D.139, it was held that a notice was bad in stating that a meeting would take place only in a certain contingency.

committee chairman, convene special meetings as circumstances may warrant. There is no provision in law, as in the case of council meetings, for members to requisition a meeting of a committee, but model standing order no. 32 is to the following effect:

> The chairman of a committee or the mayor/chairman of the council may call a special meeting of the committee at any time. A special meeting shall also be called on the requisition of a quarter of the whole number of the committee, delivered in writing to the town clerk/clerk of the council but in no case shall less than [three] members requisition a special meeting. The summons to the special meeting shall set out the business to be considered thereat, and no business other than that set out in the summons shall be considered at that meeting.

10.13. If there is no standing order to this effect and a number of members demand a special meeting the committee chairman should agree to one being convened. If he is not prepared to agree the chief executive would no doubt advise him to do so if the number of members asking was substantial; and if the number comprised the majority of members the chief executive might well feel obliged to convene a meeting irrespective of the wishes of the committee chairman. If neither committee chairman nor chief executive would act the members could always, of course, make use of their power to call a special council meeting to deal with the situation: see 5.13.

Committee agenda

General principles

10.14. The purpose of a committee agenda (indistinguishable from a council meeting agenda or, indeed, any other agenda) is:

(a) to provide advance notification of the business to be transacted at a particular meeting; and

(b) to facilitate the transaction of business at the meeting itself.

It may have practical purposes in addition (it may often provide the basis for the minutes of the meeting and, indeed, is sometimes written in a form that will aid the subsequent preparation of the minutes) but its primary objective must always be to advance the purposes for which the committee has been set up and to do so in an efficient manner. It should be regarded as a document framed to secure or at least encourage decision-making and it can only do this effectively if councillors understand what is being put before them.[6] It should not ordinarily be used merely to inform; and – a

---

[6] 'One third (of the council members interviewed) considered many committee papers to be unnecessarily difficult to comprehend: too much unnecessary technical and departmental jargon was used . . .': *Occasional Paper No. 4: Services to Elected Members: a survey of Scottish local authorities*: Planning Exchange of Glasgow (1977).

precept less often observed than it should be – the items placed before the committee should be those alone which unavoidably demand the committee's consideration. Maud critically observed in its report[7] that it saw:

> the growth of business adding to the agenda of committees and squeezing out major issues which need time for consideration with the result that members are misled into a belief that they are controlling and directing the authority when often they are only deliberating on things which are unimportant and taking decisions on matters which do not merit their attention.

It is this which brings the committee system into disrepute. The fault lies partly with members who often demand information thoughtlessly or misguidedly believing that they will fail in political responsibility if they do not keep track of triviality, or sometimes (though rarely) because they do not trust their officers. Partly, too, officers must shoulder the blame because it is they for the most part who initiate committee business and, regrettably, it is they who in some cases flinch at making decisions themselves.

Initial drafting

10.15. The buildup of committee agenda is virtually a continuous process: as soon as one meeting has been held material starts accumulating for the next. It is the committee clerk's responsibility to maintain a list of items awaiting consideration. How this 'list' is kept is a matter of personal inclination or office regulation: it may consist of a card index, a number of sheets of paper, a file of documents (but, for obvious reasons, it is preferable not to retain papers that ought to be filed away elsewhere), or merely a tray or drawer into which is placed a note of items for committee.

10.16. The material for the draft agenda will come to the committee clerk from various sources; it will comprise:

(a) Items which the committee clerk himself will have 'noted':
  (i) matters deferred or retained from previous meetings;
  (ii) periodically recurring items or reports: it is common practice for the committee clerk to look back at the committee agenda for the corresponding meeting in the previous council year to ensure that matters of annual incidence are not overlooked;
  (iii) references from other committees, the council, or other bodies.

(b) Other items:
  (i) arising out of correspondence, including departmental circulars, etc.;

---

[7] Maud Report, vol. 1, para.128. This was written, of course, before corporate management became fashionable with its emphasis upon the attainment of objectives.

(ii) initiated by other officers;

(iii) which individual councillors may ask to be included.

The extent to which councillors are permitted to call for items to be placed before committees depends upon the practice of individual local authorities. Unless standing orders provide otherwise there can be no absolute right on the part of a councillor, whether a member of the committee or not, to demand that a particular item be included;[8] and if the councillor feels aggrieved by any refusal – which the proper officer would presumably make only after consultation with the committee chairman and/or the leader of the council – he can always give notice of motion for inclusion on the council agenda (see 7.48).

10.17. It has to be accepted that items are nowadays more likely than in the past to be initiated by the leader at the request of the majority group. Practice is still developing in this respect and varies substantially between authorities. Widdicombe refers in one of its research volumes to the practice in highly politicised local authorities whereby committee chairmen exercise considerable influence over what it terms 'agenda setting'.[9] A chairman may demand the right to add items of his own (which generally reflect pressure from his party group) or to postpone, occasionally delete, items which officers intended to include, possibly ask for a change in the order of items and in extreme instances seek to bring about changes in the content of officers' reports. This sort of thing is still far from common but that it happens at all is indicative of tensions in councillor–officer relations which can develop over the control of committee agenda. Closely linked is the parallel issue of the authorship of committee reports. Instances of committee chairmen writing their own reports and presenting them to committee are not unknown; and although this, again, represents a departure from past practice it does not seem to be a particularly worrying development – provided, it may be thought, that officers have an opportunity of making their professional input, either in writing or orally, on the subject-matter of a councillor's report.

10.18. At an early stage (preferably at a prescribed date prior to the committee meeting: see 10.2) the committee clerk will prepare the agenda in draft. In some authorities this may be circulated to all officers concerned

---

[8] The council of the London Borough of Bexley's standing order no. 53(2) includes this provision: 'A member shall be entitled to have an item of business included in the agenda of the next meeting of any committee or sub-committee provided that notice of the business to be included is given to the appropriate secretary no later than 10 days before the date of the meeting concerned'. It seems that little use has been made of the standing order because members prefer to initiate business in the council chamber where it usually attracts more public interest.

[9] Widdicombe Research vol. 1: *The Political Organisation of Local Authorities*, pp. 126–30.

so that they may see what is already on the draft and add matters which they themselves wish the committee to know about or decide upon. Where this is the practice the draft should state the date by which the draft must be returned to the committee clerk together with any additional items and this date must be rigidly adhered to if the agenda is to be finalised and dispatched on time.

Editing agenda material

10.19. Because an agenda is thus compiled of material submitted from several sources some editing will be necessary on the part of the committee clerk or the final document will lack uniformity of style and layout. Mere 'verbiage' can often obscure salient facts. This editing can be an unenviable task – not solely because of bad initial preparation but because, human nature being what it is, much of the material will come in at the last minute and so place an intolerable burden and peak load of work upon the unfortunate committee clerk. Many of the problems can be reduced or avoided if the prescribed deadline for the receipt of agenda items is enforced and, of great importance, if there are prescribed rules and guidelines regulating the manner in which material is to be prepared.

10.20. It should be accepted that the agenda is the responsibility of the chief executive (or the secretary or other prescribed officer) and that he is the final arbiter of what goes on the agenda and in what form. Courtesy may demand that a departmental officer should be consulted if an item he has originated is held back, substantially amended or wholly rewritten; but the only committee papers which may properly be exempt from amendment by the committee clerk are reports in the name of a particular officer. Common practice nowadays, however, is for the agenda to be 'anonymous' in form and, if attributable to anyone at all, to the chief executive's management team collectively.

Agenda planning meetings

10.21. In some authorities – believed to be increasing in number – an agenda planning meeting[10] is held at which all officers concerned in the work of a particular committee meet together, discuss items on the draft agenda, and decide mutually whether a matter is to be submitted as drafted, modified, or left over for a future meeting.

---

[10] For a brief discussion of the pros and cons of agenda planning meetings see (1972) 136 *Local Government Review* 375.

Consultation with chairman

10.22. It is comparatively uncommon for the committee chairman to be consulted on the draft agenda in detail. Such a course might well be justified in certain circumstances, e.g. where an item of political sensitivity or major importance is concerned or where a particular member has asked for a matter to be brought before the committee.

What should be included

10.23. Local practice must determine what kind of items are included on committee agenda. As a general guide, however, it may be said that a matter should be placed before a committee only if:

(a) it is within the committee's term of reference; and
(b) it cannot be dealt with at officer level either because it:
    (i) raises an issue of policy or principle of major importance not already decided; or
    (ii) demands a decision beyond an officer's delegated authority; or
    (iii) is politically contentious;
(c) it will eventually require a resolution of the full assembly, e.g. to meet the requirements of the law or of standing orders;
(d) the committee has itself requested the information.

10.24. It should be a principle in the conduct of local authority business that everything which needs a decision should be decided at the lowest level at which it may competently be taken. Unfortunately it frequently happens in local government that decision-making is pushed upwards unnecessarily and councillors are called on to decide matters that could be dealt with at officer level. Of course there may be occasions when the good sense of the officer dictates that it might be politic to bring before a committee a matter on which he is empowered to act; but conversely there will be times when he should be well able to judge that the committee will support him in taking action in circumstances of urgency and when the committee chairman is not available for consultation. The fact that an officer can be called to account is safeguard enough as a rule against arbitrary decisions at officer level.

10.25. Among matters which do not justify inclusion on a committee agenda are reports that action has been duly taken in pursuance of the committee's instructions (though the committee may be expected to want to know if an officer has been unable to execute a decision!), and information items (e.g. statistical material or trivia – staff movements, resignations, etc.) which do not call for action. As to whether action taken by committee chairmen should be reported, either for information or confirmation, see Chapter 5.

Form

10.26. In the past a committee agenda has consisted of either:

(a) an itemised list of subject-matter headings: the 'skeleton' type of agenda; *or*

(b) a fully documented paper where all relevant information on each item of business is provided on the agenda itself or incorporated in appendices attached to the main document.

The first type is fast disappearing. It was favoured particularly by smaller authorities where the volume of business was comparatively small and matters could be dealt with – or so it was claimed – upon the oral report of the appropriate officer. There were self-evident disadvantages: it meant that members had no advance warning of the issues to be dealt with and all business was summarily dispatched by 'snap' decisions. The second type is more general but clearly the amount of material produced for members can vary considerably – more often, it seems, because of the practice of the authority rather than the weight or significance of the issue to be decided. Maud reported:[11]

> Behind . . . quite startling variations in the quantity of paper circulated lies a wide divergence of practice in the amount of written information submitted to sub-committees and committees and also in the methods of referring information and recommendations from sub-committees to committees and from committees to council. These differences in practice may in some places arise merely from a persistent adherence, for one reason or another, to different long-established traditions. On the other hand, they may well reflect elsewhere completely different philosophies. For whereas some influential officers feel that the amount of written material should be kept to a minimum so that members can concentrate on a few major issues, there are others who believe with equal conviction that it is their duty to provide members with the fullest and most detailed information possible so that they can make their own decisions as to what they feel to be significant, rather than having the selection determined for them.

It may be that the requirements now introduced as a consequence of the Local Government (Access to Information) Act 1985 (see particularly Chapter 3) will encourage the submission by officers of more detailed reports. Certainly oral reporting is no longer permissible unless it is related to an item already on the agenda or can be justified under the urgency

[11] Maud Report, vol. 5, p. 295.

provisions: an item on an agenda which merely states that a report will be made orally is out of order if it gives no indication whatsoever of the subject-matter or purport of the report to be made. There is no reason, however, why an officer cannot update orally at a meeting a report which has been properly circulated in advance, although it may be advisable for the likelihood of an updating to be referred to on the agenda.

10.27. Apart from variations in the amount of paper produced there are differences of a more fundamental character. Some authorities incorporate a formal summons as part of the agenda paper; others do not. Some make it a practice to set out the names of all members of the committee at the top of the first page or at the bottom of the formal summons; other authorities restrict this to the first meeting of a new committee.

Order of business

10.28. It is usual for the order of items to be standardised. Certain business must necessarily be dealt with first, e.g. the election of a chairman where this is called for, and confirmation of minutes; and if a deputation is to be received or a presentation made these are matters conveniently dealt with soon after the commencement of proceedings so that persons concerned can be given a definite time to attend. Some authorities prefer to deal with relatively routine or non-controversial matters first and more important business afterwards: in at least one authority the agenda is divided into two parts: first, items requiring decision or special discussion; then items submitted for information.[12] Sometimes the order is so arranged that officers are not required to sit through business which does not concern them.

10.29. There is much to commend the practice of assembling associated matters together so that members do not find themselves dealing with 'a jumble of important items of policy and trivial detail'. Maud's observations suggest that 'the amount of attention given to a particular item can often be affected by its position on the agenda and that the order of agenda items is a matter which would repay careful consideration'.[13]

First meeting of new committees

10.30. When an entirely new committee is set up or a standing committee is newly constituted with several new members it may be considered desirable:

(a) to include on the agenda a statement of the names of the members, the

[12] Maud Report, vol. 5, p. 296.
[13] *Ibid.* p. 297.

committee's terms of reference and, possibly, a résumé of the committee's activities; and

(b) to dispatch with the agenda all documents in current use relating to the work of the committee which could provide useful background or essential information for members.

As to (b) care should be taken in the selection so as to avoid including documents which soon become out of date: thus, for example, it is questionable whether the members of a staffing committee should be given copies of national schemes of conditions of service because of the cost and difficulty of updating them as changes occur.

Papers for special committees

10.31. It is obvious, no doubt, that when a special committee is set up to inquire into or investigate a particular matter or to consider a specific problem, the first meeting may need to be devoted to certain preliminaries: defining the area of inquiry, ascertaining the basic facts, planning a programme of work and so on. It will usually be helpful if a paper is circulated with the agenda for the first meeting setting out the committee's terms of reference, reciting the circumstances in which the committee came into being and providing as much factual information as can be gathered which is relevant to the task before the members.

Individual agenda items

10.32. Every agenda item has at least four principal parts:
(a) the heading;
(b) the question to be decided, succinctly expressed;
(c) the relevant facts, including – according to circumstances – a note of the authority's legal powers, of its policy on the subject matter or related topics, and of the financial considerations involved; and
(d) the courses of action open and the consequences of pursuing each alternative posed.

It may also have a fifth, i.e.:
(e) an indication of the particular course recommended.

10.33. Competence in draftsmanship will determine the brevity with which each is covered. It is not, however, enough merely to use words economically. A sense of proportion is also necessary. Routine matters of minor importance – if they must be submitted for committee consideration – can often be dealt with in a single line. There can be severe condensation in appropriate circumstances: certain knowledge, for example, can be assumed on the part of councillors, and details which members can easily look up for themselves – in past minutes, standing orders or other regulations – need not necessarily be set out in full. Only local practice and sensible judgement can provide a guide. The order of material within an item can rarely be changed, however, without sacrifice of clarity and logical exposition: the question to be decided; the facts; the courses open and the consequences; and, often, a recommendation.

Routine items

10.34. Routine or regularly recurring items should be standardised in the minimum number of words. Thus, for example, the item which deals with the submission of minutes of the previous meeting for confirmation should preferably be dealt with in one line, i.e.:

MINUTES of the meeting of . . . June, 19 . . .

rather than, e.g.:

MINUTES
To confirm the minutes of the meeting of . . . June, 19 . . .

and never embroidered to unnecessary length, as, e.g.:

MINUTES
To confirm as a correct record the minutes of the meeting of the committee held on . . . June, 19 . . .

In other words, the council members can be expected to know that the purpose of the item is to secure formal confirmation of the previous meeting's minutes.

10.35. There are several similar items which can be set out in summary fashion on the agenda: the *election* of a chairman and a vice-chairman (never the *appointment*: unless, of course, the item has been placed on the agenda for the chief executive to report formally that the full council has appointed the committee chairman); the appointment of representatives of the council to serve on other bodies; the submission of a subcommittee's report; and so on.

10.36. Apart from routine items of the kind just referred to (where the intention is self-evident), care should be taken to indicate clearly what action is expected of the committee. Thus, briefly expressed items can be introduced in the style:

To consider . . .

To decide . . .

To receive . . .

A common error, however, where agenda items are prefixed by the word 'To . . .' is to employ it carelessly and so incorrectly; thus:

TOWN CENTRE REDEVELOPMENT
To report that . . .

when what was intended was this:

TOWN CENTRE REDEVELOPMENT
Chief Executive to report that . . .

Officers report to the committee (sometimes, of course, the chairman or a particular member; and always a subcommittee) but never the committee itself!

Item or appendix?

10.37. It is not always easy in practice to determine whether particular business is better presented as an item on the agenda or in an accompanying document. Importance can be a matter of opinion and therefore an inadequate guide. Length may be more relevant: an item that can be dealt with in less than a page of type is generally more conveniently included on the main agenda while one which extends beyond, say, a page in length is probably better dealt with as an appendix. Thus, in the majority of cases a committee agenda will contain items of varying length.

Appendices

10.38. The attachment of papers to the agenda as appendices has the advantage of providing separate documents that can easily be incorporated in the subsequent minutes: it also facilitates speedy preparation of the agenda because the typing or printing work can be distributed among a number of typists; and it invariably makes for a tidier, more easily understood agenda paper.

10.39. Appendices should be identified by letter or number, i.e. either as APPENDIX A or APPENDIX 1, whichever may be preferred, and it assists members in referring to several appendices if the documents are reproduced on different coloured paper. Thus, for example, an item would appear on the agenda paper to this effect:

00. *REORGANISATION OF ARCHITECT'S DEPARTMENT*
Report of Working Party: APPENDIX A
                                              (Yellow)

and the document itself would be identified by this reference at the top right-hand corner of the first page (on yellow paper):

APPENDIX A
(see agenda item 00)

10.40. Sometimes it may be necessary for there to be documents attached to appendices. These need to be distinguished from the appendices by, for example, referring to them as ENCLOSURE or STATEMENT or ANNEXE, according to choice, and if appendices are lettered A, B, C and so on, these further attachments can conveniently be numbered – either 1, 2, 3, etc., or, perhaps, I, II, III, etc. Whatever nomenclature is favoured it should be standardised throughout the authority.

Any other business

10.41. It was once fairly common practice for committee agenda to conclude with an item: 'Any other business'. Since the coming into force of the Local Government (Access to Information) Act 1985 the practice should be discontinued because an item of business may not be considered at a meeting of a principal council unless requisite advance notice has been given: see 6.20. Some authorities now include as a matter of routine a final agenda item 'Any other business which the chairman considers to be urgent' to cover the possibility of urgent business arising.

Dispatch of committee papers

Need for efficient arrangements

10.42. There must be an efficient arrangement for the issue of notices and dispatch of committee papers to ensure:
(a) that appropriate notice, where this is necessary, is given to the Press and public;
(b) that the summons and agenda are in the hands of members by the time prescribed by standing orders;
(c) that officers required to be present and any persons invited to attend on the particular occasion are appropriately notified and advised;
and that the papers are complete in every particular and that no one entitled to receive them is omitted from the dispatch. This is secured by:
(a) strict compliance with a check-list of members' names, Press representatives and officers' names;
(b) double-checking that no one has been omitted either by:
    (i) writing the names of addressees on the front sheet of the agenda

paper and then, after separately selecting the appropriate pre-addressed envelopes, putting the papers in the envelopes; or

(ii) one officer calling out the names of the addressees and another putting the agenda papers in previously selected pre-addressed envelopes;

(c) ideally (but practicable only in the smaller authorities in compact areas) arranging for personal delivery;

(d) recording the dispatch in a book kept for the purpose.

There is no substitute for the exercise of care by the officers concerned, but a prescribed procedure and a record help to emphasise the importance of the dispatch: careless or wilful failure to serve the summons and agenda could affect the validity of the committee meeting: see 6.18.

Pre-committee briefing

General considerations

10.43. The amount of *briefing* a committee chairman may require before a meeting depends upon the type of meeting and the experience and/or knowledge of the chairman. Where business is expected to be straightforward no more may be necessary than a written brief from the committee clerk. But in the generality of committee meetings it is usual, and desirable (subject to what is said below), for the chairman to discuss beforehand with the appropriate officers the several items on the agenda. Maud said it seemed that contact between members and officers appeared to occur mostly in connection with committee meetings and, referring to the briefing of committee chairmen, commented:[14]

> The 'chairman's call-over' – a somewhat sophisticated arrangement developed in the old L.C.C. as a result of the influence of Herbert Morrison – has been described by an academic writer who studied the subject. By March, 1965, all but two of the L.C.C. chairmen held such 'call-overs' in their own offices, armed with an advance copy of the agenda, in the presence of their vice-chairman and a number of officers, the object being to ensure that they were sufficiently well briefed to be able to steer the committee into accepting the agenda.

10.44. The words 'accepting the agenda' may be significant. There are objections to the pre-committee briefing or call-over on the grounds that the chairman and officers could agree tactics to steamroller the committee into agreeing a particular course of action. This should not be the purpose. There is nothing wrong in the officer making clear to the chairman what is

---

[14] Maud Report, vol. 5, para.139.

in his mind and his own preferences or recommendations but there should be no conspiracy between chairman and officers to force a particular decision upon the committee.[15] If the chairman gains the advantage of knowing what is in the mind of the officers then the officers, for their part, become aware of the chairman's feelings. His views on a matter may well reflect the political opinion of the majority group and this, in turn, will alert the officers to the possible need to treat a matter with sensitivity and discretion.

10.45. It is for the individual chairman to determine whether there should be a pre-committee briefing, what form it should take and what officers should be present. In some cases the chairman may prefer to read through the agenda and discuss with the chief executive or chief officer concerned – possibly only with the committee clerk – those items on which he has queries or needs further information; perhaps a telephone discussion may be sufficient. Other chairmen may think it sufficient to rely on the chief executive or chief officer contacting him if circumstances merit a pre-committee briefing. But, as Maud pointed out:[16]

> whether committee briefing takes place incidentally or on a specific occasion, there is no doubt that in many instances the initiative rests entirely with the officer, who has already prepared (and in some cases already circulated) the agenda and reports.

Maud contains several paragraphs on the pros and cons of committee briefing[17]

Committee clerk should be present

10.46. It is essential for the committee clerk to be present at any pre-committee briefing. Sometimes he is not – and this seems to make his task unnecessarily difficult.

Officers and invitees

10.47. It may also be necessary to brief – primarily in relation to procedure – any 'outsider' who has been invited to attend a particular committee meeting: an officer, for example, who is required to be present to speak on an item of business but has never before attended a committee meeting; or an independent adviser who has been invited to attend; or, of course, a

[15] Some officers 'give the impression that the ventriloquist's doll is their idea of an ideal chairman': K. C. Wheare, *Government by Committee* (1955), p. 183.

[16] Maud Report, vol. 5, para.145.

[17] *Ibid.* paras.139–50.

deputation – all will feel less ill at ease if properly briefed beforehand as to what to expect when entering the committee room, where to sit, how to conduct themselves and so on. It is easy for officers intimately and continuously associated with committee work to forget that, for the member of staff who rarely attends a committee meeting, it can be a discomforting experience to be asked to attend and speak at a meeting at short notice.

Final preparations for meeting

Availability of accommodation

10.48. Before committee papers are finally dispatched to council members and others the committee clerk should check, even though the dates of meetings and accommodation have been pre-arranged, that:

(a) a suitable committee room is available with reasonable seating for the public, and table and seating for the Press;

(b) waiting room accommodation is conveniently situated for invitees to the meeting;

(c) no other committee or subcommittee with common membership has been subsequently arranged for the same time;

(d) nothing, such as noisy repair work on adjoining accommodation, is likely to interfere with the meeting;

and then, on the day of the meeting, inspect the room beforehand to ensure that:

(e) tables are appropriately arranged[18] and there are sufficient chairs;

(f) the room is properly equipped, i.e. with notepaper, blotting paper, pen and ink (for the chairman to sign the minutes), water carafes and tumblers of fresh water; and with facilities for displaying maps, etc., or other visual aids;

(g) heating, ventilation and lighting are functioning;

(h) tea or coffee will be served at the requisite time;

(i) emergency evacuation procedure is understood;

and satisfy himself that the meeting is shown on the notice-board in the foyer or entrance hall of the building concerned and that visitors will be escorted to the meeting or waiting room.

10.49. The foregoing precautions are the more important where the committee is meeting in an unfamiliar venue, in which case a map of the

---

[18] 'A long table, and a square table, or seats about the walls, seem things of form, but are things of substance; for a long table, a few at the upper end in effect sway all the business; but in the other form, there is more use of the counsellors' opinions that sit lower': Sir Francis Bacon, 'Of Counsel'.

venue might usefully be sent with the notice showing, e.g. a convenient route of access and car parks available.

What should be taken to the meeting

10.50. The documents needed at a meeting will depend upon the type of committee and the character of business: for a staffing committee, for example, it would be prudent to have ready to hand a copy of the authority's authorised staff establishment, up-to-date handbooks on national conditions of service, staffing regulations, procedure agreements and so on. All papers should be assembled beforehand and, ideally, against a standard check-list of items so that nothing is overlooked. Care must be taken to anticipate what may be required: if a plan is to be referred to, it should be displayed prominently before members begin to assemble and it should be of a scale clearly visible from every seat. Sometimes it may be desirable to draft out alternative versions of likely resolutions.

10.51. The items likely to be included in a check-list are these:

(a) Minutes of the previous meeting for signature after confirmation;

(b) Current minute book;

(c) Attendance book;

(d) Spare copies of the agenda (now a statutory obligation: see 3.5) and other circulated papers;

(e) Committee clerk's notebook (and spare pencils);

(f) Standing orders; and any rules or regulations (including earlier policy decisions) governing matters within the particular committee's terms of reference;

(g) Current constitution of the committee: the list of members of the committee and any associated subcommittees, its terms of reference, timetable of future meetings, etc.;

(h) Forms or plain paper in case of a ballot;

(i) Schemes, plans, by-laws, files and other papers relating to the business to be transacted, assembled in agenda order, with particular documents flagged for easy reference;

(j) Standard reference books, year-book, relevant statutes, etc.

11

WORK AT MEETINGS

Introduction

Business must proceed

11.1. It is good practice and administratively convenient to adopt the principle that business must proceed as planned once a committee meeting has been convened – provided there is no overriding reason why it should not. The general rule is that a meeting which has been properly convened cannot be postponed (see 6.31) – although in practice this is often done – but there can be failure to make a meeting, i.e. where, for example, a quorum is not present when the meeting should begin: see 6.33. It is also a general rule that the proceedings of any meeting are invalid if the meeting has not been properly constituted: see 1.31. Strictly speaking, the chairman of a committee should satisfy himself that these requirements are fulfilled before the committee proceeds to business: see 7.30. In practice the chairman assumes that due formalities have been met unless he is advised to the contrary or it is self-evident that, for example, there is no quorum. It is submitted that this principle should be extended so that there shall be a presumption, until the contrary is shown to be the case, that a committee has been validly convened and is properly constituted and that the meeting can properly proceed with the transaction of business.[1] And the business to be transacted can only lawfully be that of which notice has been given on the agenda (see 6.19 *et seq.*) unless (a) the chairman accepts it as urgent or (b) whether written or presented orally it merely updates an item already on the agenda without introducing wholly new matter: an agenda item *Report to be laid on the table* is strictly no longer permissible unless it comes under one or other of these headings.

---

[1] The provisions of Local Government Act 1972, sch.12, para.41(3) help to substantiate this view. See 8.30.

Record of attendance

Attendance of members

11.2. The law provides that the names of council and co-opted members present at a local authority meeting must be recorded[2] This is best and usually done in practice by providing an attendance book for signature by those present: the book can be passed round at the meeting (in which case the committee clerk in attendance must be alert to ensure that the book is placed in front of latecomers) or, preferably in the case of large committees, placed at the entrance to the committee room so that those attending can sign before they enter the meeting.

11.3. The attendance book can be an ordinary hard-covered book of ruled pages in which the committee clerk writes as necessary the name of the committee and date of meeting at the top of the page on which members are required to sign. Or, preferably, it can be a prepared two-column loose-leaf sheet headed with the name of the committee and date of meeting, with the names of members typed in the left-hand column; each member is expected to sign on the appropriate line in the right-hand column. This helps in the case of illegible signatures and in determining quickly in the case of large committees who is present and who is absent.

11.4. The importance of an accurate record of attendance lies in the fact that this will be prima-facie evidence for purposes of determining disqualification in the event of failure to attend for a consecutive period of six months (see 5.76) and may be used for other purposes: in checking council members' attendance allowances, etc. Councillors themselves may wish to avail themselves of the record: for political purposes, or for evidence that they were not at a meeting at which unlawful expenditure had been approved: see 5.42.

11.5. Standing orders will usually place upon members an obligation to sign the attendance book. Thus model standing order no. 17 is to this effect:

> Every member of the council attending a meeting of the council, or of any of its committees of which he is a member, shall sign his name in the attendance book or sheet provided for that purpose. [And every member attending some other meeting, conference or inspection on approved duty shall sign his name in the register kept for that purpose.]

The committee clerk would be wise, however, to keep his own check on members' attendance by, for example, ticking against the list of members of the committee as each one enters.

11.6. Councillors who attend a meeting of a committee of which they are

---

[2] Local Government Act 1972, sch.12, para.40, extended to committee meetings by s.99.

not members in exercise of a right conferred upon them by standing orders or of their common law 'need to know' will not ordinarily be credited with an attendance (nor may they take part in the proceedings unless expressly permitted to do so). A standing order governing the attendance of non-committee members might be to this effect:

> Any member of the council may be present during a meeting of any committee or subcommittee but unless he be a member of that committee or subcommittee he shall not (except with the permission of the chairman) take part in the proceedings thereof, neither shall he be entitled to sign the register of attendance nor to have his attendance reckoned for any purpose of these standing orders.

11.7. On the other hand, a non-committee member present at a meeting by express invitation ought to be credited with an attendance. Standing orders should state specifically the rights of council members in this respect. Model standing order no. 37 is to this effect:

> A member of the council who has moved a motion which has been referred to any committee or sub-committee shall have notice of the meeting of the committee or sub-committee at which it is proposed to consider the motion. He shall have the right to attend the meeting and if he attends shall have an opportunity of explaining the motion.[3]

Return of attendances

11.8. It is usual for a return of members' attendances to be prepared as soon as practicable after the end of the council year – for circulation to members and the Press and for the guidance of the selection committee in determining committee membership for the ensuing year.

Appointment of committee chairman

Election procedure

11.9. The chairman of a committee is ordinarily elected by the committee itself at its first meeting (although in a few authorities the council makes an appointment[4]) and the term of office is usually for the ensuing council year. Model standing order no. 31 is to this effect:

> Every committee shall, at its first meeting, before proceeding to any other

---

[3] It would not be necessary for the council member concerned to move the motion afresh at the committee meeting; indeed, as a non-member of the committee he could not properly do so.

[4] The term *election* is appropriately used where the committee chooses its chairman; and the term *appointment* where the council makes the choice.

business, elect a chairman for the year, and may at any time elect a vice-chairman. In the absence from a meeting of the chairman (and vice-chairman if elected) a chairman for that meeting may be appointed.

No special formalities are necessary, unless standing orders prescribe any, and if the committee is making the appointment it may choose any of its members including a co-opted member.[5] An elaboration of model standing order no. 31, covering other contingencies, is this one adopted by Surrey County Council:

(1) A chairman shall, and if the committee thinks fit, a vice-chairman may, be elected by each committee at its first or, in the case of a vice-chairman, a subsequent, meeting and, where more than one member is proposed, such election shall be by ballot:
   Provided that during the interval between the appointment and first meeting of a committee the retiring chairman (if a member of the committee) shall continue to act as chairman.
(2) A member of the committee proposing to nominate another member as chairman or vice-chairman of the committee may communicate in writing the name of such member to the clerk before the meeting of the committee at which the election is to be held. The clerk shall inform the committee of the nominations so submitted to him.

Who presides at the election?

11.10. A person cannot preside at his own election (see 7.18) and therefore it is necessary for someone other than the prospective chairman to take the chair at the outset of the meeting. This may be prescribed by standing orders but it is more likely to be a matter of local practice. Thus the chairman of the council may attend the initial meeting of all committees each year expressly for the purpose of presiding over the election of a committee chairman. In the absence of the chairman or mayor the committee should appoint a chairman pro tem (the outgoing chairman or the senior member present) and the senior officer present could quite properly ask for nominations for the temporary chairman.[6] Where the council appoints the committee chairman he assumes the chair from the outset.

Eligibility for committee chairmanship

11.11. Some local authorities place restrictions on the eligibility of council

---

[5] Some disadvantages flow from the choice of a co-opted member: see 5.52, 11.12.
[6] The officer in effect acts as a returning officer but the pedantic view could admittedly be taken that it is not appropriate for an officer to call for nominations for chairmanship on the grounds that a meeting cannot be constituted until a 'proper' person is in the chair.

and co-opted members (see 5.49, 11.12) for the chairmanship of committees. Thus, for example, these two standing orders adopted by the former Surrey Council Council:

> The chairman of the council shall not be appointed as the chairman of any committee of the council except of the selection committee or of any committee specially appointed from time to time.
>
> No member of the council shall be chairman of more than one committee at the same time, nor shall any chairman of a committee act as vice-chairman of another committee at the same time:
>
> > Provided that this standing order shall not (a) apply to any committee specially appointed or (b) be deemed to prevent the chairman of a standing committee from being vice-chairman of the Law and Parliamentary Committee so long as he is a member of either House of Parliament.

11.12. A co-opted member as a full member of a committee can be elected as its chairman. There are, however, some disadvantages in this. A co-opted-member chairman has not the political responsibility of a councillor chairman and this could be regarded as a reason for not choosing a co-opted member for that office: in practice a committee chairman has responsibilities going far beyond his duty to preside at meetings of his committee. It is not possible, either, for a co-opted member to present his committee's report or minutes at the full assembly and pilot through or defend the committee's proposals or answer questions on his committee's work: but a vice-chairman could, of course, perform these tasks on his behalf at the council meeting.[7]

Vice-chairman

11.13. There is much to commend the election of a vice-chairman of a committee because there can then be no doubt who should act in the chairman's absence: it eliminates the need for a separate election of an acting chairman wherever the chairman is absent from a meeting (because the vice-chairman automatically takes the chair in the absence of the chairman at a committee meeting) and it provides training for prospective chairmen.

There must always be a chairman

11.14. A meeting is never properly constituted without a chairman: see 1.8, 1.31. This means that if the chairman and the vice-chairman are both

---

[7] A somewhat analogous situation arises where the chairman of the police committee is a magistrate and not a member of the county council: see 9.31.

absent at the commencement of a meeting the committee must proceed forthwith to elect a chairman for the time being. If, later, the chairman or vice-chairman arrives it is usual – but not essential (as in the case of a meeting of the full assembly where the chairman or mayor, if present, must preside: see 7.24) – for the acting chairman to relinquish the chair in favour of the chairman or vice-chairman as the case may be. He will not do this immediately as a rule but will wait until the conclusion of the item of business under discussion at the time.

Chairman has casting vote

11.15. The chairman or vice-chairman or whoever else may be presiding at a committee or subcommittee meeting has a second or casting vote.[8]

Quorum

None prescribed by statute

11.16. No quorum is prescribed by statute in the case of committee meetings but the local authority has power to prescribe one by standing orders: if it does not do so the committee may determine its quorum.[9]

11.17. Model standing order no. 34 is to this effect:

(1) Except where authorized by a statute or ordered by the council, business shall not be transacted at a meeting of any committee unless at least [one quarter] of the whole number of the committee is present.

Provided that in no case shall the quorum of a committee be less than [three] members.

(2) Except as aforesaid or otherwise ordered by the committee which has appointed it, business shall not be transacted at a sub-committee unless at least [one quarter] of the whole number of the sub-committee is present.

Provided that in no case shall the quorum of a sub-committee be less than [two] members.

Absence of quorum

11.18. On the principle put forward earlier (see 11.1) that committee business should proceed rather than not – that the objective always should be to transact business rather than delay it – then the following courses might usefully be pursued when at the time fixed for the commencement of a meeting there is no quorum present:

(a) If it is known for certain or there is reasonable cause to believe that

---

[8] Local Government Act 1972, sch.12, para.39(2).
[9] *Ibid.* s.106.

additional members will be present later, the members present could proceed to discuss the business on the agenda on the understanding that, as soon as a quorum is present, the business already transacted will be affirmed by those then present and so legitimise what has been done.[10]

(b) If a committee has power merely to consider and report there seems no reason why business should not proceed provided it is made clear at the time of report to the parent body (the full assembly in the case of a committee; the committee in the case of a subcommittee) that any recommendations put forward are those of the members concerned and not of the fully constituted committee or subcommittee: the decision of the parent body if it chooses to adopt the recommendations thereby validates what has been done.

(c) If a committee has delegated powers then, somewhat similarly, the members present could, notwithstanding the absence of a quorum, proceed to discuss business on the agenda and, instead of taking executive decisions, put forward recommendations for consideration on the same basis as in (b).

As suggested above the temporary absence of a quorum should be ignored unless the attention of the chairman and, therefore, the committee is drawn to it expressly.

Confirmation of minutes of previous meeting

General

11.19. What has been said about confirmation at a council meeting of the minutes of the council's previous meeting[11] applies for the most part in respect of confirmation of minutes at a committee or subcommittee meeting. The agenda should provide for this item to be taken as first business (except where there is need to elect a chairman) and the only matters which may properly be raised on the confirmation of minutes are questions as to their accuracy. It is no bad thing to cover this specifically in a standing order:[12]

No motion or discussion shall be allowed upon the confirmation of minutes,

---

[10] See 11.35 as to whether a committee's deliberations are properly regarded as finalised until the conclusion of the meeting.

[11] See 8.25, where the ambiguity of the expression 'confirmation of the minutes' is discussed.

[12] Although it is not unreasonable to expect only those members present at the meeting concerned to vote on the 'confirmation' of the minutes it may be that a standing order in these terms is invalid because it seeks to infringe the statutory rule that all questions coming before a local authority shall be decided by a majority of those present and voting (Local Government Act 1972, sch.12, para.39).

except as to their accuracy, and any question upon this point shall be determined by a majority of the members of the committee present when the matter in question was decided.

11.20. Whereas minutes of a council meeting are usually printed and circulated to council members it is the exception rather than the rule for minutes of a committee meeting to be circulated (unless, of course, the committee minutes have been submitted in their entirety to the council – a practice which is falling into disuse: see 12.41). This means that some other arrangement is desirable in order that members may be satisfied as to the accuracy of the minutes before agreeing to their confirmation. As in the case of council minutes it is usual to obtain the chairman's approval to the draft committee minutes and to lay the minutes 'on the table' before the commencement of a meeting so that members who wish may have the opportunity of inspecting them. A standing order to the following effect is useful:

> At every committee meeting the minutes of the previous meeting shall be taken as read, provided the person presiding at the meeting shall have previously examined them and shall vouch for their correctness, but shall be read, either in part, or in their entirety, before signature, if a majority of members of the committee then present so require.

Minutes must be of previous meeting

11.21. The law requires that minutes must be 'confirmed' at the same or next following meeting.[13] This was so also under the Local Government Act 1933, sch.3, para.3(1) of Part V, but there was a useful amendment made by the London Government Act 1963, sch.4, para.44 – not, unfortunately, carried forward into the 1972 Act – which permitted the minutes of *committee* meetings (but not of council meetings) to be lawfully confirmed *at any subsequent meeting*, i.e. not necessarily the same or next meeting.

Recording the proceedings

Introduction

11.22. Because of the informality of committee proceedings, where discussion is discursive and not always directed towards a specific proposition before the meeting, considerable skill is demanded of the committee clerk whose task it is to grasp the collective 'sense' of the committee and to

---

[13] Local Government Act 1972, sch.12, para.41(1).

record the decision which emerges out of the debate. Only very rarely will the chairman ask for a proposition to be moved: it is far more usual for him to say at a particular stage in the proceedings, 'We're agreed then', or words to that effect, and move on to the next business – in confident expectation that the committee clerk will get down on paper a form of words which will fairly reflect the views of the majority. It is this which distinguishes proceedings in committee from proceedings in the full assembly and makes greater demands upon the competence of the committee clerk.

Sense-taking

11.23. A committee clerk is unlikely to be able to crystallise at any particular point the emergent view of the committee collectively if he is engrossed in extensive note-taking, even less so if he is making a scrupulously accurate shorthand record of all that is being said. It is of little value to the chairman if he turns to the committee clerk for recapitulation of the committee's views to be told that the only guidance available is a verbatim note of what was said by the last speaker. Admittedly it is the chairman's responsibility to 'hold the thread of the discussion, summing it up at intervals if necessary'[14] but not all chairmen do so. The late Lord Normanbrook, who was secretary to the Cabinet until 1962, is reported to have said:

> I used to take the Cabinet notes in long-hand, just with an old-fashioned fountain pen. I rarely wanted to get down what was said, except perhaps when they were trying to formulate the wording of an announcement and various people had different versions. What I was trying to get was the sense of a Cabinet meeting.

This is precisely what the effective committee clerk should strive to do: to capture *the sense of the meeting.*[15] It is all too easy sometimes for a committee clerk to allow his knowledge of what a committee chairman was briefed to say or a chief officer intended to say – but in fact failed to say explicitly – to influence his view of the consensus reached at a meeting. This is less likely, admittedly, at a committee meeting but can happen when, for example, a committee chairman may be meeting representatives of an outside body. It is a common fault, a serious one, which must be guarded against.[16]

[14] Civil Service booklet, *Committee Procedure* (1958) 36 *Public Administration* 252.
[15] 'The secretary should not try to reproduce what the speaker said: he should get down to the essential core of the discussion and record that as briefly and as clearly as possible': Civil Service booklet, *Committee Procedure, ibid.* p. 254.
[16] It was possibly what happened in the dispute over what had transpired at a meeting to discuss the Conservative Government's handling of the Westland helicopter affair which

Note-taking

11.24. Just how best to take notes at a committee meeting is very much a matter of personal preference. Some local authorities insist that the committee clerk keeps his notes in a book (which is often preserved: see 12.49), sometimes requiring the agenda to be pasted on to the left-hand pages and the notes to be recorded on ruled pages opposite; others leave the decision to the committee clerk who may be content merely to make manuscript notes in the margin of the agenda paper. In general terms the clerk must note down each possible decision as it begins to emerge and then cross it through as the discussion swerves to some other proposition. Apart from keeping track of the discussion the committee clerk should carefully record:

(a) specific motions with the names of the mover and any seconder and, necessarily, any amendments similarly;[17]

(b) the name of any individual member who expressly asks that his dissent be recorded: see 5.42;

(c) the names of members who vote for and against a motion and of those who abstain upon a requisition for the voting to be recorded: see 7.109;

(d) any incidental happening, e.g. a member's declaration of interest; the chairman's vacation of the chair for a specific item; a temporary adjournment; and so on.

11.25. If there is doubt in a committee clerk's mind about a decision he should ask for clarification immediately from the chairman, i.e. before the committee proceeds to the next business. This is vitally important because it is useless, after the conclusion of a meeting, to canvass opinion as to what the decision on a particular item of business might have been:[18] apart from dereliction of duty (because the recording of decisions is the committee

---

16 cont.

led to the resignation in January 1986 of the then Defence Secretary, Michael Heseltine. One civil servant, not himself involved, said at that time of meetings at which a minister is present: 'You do not take notes if your minister says something that he did not mean to say, especially if that contradicts what he has said publicly on an issue. You try to improve what is said and put it in a better order. You are always tactful.' That viewpoint has no relevance within local government!

17 Not to be recorded necessarily in the minutes but to jog the memory if the chairman suddenly asks 'Was the motion formally proposed [or seconded]?'

18 Or, for that matter, for the committee clerk to decide himself what he believes was decided on the analogy of the following, variously attributed, as the task of the Cabinet secretary:
    And so while the great ones repair to their dinner,
    The secretary stays, getting thinner and thinner,
    Racking his brains to record and report
    What he thinks they will think that they ought to have thought!

clerk's responsibility) there is unlikely to be unanimity of opinion among those whose views are sought! If a competent committee clerk does not understand the committee's decision it may safely be assumed that no one else does either. On the other hand, if the sense of the meeting is abundantly clear to the members, neither the chairman nor the majority on the committee will thank the committee clerk in seeking clarification for providing an opportunity for discussion to be reopened on a matter already decided.

11.26. A somewhat different approach in note-taking is necessary if a committee is considering a long-term matter in the course of a series of meetings. Here the committee clerk will not be concerned in minuting the proceedings but in collecting material from which to frame the committee's ultimate report, in devilling for facts, in submitting papers on particular aspects of its terms of reference, and so on.

Voting

Ordinary mode

11.27. Model standing order no. 35 – reflecting widespread practice[19] – is to this effect:

> Voting at a meeting of a committee or sub-committee shall be by show of hands.

Counting a vote

11.28. In practice the chairman will call for a show of hands only if unsure of the collective sense of the meeting. When a show of hands is asked for it is a wise precaution for the committee clerk to count the raised hands both for and against and to count aloud as he points to each member so that members can check the voting if they wish. It is, however, for the chairman to declare the decision and thus the committee clerk, after counting, should pause after voicing the total numbers and – even when the decision is obvious – leave it to the chairman to say whether the motion or amendment is carried or lost. Thus the sequence should be to this effect:

> *Chairman:* Those in favour?
> *Committee clerk:* One, two, three, four, five: five, Mr Chairman.
> *Chairman:* Those against?
> *Committee clerk:* One, two, three: three, Mr Chairman
> *Chairman:* The motion is carried.

[19] The law does not prescribe the method of voting at committee or subcommittee meetings.

11.29. The importance of this procedure is underlined where there is an equality of votes and the chairman must decide whether to use his second or casting vote. Thus:

> *Chairman:* Those in favour?
> *Committee clerk:* One, two, three, four, five: five, Mr Chairman.
> *Chairman:* Those against?
> *Committee clerk:* One, two, three, four, five: five, Mr Chairman.
> *Chairman* (after, no doubt, momentary hesitation): The motion isn't carried
>   OR
>   I shall use my casting vote. The motion is carried.

11.30. Not all members present at a committee meeting are necessarily entitled to vote. There may be members present who have declared an interest and who should thereafter abstain; and council members, not members of the committee, who are attending by invitation or under a claim of a 'need to know' (see 5.12), or under the provisions of a standing order which permits non-members to be present at any committee but does not allow them to take part in the discussion, except by leave of the committee, or to vote. It is often difficult for the chairman in a large committee to recognise whether those voting are all in fact entitled to vote. The committee clerk ought to draw attention to any vote by someone not entitled to vote but, of course, the difficulty may be no less for him. The chairman might well be advised to remind the assembled gathering – particularly if the vote is on a crucial matter – that only members of the committee may vote. Difficulties of this kind can be overcome by requiring non-members to occupy seats apart from the committee members.

Voting rights of non-members

11.31. As indicated earlier (see 5.12), persons present at a committee meeting who are not appointed members of the committee do not possess a right to vote. That, at least, is the position ordinarily. Some local authorities, however, in carefully regulated circumstances, permit a councillor to be present with full voting powers when substituting for an appointed councillor who is absent from the particular meeting: see 9.64. There is also the exceptional position in some authorities where, usually in the case of a planning committee, the authority confers a right on any member of the council, whether or not appointed to the committee, to attend and speak and vote on any matter concerning the area which the councillor represents. Strictly, this practice contravenes the principle that a committee must have a fixed and not a fluctuating membership (see 9.5); and it obviously poses practical problems. It makes for difficulties for the chairman. How can he know on each item of business whether the individual councillor is entitled to vote or not? The onus of 'playing fair' may well rest upon the individual councillor under standing orders but it could be that a councillor might unwittingly vote on an item in which he may not be concerned as the representative of a ward or electoral division.[20] And how should the quorum be calculated? The answer would appear to be by reference to the number of appointed members. But the fact that these questions arise surely casts doubt on the wisdom if not the propriety of such a practice.

11.32. Suppose a councillor is summoned to a committee meeting in error (e.g. because of a confusion over similar surnames) and that councillor attends and actually votes and the voting error is not detected at the time? What is the position? First, the proceedings are not invalidated solely on that account,[21] nor can the constitution of the meeting be easily challenged subsequently because of the presumption that after the minutes have been confirmed the meeting was properly constituted.[22] But a vote which is an invalid vote is no vote at all and if such a vote was critical, e.g. if a proposition was carried by one vote, then the decision is open to challenge.[23]

Chairman's second or casting vote

11.33. The statutory power of a chairman of any local authority meeting, including that of a committee or subcommittee, to give a second or casting vote has already been discussed (see 7.114). Some authorities, no doubt to avoid uncertainty, provide specifically in standing orders for a second or casting vote by the person presiding:

> In the case of an equality of votes at a meeting of any committee or subcommittee the chairman presiding thereat shall have a second or a casting vote.

Reversal or variation of decision at same meeting

11.34. The ordinary rule is that when a meeting has resolved upon a certain issue the resolution cannot at the same meeting be extinguished or

---

[20] Decisions of a committee not properly constituted are nevertheless deemed valid by the Local Government Act 1972, sch.12, para.44(2).

[21] Local Government Act 1972, sch.12, paras.4(4), 10(3), 26(3).

[22] *Ibid.* para.44(2).

[23] See *Nell* v. *Longbottom* (1894) 1 QB 767, in which it was held that an invalid vote could not be regarded as having been cast: see 7.102.

changed by a second resolution purporting to rescind or reverse or vary the first.[24] The rule should be observed inflexibly in the case of council meetings.[25]

11.35. The view could be taken, however, that (subject necessarily to standing orders) in the case of committee deliberations, where procedure is informal and a strict order of debate is rarely observed or needs to be, the conclusions or decisions of the committee are not settled until the chairman declares the sitting at an end. Much depends upon the character of the committee and the business being transacted. In the case of a committee appointed for a specific or one very general purpose (as in the case of a committee of inquiry), the discussion may range over the whole terms of reference and such conclusions as may emerge during the course of the discussion are purely tentative ones which are not finally settled until the concluding stages of the proceedings. In such cases there seems nothing to prevent the committee from changing its mind several times.

11.36. This view could hardly be sustained, however, in the case of the ordinary local authority committee sitting to consider an agenda with quite separate items of business. It would not be logical to regard the committee meeting as sitting in continuous session to deal with the business *en bloc* because in fact each item of business discussed and not deferred is settled there and then by a decision expressly stated or implied. Nevertheless, the wishes of committee members are paramount and, provided that the members present when the business was first dealt with are still present and no others have come into the room and no executive action has been taken on the resolution by a zealous officer, i.e. the circumstances are precisely as they were at the time when the original decision was taken, it would not seem unpardonable for the chairman to permit the matter to be reopened.

11.37. Where exceptionally an earlier decision is reversed or varied later the minutes should record only the second resolution as being the properly considered decision of the committee. Where, however, it is the practice to prepare minutes to reflect precisely the order of business and the movement of members in and out of the committee, the minutes would misrepresent the proceedings if the first resolution was not recorded. The dilemma then is that the minutes themselves would record if not an irregularity at least a departure from conventional procedure which might provide evidence upon which the validity of the second resolution could be

---

[24] Although the question does not appear to have been before the courts this view is taken by several textbook writers, e.g. Shaw and Smith, *The Law of Meetings*, p. 78.

[25] If specific procedure is made for the rescission of resolutions the prescribed procedure must be stringently observed or the purported rescission will be ineffective: *R. v. Tralee UDC* (1913) Ir. KB 59.

challenged. This may be thought further justification for the generally accepted view that a question once settled cannot properly be reopened at the same meeting.

Duration of committee meetings

Setting a time limit

11.38. Although it is not uncommon for standing orders to set a limit upon the duration of council meetings (or at least set a time at which members must decide whether or not to continue the sitting: see 7.132) it is rare for committee meetings to be so regulated. Nevertheless, there is much to be said for limiting the duration of committee sittings because long meetings are not conducive to good decision-making: members excuse themselves and leave if the meeting is long drawn out, the attention of others wavers as time goes by and concentration on business becomes difficult as members grow tired and possibly hungry too. Some committee chairmen (and a chairman's competence is usually critical)[26] will set themselves or agree with members a target time for completion of business: there is widespread agreement that the efficiency of any meeting dwindles after an hour and a half.

11.39. The morning is no doubt the ideal time for business (though few meetings seem to take place then) and at least the need for lunch provides automatically for a break in proceedings if not for the termination of the meeting. Afternoon meetings suffer the disadvantage of there not being a natural break and evening meetings (common particularly among district councils) suffer every possible disadvantage: they tend to go on for far too long and very often members and officers have already worked for a full day beforehand.

Conclusion of meeting

'That concludes the business'

11.40. The chairman should always end the meeting by saying expressly, 'That concludes the business of the meeting' or words to like effect. There can then be no doubt that the meeting has terminated and less likelihood

---

[26] 'The . . . officer emphasized the effect of the mode of chairmanship on the pace of a meeting by stating that if the chairmen of two of his authority's committees which each averaged one hour in length were to change places, one of these committees would average only 10 to 20 minutes but the other some three hours. We have watched extreme cases of a committee being thrust along through the business so fast that some members hardly ever seemed to find their places on the agenda, and of a committee in a doldrums for half an hour or more without any sense of purposefulness or sign of progress.': Maud Report, vol. 5, p. 153.

that continuing discussion between members after the end of official business may be misinterpreted as part of the meeting.

Noting the time

11.41. The time at which the chairman declares the meeting at an end should be recorded – as evidence of the period of attendance for purposes of members' allowances (see 5.25) and for similar purposes in the case of officers entitled either to overtime payment or honorariums for planned overtime or subsistence allowances.

Collection and disposal of committee papers

11.42. It should be the committee clerk's responsibility to gather up committee papers left behind by members and officers after the meeting. This is particularly important in the case of papers relating to business conducted while proceedings were not open to the public and Press.

12

WORK AFTER MEETINGS

Introduction

12.1. At the conclusion of a committee meeting it is the committee clerk's responsibility to do the following things, the order of priority and urgency depending upon circumstances:

(a) draft the *minutes* of the proceedings;

(b) prepare a *report* for submission to the full assembly (where the practice locally is to submit reports instead of the full committee minutes to the council: see 12.38);

(c) transmit a note immediately to the committee clerk concerned of any matter referred to another committee;

(d) notify other officers by the preparation and circulation of an *action sheet* of action which it is their responsibility to take in pursuance of the committee's decisions;

(e) implement the decisions of the committee which fall to the committee clerk to carry out personally;

(f) record in a *noter-up or bring-forward system* any matters which need to be followed up or reported to a later meeting of the committee;

(g) record each decision in the appropriate correspondence file;

(h) update the *index* to the committee's proceedings in the minute book.

Matters requiring immediate action

Action sheets

12.2. It is the practice in some authorities for the committee clerk to prepare as soon as practicable after each meeting a brief summary of proceedings or *action sheet* (the description varies according to the purpose). In most instances the aim is to provide for easy reference an immediately available guide to the decisions made and, in some instances, an indication of the officer expected to take executive action. While this has its advantages – and officers accustomed to the practice think it indispensable – it may be thought preferable to avoid preparation of any document which must delay the drafting of the minutes (or the report) for the full council: indeed, the practice may encourage tardiness in writing up minutes.

12.3 An example of an action sheet is set out hereunder:

London Borough of . . . . . .
Housing Committee: 10 June 19 . . .

Decision/Action Sheet

Agenda Item No.	Subject	Decision	For action by
1	Minutes: Meeting of 10 May, 19 . .	Confirmed.	—
2	Apologies	Clrs. Brown, Smith, and Robinson. Best wishes to be sent to Clr. Brown for speedy return to health.	Borough Secretary
3	Membership of . . . Housing Association: appointment of council representative	Clr. Jones to be nominated.	Borough Secretary
4	Housing estate, Southfield Road: naming.	To be named Robinson Retreat.	Borough Housing Manager

In some cases there is a fifth column which gives a *target date* by which executive action is expected to be taken. Items subject to council approval need to be clearly indicated.

References to other committees

12.4. This will ordinarily be a matter of first priority because where committees follow in quick succession there is always the possibility of a reference failing to reach the other committee in due time if the committee clerk is slow in transmitting the necessary information to the other committee clerk or clerks concerned. Often the probability of a reference from one committee to another can be foreseen: and in that event it is prudent to include an appropriate item on the agenda of the 'recipient' committee.

12.5. References from one committee to another are of three types:

(a) those on which the views of another committee are sought before the originating committee resumes or completes its consideration of the matter concerned;

(b) those which, as a matter of routine, stand referred to other committees, e.g. staffing matters to a personnel committee or financial proposals to a finance committee, before consideration by a policy committee or the full assembly;

(c) those which involve matters of policy or important principle which either must be by standing orders, or are thought desirable to be, placed before a policy committee.

12.6. Unnecessary references between committees can and ought to be avoided by careful arrangement of committee business. The general principle should be to place an item only before the committee which has the power to make a decision or frame a recommendation. The Mallaby Committee on *Staffing of Local Government* had this comment to make about the consideration of staffing proposals:[1]

> The procedure whereby an establishment revision is first worked out between a service department and its committee and is then submitted to an establishment committee whose staff cover the ground again is clearly wasteful; it can result in much controversy and bad feeling if there is a conflict of advice. Establishment specialists should be consulted as soon as a need for a change is realized or from the beginning of a periodic review of establishments. A joint report should be prepared after consultation between the departments concerned and the clerk or establishment officer; this report should be submitted to the committee which has authority to take a decision or make a recommendation to the council.

Urgent executive action

12.7. Next after references to other committees attention should be given to matters of urgency where failure to take action immediately could frustrate the committee's intention or otherwise prejudice the council's interests. These include:

(a) items of business on which the committee has expressly instructed that executive action should be taken as a matter of urgency;

(b) anticipatory action on recommendations to another committee or the full assembly where delay could nullify the eventual decision.

A committee clerk should be alert to the need to take action to secure due performance of his committee's instructions, e.g. if a committee is propos-

---

[1] Mallaby Report, para.433.

ing to nominate an officer to attend a study course and the nomination requires the approval or affirmation of another committee, the committee clerk should make a provisional booking without commitment if there is likelihood otherwise that the course will be fully booked before a final decision can be taken. Where immediate action may be called for on matters not within the committee's delegated powers the approval of the chairman of the council may be necessary.

Minutes or reports?

12.8. If minutes are used as the means of reporting every committee's proceedings to the full assembly, the preparation of these will be a matter of priority for the committee clerk after conclusion of the meeting: the minutes will need to be drafted, approved by the officers concerned, submitted for the chairman's agreement and printed for inclusion in the council meeting agenda. If, on the other hand, the authority has adopted the report system, it will be the committee clerk's responsibility to prepare the report first and the minutes subsequently: the report will similarly need to be drafted, approved and printed. These differing methods of reporting upwards are discussed later: see 12.38.

Preparation of the minutes
Objectives

12.9. The minutes of a committee meeting cannot be successfully written up without a clear understanding of the purposes which the minutes are to serve. These include the need:
(a) to establish an accurate record of the decisions taken;
(b) to comply with legal requirements;
and, where minutes are used as the vehicle to bring committee proposals before the full assembly, the need also:
(c) to ensure that the record is sufficiently self-explanatory to enable the council to make a decision in full possession of the relevant facts;
(d) to provide adequate information about the authority's business for Press and public.

12.10. In practice it is difficult, if not impossible, to meet satisfactorily these several and sometimes conflicting objectives. The obligation upon local authorities to keep minutes of proceedings could be met by notes of extreme brevity, consistent with intelligibility, for the law does not prescribe the form in which minutes shall be written up: but the authority may need to substantiate what has been done in its name by production of the minutes authorising the action taken and the minutes must be drawn up in terms which will satisfy legal requirements. However, although the law imposes constraints, administrative and public relations needs provide scope for skilful and imaginative drafting.

12.11. The factor most likely to influence the style, form and content of committee minutes is the need to secure council approval of committee proceedings. Indeed, it was a recognition of the irreconcilability of preparing minutes to satisfy legal *and* procedural needs that led local authorities to adopt what is termed the *report method* of advising the full assembly of committee business. This method involves the preparation of two documents: the actual *minutes* in which are recorded the whole of the committee's proceedings; and a *report* which, in wholly different style, sets out only those items of business which must be submitted to the full assembly for information or approval. The advantages and disadvantages of the report system and the several ways in which it is operated in practice are referred to later: see 12.38.

Drafting minutes

12.12. There is no right or wrong way of drafting minutes: the form adopted by any particular local authority is a matter of individual choice or local custom. The obligation to keep minutes does not mean that the minutes must be written up during the course of the meeting. This could be done[2] and there are advantages where it is practicable, but it is usual and perfectly permissible for the minutes to be transcribed from rough notes taken at the meeting.[3]

12.13. In course of time a number of cardinal principles of good practice have become widely accepted. Thus, for example, a minute should be:

(a) *brief*, i.e. precise and concise, recording exactly what was done and no more;[4]

(b) *self-contained*, i.e. complete in itself and intelligible without reference to other documents (but see below); and

(c) *decisive*, i.e. there must be no ambiguity or doubt as to the committee's

---

[2] Indeed, the terms of the Local Government Act 1972, sch.12, para.41, that minutes shall be signed *at the same* or next ensuing meeting envisages that this might be done.

[3] *Re Jennings* (1851) 1 I. Ch. Rep.236.

[4] Sometimes precision demands more rather than fewer words and thus, unfortunately, matters of comparative triviality sometimes need to be expressed at greater length than pronouncements of high policy or principle. Thus Congressman Arthur Miller of Nebraska, speaking before the United States Senate: 'Lincoln's Gettysburg Address contained 266 words. The Ten Commandments contain 297 words. The Declaration of Independence contains about 1,500 words. But the Office of Price Stabilisation Order fixing prices for cabbages contains 26,911 words.'

intention; and thus clarity is an indispensable part of the accuracy of the record.

Brevity can be secured by being selective: a minute is not a verbatim record but a summary of the proceedings which includes only the essence of the discussion[5] – not always that – and the decision. It is rarely necessary to reproduce, however summarily, what a particular speaker said; but helpful, as a rule, to pick up the main threads of the discussion which lead to the conclusion. To be *self-contained* does not mean that a minute cannot properly refer to supporting material, e.g. an officer's report incorporated as an appendix, a plan, deed or other significant document which cannot physically be made part of the minute book: but a minute must not rely on extraneous material for its understanding or interpretation. *Decisiveness* can be facilitated by a crisp style, eschewing adjectives.

12.14. Minutes collectively should be complete in the sense that they include at least a brief reference to every item of business dealt with, so that it may safely be assumed that any matter not mentioned was not before the meeting.

Skill in draftsmanship

12.15. Skilful use of the written word comes generally from practical experience: what is demanded of those who write minutes and reports is workmanlike competence. The author has said elsewhere:[6]

> Minute writing is conditioned by two antagonisms. On the one hand there is insistent necessity for speedy work. On the other, there is a demand for less paper – for economy of words and accuracy of expression that are its prerequisites. These two divergent extremes are seemingly irreconcilable. The hardpressed secretary must *dictate* his draft minutes and despatch them for approval with perhaps the minimum of revision and with no time to seek the polished phrase. Lack of time demands the greatest expedition. But it is not given to everyone to dictate both fluently and with economy of words. The only way for most mortals to achieve impeccable phraseology – and secretaries, of whom infallibility is generally expected, are the most human of mortals – is the hard grind of pen to paper for with it comes the possibility of

---

[5] 'The secretary should make use of any striking phrases used in the discussion – this will help to reflect the tone of the meeting – but should not attempt to set out the course of the arguments as they were developed by the speakers, as this will usually lead him into an unnecessarily diffuse style. He will find it easier to be concise if he dictates the minute without following too closely the rough notes taken at the meeting': Civil Service booklet on *Committee Procedure, ibid.* p. 253.

[6] 'Reflections on Minute Writing', *Secretaries Journal* (19 July 1952), p. 56. And *The Complete Plain Words* by Sir Ernest Gowers quotes a one-time Foreign Office memorandum on drafting: 'It is a common-place that . . . simplicity does not always come with a first draft even to the greatest stylists'.

detecting at the instance of birth the superfluous word, the ambiguous phrase. . . . But lack of time generally militates seriously against maximum care.

Though conformity with a pattern may help in producing good work (see, e.g. the next following paragraphs on *form*), this cannot of itself produce the clarity and precision characteristic of the expert draftsman. Constant attention to the construction of sentences is necessary. All adjectives must be eliminated. The simplest word rather than the unusual must be preferred, the active rather than the passive style, positive rather than negative construction. Every word must contribute something material to the meaning of the minute: the article *the*, for example, can almost always be omitted before dates and in many other instances. And there is always something additional to learn. With increased skill in drafting comes an appreciation of layout, and then importance begins to be attached to the visual appearance on paper, to the proper balance between the long and the short paragraph. The author has found it useful to make a special reading of all draft minutes before final approval specifically for the purpose of adding that finesse, that plus something, which distinguishes the competent from the pedestrian and which is invariably achieved by taking something away – the unnecessary words.

12.16. An example of mindless use of unnecessary words was given a few years ago in an editorial comment in one of the local government weekly periodicals:[7]

> The fault (of verbiage) is so common that I don't want to pillory any single authority but I offer some samples in which I have italicized the unnecessary words:
>
> 'That the total amount of any one advance be restricted to *a maximum of* £10,000.'
>
> 'That, *by confirming this minute*, the council endorse . . .'
>
> '. . . including the implications of the *provisions contained in the* Community Land Bill.'
>
> 'That the officers be requested to report *to a subsequent meeting* . . . concerning the *possible* involvement of the work force.'

This kind of thing can add enormously to the length of a document with consequent waste of typing and printing time and paper.

Form
Minutes individually and collectively

12.17. In considering the structure of minutes there needs to be examined both the form of the *individual minute* covering a particular item of business

---

[7] Chronicler in *Local Government Chronicle* (26 September 1975), p. 884.

(which, as already indicated, must be complete and self-contained: see 12.13), and that of the *'set' of minutes* which collectively relate to the proceedings of a meeting as a whole.

'Set' of minutes

12.18. Each 'set' of minutes, i.e. the minutes which collectively relate to a particular meeting, will ordinarily follow a prescribed pattern. It will first identify the committee concerned and the date of the meeting and also, possibly, the time of commencement and the place of meeting, e.g.:

> MINUTES of a meeting of the POLICY COMMITTEE held at the Blanktown Town Hall on Monday, the 1st May, 19 . ., at . . . p.m.

Thereafter will usually be recorded[8] the names of council members and, if any, co-opted members present, distinguishing between the two as a rule: with the chairman's name appearing first and the names of the others in alphabetical order, e.g.:

> Present: Councillor John Smith (Chairman); Councillors Jones, Robinson, Smith T. J., and White; and Messrs. Black, Brown, and Gray.

If someone other than the committee chairman is presiding that member's name will still appear first but followed with an appropriate description: (in the chair), or (presiding), according to local practice. Whether or not members' initials are included is, again, a matter of custom. Some authorities prefer to list the names of all members of the committee and to indicate attendance by an asterisk. It is not good practice to include the names of officers who are in attendance because the officers are not part of the membership of the committee.

12.19. The minutes should be prepared to reflect the order in which business was transacted. This is also a logical order because it is often convenient to record, for example, a change in chairmanship e.g.:

> Councillor John Brown relinquished the chair at this point and Councillor Jack Smith assumed it.

or some other happening, e.g.:

> Councillor White declared his interest in the next succeeding item of business and, in accordance with standing order no. ——, left the meeting before the commencement of discussion.

These items could not very well be inserted in the minutes unless the

---

[8] The names of members present at a meeting must be recorded though not necessarily in the minutes: Local Government Act 1972, sch.12, para.40.

minutes followed the actual sequence of business. There is, however, a body of opinion which favours following the order of the agenda; and there is much to commend it if it is the practice of the particular authority to incorporate the agenda paper in the minute book in order to shorten the text of minutes by cross-referencing to material in the agenda. It is submitted that this is not good practice, no matter how convenient it may be administratively, because (a) the agenda is a document of no legal significance (though it must now be kept open for public inspection: see 8.38) and a meeting can refuse to discuss or receive an item on the agenda, and (b) it may encourage the drafting of resolutions which are intelligible only when read with the agenda, and this may be thought bad practice.

Individual minutes

12.20. An individual minute should consist of:
(a) a heading;
(b) a preamble or narrative; and/or
(c) a resolution;
and must be numbered distinctively.

12.21. The shorter the minute the greater its precision is likely to be. The main purpose is to record the committee's decision and therefore a minute which comprises heading and resolution only is often a sufficiently good minute. Sometimes, however – and these matters are questions of individual preference – it may be thought desirable to include a preamble, separate and distinct from the formal resolution, to show how the item of business originated (see 12.27) or to indicate the reasoning which persuaded the committee to reach its conclusion. Sometimes, again, it may be thought desirable to make the minute one of narration only which merely indicates the general sense of the meeting and the broad conclusion which it reached. Just as there is no right or wrong way of writing a minute, so there is no one method of approaching the task better than another.[9]

12.22. There should, however, be uniformity of practice. Guidelines should be laid down locally to govern style and phraseology. Thus, for example, it would seem inappropriate in some instances to record a decision in terms such as:

The committee thereupon decided to . . .

---

[9] 'It is a good rule to think out the sequence of a minute before beginning to dictate it, and to work backwards from the conclusions.': Civil Service booklet on *Committee Procedure, ibid.* para.28.

and at other times:

> Resolved: That . . .

Inexpert drafting of this character may persuade a critical reader to suspect there is significance in a difference which may be no more than a committee clerk's quirk of inconsistency.

Heading

12.23. A minute heading or title should be brief and explanatory of the subject-matter: once settled it should be retained unaltered to facilitate indexing, at least in its main wording, for all subsequent minutes on the same subject. There is advantage in referring immediately after the heading to previous minutes or the last minute on the same subject.

12.24. It is not always easy, however, to determine the wording of the heading. Take, for example, the following:

> 908. *Flooding: Riverside Area* (see Minute 866)
>   The Borough Engineer reported on the flooding which had occurred in
>   . . .

It is a matter of judgement in relation to the particular circumstances whether the heading might more appropriately be reversed so that it becomes:

> 908. *Riverside Area: Flooding* (see Minute 866)

If the subject of *Flooding* is a continuing problem before the committee then this might fairly be chosen as the main part of the heading. If, on the other hand, the committee has a special interest in the *Riverside Area* it is preferable that this should form the main part. In either case, despite the merit of brevity, a heading of one or the other alone would not be satisfactory: if *Flooding* is used by itself it implies that flooding in general is the subject-matter of the minute; and if *Riverside Area* is used alone the heading could mean anything.

12.25. A common error is to use a wholly inappropriate heading. Thus, encouraged no doubt by the obsessive concern of some authorities with legal technicality, is this example of using an Act of Parliament as the heading to a minute which is not in any way concerned with the statute as such:

> 418. *Food and Drugs Act 1955*
>   The Chief Executive reported that at Little Muddington Magistrates
>   Court on 1st January 19 . ., the firm of . . . had been fined for selling a
>   loaf of bread which . . .

12.26. There is some justification for the view that – as neither heading nor preamble is admissible to explain a resolution (which must stand or fall by its own terms) – a *heading is not really part of a minute* and should, if it appears at all, be placed in the margin of the minute book in this fashion:

Flooding: *Riverside* *Area (see* *Minute 866)*	908. The Borough Engineer reported on the flooding which had occurred in . . .

Whatever merit there may be in this view, the practice is not generally followed in English local government although favoured by some authorities in Scotland.

Preamble

12.27. A preamble, or narrative, should be included only if it serves a purpose. It may be necessary, but rarely is, to indicate who brought a particular matter before the committee but if the officer's act is no more than procedural there is no need to recite it. An example of an entirely superfluous preamble is this:

> 123. *Association of County Councils: Annual Conference, 19 . .*
> The Chief Executive submitted an invitation to the Council to appoint delegates to the 19 . . annual conference of the Association of County Councils to be held at Brighton from . . . to . . .
> *Resolved*: That Councillors Smith, Brown and Robinson be appointed as the Council's delegates to attend the 19 . . annual conference of the Association of County Councils to be held at Brighton from . . . to . . .

If, however, the officer is making a recommendation or tendering advice there is virtue in including a reference to the recommendation or advice so submitted, e.g.: 'The Chief Executive advised the Committee that . . .'; and, vitally important, that the advice should be minuted if an officer tenders advice which he considers it his duty to give and the committee chooses to disregard it:

> The Borough Solicitor advised the committee that in his view there was no legal authority for the expenditure which the committee wished to incur . . .

12.28. The preamble can properly be used to record in narrative form the tenor of the discussion on the particular item of business but in an impersonal way,[10] i.e. not attributing views to individual members. This

---

[10] 'The main advantages of this form are: first, that it makes for brevity – a point can usually be recorded more concisely in an impersonal form. Secondly, a point raised by one speaker will often be taken up and developed by others; in an impersonal minute the secretary

can be done, for example, in this way, not necessarily following the order in which the points were made:

> The following points were raised in discussion:
> (a) . . . . .;
> (b) . . . . .; and
> (c) . . . . .

or, where there was broad agreement on the points raised:

> The committee had regard to/took account of the following points made in the course of discussion:
> (a) . . . . . .;
> (b) . . . . . .; and
> (c) . . . . . .

What must be avoided – at all costs! – is this form: 'Mr A. said . . . . . .; Mr B. replied . . . . . .; and Mr C. then pointed out that . . . . . .' Such a discursive description in conversational style obscures the thread of discussion and leaves the minute-writer open to charges that he has misinterpreted what Mr A. or Mr B. said or unfairly summarised their contribution.

12.29. It is doubtful whether there is merit in recording that discussion preceded the decision without indicating the gist of it, e.g.:

> After discussion [it was]
> *Resolved*: That . . .

Admittedly it conveys to a reader that at least the committee did not merely accept unquestioningly the advice of a chief officer or rubber-stamp a recommendation of a subcommittee; but it does little else. In a set of minutes the presumption must be, in the absence of an indication to the contrary, that no discussion preceded the decision, i.e. it is reasonable to assume that when the committee reached each particular item on the agenda the chairman said 'Agreed?' and the members, in effect, replied 'Aye' – and the meeting passed to the next item of business.

12.30. It is not usual to record in the preamble the procedural steps through which the members reached their decision. Thus, for example, the names of proposers and seconders of motions, whether passed or not, are not normally recorded; nor, ordinarily, is any record kept – as already indicated – of the contribution of particular members to the discussion.

10 cont.

need record it only in its final form; if he attributes it to the original speaker he will have to add the comments and re-state it. Thirdly, it is often convenient to weld together into a single paragraph a number of points made by various speakers. Fourthly, the impersonal style tends to avert suggestions for amendment of the minute, for members naturally look with special care at paragraphs which attribute statements to them personally, and tend to ask for additions and modifications which are not strictly necessary for the purpose of a minute.': Civil Service booklet, *Committee Procedure, ibid.* p. 255.

Unsupported statements

12.31. Care needs to be taken, in drafting a preamble which goes to some length, not to include independent sentences which represent statements unidentified as to their source. This is permissible in a committee *report* because of the presumption that all that is included represents the collective view of the committee unless otherwise indicated. In the case of a minute this is not so. For example, a narrative may begin in this way: 'The Chief Executive explained that . . .' and continue at length. When, however, the Chief Executive's reported statement goes on to a new point it is never sufficient just to begin a new paragraph but, in order to avoid an unsupported statement, i.e. one not clearly attributable to anyone in particular, it is necessary to write either 'The Chief Executive went on to say . . .' or 'The Chief Executive further reported that . . .' or words to like effect.

Conclusions

12.32. It is ordinarily inappropriate to record the reason for a decision (unless, of course, a reason is expressly stated by the committee) because members are not necessarily actuated by the same motives though they may agree on the same course of action. Nevertheless there is merit, where circumstances justify it and there is no possibility of misinterpreting the collective view of the committee, in recording a committee's conclusions properly drawn or inferred from the facts before them which lead finally to the decision. This might be expressed:

> The committee [concluded] [took the view] [were of opinion] that . . . and [accordingly] [for that reason] [on those grounds]
> *Resolved:* That . . .

or, less positively:

> The committee [inclined to the view] [felt the balance of advantage suggested] [considered it prudent] that . . . and [accordingly] [for that reason] [on those grounds]
> *Resolved:* That . . .

See further, however, 13.18.

Decisions

12.33. The decision should ordinarily be set out at the end of the individual minute in the form of a resolution. If, however, the minute falls naturally into different sections the resolutions may properly be interspersed appropriately at the end of each section rather than brought together at the end. In every case each resolution should commence with the word *That*, preferably indented from the margin of the text, and preceded in capital letters or underlined or in heavy type or some other distinctive manner by the word *RESOLVED*.

12.34. There are rules ordinarily to be observed in framing resolutions apart, of course, from what has been said about clarity and brevity:

(a) The introductory phrase *RESOLVED: That* governs all that follows. Thus it is correct to write:

RESOLVED: That the Chief Personnel Officer be empowered:
> (a) to make all appointments of clerical and administrative staff within the council's authorised establishment;
> (b) to sign on behalf of the council contracts of employment in respect of such appointments;
> and be required to submit periodically to the committee a list of all such appointments made.

but not:

RESOLVED: That the Chief Personnel Officer be empowered:
> (a) to make all appointments of clerical and administrative staff within the council's authorised establishment;
> (b) that he be authorised to sign on behalf of the council contracts of employment in respect of such appointments; and a list of all such appointments be submitted to the committee periodically.

(b) Because a resolution should be self-contained it is bad practice to employ such phrases as:

RESOLVED: accordingly.

or:

RESOLVED: That the matter be dealt with accordingly.

or, though with less objection, to make use of the heading:

Clerical and administrative staff
RESOLVED: That the Chief Personnel Officer be empowered to make all appointments of this character within the council's authorised establishment.

(c) Resolutions can be numbered serially (at least through each set of minutes) as an additional safeguard against tampering with the minute book by deletion:

RESOLVED: 1. That . . .

12.35. There are also matters of individual style. Thus, for example, the resolutions of, say, a subcommittee or committee without delegated powers may be preceded by either:

RESOLVED TO RECOMMEND: That . . .

or

RECOMMENDED: That . . .

or

 · *RESOLVED:* That the council be recommended to . . .

or, preferably, because the resolution can then be identifiable as the council's resolution without alteration of the words:

RESOLVED: That it be recommended to the council that . . .

And there is advantage often in clearly indicating which officer is to take executive action:

RESOLVED: That . . . and that the Chief Executive be empowered to take all such steps as may be necessary to secure compliance therewith.

Some authorities favour the style:

RESOLVED UNANIMOUSLY . . .

on particular occasions of formality or when desirous of indicating to a recipient of the authority's sympathy or congratulations that the council is patently 'at one'. On the other hand, the use of 'Resolved unanimously' might imply some lesser value of resolutions not so distinguished. Also favoured on special occasions are what otherwise might be regarded as unnecessarily ponderous:

RESOLVED: That the council do hereby . . .

although the use of 'hereby' may be thought to indicate beyond doubt that the resolution is immediately effective and not dependent on some subsequent administrative or legal formality: see 1.46.

Procedural considerations

12.36. Where full committee minutes are submitted to the parent body it is desirable that the attention of the council in the case of committee minutes, and the attention of the committee in the case of subcommittee minutes, is directed to matters of significance.[11] Where there is no delegation of executive powers this may be sufficiently evident by the use of

[11] Maud Report, vol. 5, p. 311.

heavy type to denote recommendations, but there are other methods, e.g.
by sidelining recommendations in the margin or (a practice not to be
commended because it increases the volume of paper) by extracting and
listing together separately all recommendations for the parent body's
consideration. Even in the case of reports, as distinct from minutes, it is
desirable that recommendations should be clearly distinguished from the
main text. One local authority's standing orders provide that:

> Every paragraph . . . containing a recommendation shall be marked with an
> asterisk, and the paragraph and recommendation shall be called from the chair
> simultaneously.[12]

12.37. Some local authorities divide each set of committee minutes (or
reports) into two parts and so distinguish between matters dealt with
under delegated and referred powers respectively. Whether there is virtue
in such an arrangement is a matter of opinion, but it can facilitate
proceedings at the council meeting.

Reporting upwards

Minutes or reports?

12.38. The minutes of a committee can be used to report the committee's
proceedings to the full assembly. Similarly, at a lower level, a subcommittee's minutes can be the medium through which the subcommittee reports
to its parent committee. The view is taken by many local authorities
(probably decreasing in number since reorganisation) that this is an
efficient and economical arrangement: minutes must be prepared in any
case as a matter of administrative and legal necessity and thus it is thought
unnecessary and time-consuming for another, different, document to be
produced either to advise the parent body of action taken in pursuance of
delegated powers or to bring before it matters upon which the parent body
alone can make the final decision. Other authorities (in the past mostly the
larger authorities and those which have conferred wide executive power
upon committees) prefer the report system as the method of bringing
before the parent body the proceedings of committees or subcommittees,
as the case may be, for purposes of information or consideration.

12.39. Minutes record, in the past tense, the business actually transacted
at a particular meeting: very often an individual minute (as distinct from a
resolution) may be intelligible only by reference to preceding minutes on

---

[12] This, as drawn, may demand of the chairman an accomplishment beyond his capacity! But
the intention is clear. See also 7.86 *et seq.* as to the procedure for dealing with committee
reports at the council meeting.

the same subject-matter and it may or may not recite the reasons which influenced the meeting in reaching its decision or the alternative courses of action considered and rejected. A report, on the other hand, normally written in the present tense, need not limit itself to matters actually dealt with at a particular meeting: it can deal with an issue comprehensively, covering proceedings at several past meetings, and so present to the parent body a full account in readable, intelligible form. The style, too, is different: e.g. 'The Committee have considered . . .', or 'We have considered . . . and now *recommend*'.

Challenge to committee minutes at full council

12.40. It can happen, where a local authority submits committee minutes rather than reports to the full assembly, that the committee minutes will be before the council in advance of their confirmation by the committee. What, then, should happen if a councillor questions the accuracy of a committee minute and the question of accuracy is critical either to the council's understanding of what has been decided or could affect what is proposed? The minute – even if its inaccuracy is evident to the full assembly – cannot properly be corrected because that can only be done by the committee when the minutes come before it for confirmation. The correct procedure would be for the member who is challenging the accuracy of the minute to move its reference back to the committee. If the motion is approved it will be for the committee to consider the objection when it comes to confirm the minutes at the next meeting. In practice it seems unlikely that such a motion would be approved: after all, the minutes will have been drawn up by the officers and probably approved by the committee chairman; and the chairman is likely to oppose the reference back and will conceivably be supported by committee members present at the council meeting. If, of course, the report system is adopted a procedural problem of this kind cannot arise: it would be perfectly proper for the full assembly to debate a motion seeking to refer back a paragraph in the report or to amend a recommendation contained in it.

Advantages and disadvantages of the report system

12.41. The comparative advantages and disadvantages of the contrasting systems may seem self-evident: they have, in any case, been thoroughly discussed elsewhere.[13] If business dealt with in committee or subcommit-

---

[13] Warren, *Municipal Administration*, 2nd edn, p. 127, which refers to and summarises discussion on the matter in the *Justice of the Peace* in 1944.

tee is considerable and does not involve questions of major policy, there may seem little advantage in submitting the full minutes of proceedings to the parent body: the sheer bulk of paper in some cases may make it difficult for the parent body to distinguish between the important and the trivial and to concentrate attention upon matters of major policy or principle.[14] If, however, the position is otherwise: if the committee or subcommittee only discusses important questions (i.e. where there is substantial delegation to officers) it could fairly be argued that the preparation of a report in addition to the minutes is unnecessary. Clearly it would be impracticable to leave it to be decided in each instance whether the parent body should sometimes be advised by minutes and sometimes by report: there must be one system laid down and properly regulated.[15] Unless, indeed, the arrangement is controlled the parent body may find itself deprived of essential information whether advised by a report or by minutes. It is the content rather than form which matters in this respect. In an inquiry into certain irregularities in Newcastle's ARP services during World War II, Sir Roland Burrows, QC, suggested that the submission of a committee report rather than the full minutes to the city council was partly the reason why the council had failed to detect what was going on;[16] on the other hand, a minute can be equally inadequate (see 9.26 with regard to a case where the decision of a local education authority was held to be *ultra vires* largely because the authority had not been provided with sufficient information in a committee minute on which to reach a decision). Or, of course, if committees are not compelled to report periodically the council may get the impression that a committee is doing nothing at all (the Maud Committee refers to the disquiet of an officer that because his committee's business rarely featured in the council agenda, 'council members as a whole were unfamiliar with the service he represented and that this prejudiced his case when priorities were being settled'[17]).

12.42. Criticism from individual council members that the report system

---

[14] 'Submission of reports . . . tends . . . to direct the minds of members to policy, whereas the submission of full minutes is apt to result in debates upon many relatively unimportant questions of detail to the exclusion of discussion upon the important matters of policy.': County Councils Association memorandum on *Simplification of County Administration* (1951).

[15] There might not be much objection to the adoption by a local authority of one system in respect of subcommittees (where it might be thought appropriate for minutes to be submitted to the parent committee) and another in respect of committees (where, because of different considerations, the report system is considered desirable): the practice ought, however, to be clearly prescribed and adhered to. The Maud Committee thought there might be grounds for distinguishing the education committee and its subcommittees as a special case: Maud Report, vol. 5, p. 309.

[16] Quoted in Warren, *Municipal Administration*, 2nd edn, p. 128.

[17] Maud Report, vol. 5, p. 310.

denies them full knowledge of the council's activities stems from the belief that a comprehensive knowledge is necessary for proper performance of their duties as councillors. Most people would think this a mistaken view. Council members should, however, be able to obtain the information they want and obtain it easily if it is information to which they are entitled. Where the report system is adopted committees, and subcommittees, should be under an obligation to report upon their deliberations. How frequently is a matter for decision but it may be thought prudent to impose an obligation to report in each cycle by a standing order to this effect:

> Every committee of the council shall report their proceedings to the next available council meeting.

This at least provides an opportunity for a council member to ask questions about progress on a matter in which he is interested or even to challenge the adequacy of the report submitted.

Hybrid systems

12.43. Some authorities attempt, with varying degrees of success or lack of it, to combine the advantages of the report system with the advantages of submitting full minutes to the parent body. Thus an authority will submit to the full assembly 'only certain sections of the minutes',[18] the choice being made administratively, sometimes on the basis that only non-delegated business will be reported selectively,[19] or by the committee itself; or, where the practice of submitting full minutes means that minutes on confidential matters must be drawn in general terms only, certain *unreported minutes* will be written up solely for recording in the committee minute book.

Methods of reproduction

12.44. Some local authorities cling to traditional methods of reproducing the council meeting agenda. Apart from the substantial cost involved this brings problems in finalising and printing committee reports in time for incorporation with the agenda. Word processors have revolutionised the preparation of council and committee papers, but the heavy peak load of work in the committee cycle often taxes the authority's resources.

12.45. A discussion of the economics of differing methods of reproduction would be beyond the scope of this book. The efficient organisation of

[18] Maud Report, vol. 5, p. 311.
[19] *Ibid.* p. 309.

committee work involves necessarily careful regard to the demands made upon the authority's administrative machinery. Some years ago the (now Royal) Institute of Public Administration produced a pamphlet on *Local Authorities Minutes and Reports.*[20] It is now rather dated but the following steps recommended in seeking a solution to this problem still have some relevance:

(a) Lower the height of the peak by reducing as far as possible the amount of text to be reproduced;

(b) Seek to spread this peak over the maximum possible period, perhaps by some rearrangement of the committee cycle;

(c) See how far existing resources of staff and machines can be pooled for this particular operation without causing undue dislocation of normal work;

(d) Assess the amount of overtime that might be forthcoming each month from typing and non-typing staff to make internal reproduction practicable;

(e) Determine what additional staff and machines would be required to bridge any gap that may still remain between the desirable and the practicable;

(f) Investigate the cost and speed of service to be obtained from firms that undertake duplication commercially and might be employed to supplement the council's own resources.

Other work involved
Implementation of decisions

12.46. It is ordinarily the committee clerk's responsibility to see that committee decisions are implemented either by ensuring that the appropriate officer is advised of the action to be taken or by himself performing certain of the executive work. Reference has already been made to the importance of taking urgent executive action immediately after a committee meeting and to the practice of some authorities in circulating an *action sheet* (see 12.2). On many items, however, action will need to be delayed until the committee's recommendation has been accepted by the council or, prudently, until the minute has been written up.

12.47. Practice varies widely in this respect.[21] In some cases a memorandum is circulated to chief officers indicating the action that is

---

[20] Studies in Administrative Methods No. 2: *Local Authorities Minutes and Reports: Their Preparation and Reproduction* (Institute of Public Administration, 1950).

[21] Maud Report, vol. 5, p. 312.

expected of them; in others it is well established that officers will automatically take action on the minutes as soon as they are promulgated – and on the basis, say, of any action sheet already circulated. This latter is probably the ideal situation provided the committee clerk chases those items which may require further report to committee.

12.48. It is not usual for the committee clerk to go to the length of satisfying himself that a particular chief officer has done what is expected of him. Most officers do not appear to think that the arrangements for ensuring that action is taken on council and committee minutes constitute a problem.[21]

Destruction of committee clerk's notes

12.49. Once the minutes have been confirmed the committee clerk's notes should be destroyed. The reason for this is that there should be no other record, however informal, which might cast doubt upon the correctness of the official record. If the notes are known to be retained (and many authorities do seem to favour keeping them) there is always the likelihood that they may be required to be produced. If, which is unlikely, the notes constitute a verbatim shorthand record there should, of course, be no possibility of their contradicting the minutes (indeed, it could be argued that the notes are of value in supporting the minutes if challenged), but otherwise rough notes are capable of misinterpretation and could in that event be capable of proving the opposite!

Indexing

12.50. Minute books must be indexed, for self-evident reasons. Unless it is possible to trace the minute on a particular matter the decision, at least as a record, might as well not be passed. Indeed, there is much to commend the practice of recording separately, possibly bound up as an addendum to standing orders, a copy of minutes on matters of policy or important principle which are of continuing effect.[22]

12.51. The indexing should be carried out in a systematic manner in accordance with prescribed guidelines formulated by each local authority to meet particular needs and entrusted to someone with knowledge and understanding of the subject-matter and the purposes for which the index

---

[22] 'Minutes should be written in a clearer, more understandable form with better indexing, and policy items should be identified distinctly': *Occasional Paper No. 4: Services to Elected Members*: a survey of Scottish local authorities by the Planning Exchange of Glasgow (1977).

is likely to be used. There are many minutes which do not merit indexing: the record of apologies for absence (if, indeed, these are minuted at all); the confirmation of minutes; matters of purely procedural or transitional interest. And where full committee minutes are submitted to the council there seems no advantage in duplicating in the index to the council minute book the individual items in committee minutes which are more appropriately indexed in the minute books of the respective committees.

12.52. It is usual to bind up sets of minutes in volumes covering a year or half-year (perhaps multiples of a year for committees which seldom meet) according to the amount of business transacted. Each minute book should have an index relating exclusively to the minutes therein. The easiest way to build up an index is on a loose card system which can then be transcribed for incorporation in the binding. The task is facilitated if each minute has a standardised heading and explanatory subheading: see 12.23.

Minute numbering

12.53. Each minute should be numbered consecutively: this facilitates indexing, reference and cross-reference from one minute to another, and makes more difficult any tampering with the minute book, i.e. it is impossible then for a new page to be fraudulently substituted or a particular minute omitted altogether (although, of course, a spurious minute could be written in to replace the authentic one).[23]

12.54. It is a matter of individual choice or local practice whether the numbering is recommenced for each 'set' of minutes, i.e. the minutes relating to a particular meeting, or is continued throughout, say, the council year (of advantage if the minutes are bound annually). There is simplicity in beginning with 1 again for each 'set' of minutes though cross-referencing is necessarily lengthier (assuming cross-referencing is favoured), as indeed it is if there is renumbering for each year. It means, for example, that the reference to a previous minute on the same subject will need to be *See minute no. 10 of 1st May 19 . .* or *See minute no. 100 of 197–/7–* instead of merely *See minute no. 1000.* On the other hand, the reference to date may facilitate retrieval of the particular minute required.

---

[23] But see 12.34 as to the advantage also of numbering *resolutions.* In any case each page of a minute book should be initialled by the person who signs the particular 'set' of minutes to which the pages relate.

Inspection of committee minutes

12.55. Since 1 April 1986 the minutes of committees and subcommittees of principal councils have been open to public inspection on the same terms and subject to the same limitations as in the case of council minutes: see 8.38. and 8.39. Prior to that date only the minutes of the education committee were open to inspection and only by local government electors: the minutes of other committees and subcommittees were (and, strictly speaking, still are) only open to inspection so far as they were laid before the council meeting for approval. The minutes of committees and subcommittees of parish and community councils are still not required to be open for inspection. Where an embargo continues it is nevertheless open to the local authority to allow inspection at its discretion. Councillors have always possessed a common law right to inspect committee and subcommittee minutes so far as it may reasonably be necessary to enable them to carry out their council duties: see 8.35.

12.56. What has been said earlier about the times when council minutes may be inspected applies also to committee and subcommittee minutes (see 8.42) – as it does regarding obstruction of the right of inspection (see 8.44 and 8.45).

PART FOUR

MISCELLANEOUS MEETINGS

13

MEETINGS FOR SPECIAL PURPOSES

Introduction

13.1. This chapter deals with a number of specialised committees and panels and somewhat similar groups whose meetings call for special treatment. There can be no exhaustive list of these because many local authorities have set up special committees and the like for purposes that arise out of peculiarly local circumstances, but the examples selected are thought to cover the more important of those of concern to the majority of authorities.

13.2. In several of these cases the rules governing meetings are not substantially different from those applicable to local authorities and what might be termed their conventional committees. This is certainly so as regards joint committees and joint boards set up by two or more authorities; and the practices associated with meetings of most other groups considered here are not dissimilar from those adopted by local authorities. However, certain of the specialist committees or panels, either in their constitution or their functions or in the procedure which they must follow, differ significantly from the generality of local authorities and other bodies. Also included in this chapter are election meetings and some quasi-meetings, such as public inquiries, etc., with which local authorities are concerned indirectly.

Joint committees

Power to appoint

13.3. Among the several arrangements which local authorities may make for the discharge of their functions is that which provides for two or more authorities to discharge functions jointly[1] so long as it is not a function

---

[1] Local Government Act 1972, s.101(5).

which the law requires to be discharged by a specified committee.[2] For purposes of discharging a function jointly the authorities may appoint a *joint committee*.[3] The number of members of the joint committee, their term of office (which must not extend beyond their term of office with the appointing authority), and the area within which the joint committee shall exercise its authority must be fixed by the appointing authorities:[4] the membership may include persons who are not members of the appointing authorities[5] (so long as they are not disqualified for membership).[6] Local planning authorities in Greater London are *required* to establish a joint committee to consider and advise those authorities on matters of common interest and to represent their views to the Secretary of State and other planning authorities in the vicinity of Greater London.[7]

Executive and advisory powers

13.4. Two or more authorities, in discharging any of their functions through a joint committee, may delegate executive powers to the joint committee[8] other than the function with respect to levying or issuing a precept for a rate or borrowing money.[9] There is separate statutory power (although the terms are substantially the same) enabling two or more authorities to join in appointing a joint committee 'to advise the appointing authorities on any matter relating to the discharge of their functions'.[10]

Expenses

13.5. The expenses incurred by a joint committee of two or more authorities, whether appointed under the Local Government Act 1972 or any other enactment,[11] are to be defrayed by those authorities in such proportions as they may agree or in case of disagreement as may be determined (a) in any case in which those authorities are the councils of parishes or

---

[2] *Ibid.* s.101(10).
[3] *Ibid.* s. 102(1). To be distinguished from a *joint board* and *joint authorities*: see 13.7.
[4] Local Government Act 1972, s.102(2).
[5] *Ibid.* s.102(3).
[6] *Ibid.* s.104.
[7] Local Government Act 1985, s.5. The Act is silent as to the constitution and proceedings of such joint committees.
[8] Local Government Act 1972, s.101(5).
[9] *Ibid.* s.72, 101(6).
[10] *Ibid.* s.102(4).
[11] The expenses of the joint planning committee for Greater London, if incurred with the approval of at least two-thirds of the local planning authorities, are to be defrayed by those authorities in such proportions as they may decide or, in default, as the Secretary of State may determine: Local Government Act 1985, s.5(3).

communities or groups of parishes or communities situated in the same district, by the district council, and (b) in any other case, by a single arbitrator agreed on by the appointing authorities or, in default of agreement, by the Secretary for the Environment.[12]

Standing orders

13.6. Standing orders regarding a joint committee of two or more local authorities (irrespective of the statute under which the joint committee is appointed) may be made by those authorities, dealing with the quorum, proceedings and place of meeting of the joint committee (including any subcommittee); but, subject to any such standing orders, the quorum, proceedings and place of meeting can be such as the joint committee itself may determine.[13]

Joint boards and authorities

Distinguishable from joint committees

13.7. A joint board or, as it is sometimes called, a joint authority, is fundamentally different from a joint committee. There is no general power permitting the establishment of joint boards, but specific power is contained in a number of statutes and in each case the rules as to the constitution are prescribed.

Joint boards

13.8. A joint board is a corporate body, created by order of a minister, requiring in many cases the approval of Parliament: it has perpetual succession, a common seal, and it can hold land. Unlike a joint committee a joint board cannot be dissolved by agreement; it has independent financial powers, including the power to borrow money, and obtains its revenue from constituent authorities by means of precepts.

13.9. The order or other instrument creating the joint board will ordinarily prescribe its constitution and the rules governing meetings procedure. As to the unique position of local authority members on a joint planning board (and other joint boards where members hold statutory office: see Chapter 5) and as to the new statutory joint authorities, see 13.10.

[12] Local Government Act 1972, s.103.
[13] *Ibid.* s.102.

Joint authorities

13.10. As a consequence of the abolition of the Greater London Council and the metropolitan county councils, provision was made in the Local Government Act 1985 for the establishment of joint authorities to administer county-wide a number of former county functions which it was considered could not be discharged effectively and efficiently at borough or district level. In each case the joint authority is a corporate body, similar in most respects to a joint board – except that it owes its existence to an Act of Parliament rather than to a ministerial order and its members do not hold a statutory office – and in general they are treated as local authorities: their members are subject to the same rules as to disqualification, and the statutory provisions in regard to meetings procedure apply[14] to them, including the obligation to admit the public and Press to their meetings.[15]

13.11. The joint authorities established under the Local Government Act 1985 are:

(a) metropolitan county police authorities, except in the case of Tyne and Wear which is part of a combined police authority with Northumberland County Council;[16]

(b) Northumbria Police Authority for Tyne and Wear and Northumberland;[17]

(c) metropolitan county fire and civil defence authorities;[18]

(d) London Fire and Civil Defence Authority;[19]

(e) metropolitan county passenger transport authorities.[20]

The 1985 Act also set up a directly elected Inner London Education Authority, distinguishable from all other *ad hoc* bodies.

Membership

13.12. The members of the joint authorities are the elected members of the constituent borough or district councils nominated to serve thereon plus, in the case of police authorities, magistrates appointed by the joint committee of magistrates for the county. The numbers to be appointed are prescribed[21] and subject to alteration by ministerial order, having regard to

---

[14] Local Government Act 1985, s.84. There were transitional provisions for the first meetings of the new authorities: s.86.

[15] Local Government Act 1972, s.100J, added by Local Government (Access to Information) Act 1985.

[16] Local Government Act 1985, s.24.

[17] *Ibid.* s.25.

[18] *Ibid.* s.26.

[19] *Ibid.* s.27.

[20] *Ibid.* s.28.

[21] *Ibid.* s.29 and sch.10.

the number of local government electors in the constituent authorities' areas. It is expressly provided – distinguishing a joint authority from a joint board in this respect – that a constituent council may at any time terminate an appointment and appoint another member of the council in his place, but where this power of replacement is exercised the council must give notice one month in advance of the new appointment and of the termination of the previous appointment to the joint authority concerned.[22] The provisions as to the filling of vacancies follow substantially the usual pattern of such arrangements for joint committees and joint boards. What is unusual – indeed, it is the first time that any statute has recognised that politics is a reality in local government! – is that each constituent council must, as far as practicable, ensure in making or terminating appointments to joint authorities 'that the balance of parties for the time being prevailing in that council is reflected in the persons who are for the time being members of the [joint] authority and for whose appointment the council is responsible'.[23] The joint authority is required to give public notice of changes in its membership.[24]

Judicial and quasi-judicial business

General considerations

13.13. There are occasions when a meeting is required to conduct business which is judicial or quasi-judicial in character: invariably a meeting of a committee because the full assembly could not effectively exercise such a role. Examples include: the grant of licences where there is scope for or the need to exercise discretion[25] (as opposed to instances where a licence issues automatically given the fulfilment of specified conditions); the exercise of powers which affect the interests of individuals whether or not they have a right to be heard;[26] and the hearing of appeals by the authority's employees against disciplinary measures.[27] Within the National Health Service there are the several service committees of the family practitioner committee charged with responsibility for considering complaints against a doctor, an ophthalmic medical practitioner, a chemist or an optician: see 14.13. In all such cases the committee must observe the principles of natural justice.

---

[22] *Ibid.* ss.29–32. This power of replacement does not exist in the case of joint boards: see 5.59.
[23] *Ibid.* s.33.
[24] *Ibid.* s.36.
[25] See *R.* v. *London County Council ex-parte The Entertainment Protection Association* [1931] 2 KB 215.
[26] See *R.* v. *Hendon RDC ex-parte Chorley* [1933] 2 KB 696.
[27] See *Ridge* v. *Baldwin* [1964] AC 40 and see 13.41.

13.14. In most instances where a committee or subcommittee is exercising a judicial or quasi-judicial function it can properly meet in private because the subject-matter will be exempt information.[28]

13.15. It is a cardinal principle that not only must justice be done but it must manifestly be seen to be done. There is, therefore, a responsibility on councillors when acting in a judicial or quasi-judicial capacity (and officers, too, if present on such an occasion) to conduct proceedings in such a way that parties appearing before them have no reason to suspect bias or be encouraged to challenge the proceedings on some grounds of impropriety.[29] Apart from the above, it is important that members of the committee should be present in the committee room at the outset of the meeting and remain there until a decision has been reached: it would be wholly improper for a councillor to participate in reaching the decision if he had not heard all the evidence; improper, too, it is submitted, for any councillor to be present who is not an appointed member of the committee even if he purports to claim a 'need to know'. And where an officer remains in the committee room after the parties have withdrawn it is important that the chairman should advise the parties beforehand that the officer's presence is for purposes solely of advising on the law and/or procedure and will not himself be influencing the decision.

Natural justice

13.16. Where in the exercise of a discretion by a local authority the rights and interests of an individual are affected, the authority – through a committee in practice – is under a duty to exercise its discretion fairly and without whim or bias:[30]

> . . . they must fairly consider the application and exercise their discretion on it fairly, and not take into account any reason for their discretion which is not a legal one. If people who have to exercise a public duty by exercising their discretion take into account matters which the courts consider not to be proper for the guidance of their discretion, then in the eyes of the law they have not exercised their discretion.

[28] See the descriptions of exempt information set out in sch.12A of the Local Government Act 1972. In the case of school admission appeals it is expressly provided that the hearing shall ordinarily be in private: Education Act 1980, sch.2, para.10.

[29] If there is a defect in procedure the court will intervene. Thus in *Ex-parte Ladbroke Group* (1969) 119 NLJ 225, the decision of a committee was quashed where, when considering a contested application for renewal of a licence under the Betting, Gaming and Lotteries Act 1963, the chairman twice announced that he was ready to give a decision before counsel had completed cross-examination and then appeared to reach a decision without consulting the other members of the committee.

[30] Lord Esher in *R. v. West Vestry of St. Pancras* [1890] 2 QBD 371 p. 375.

An authority, or indeed any body of persons, which has a duty in law to determine questions affecting the rights of subjects must act judicially and this means in general terms (because a dissertation on the relevant law is beyond the scope of this book)[31] that it must comply with the principles of natural justice.

13.17. These principles, as evident from decisions of the courts, are that the local authority must reach its decision fairly, without bias and in good faith, and must give a reasonable opportunity to the parties concerned to put their case, though not necessarily in person or by representative, and it may not act as a judge in its own cause. If the statute under which the authority is purporting to act lays down a procedure then that procedure must be followed; but otherwise it is not necessary for the procedure of a court of law to be followed:[32] any procedure which does not offend the principles of natural justice may be employed. The courts can review a decision made in a judicial or quasi-judicial capacity if there is an error in law disclosed on the face of the record[33] – except where the statute concerned provides that an order made thereunder may not be questioned in legal proceedings. In several instances a statute gives a right of appeal to a person aggrieved by a decision of a local authority, either to a Minister or to a court of law.

Reasons for decisions

13.18. This may be the appropriate point at which to examine the question whether the reasons for a decision of a local authority or one of its committees or subcommittees should be minuted as well as the resolution itself. If an authority can show the reasons why it reached a particular decision, the authority's act can be expected to have greater credibility in the minds of those affected by the decision; but, on the other hand, it provides evidence for those who may wish to dispute the decision to show that the decision was an unreasonable one in the light of the considerations which influenced the authority in reaching it. Nevertheless, it would seem a good principle that an authority should always be prepared to justify its action by giving a reason unless there are overriding considerations which suggest it should not do so. It may be that it would be against the council's interests (and, therefore, it may be presumed, against the public interest) for a reason to be disclosed; or it may be that the reason is far from certain:

---

[31] As to review by the courts of the exercise of discretion by local authorities see S. H. Bailey, C. A. Cross and J. F. Garner, *Cases and Materials in Administrative Law* (1977), p. 215.

[32] *R.* v. *Electricity Commissioners* [1924] 1 KB 171, *per* Atkin LJ p. 205.

[33] *Local Government Board* v. *Arlidge* [1915] AC 120, *per* Lord Shaw, p. 138.

the fact that a decision has been reached even unanimously does not necessarily mean that all those who voted were similarly motivated or influenced by the same considerations. There are thus often sound grounds for not minuting a reason; and it would seem to follow that if a reason is not minuted no officer should presume to give his interpretation of the reason which influenced the local authority or committee or subcommittee collectively.

13.19. Where, however, an authority is bound by law to disclose the grounds for a decision then the reason for the decision should be minuted. There are comparatively few such instances, but one example is a decision to dismiss an employee in circumstances where the local authority may be called upon to defend a complaint of unfair dismissal because the onus is on the council as employer to show that the dismissal was fair.

Staff consultative committees

General principles

13.20. Two important general principles govern committees of this character: one is that their function is *advisory* (such a committee can have no executive power to commit the employing authority); and the other – in conformity with the practice of all collective bargaining – is that decisions can only be reached upon the affirmative vote of a majority on each side voting separately.[34]

13.21. If, however, the process of consultation is to have the confidence of the staff or workpeople's sides the employing authority should take care to ensure that its representatives are knowledgeable and can speak with authority and in expectation that when they join with the other side in commending a course of action to the local authority it is likely to accept the proposal.[35] Somewhat similarly the staff or workpeople's sides should be truly representative of the workforce for whom they purport to speak.[36]

---

[34] Although it might be thought that committees of this character could be set up under the provisions of the Local Government Act 1972, s.102(4), which empower the establishment of committees 'to advise . . . on any matter relating to the discharge' of an authority's function, the obligation to decide questions 'by a majority of the members . . . present and voting thereon' (sch.12, para.39(1), as applied to committees by para.44) would make this impracticable. These committees are not, therefore, committees of the local authority in the ordinary sense: in a way they exist in limbo.

[35] There is thus advantage in the selection by the local authority of representatives who are members of the authority's staffing committee: on the other hand, some authorities think it desirable that the chairman of the staffing committee should never sit on a consultative committee to avoid embarrassment if that committee decides not to accept a recommendation from a consultative committee.

[36] This in practice can usually best be secured if the representatives are selected by the trade unions concerned in such proportions as may be agreed.

Such a committee's deliberations must take place in an atmosphere conducive to free and meaningful discussion. Thus it is usual for the chairman to be chosen in turn from each side, and when an employer's side representative is serving as chairman the other side should select a vice-chairman and *vice versa*.

13.22. Although the aim should be to embrace within the scope of each consultative committee as many categories of employee as practicable it is usual – because of their differing interests and conditions of service – for there to be separate committees with respect to officers and manual workers respectively: often termed a *joint staff committee* for the former and a *joint works committee* for the latter. Exceptionally there may be justification for setting up a separate consultative committee for a specific purpose: some local authorities have established *safety committees* (often covering both officers and manual workers) for purposes of s.2(7) of the Health and Safety at Work, etc. Act 1974: see 13.26.

Model constitutions

13.23. The constitution and rules of procedure of consultative committees vary considerably in detail and are always settled by agreement between the employing authority and employee representatives.

Clerking the committees

13.24. The committee's constitution will provide for the appointment of either a single secretary to clerk the committee's proceedings or joint secretaries, i.e. one appointed by each side, whose respective responsibility is to frame the matters to be placed on the agenda and to take appropriate executive action on decisions. Where there are joint secretaries it is usual, nevertheless, for the employer's side secretary to take charge of the dispatch of agenda, preparation of draft minutes, and servicing the committee generally.

13.25. Where there is only one secretary of the committee that officer – even if a council officer (and especially if the authority's personnel officer) – should regard himself *as the servant of the committee collectively*. If the personnel officer is secretary he must in acting in that capacity be at pains to be impartial, to facilitate the process of consultation and, so far as he may deem it advisable to intervene in discussion, should do so in a conciliatory role; and in drafting the minutes (which must be approved by both sides) must see to it that the arguments put forward by each side are fairly summarised.[37] The secretary-cum-personnel-officer will ordinarily advise the employer's side either in writing beforehand or at a pre-committee briefing (it is usual for each side to meet separately before the meeting of the full consultative committee); but it may be necessary for him to express an employer viewpoint during the course of proceedings and in that event he must make it clear that he is then speaking as the personnel officer. The combined task obviously calls for diplomacy and skill.

Safety committees

13.26. The Health and Safety at Work, etc. Act 1974 makes it the duty of every employer – and that includes, of course, every local authority (except perhaps the smallest), health authority and water authority – to ensure, so far as reasonably practicable, the health, safety and welfare at work of all its employees.[38] The employer has a duty to consult safety representatives, i.e. representatives of the employees,[39] with a view to the making and maintenance of arrangements enabling the employer and the employees to co-operate effectively in promoting and developing measures for this purpose[40] and may be required by the safety representatives or may itself so elect to establish a *safety committee* or committees to keep health, safety and welfare measures under review.[41]

13.27. The Safety Representatives and Safety Committees Regulations 1978,[42] operative from 1 October 1978, provide that an employer must establish a safety committee within three months of being requested in writing to do so by at least two safety representatives. The employer must consult with the safety representatives who made the request and with representatives of recognised trade unions whose members work in any workplace in respect of which the committee is to function; and is required to post a notice stating the composition of the committee and the workplace or workplaces covered by it in a place where the notice may be easily read by employees. The Health and Safety Commission has produced guidance notes[43] which provide advice on the objectives and functions of

---

[37] In drawing up the minutes or report of a consultative committee it will never be sufficient as a rule to limit the document to a record of decisions alone.

[38] Health and Safety at Work, etc. Act 1974, s.2(1).

[39] These representatives must be appointed by recognised trade unions from among the employees (*ibid.* s.2, as amended by the Employment Protection Act 1975, s.116, sch.15, para.2).

[40] *Ibid.* s.2(6).

[41] *Ibid.* s.2(7).

[42] Made under *ibid.* s.2(4).

[43] These notes are of no legal significance: they do not even have the same status of codes of practice under the 1974 Act. A local authority's standing orders do not ordinarily apply to local consultative committees because such committees are not committees of the local authority: see footnote 34 to 13.20.

safety committees, their membership and conduct. The notes suggest, for example, that each safety committee ought to have a separate identity, i.e. it ought not to form part of an existing consultative committee for more general purposes, and that it is more likely to prove effective if related to a single establishment rather than a collection of geographically distinct places – although it is recognised that there may be a place for a safety committee at higher level in large organisations. The constitution, rules and procedure of the committees should be settled by joint consultation between management and trade unions: see 13.23.

13.28. A safety committee will be advisory in character and will function in much the same way as other consultative committees, i.e. decisions will be made by majority vote on either side and the decisions will be recommendations – ordinarily to the staffing committee.

Staff selection panels

General considerations

13.29. The Maud Committee's investigations showed that there was 'considerable variation in the extent to which procedures are precisely defined' for the appointment of staff and that there are 'discrepancies in the degree of precision in different departments of the same authority'.[44] The Mallaby Committee was uncompromisingly critical:[45]

> . . . a committee may have among its members one who is an expert in staff selection technique and has a knowledge of the work involved in the post for which a selection is being made, but this is usually by chance rather than by design.

It may be, with greater importance currently attached to personnel management and growing professionalism in its practice, that the appointments procedure will be improved within local government. It would, however, be beyond the scope of this book to discuss the virtues of differing methods of appointing staff or to examine the selection process as a whole, i.e. including advertisement of vacancies, shortlisting, and the documentation that must ensue following an appointment. Whatever the method of appointment it should be one which is systematic and properly prescribed, i.e. in standing orders or staffing regulations, and – if appointments of a certain level of seniority are made by council members[46] – the powers of

[44] Maud Report, vol. 5, pp. 315–16.
[45] Mallaby Report on *Staffing of Local Government.*
[46] Widdicombe has suggested that the chief executive should be empowered to make all staff appointments below principal officer level, both manual and non-manual (except where staff are appointed to serve the political groups and their leaders) and that a statutory code of practice should be introduced to ensure that all appointments are based on merit and open competition: Widdicombe Report, paras.6.163–6.165, 6.196–6.198.

the appointments committee, subcommittee, panel or board should be defined, i.e. whether it is empowered to make the choice of candidate or (and there are disadvantages in this) merely interview, provisionally select, and recommend a selected candidate for appointment.

Standing orders

13.30. Some local authorities' standing orders incorporate staffing regulations including detailed procedure for the selection and appointment of staff. Model standing order no. 16 (see 5.55) is often used to decide the choice of candidate when interviewers cannot agree. Other model standing orders relate to staffing matters. Model standing order no. 19 deals with the interest of officers in contracts in these terms:

> The town clerk/clerk of the council shall record in a book to be kept for the purpose particulars of any notice given by an officer of the council under s.123 of the Local Government Act 1933[47] of a pecuniary interest in a contract and the book shall be open during office hours to the inspection of any member of the council.

Model standing order nos. 20 and 21 are concerned with the appointment of staff:

Canvassing of and recommendations by members
(1) Canvassing of members of the council or any committee of the council directly or indirectly for any appointment under the council shall disqualify the candidate concerned for that appointment. The purport of this paragraph of this standing order shall be included [in every advertisement inviting applications for appointments or] in any form of application.
(2) A member of the council shall not solicit for any person any appointment under the council, but this shall not preclude a member from giving a written testimonial of a candidate's ability, experience or character for submission to the council with an application for appointment.

Relatives of members or officers
(1) A candidate for any appointment under the council who knows that he is related to any member or senior officer of the council shall when making application disclose that relationship to the town clerk/clerk of the council. A candidate who fails to disclose such a relationship shall be disqualified for the appointment and if appointed shall be liable to dismissal without notice. Every member and senior officer of the council shall disclose to the town clerk/clerk of the council any relationship known to him to exist between himself and any person whom he knows is a candidate for an appointment under the council. The town clerk/clerk of the council shall report to the council or to the appropriate committee any such disclosure made to him.

[47] Now the Local Government Act 1972, s.117.

(2) The purport of this standing order shall be included [in every advertisement inviting applications for appointments or] in any form of application.

(3) For the purpose of this standing order 'senior officer' means any officer under the council so designated by the [council] [or] [. . . committee], and persons shall be deemed to be related if they are husband and wife or if either of them or the spouse of either of them is the son or daughter or grandson or granddaughter or brother or sister or nephew or niece of the other, or of the spouse of the other.

So, too, is model standing order no. 22 (primarily concerned with the authorised staffing establishment of a local authority and the advertisement of staff vacancies) but its provisions are not directly relevant to the issues being discussed here. Widdicombe's proposal that there should be a statutory code of practice governing staff appointments (see 13.29) would, if ultimately agreed, presumably cover all the matters on which the model standing orders make provision as well as current practices of most local authorities. What follows in the next several paragraphs is related to present arrangements where councillors are involved in staff appointments.

Summons and agenda

13.31. The summons and agenda for a selection panel will comprise:

(a) the usual notification of date, time and place of the meeting;

(b) an indication of the panel's terms of reference and powers, e.g. to this effect if the panel possesses delegated power:

> to interview selected candidates for appointment to the post of . . .

or to this effect if not possessing such power:

> to interview selected candidates and to recommend an appointment to the post of . . .

(c) such documents as may be thought appropriate to enable the members to study in advance: the *job description*[48] of the post; the *job specification*[49] of the kind of candidate sought; and a copy of the applications and/or a summary of them.

13.32. The candidates, too, will need to be invited to attend for the interview before the selection panel: they should be given advance notice

[48] The *job description* is a statement, in whatever detail circumstances may require, of the content of the job; the duties and responsibilities, its place in the organisation, the salary grade and so on.

[49] The *job specification* lists the personal qualities required in the candidate who can be expected to perform the job to the prescribed standard.

(indeed, there is much to commend the practice of thinking out the programme sufficiently far ahead to enable candidates to be advised of the probable date of interview when they first apply for an application form and particulars of the post), asked to come at staggered times, and told how best to get to the town hall or offices concerned. A comfortable waiting-room should be available for them when they arrive.

Purpose of selection interview

13.33. It would be an over-simplification to say that the object of the selection interview is to select and appoint a candidate to the job concerned. The interview, in any case, is only part of the total selection process: there are enquiries to be made beforehand and formalities to be dealt with subsequently before the contract of employment is finalised: the taking up of references, medical clearance and so on. Nevertheless, the interview is in most cases the critical stage in the process and will usually result in the selection of a favoured candidate.

13.34. The purposes of the interview may be summarised thus:

(a) To give the candidate information about the job (although ideally most of the information he will require should have been provided by the written particulars of the appointment);

(b) To obtain or check the basic facts about the shortlisted candidates;

(c) To permit observation of the candidates' outward appearance and manner;

(d) To test, by oral question and answer, the candidates' capabilities as relevant to the job;

(e) To enable an assessment to be made of the personality of the candidates (using this term in the most general sense to include both intelligence and personal qualities);

(f) To influence the favoured candidate towards accepting the job if the panel wishes him to take it.

The ultimate choice of candidate ought to be a matter of mutual agreement between members of the interviewing panel. There is risk of making an unsatisfactory decision where the choice is decided on a formal vote. If the panel is a sizeable one – as, regrettably, is still the case in some authorities, especially for chief officer appointments – a candidate chosen on the basis of having secured most votes may have been selected as a minority choice if the majority of interviewers have spread their votes among other candidates. If voting there must be it may be preferable to proceed on the basis of model standing order no. 16, already referred to: see 5.55.

Conduct of the interview

13.35. It would be impossible here to deal comprehensively with the considerations to be borne in mind in conducting an interview for the selection of staff. Essentially, of course:[50]

> The right *rapport* must be established between interviewers and interviewee – something more easily secured in the informality of a one-to-one conversation but difficult sometimes in the case of a panel. It is the chairman's responsibility to seek the candidate's co-operation, reduce the tension that must exist in such a situation, and ensure that the interview is conducted courteously and efficiently.

The candidate should be greeted in a cordial manner, told the names of his interviewers (if these are not displayed on name-plates in front of them), treated with utmost consideration during questioning, and given an opportunity at the end of asking questions and of adding anything he may wish in support of his candidature:[51]

> Throughout the chairman must be firm and see that neither he nor any of the panel are being put in the position of interviewee. He should ensure that council members (and officers) give full attention to the business in hand, that nothing occurs which may disconcert the candidate or put him at a disadvantage: he should not be required to sit facing the light so that members of the panel are mere faceless silhouettes against a window nor at the far end of a long table so that he has difficulty in hearing questions from the distance. At best the interview is an artificial situation in which, as a rule, neither interviewers nor candidates behave as they would in other circumstances. There must, of course, be no telephone or other interruptions, nor – quite unpardonable – must tea be served in the middle of an interview. It is no bad thing, however, to break off for refreshments at a convenient time.

The proceedings must be businesslike:[51]

> Sometimes well-meaning attempts at informality can be disastrous. It is better to sit the candidate on the other side of the table than in an easy chair where he will either perch uncomfortably on the edge or sink into its depths. The offer of a cigarette can pose for a candidate, even if a smoker, a dilemma whether to accept or not. The best interviews, given the drawbacks, are those conducted in a traditional but wholly friendly and businesslike manner.

13.36. It used to be said that there is no restriction on the type of questions which may be put to candidates save those which relate to religious or political views. That must now be modified. Questions which may imply that the selection could be biased on grounds of sex or race are likely to

---

[50] See E. Anstey and E. O. Mercer, *Interviewing for the Selection of Staff* (1956).
[51] Raymond S. B. Knowles, *Staff Selection: A handbook for councillors* (1973), p. 12.

involve the employing authority in challenge subsequently before an industrial tribunal if the candidate concerned is not appointed. On the other hand, it has to be recognised that in the case of certain authorities questions may be put about the 'social awareness' of the candidate which could be interpreted as politically orientated.[52] Clearly the interviewing process needs to be conducted in a way which will detect fitness for the job and to persuade candidates that that has been the overriding criterion.

13.37. The following is suggested as a check-list on procedure:

(a) Preliminary discussion: clarify key qualities being sought; decide systematic approach: time to be devoted to each candidate, when to break for refreshments, apportionment of questioning, etc.; ensure no likelihood of interruptions.

(b) Receive candidate: introduce panel;

(c) Check that candidate is a firm applicant and willing to accept the job if offered;

(d) Invite candidate to:
  (i) give outline of experience, stressing that which he considers relevant; or
  (ii) say what he does in present post;

(e) Ask questions of candidate; invite:
  (i) panel members to ask questions;
  (ii) officers to ask questions;

(f) Ask candidate whether:
  (i) he wishes to add anything in support of his candidature;
  (ii) he has any questions;

(g) Thank candidate for attending, ask him to retire and either:
  (i) tell him to wait; or
  (ii) say he will be advised of the panel's decision in due course;

(h) Consider decision in light of:
  (i) written applications; and
  (ii) impression gained at interview; and
  (iii) result of any aptitude or other test; and – with reserve –
  (iv) references; against job specification;

(i) Call back successful candidate and offer appointment subject to clearance of formalities;

(j) Tell unsuccessful candidates of decision and thank them for attending.

For action by the panel chairman, who should keep a check on time devoted to each candidate and ensure that all areas of necessary investigation are adequately covered by questions.

Staff appeals tribunals

General considerations

13.38. A staffing committee (or a personnel subcommittee of a policy and resources committee) will need to provide appeals machinery to deal with three types of hearing:

(a) *appeals against disciplinary measures;*

(b) *appeals against salary grading* in respect of certain categories of officer; and

(c) *unresolved grievances;*

and to set up a subcommittee, panel or tribunal to deal with each or all three types of case. The term *tribunal* has merit because of its judicial connotation: council members in reaching a decision in appeal cases are exercising a quasi-judicial role: see 13.13.

13.39. The membership should be small (three is a popular number), the council members chosen should ideally be ones who enjoy the confidence of both council and employees, and they should be empowered to make the final decision so far as the local authority is concerned. There is advantage in always choosing the same members because of the expertise which is built up by their experience and the greater likelihood of uniformity of approach.

13.40. The constitution of the tribunal and the procedure adopted at its meetings will depend to some extent upon local arrangements governing employee appeals. For example, where, as is usual, the power to take disciplinary measures is delegated to chief officers, the appeals tribunal can be appointed by and out of the establishment or staffing committee (or personnel subcommittee); but if only the establishment or staffing committee (or personnel subcommittee) can dismiss an employee the tribunal will need to be comprised of members who are not members of the committee or subcommittee which made the original decision, and this makes for anomalous situations. It means that the establishment committee or personnel subcommittee does not have the final say but that council members with ordinarily no staffing responsibility are empowered to settle an appeal from a decision of members charged with that responsibility on behalf of the local authority. Much the same dilemma can arise on appeals

---

[52] Many of Widdicombe's recommendations relating to local authority staffing – not all relevant to the subject-matter of this work – are designed to eliminate the possibility of political bias in the appointment, discipline and dismissal of staff.

on salary questions (which ordinarily only affect staff within the purview of the National Joint Council for Local Authorities' Administrative, Professional, Technical and Clerical Services[53]): but in these cases the position can more correctly be regarded as a matter of an appeals tribunal reviewing a decision made by its parent committee or subcommittee in the light of representations of the officer aggrieved. In the case of the dismissal of an employee there may be further appeal outside the local authority – to an industrial tribunal if the employee, having the requisite service, challenges the disallowance of his appeal and alleges unfair dismissal.[54] In the case of the rejection of an appeal made locally by an officer in a grading dispute there may be a right to appeal to the appeals committee of the provincial council of the NJC. No particular procedural problems arise, as a rule, where a tribunal seeks to settle an unresolved grievance because most grievances arise out of the local authority's general practices or a chief officer's act or omission.

Disciplinary hearings

13.41. An appeals tribunal set up to hear appeals against disciplinary measures does not begin to function, of course, until an appeal is submitted and is due for hearing. The preliminary stages should be governed by the authority's procedure agreement, which should incorporate provisions on the lines of these in para.71 of the Scheme of Conditions of Service of the officers' NJC:

> The chief officer of each department shall be responsible for the management and discipline of his department. In this connexion, it is recommended that a 'warning' procedure should be adopted where an officer's work, conduct or omission are such as to warrant disciplinary action.
>
> A chief officer may suspend any member of his staff for gross misconduct and such action shall be reported forthwith to the appropriate committee. Where, on grounds related to discipline or efficiency, it is proposed either (i) by an appropriate committee of the employing authority, or (ii) by a chief officer acting under delegated powers to relegate or dismiss an officer (except for a criminal offence for which he has been prosecuted and convicted) then such proposal when formulated shall be conveyed to the officer concerned by letter over the signature of the chief officer stating the grounds on which the proposed action is based.

---

[53] Exceptionally, local government officers within the purview of the NJC have a right of appeal in the first instance to their employing authority and subsequently to the provincial council when their salary grading is varied and they are dissatisfied with the grading awarded, or where there has been a substantial change in the general character of the duties and level of responsibility of their post and the grading has not been increased.

[54] See Trade Union and Labour Relations Act 1974, sch.1.

Upon receipt of such a communication, the officer concerned may appeal within seven days, either individually, or through his association or trade union, to an appeals committee of the employing authority and shall have the right of appearing before such committee (with or without a representative of his association or trade union or other representative of his choice).

13.42. The employee should be given advance notice (at least seven days) of the time and place of the hearing and should be supplied with all the papers to be placed before the tribunal: a copy of the letter of dismissal and/ or the written statement setting out the reasons and any written submissions which the appellant may wish to have considered. The procedure to be followed at the hearing is prescribed in general terms by the national schemes of conditions of service but it is good practice for the procedure to be set down in detail so that all concerned – the chairman of the appeals tribunal, the chief officer (or council's representative), and the appellant and his representative – know what is to happen at every stage. Too much formality should, however, be avoided.

Natural justice

13.43. When an appeals tribunal is hearing an appeal against disciplinary action (or against a salary grading claim or seeking to settle a grievance), it is acting, of course, in a quasi-judicial capacity and must observe the principles of natural justice. These principles in relation to judicial and quasi-judicial business in committee have already been discussed (see 13.13) but their application specifically to the conduct of disciplinary proceedings was considered in *Khanum* v. *Mid-Glamorgan Area Health Authority* (1978)[55] in which the Employment Appeal Tribunal said:

> . . . in the end how nearly a domestic disciplinary inquiry, a statutory inquiry by a statutory body, a public statutory inquiry, or any other inquiry which has to make decisions, must approach to the full-blown procedure of a court of justice is, no doubt, a matter of degree. But in our judgment as regards the sort of domestic tribunal with which we are concerned in this case [a domestic inquiry and disciplinary hearing by an area health authority] the law is as it was expressed by Harman, J., in *Byrne* v. *Kinematograph Renters Society Ltd* [1958] 1 W.L.R. 762, and approved and applied by the Privy Council to the conduct of a university vice-chancellor's inquiry into cheating in examinations in *Fernando's Case*:
>
> > 'What then are the requirements of natural justice in a case of this kind? First, I think that the person accused should know of the nature of the accusation made; secondly, that he should be given an opportunity to

[55] (1978) IRLR 215.

state his case; and thirdly, of course, that the tribunal should act in good faith. I do not myself think that there is really anything more.'

13.44. It must be obvious that a tribunal cannot be regarded as acting in conditions of complete impartiality because it will always be reviewing a decision already made by the 'management' of which it forms part. This was well expressed in another EAT case, *Corina* v. *Berkshire County Council* (1979):[56]

> It is a fallacy to suppose that in the course of internal grievance or disciplinary procedures you can have a neutral disciplinary or appellate 'tribunal' short of an express provision for recourse to outside arbitration through ACAS or otherwise, something which involves its own disadvantages. The people who have to hear and decide on the matter, in internal procedures, are limbs of the employer and so not 'impartial' in any true sense. What, as a matter of natural justice you are entitled to, is that they shall come to their decisions honestly.

Who should represent the parties?

13.45. The officer who is to represent the council at a disciplinary or grievance hearing should, ideally, be the officer who took the initial disciplinary decision against the appellant or heard his grievance at first instance (and this will ordinarily be the chief officer or, conceivably, a senior officer in the department). It ought not to be the personnel officer because, among other reasons, he may well be the appeal tribunal's adviser. The personnel officer must remain impartial until a final decision has been taken on behalf of the employing authority, i.e. after the decision of the tribunal in a disciplinary matter, when he may well represent the local authority before an industrial tribunal. The expression *council's representative* used in para.13.47 below should thus be interpreted to mean the departmental chief officer or his representative.

13.46. The ACAS *Code of Disciplinary Practice and Procedures in Disciplinary Practice and Procedures in Employment* says that the employee should be accorded the right to be accompanied by a trade union representative or a fellow employee of his choice; and most local authority codes – likely in every case to have been agreed with employee representatives – will contain similar provisions. What, however, if notwithstanding such provisions an employee wishes to be accompanied or represented by a lawyer or a relative? Most authorities would probably not wish to place any restriction on the freedom of the individual to be represented by whom-

---

[56] (1979) EAT 15/79.

soever he wishes. Nevertheless, there is support for the view that a tribunal, which is entitled to regulate its own procedures, could properly refuse to allow legal representation – at least if the applicable code expressly forbids it. Lord Justice Cairns expressed the view in *Enderby Town Football Club Ltd* v. *Football Association Ltd* (1971)[57] that 'it is open to an organisation to make an absolute rule that a tribunal set up by it is not to hear legal representations'. This view was cited by Lord Justice Orr in *Maynard* v. *Osmond* (1977),[58] which concerned an appeal by a police constable against a decision that he was not entitled to be legally represented in disciplinary proceedings against him under the Police (Disciplinary) Regulations 1965:

> No authority cited to us lends support to the view that the denial either of a right to legal representation or of a discretion to allow it contravenes the rules of natural justice and while we are concerned in this case with regulations made by a minister under statutory powers and not with a domestic tribunal constituted by contract, I am inclined to agree with the view provisionally expressed by Lord Justice Cairns in *Enderby Town Football Club Ltd* v. *Football Association Ltd* . . .

In this same case, Lord Denning considered that, even if a man was not entitled as of right to be legally represented in disciplinary proceedings, the disciplinary body should have discretion to allow it:

> Legal representation should not be forbidden altogether. The tribunal should have discretion so as to permit him to have a lawyer if they think it would assist. They are the masters of their own procedure; and, unless expressly forbidden, should have a discretion to permit it.

Despite these differing views the Court of Appeal ruled in the *Maynard* case in favour of allowing a police constable to be legally represented in disciplinary proceedings and thought that in principle such a right should be accorded to other individuals in other disciplinary proceedings:

> On principle, if a man is charged with a serious offence which may have grave consequences for him, he should be entitled to have a qualified lawyer to defend him. Such has been agreed by the Government of this country when it adhered to the European Convention on Human Rights. But also, by analogy, it should be the same in most cases when he is charged with a disciplinary offence before a disciplinary tribunal, at any rate when the offence is one which may result in his dismissal from the force or other body to which he belongs; or the loss of his livelihood; or, worse still, may ruin his character for ever.

[57] [1971] Ch. 591, p. 609.
[58] [1977] 1 All ER 64.

Procedure

13.47. The following is an example, couched in terms of advice for the chairman, of the procedure which should be followed at the hearing of an appeal. The council's representative (CR) – the departmental chief officer or his representative: see 13.45 – puts his case first and the appellant's representative (AR) puts the case for the appellant (A) afterwards:

(a) *Call in* together CR, AR, and A.

(b) *Invite* CR to put the council's case.

(c) After each of the CR's witnesses (if any) has given evidence:
Ask AR whether he (or A) wishes to ask questions of the witness;
Ask whether members of the tribunal wish to ask questions of the witness;
Ask CR whether he wishes to re-examine his witness.

(d) After CR has completed his case:
Ask AR whether he has any questions he wishes to put to CR;
Ask whether members of the tribunal wish to ask questions of the CR.

(e) *Invite* AR to put A's case.

(f) If AR calls witnesses then after each has given evidence:
Ask CR whether he wishes to ask questions of the witness;
Ask whether members of the tribunal wish to ask questions of the witness;
Ask AR whether he wishes to re-examine his witness.

(g) After AR has completed his case:
Ask CR whether he has any questions to put to either AR or A;
Ask whether members of the tribunal wish to ask questions of AR or A.

(h) *Invite* CR to sum up the council's case if he wishes to do so.

(i) *Invite* AR to sum up A's case if he wishes to do so.

(j) *Ask* all parties to withdraw except the tribunal's adviser.

(k) *Deliberate* upon the case.
The tribunal may confirm, amend or reject the original decision; and may recall both parties to clear points of uncertainty on the evidence given, but if recall is necessary both parties are to return notwithstanding that only one is concerned with the point giving rise to doubt.

(l) After a decision has been reached:
Call back both parties and *announce* either:
(i) the tribunal's decision if it possesses delegated power; or
(ii) that the decision will be communicated to the parties as soon as possible:
in either case the decision must be confirmed in writing.

Meetings of governing bodies

Introduction

13.48. There is within local government an immense variety of governing bodies. These include, for example, informal groups of council and co-opted members (sometimes local residents also) appointed by a social services committee to visit residential establishments, and the formally constituted boards of governors of schools set up by local education authorities (see 13.50). It would be unprofitable to attempt to refer to each one of the many types of such bodies that exist. Whatever their type, however, it is a matter of good practice and convenience where such matters are not prescribed by law that each should be accorded clearly defined terms of reference, so that even if the precise constitution has not been set down on paper at least there is no uncertainty about the powers and duties of members individually and the body collectively; preferably, too, each meeting should be minuted even if the note of proceedings is no more than a brief *aide-mémoire*. Ideally, standing orders or rules of procedure should be drawn up as well.

13.49. If the governing body has not been formally constituted and no rules, regulations or standing orders have been laid down then necessarily the common law rules of meetings procedure will apply. If the body is a subcommittee of a local authority committee (and not all will be), then unquestionably the appropriate statutory provisions and the authority's standing orders will apply to its meetings, which must be open to the public.

School governors

13.50. The law requires[59] that there shall be for every primary and secondary school an instrument of government providing for the constitution of a representative body. The instrument is made in the case of county schools by the local education authority and in the case of voluntary schools by order of the Secretary of State for Education and Science. All school governing bodies must include governors appointed by the local education authority by whom the school is maintained: in the case of schools with fewer than 300 registered pupils there must be at least one teacher governor; if there are 300 or more pupils there must be at least two. The teacher governors are elected by teachers at the school from among

---

[59] Education Act 1944, s.17, as amended by the Education Act 1980, s.1, which provided that the representative body for primary schools are to be called governors, as in the case of secondary schools, instead of managers.

their own number, with the head teacher ex officio a member unless he or she chooses otherwise. In the case of an aided or special agreement school there must be at least one parent governor; in the case of a county or controlled school there must be at least two. Parent governors are persons elected by parents of registered pupils at the school and who are themselves such parents when elected. Elections of parent and teacher governors are arranged by the local education authority for county and controlled schools and by the governors for aided and special agreement schools. The governing body of a county or voluntary primary school must include at least one governor appointed by the local authority in which it is situated, i.e. of the parish or community council or non-metropolitan district council. There must also be in the case of a voluntary school foundation governors appointed by the local education authority or the non-metropolitan district, parish or community council. In controlled schools at least one-fifth of the governors must be foundation governors and in aided or special agreement schools they must outnumber the other members by two if the governing body has 18 or fewer members and by three if it has more; and at least one of the foundation governors must be a parent of a registered pupil at the school at the time of appointment. Schools may be grouped under a single governing body.

13.51. The meetings and proceedings of governors, previously regulated by the Education Act 1944, s.21 and sch.4, are now dealt with under regulations made by the Secretary of State under the Education Act 1980, s.4. The current regulations (Education School Governing Bodies Regulations 1981, as amended) contain provisions relating to the disqualification of persons from membership of governing bodies (for bankruptcy, etc., and criminal convictions, or failure to attend meetings over a period of 12 months); the resignation and removal of governors and the filling of casual vacancies; the election of a chairman and vice-chairman; the tenure of office of governors; and, particularly in relation to meetings and the proceedings thereat, as follows:

1. The governing body of a school must hold a meeting at least once in every term;

2. Any three members of the governing body may requisition a meeting and it is the duty of the clerk to convene a meeting which is so requisitioned;

3. The quorum for a meeting is not less than three or, where greater, a third (rounded up to a whole number) of the membership of the governing body when complete;

4. A meeting may be convened by the clerk though he must comply with any direction in the matter:

   (a) given by the governing body at a previous meeting, or

(b) given by the chairman, or in his absence, the vice-chairman so far as such direction is not inconsistent with a direction given as in (a);

5. Every member of the governing body, the head teacher (if not an *ex officio* governor) and the chief education officer of the local education authority by whom the school is maintained must be given, at least seven clear days before the date of a meeting:

(a) written notice thereof, signed by the clerk, and

(b) a copy of the agenda for the meeting;

provided that where the chairman or, in his absence, the vice-chairman, so directs on the ground that there are matters demanding urgent consideration, it is sufficient if the written notice convening a meeting, and the copy of the agenda therefor, are given within such shorter period as he specifies: the notice and the agenda may be given to a person by leaving it at, or sending it by post to, his usual place of residence;

6. The convening of a meeting and the proceedings conducted thereat are not invalidated by reason of an individual not having received written notice of the meeting or a copy of the agenda;

7. The proceedings of the governing body of a school are not invalidated by any vacancy among their number or by any defect in the appointment, election or qualification of any member;

8. Any question coming or arising before the governing body must be decided by a majority of the members present and voting on the question at a meeting of the governing body except that, in the case of an equality of votes, the chairman has a second or casting vote;

9. Subject as elsewhere provided, the schedule to the regulations [which relates to withdrawal from meetings, etc., because of a pecuniary or other interest in the business about to be transacted: see 13.52] has effect as to the circumstances and cases in which a member of the governing body, head teacher, chief education officer or other person present at a meeting must (a) withdraw from the meeting, (b) not take part in the consideration or discussion of specified matters, (c) in the case of a member, not vote on any question with respect to a specified matter;

10. Where the governing body is considering disciplinary action against a teacher or other person employed at the school, against a pupil, or arising out of an alleged incident involving a pupil, nothing in the schedule is to be construed as precluding the governing body, at any disciplinary hearing conducted by the body (including the hearing of an appeal) from allowing:

(a) that teacher or other person, the pupil concerned, or his parent, to attend the hearing and to be heard in the matter;

(b) a person who has made relevant allegations, to present those allegations at the hearing; or

(c) a person who is a material witness, to give relevant evidence;

11. A resolution to rescind or vary a resolution carried at a previous meeting cannot be proposed at a meeting of the governing body unless the consideration of the rescission or variation of the previous resolution is a specific item of business on the agenda;

12. If the number of governors assembled for a meeting of the governing body does not constitute a quorum therefor, the meeting must not be held: if in the course of a meeting (a) it is so resolved, or (b) the number of members present ceases to constitute a quorum therefor, the meeting must be terminated forthwith;

13. If a meeting is not held or is terminated as aforesaid before all the proposed business has been transacted, a special meeting must be convened as soon as is reasonably practicable;

14. If it is so resolved, a meeting of the governing body must stand adjourned until the time and date specified in the resolution for the resumption thereof; and, in such a case, the clerk must endeavour to ensure that any member not present when the resolution was carried is informed of its terms;

15. Minutes of proceedings of meetings must be drawn up and entered in a book kept for the purpose and must be signed at the same or a following meeting held not later than the end of the next following term by the person who is the chairman thereof: but the minutes may be entered on loose leaves consecutively numbered but in such case the person signing the minutes must initial each leaf;

16. Subject to 17, copies of the agenda and signed minutes relating to any meeting must, in each case as soon as may be, be readily available at the school for inspection by any teacher or other person employed at the school, any parent of a registered pupil or any registered pupil;

17. There may be excluded from the copies of the minutes so made available any minute relating to:

    (a) a named teacher or other person employed or proposed to be employed at the school;

    (b) a named pupil at, or candidate for admission to, the school;

    (c) any matter which, by reason of its nature, the governing body considers should be dealt with on a confidential basis;

18. Not only must the minutes of any meeting of the governing body be open to inspection by the local education authority by whom the school is maintained but, on request made in that behalf by the chief education officer either generally or in relation to a particular meeting, that authority must be supplied with a copy of the signed minutes of such a meeting;

19. The names of the members of the governing body present at a meeting and of the head teacher if he attends must be recorded alongside the minutes of the meeting drawn up and entered as mentioned in 15.

Exclusion from meetings

13.52. In *R.* v. *London Borough of Croydon ex-parte Lockett and Another* (1986)[60] it was held that teacher governors could properly in such circumstances be excluded from a meeting of a school's governing body under the instrument of government which provided that members of staff

[60] (1986) 150 LG Rev. 234.

who were governors of the school should withdraw from meetings when, *inter alia,* 'the appointment or promotion of a person to a post at the school is senior to that which is being held by the staff member concerned'. The court ruled that the schedule to the 1981 Regulations (see 13.51), which provide for the withdrawal in specified circumstances of governors from meetings of the governing body, contained only a core of instances in which withdrawal could be required and was not exhaustive.

Appeals against school admission decisions

Appeal committees

13.53. There is statutory provision[61] allowing parents of a child to make representations when their expressed preference for a certain school or college is not complied with by the local education authority or the governing body of a voluntary school. An appeal committee must be set up for this purpose, constituted in accordance with the statutory regulations which also prescribe the committee's procedure.[62] The decision of such a committee is binding on the local education authority and governing body,[63] save that an aggrieved parent may in limited circumstances resort to the Secretary of State.

13.54. The appeal committee is not a committee or subcommittee of the local authority.[64] That is clear from several of the statutory provisions which, for example, expressly exclude the application of the provisions of the Local Government Act 1972 relating to local authority committees,[65] and from the fact that the committee is subject to the Tribunal and Inquiries Act 1971[66] and to the supervision of the Council on Tribunals, which has drawn up an advisory code of practice for the guidance of local education authorities in determining their arrangements for appeal procedures.[67] The committee is within the jurisdiction of the local government ombudsman.[68]

13.55. The statutory provisions relating to the constitution of the committee and its proceedings and the code of practice are set out in the appendix to this chapter.

---

[61] Education Act 1980, s.7 and sch.2.
[62] *Ibid.* sch.2, set out in the appendix to this chapter.
[63] *Ibid.* s.7(5).
[64] The committee's meetings, therefore, are not open to the public or Press.
[65] Education Act 1980, sch.2, para.11.
[66] *Ibid.* s.7(6).
[67] An example of the code is set out in the appendix to this chapter.
[68] Education Act 1980, s.7(7).

Chief executive's management team

Its character

13.56. It has long been a practice in many authorities for the chief executive (formerly, of course, the clerk or town clerk) to hold regular meetings with his chief officer colleagues. In the past these have varied in character, according to local custom, from mere social gatherings for the exchange of opinion and information largely about the officers' respective areas of involvement, to more purposeful but still informal meetings concerned with high-level co-ordination and the discussion of matters of policy or important principle. These meetings have now been supplanted in most instances by more formal meetings of properly constituted *management teams* of the kind originally envisaged by the Maud Committee but modelled more specifically on that sketched out by Bains: they are distinguishable from their forerunners by the fact that the management team is usually an integral part of the management process of decision-making and control.

13.57. Maud recommended that 'the principal officers' should:[69]

> Work as members of a team of managers and specialist advisers and see that the same approach is adopted by their staff at all levels;

and it saw the principal officers:

> working together on . . . matters which transcend the purely professional and departmental considerations under the clerk's leadership and producing agreed and co-ordinated recommendations

to be put to Maud's management board.[70] Bains believed that the officers' management team:[71]

> should have a corporate identity and a positive role to play in the corporate management of the authority. It is the counter-part, at officer level, of the policy and resources committee. Its members do not attend primarily as representatives of particular departments, though on occasion it will be necessary for them to speak in that capacity; they are there as members of a body created to aid the management of the authority as a whole.

Bains discussed the role of the management team[72] and its size,[73] the support it would need from inter-departmental working groups and its terms of reference:[74] it thought the team had two broad functions:[75]

---

[69] Maud Report, vol. 1, para.182.
[70] *Ibid.* para.177.
[71] Bains Report, para.5.38.
[72] *Ibid.* para.5.42.
[73] *Ibid.* paras.5.43–5.47.
[74] *Ibid.* para.5.44.
[75] *Ibid.* paras.5.42, 5.47.

The first is the long-term strategic function of considering and advising on what policies the council should be adopting to cope with changing needs and circumstances and the second the overall management co-ordinative and progress-chasing role.

Proceedings and business

13.58. The business of the management team should be transacted with some measure of, but not too much, formality. There should be a pre-arranged timetable of regular meetings and a notice and agenda circulated on each occasion to those entitled to attend: individual officers should have the opportunity of originating matters for discussion but the agenda should be controlled by the chief executive; minutes should be kept and copies circulated. The distinguishing feature of management team meetings is that business is conducted as in a cabinet: the chief executive will occupy the chair as of right and there will ordinarily be no voting (or the team could vote the chief executive out of the chair!). The chief executive will make the decisions either on the basis of a consensus of opinion or on his view of the balance of argument on a particular issue, or may make his own judgement of what needs to be decided after taking account of what is said by his colleagues. Members of the team will usually accept collective responsibility for the advice which in the final resort the chief executive tenders to the council.[76]

13.59. One of the by-products, as it were, of compiling an agenda is that the chief executive can examine it in draft and delete any items he thinks do not warrant the attention of the management team. It is important that meetings of the team should not be cluttered up with matters that can be competently dealt with elsewhere – by chief officers individually or in consultation with others either in company or not with the chief executive – otherwise the team will fail constantly to perform its corporate role. The mere fact that a proposal of one officer may impinge on the work of others is not itself sufficient justification for bringing the matter to the management team (or almost everything, important or otherwise, that, for example, the treasurer or chief personnel officer wants to do could be held up for management team consideration): the matter must be of major importance or affect council policy to warrant the formal attention of the team as a whole. The team exists to facilitate the business of the local authority, not to obstruct progress.

[76] Maud, however, believed that 'where a principal officer is in disagreement with recommendations being put to the management board (of members) his dissenting opinion should be made known to the board and further that the principal officer should be heard': Maud Report, vol. 1, para.177.

13.60. Bains thought it 'difficult to lay down specific terms of reference' for the management team;[77] but the following is a suggested shortlist of the kind of items that would need to come before the team:

(a) Important questions of a corporate character and matters of major importance that cannot properly be dealt with by the individual officer or officers concerned;

(b) Matters referred to the team for consideration from the policy and resources committee;

(c) Policy matters on which advice is to be submitted to council or committee;

(d) Formulation of proposals for linking presentation of objectives, programmes and budgets;

(e) Identification and review of objectives and priorities;

(f) Monitoring progress against plans;

(g) Strategic questions concerning the acquisition, use, motivation, development and levels of manpower resources;

(h) Monitoring and co-ordinating land acquisition programmes and considering matters of policy affecting the acquisition, holding and disposal of land and premises.

Election meetings
Use of local authority premises

13.61. The Representation of the People Act 1983, consolidating previous enactments to like effect, obliges a local authority to permit the use of certain schools and halls for meetings for purposes connected with Parliamentary and local government elections. A local authority cannot refuse the use of such premises even if the candidate's views are offensive to many people.[78]

Parliamentary elections

13.62. A candidate at a Parliamentary or European Assembly election is entitled,[79] for the purpose of holding public meetings in furtherance of his candidature, to the use at reasonable times between the receipt of the writ for the election and the date of the poll, of (a) a suitable room in the school premises, i.e. at a county school or voluntary school situated in the constituency or an adjoining constituency if more reasonably accessible,

[77] Bains Report, para.5.47.
[78] See *Webster* v. *Southwark London Borough Council* [1983] 2 WLR 217.
[79] Representation of the People Act 1983, s.95.

and (b) any meeting room situate in the constituency the expense of maintaining which is payable wholly or mainly out of public funds or of any rate or by a body whose expenses are so payable.[80]

13.63. Where a room is thus used the person by whom or on whose behalf the meeting is convened may be required to pay for expenses incurred in preparing, warming, lighting and cleaning it, in providing attendants for the meeting and restoring the room to its usual condition, and for any damage caused.

13.64. A candidate is required to give reasonable notice if he wishes to take advantage of these rights, but there cannot be any interference with the hours during which a room in school premises is used for educational purposes or with the use of a meeting room either for the purposes of the person maintaining it or under a prior agreement for its letting.

Local government elections

13.65. Similar statutory provisions apply in respect of local government elections.[81] A candidate is entitled to the use of school rooms during the period between the notice of election and the day preceding election day, free of charge, except that expenses incurred by the person having charge of the room and payment for any damage must be made.

Disturbance at election meetings

13.66. Anyone who, at a lawful public meeting held for the foregoing purposes, acts or incites others to act in a disorderly manner for the purpose of preventing the transaction of the business for which the meeting was called is guilty of an illegal practice. This applies[82] to:

(a) a political meeting held in any constituency between the date of the issue of a writ for the return of a Member of Parliament for the constituency and the date at which a return to the writ is made;

(b) a meeting held with reference to a local government election in the electoral area for that election on, or within three weeks before, the day of election.

Public inquiries

Types of inquiry

13.67. There are several occasions when a local authority may become

[80] Local education authorities, district councils and London borough councils must prepare lists of suitable available rooms: *Ibid.* sch.5.

[81] *Ibid.* s.96.

[82] *Ibid.* s.97, applied, with modifications, to elections of the European Assembly by the European Assembly Regulations 1984.

involved in the organisation of a public inquiry. The authority may:

(a)   need to provide appropriate facilities for the holding of:

   (i)   a statutory public inquiry, i.e. one held 'by or on behalf of a Minister';

   (ii)   a non-ministerially appointed mandatory inquiry; or

   (iii)   a discretionary inquiry which may be appointed by the appropriate Minister; or

(b)   decide itself to set up an inquiry for some purpose relating to one or other of its functions.

The distinctions are important. Those inquiries which qualify as 'statutory inquiries' within the meaning of s.19(1) of the Tribunals and Inquiries Act 1971 fall under the supervision of the Council on Tribunals and are subject to prescribed procedural rules: these include inquiries constituted to inquire into and report upon objections to compulsory purchase orders and inquiries held prior to the determination of appeals against refusal of planning permission. Non-ministerially appointed mandatory inquiries are not subject to this supervision: an example is one conducted by the Boundary Commission (i.e. not held 'by or on behalf of a Minister') into local objections to proposed alterations to constituency boundaries. Discretionary inquiries set up by a Minister include, e.g. one into matters connected with the policing of an area.[83]

13.68. In all instances where the local authority is not itself initiating the inquiry the authority will nevertheless be involved often in providing accommodation for the inquiry and the requisite facilities for its conduct, including such administrative duties in connection with it as the minister or an inspector on his behalf may require. In the case of a major inquiry – though necessarily depending on its character – the authority may need to designate a member of staff as a programme officer to assist the inspector over a wide sphere of tasks including, possibly, the recording of objections and representations received and corresponding with objectors over the clarification of their objections, availability for attending the inquiry, the number of witnesses who will be called and so on. In cases, however, where the local authority decides to hold an inquiry, public or otherwise, the authority itself has responsibilities which extend much wider because the authority will need to determine the terms of reference and appoint someone or a committee to hold the inquiry: see 13.71.

---

[83] In an article in *Local Government Chronicle* (1986) No. 6206, p. 589, Charles Arnold-Baker argued the need for a properly equipped permanent building in a number of centres throughout the country for the holding of public inquiries.

Procedure

13.69. The procedure at an inquiry will be at the discretion of the inspector or whoever else may have charge of the proceedings. Most statutory inquiries are by their character adversarial because the issue will ordinarily be argued out by supporters of and objectors to a proposed scheme or course of action or whatever it might be.[84]

Practical arrangements

13.70. There is, as it were, no standard layout of a room in which an inquiry is to be held but the room must be adequate for the purpose, easy of access, and reserved for the likely duration of the proceedings. Essential points to be borne in mind include the following:

(a) Seating and tables must be provided in a convenient arrangement for the participants, e.g. parallel facing tables and chairs for supporters and opponents respectively with the inspector/chairman's table between them forming a square U is the usually preferred layout, but the size and shape of the room itself will be governing constraints.

(b) Reasonable facilities should be provided: notepaper, pencils, water carafes and tumblers with fresh water, display boards for maps, etc., possibly visual aid equipment. Direction signs should be displayed at the entrance to the building indicating the room in which the inquiry is being held, and to car parks, lavatories, etc., but attendants should also be on duty to assist those attending.

(c) Ample seating must be provided for witnesses and others behind the front tables for the advocates on the respective sides.

(d) Provision should be made for accommodating members of the public and Press with easy access to telephones, etc.

13.71. Where the local authority has set up an inquiry there are important preliminary steps to be taken:

(a) The terms of reference of the inquiry must be settled;

(b) A chairman must be appointed and, if desired, a committee or commission to assist him, and the fees or remuneration to be paid must be set;

(c) The date when the inquiry is to begin must be fixed, as well as the period within which the inquiry's report is to be submitted;

(d) Evidence should be invited from interested parties by such means as may be appropriate.

---

[84] The Secretary of State is given power to direct inquiries wherever any minister is authorised to make decisions under the Local Government Act 1972 or any other enactment relating to the functions of local authorities: s.250.

APPENDIX TO CHAPTER 13

School admission appeals

Schedule 2 of the Education Act 1980, set out hereunder, provides for the composition and procedure of appeal committees constituted under s.7 of the Act to hear appeals against decisions of local education authorities and governing bodies of voluntary schools concerning the admission of children to schools: see 13.53–13.54.

Part I: Constitution of appeal committees

1.–(1) An appeal pursuant to arrangements made by a local education authority under s.7 of the Act shall be to an appeal committee constituted in accordance with this paragraph.[a]

(2) An appeal committee shall consist of three, five or seven members[b] nominated[c] by the authority from among persons appointed by the authority under this paragraph; and sufficient persons may be appointed to enable two or more appeal committees to sit at the same time.

(3) The persons appointed shall comprise:

    (a) members of the authority[d] or of any education committee of the authority; and

    (b) persons who are not members of the authority or of any education committee of the authority but who have experience in education, are acquainted with the educational conditions in the area of the authority or are parents of registered pupils at a school;[e]

but shall not include any person employed by the authority otherwise than as a teacher.[f]

(4) The members of an appeal committee who are members of the authority or of any education committee of the authority shall not outnumber the others by more than one.[g]

(5) A person who is a member of an education committee of the authority shall not be chairman of an appeal committee.

(6) A person shall not be a member of an appeal committee for the consideration of any appeal against a decision if he was among those who

---

[a] The appeal committee is not a local authority committee in the usual sense: see 13.54. It is subject to the supervision of the Council on Tribunals: s.7(6).

[b] These numbers mean that – in a situation where a member of the committee cannot be expected ordinarily to abstain, i.e. he must either be for allowing or not allowing the appeal – an equality of votes is unlikely to arise: but see para.8.

[c] *Nominated* here must mean *appointed* or *selected*.

[d] I.e. councillors who are *not* members of the education committee.

[e] Not necessarily a maintained school.

[f] But see para.1(7).

[g] This paragraph, along with paras.1(5)–(6), helps ensure the committee's impartiality: it means that the local education authority cannot 'pack' an appeal committee with its own members.

made the decision or took part in discussion as to whether the decision should be made.

(7) A person who is a teacher at a school shall not be a member of an appeal committee for the consideration of an appeal involving a question whether a child is to be admitted to that school.

2.–(1) An appeal pursuant to arrangements made by the governors of an aided or special agreement school under s.7(2) of this Act shall be to an appeal committee constituted in accordance with this paragraph.

(2) An appeal committee shall consist of three, five or seven members[h] nominated[i] by the governors from among persons appointed by them under this paragraph; and sufficient persons may be appointed to enable two or more appeal committees to sit at the same time.

(3) The persons appointed:

    (a) may include one or more of the governors;

    (b) shall include persons appointed from a list drawn up by the local education authority by whom the school is maintained;[j] and

    (c) shall not include any person employed by the authority otherwise than as a teacher.

(4) Half the members of an appeal committee (excluding the chairman) shall be nominated from among such persons as are mentioned in sub-paragraph (3)(b) above.

(5) None of the governors shall be chairman of an appeal committee.[k]

(6) A person shall not be a member of an appeal committee for the consideration of any appeal against a decision if he was among those who made the decision or took part in discussion as to whether the decision should be made.

(7) A person who is a teacher at a school shall not be a member of an appeal committee for the consideration of an appeal involving a question whether a child is to be admitted to that school.

3. An appeal pursuant to joint arrangements made by virtue of s.7(3) of the Act by the governors of two or more schools shall be to an appeal committee constituted as provided in paragraph 2 above, taking references to the governors as references to the governors of both or all the schools.

4. An appeal committee constituted in accordance with paragraph 2 or 3 above shall be included in the bodies to which sections 173(4) and 174 of the Local Government Act 1972 apply.[l]

Part II: Procedure

5. An appeal shall be by notice in writing setting out the grounds on which it is made.

[h] See footnote b *supra.*
[i] See footnote c *supra.*
[j] See footnote e *supra.*
[k] These paragraphs are designed to help ensure the committee's impartiality.
[l] These sections of the 1972 Act relate to the payment of allowances.

6. An appeal committee shall afford the appellant an opportunity of appearing and making oral representations[m] and may allow the appellant to be accompanied by a friend or to be represented.

7. The matters to be taken into account by an appeal committee in considering an appeal shall include:

   (a) any preference expressed by the appellant in respect of the child as mentioned in section 6 of the Act;[n] and

   (b) the arrangements for the admission of pupils published by the local education authority or the governors under section 8 of the Act.

8. In the event of disagreement between the members of an appeal committee the appeal under consideration shall be decided by a simple majority of the votes cast and in the case of an equality of votes the chairman of the committee shall have a second or casting vote.[o]

9. The decision of an appeal committee[p] and the grounds on which it is made shall be communicated by the committee in writing;[q] and to:

   (a) the appellant and the local education authority; and

   (b) in the case of an appeal to an appeal committee constituted in accordance with paragraph 2 or 3 above, to the governors by or on whose behalf the decision appealed against was made.

10. Appeals pursuant to arrangements made under s.7 of the Act shall be heard in private[r] except when otherwise directed by the authority or governors by whom the arrangements are made but, without prejudice to paragraph 6 above, a member of the local education authority may attend as an observer[s] any hearing of an appeal by an appeal committee constituted in accordance with paragraph 1 above and a member of the Council on Tribunals may attend as an observer any meeting of any appeal committee at which an appeal is considered.

11. Subject to paragraphs 5 to 10 above, all matters relating to the procedure

---

[m] I.e. there must be a hearing and it is to this which the code of practice mainly relates.

[n] Section 6 of the 1980 Act imposes on local education authorities, among other things, duties to make arrangements for parents of children in their area to be able to express a preference for a school at which they wish their child to be educated, and on both local education authorities and governors of voluntary schools to comply with the preferences subject to (a) provision of efficient education and efficient use of resources, (b) arrangements made by voluntary aided or special agreement schools with the local education authority for the admission of pupils, and (c) any arrangements for selection by aptitude and ability.

[o] As indicated above, the likelihood of an equality of votes is reduced by the provision in para.1(2), but obviously a decision must be made one way or the other and thus the power of the chairman to give a second or casting vote.

[p] The decision is binding on the local education authority or governors as the case may be: Education Act 1980, s.7(5).

[q] In practice the decision will be communicated by the officer, usually of the local education authority, who attends and advises the committee.

[r] This excludes the application to appeal committees of the statutory provisions relating to the admission of the public and Press to local authority meetings but, in any case, an appeal committee is not a committee or subcommittee of a local authority.

[s] Observers have no power to intervene in the proceedings or to take part in the formulation of the decision.

on appeals pursuant to arrangements made under s.7 of the Act, including the time within which they are to be brought, shall be determined by the authority or governors by whom the arrangements are made;[t] and neither section 106 of the Local Government Act 1972 nor paragraph 44 of schedule 12 to that Act shall apply to an appeal committee constituted in accordance with paragraph 1 above.[u]

Code of practice

As indicated above a code of practice for the guidance of local education authorities in determining arrangements for appeal procedures has been drawn up and approved by the Council on Tribunals. An outline of the code, in the form in which it has been adopted by the particular local authority, must be provided for appellants. The following is an extract from the relevant information in the papers provided for appellants by Surrey County Council:

How the committee reaches its decision

There are two stages involved in the appeal committee's decision-making process. The following is a summary of the two-stage process as suggested by the guidance contained in the code of practice:

1. It is for the authority to satisfy the committee that the duty to allocate the child to the school preferred by the parent does not apply because compliance with the preference would prejudice the provision of efficient education or the efficient use of resources. If the authority fails to satisfy the committee on the above point, the committee must allow the appeal by allocating the child to the school of the parent's choice.

2. If the authority does satisfy the committee on the above point then the committee must balance this against the parent's preference and decide which should prevail. This involves consideration of the reasons given for the parent's preference and the authority's published admission arrangements. It will then be necessary to consider the consequences for the authority of complying with the parental preference and how serious they would be. The committee must then balance these conflicting factors and reach a decision. Where two or more appeals are being decided together in respect of the same school, this process may involve considering the consequences of allowing all or only some

---

[t] The procedure followed by local education authorities is that laid down in the code of practice: see below.

[u] These provisions of the Local Government Act 1972 relate to standing orders (s.106) and therefore exclude the application of the local education authority's standing orders to appeal committees, and to local authority committees (para.44 of sch.12), which means that the statutory provisions relating to local authority committees shall likewise be excluded from application to appeal committees.

appeals. If, as a result, it is thought right to allow some but not all the appeals this may involve comparing the circumstances of one parent with another to establish which appeals should succeed.

Procedure for the day

1. Grouped appeals: generally speaking, all appeals will be grouped according to the school/college named as the preferred school/college. Individual appeals: where there is only one appeal for the school/college named as the preferred school/college the appeal will be conducted on an individual basis.
2. The clerk will explain to the parties the order of presentation of the case.
3. Cases will be called by the clerk.
4. Hearings will be in private except when otherwise directed by the chairman of the appeal committee at the request of the parents.

Grouped appeals where some cases are presented by parent in person or by representative

5. Appeals will be heard in alphabetical order subject to variation on request from parents or their representatives: such variation will be at the discretion of the clerk to the committee.
6. On the day of the appeals, appellants will be addressed as a group by the area education officer or his representative presenting the local education authority's case before the committee. He will explain the county council's general policy on admissions and will present the local education authority's case as far as it is of general application to all the appellants' cases. The area education officer will invite and answer questions from those present on the general policy and on the authority's general case. He will not be able at this stage to answer questions on nor comment on matters arising from a particular case. Thereafter each appellant's case will be heard in turn in private.
7. The appellant will then present his case.
8. The appellant may be questioned on points arising from the presentation of his case by the area education officer or his representative and the committee.
9. The local education authority, represented by the area education officer or his representative, will present its case as briefly as possible, establishing the application of the local education authority's admission arrangements to the particular case.
10. The area education officer or his representative may be questioned by the appellant and by the committee.
11. The area education officer or his representative will sum up the local education authority's case.
12. The appellant will sum up his case.

Individual appeals where the case is presented by parent in person or by representative

13. The area education officer or his representative will present the local education authority's case before the committee. This will include an explana-

tion of the county council's general policy on admissions and the application of the local education authority's admission arrangements to the particular case which is the subject of the individual appeal.

14. The area education officer or his representative may be questioned by the appellant and by the committee.

15. The appellant will then present his case.

16. The appellant may be questioned on points arising from the presentation of his case by the area education officer or his representative and the committee.

17. The area education officer or his representative will sum up the local education authority's case.

18. The appellant will sum up his case.

General

19. Matters not included in the parties' written statements which have been submitted prior to the hearing may not be raised before the committee unless the committee is satisfied that the other party has been given an opportunity to answer those additional matters.

20. The committee will retire or ask those present to retire whilst they consider the case. At this stage the clerk remains with the committee to offer independent advice on points of law or of procedure arising, assisting on points of evidence and recording decisions and reasons.

Cases dealt with by written statement

21. The written statements submitted by both parties will be read by the committee.

All cases

22. In addition to the oral or written information received during the course of the appeal, the committee will have before them and are to take into account the information contained on the preference form originally submitted by the appellant, the form of notice of appeal and the local education authority's written statement. They are also to take into account the arrangements for admission of pupils published by the local education authority.

23. The appeal committee includes county councillors and others who are not members of the local education authority. No members of the committee will have had any involvement in making the decision against which the appeal is made.

24. Equal consideration will be given by the committee to all appeals whether conducted in the presence of the parties or dealt with by written statement.

14

MEETINGS OF OTHER PUBLIC BODIES

Introduction

14.1. There are many bodies, statutory and otherwise, which operate within the sphere of local government, apart from local authorities themselves, either on the fringe of local government or with functions which were at one time the responsibility of local authorities. It seemed appropriate that there should be some brief reference to the meetings procedure of certain of these bodies: in some cases their practices are indistinguishable from those which have long been part of the management process of local government, but in others there are distinctive features.

14.2. The statutory bodies which have been selected for special reference in this chapter are the authorities through which the reorganised National Health Service operates and the water authorities which became operational – at least in their present form – co-incidentally with the reorganisation of local government in England and Wales on 1 April 1974.

14.3. There are also many quasi-official and voluntary bodies in which local authorities have an interest and/or to which they provide grant aid. Among the first category are the local authority associations and the national negotiating bodies regulating the pay and conditions of service of local authority staffs, and bodies such as the Local Authorities Conditions of Service Advisory Board, the Local Authorities Management Services and Computer Committee, and the Local Government Training Board. All these bodies substantially follow local authority practice as regards their meetings procedure. Of the others, too numerous to mention, are bodies such as councils of social service, community relations councils, council tenants' liaison committees, neighbourhood councils and so on.

Residuary bodies

Constitution and purposes

14.4 When in 1986 the Greater London Council and the former metropolitan county councils were abolished the Local Government Act 1985 provided for the establishment of a residuary body for each of the seven areas as legatees of the abolished local authorities.[1] The principal task of the residuary bodies is to tidy up unfinished business, dispose of surplus property and make compensation payments to staff made redundant or re-employed on less favourable terms at abolition. They are also responsible for debt management and superannuation except where the borough or district council agrees other arrangements, and have a particular role in relation to specialist teams providing professional and technical services.

14.5. The residuary bodies are non-elected bodies corporate,[2] government-appointed (though neither their members nor their staff are Crown servants; indeed, the staff are deemed to be within the local government service). Although legally defined as principal councils for some local government purposes, and while certain local government statutory provisions apply to them,[3] they are not local authorities in any other sense. They are under a remit to wind themselves up as soon as practicable within five years of abolition. They finance themselves by charges and through precepts on the borough and district councils within their respective areas of jurisdiction[4] and possess such powers as are necessary to enable them to discharge their functions.

14.6. The residuary bodies consist of not less than five and not more than ten members, appointed by the Secretary of State, who may vary the numbers by order and remove any members, and who has power to fix their remuneration. The chairman is selected by the Secretary of State from among the members and he may appoint a member to act as deputy chairman.

Regulation of proceedings

14.7. The residuary bodies are empowered to regulate their own proceedings – which means that, except in the limited extent to which the Local Government Act 1985 affects their constitution, they are subject to common law rules as regards meetings procedure. Thus, for example, the

[1] Local Government Act 1985, Pt VII and sch.13.
[2] *Ibid.* s.57.
[3] *Ibid.* s.57(7), sch.13, para.1.
[4] *Ibid.* s.74.

chairman or whoever presides at their meetings will not have a second or casting vote unless the body so decides. Nevertheless, the residuary bodies appear to be following well-established local government practices. The validity of any proceedings of a residuary body is not affected by any vacancy among its members or by any defect in the appointment of any of them.[5]

Seal

14.8. The application of the seal of a residuary body must be authenticated by the signature of the chairman or some other member authorised either generally or specifically for that purpose. And any document purporting to be a document duly executed under the residuary body's seal is good evidence and must, unless the contrary is proved, be deemed to be so executed.[6]

National Health Service

Introduction

As a consequence of the reorganisation of the National Health Service in 1974, local authorities lost the last of their duties and responsibilities as one of the agencies through which the health service was administered. On 1 April 1974 – coinciding with the reorganisation of local government in England and Wales – the county and county borough councils (and the London borough councils in Greater London) ceased to be local health authorities and their functions under the now repealed National Health Service Act 1946 (for which the local health authorities were required to set up a statutory health committee) were transferred to the new or reorganised authorities established under the National Health Service Reorganization Act 1973: see now the consolidating National Health Service Act 1977 and the Health Services Act 1980. Not surprisingly, because the present-day National Health Service had its pre-1946 origins in local government, much of the practice relating to meetings of the regional and area health authorities follows well-established local government practice, and certain of the statutory provisions can be seen also to stem from the statutory provisions regulating local authority practice, meetings and procedure.

14.10. The basic difference between local authorities and the National

[5] *Ibid.* s.57(3), (5).
[6] *Ibid.* s.57(7), sch.13.

Health Service authorities is, of course, that the latter are responsible to a Minister of the Crown (the Secretary of State for Social Services, as respects England, and the Secretary of State for Wales, as respects Wales) and are *appointed* bodies, whereas the former are *elected* bodies, independent of the central government; and this difference is reflected in the constitution of the respective bodies concerned and their committees. It was largely because of a recognised need to make the National Health Service more responsive to the views of the people whom it serves (although, of course, the Secretary of State is democratically responsible to Parliament) that provision was made for the establishment of community health councils as forums to reflect consumer views and provide for a measure of local participation in the running of the service. There is a duty on the health authorities and local authorities to co-operate with one another in order to secure and advance the health and welfare of the people of England and Wales: see 14.19.

Regional and district health authorities

14.11. England is divided, for purposes of administering the National Health Service, into 14 regions and the regions into districts.[7] Regional health authorities administer the first and district health authorities the second. In Wales the district health authorities are in direct relationship with the Welsh Office. Each regional authority consists of a chairman appointed by the Secretary of State and of such number of other members appointed by him as he thinks fit after consultation with various bodies. District health authorities consist of a chairman appointed by the regional authority after consultation, and a specified number, not fewer than four, of members appointed by the corresponding local authorities. The term of office of members, their eligibility or disqualification for appointment, the termination of their membership and matters relating to the constitution and proceedings of the authorities (the appointment of committees and subcommittees, meetings and procedure) are all settled by the Secretary of State by regulation.

Special health authority

14.12. If the Secretary of State considers that a special body should be established for purposes of performing any functions which he may direct the body to perform on his behalf, or on behalf of a district health authority

---

[7] National Health Service Act 1977, s.8, as amended by the Health Services Act 1980, s.1, and ss.8, 10, 12, and sch.5 as regards membership of the authorities.

or a family practitioner committee (see next paragraph), he may by order establish such a body, to be called a *special health authority*.[8]

Family practitioner committees

14.13. Each district health authority is required to set up a *family practitioner committee*.[9] The membership of the committee, the appointment and terms of office of its members and the rules as to meetings and proceedings are prescribed by regulations made by the Secretary of State. Each such committee is required to establish a *medical service committee*, a *pharmaceutical service committee* and a *joint services committee*.

Local advisory committees

14.14. Provision is made for the recognition by the Secretary of State of certain *advisory committees* representative of persons who provide services forming part of the National Health Service.[10] Thus a committee representative of (a) medical practitioners, (b) dental practitioners,(c) nurses and midwives, (d) registered pharmacists, and (e) ophthalmic and dispensing opticians, called either the regional or area medical, dental, nursing and midwifery, pharmaceutical or optical committee, as the case may be, must – subject to some discretion otherwise – be recognised by the Secretary of State. Committees representative of other categories of person may also be recognised.

Community health councils

14.15. The Secretary of State is required to establish a *community health council* for the area of each district health authority or separate such councils for separate parts of the areas of those authorities,[11] or, if he thinks fit, a council for a district which includes the areas or parts of the areas of two or more authorities. There must, however, be no part of the area of a district health authority which is not included in some community health council's district.

14.16. The councils are, in effect, consumer councils: it is their duty to represent the interests in the health service of the public in their respective

---

[8] National Health Service Act 1977, s.11.
[9] *Ibid.* ss.10, 15, as amended by the Health Services Act 1980, s.2, and the Health and Security Act 1984, s.5.
[10] *Ibid.* s.19 and schs.6 and 7.
[11] National Health Service Act 1977, s.9(1).

districts and to perform such other functions as may be conferred upon them by regulation.

14.17. The establishment of community health councils; their number, size and composition; the term of office of members; their appointment and reappointment and termination of membership; the constitution and proceedings of the councils; and matters relating to the performance of their functions: all these are matters prescribed by regulation.

14.18. The term of office of members of a community health council is fixed at four years 'expiring at the relevant date in any year',[12] and this means that the only termination of membership provided for is resignation – or death, of course – or failure to attend meetings for six months. Thus in *R. v. Lambeth London Borough and Another ex-parte Parker* (1983)[13] it was held that the borough council, though it had *appointed* and not merely nominated a representative (see 5.56), had no power to rescind the appointment of one of its representatives, which it wished to do as a consequence of a change in political control.

Joint consultative committees

14.19. There are required to be *joint consultative committees* to advise district health authorities and associated authorities in securing co-operation with one another 'in order to secure and advance the health and welfare of the people of England and Wales'[14] and on the planning and operation of services of common concern to those authorities. Again there is power enabling the Secretary of State to make an order on any matter relating to joint consultative committees after consultation with such associations of local authorities as appear to him to be concerned and with any local authority with whom consultation appears to him to be desirable.

Water authorities

Central and local organisation

14.20. Coinciding also with the reorganisation of local government in England and Wales and of the National Health Service there was introduced under the Water Act 1973 a new system (under the Secretary of State for the Environment in England and the Secretary of State for Wales in Wales, jointly with the Minister of Agriculture, Fisheries, and Food) for

[12] National Health Service (Community Health Councils) Regulations 1973, reg.5.
[13] *The Times*, 1 March 1983.
[14] National Health Service Act 1977, s.22, as amended by Health and Social Services and Social Security Adjudications Act 1983, s.12 and sch.5.

the administration of a number of matters relating to water: water conservation, water supply, sewerage and sewage disposal, prevention of river pollution, fisheries, land drainage, and recreation in relation to water. Local authorities were affected in particular by the integration of their sewerage functions with the new system, although for sewerage (as distinct from sewage disposal) they retained agency powers.

14.21. New bodies were established, known as *water authorities* – nine in England and one for Wales – to replace[15] the former Water Resources Board, the Central Advisory Water Committee, all river authorities, the Conservators of the River Thames and the Lee Conservancy Catchment Board, the Isle of Wight River and Water Authority, all statutory water undertakers existing immediately before the passing of the Act (except statutory water companies, joint water boards, joint water committees and existing local authorities and other bodies exercising functions not affected by the Act[16]), all joint sewerage boards and joint committees of sewerage authorities existing immediately before the passing of the Act, and the Water Supply Industry Training Board.[16] Also set up was the *National Water Council* with broad advisory functions over the whole area of water policy;[17] and the *Water Space Amenity Commission* with advisory functions in the particular fields of recreation and amenity.[18]

14.22. Under the Water Act 1983 the water authorities were reconstructed, each with a smaller number of members, and the National Water Council and the Water Space Amenity Commission were dissolved. The reconstituted water authorities have between nine and 15 members, all appointed by ministers, although local authorities are able to nominate people for between two and four of the board appointments. The new boards, now run on conventional nationalised industry lines, are required to establish a consumer consultative committee for each of their divisions which include representatives of local authorities and consumers. A White Paper, *Privatisation of the Water Authorities in England and Wales* (Cmnd 9734), published in February 1986, foreshadows legislative proposals for the transfer of the ten water authorities in England and Wales to private ownership.

Meetings and procedure

14.23. There was formerly some similarity with local authority practice in the rules relating to water authority meetings and procedure, although the

[15] Water Act 1973, s.33.
[16] Defined in *Ibid.* s.38(1).
[17] Water Act 1973, s.4, *post.*
[18] *Ibid.* s.23, *post.*

authorities have always been far less regulated by statutory prescription in this respect. Now these procedural ties with local government have ended. The water authorities are no longer required to hold main authority and committee meetings in public. The water authority chairmen have, however, drawn up a code of practice to ensure that the Press and public continue to be provided with information. There are now regular press conferences after water authority and main committee meetings, and the meetings of the consumer consultative committees are held in public. The jurisdiction of the local ombudsman in all water authority matters has been retained.

INDEX

·